W9-BWN-669

The Triumph of Democracy in Spain

PAUL PRESTON

The Triumph of Democracy in Spain

Methuen
London and New York

First published in 1986 by
Methuen & Co. Ltd
11 New Fetter Lane, London EC4P 4EE

Published in the USA by
Methuen & Co.
in association with Methuen, Inc.
29 West 35th Street, New York, NY 10001

Typeset by AKM Associates (UK) Ltd
Ajmal House, Hayes Road, Southall, London
Printed in Great Britain
at the University Press, Cambridge

British Library Cataloguing in Publication Data
Preston, Paul, *1946–*
   The triumph of democracy in Spain.
   1. Spain——Politics and government——1939-1975
   2. Spain——Politics and government——1975-
   I. Title
   320.946   JN8203

   ISBN 0-416-36350-4

Library of Congress Cataloging in Publication Data
Preston, Paul.
   The triumph of democracy in Spain.
   Bibliography: p.
   Includes index.
   1. Spain——Politics and government——1975-
  2. Spain——Politics and government——1939-1975.
  3. Government, Resistance to——Spain——History——20th century.
  I. Title.
DP272.P74   1986   946.082   85-28477

   ISBN 0-416-36350-4

For *Gabrielle*

Contents

Preface

This book begins in 1969, the year in which I went to live in Spain. At the time, much less interested in contemporary Spanish politics than in the Second Republic and the Civil War, my purpose was to carry out research for a D. Phil. in history. Although the research trip was supposed to be of not more than twelve months' duration, I ended up staying for more than three years. I loathed the Franco regime but my immersion in archives and newspaper libraries was such that I lived more in the 1930s than in the present. However, the restrictions on sources for my work made it difficult to ignore for long the daily reality of living under a dictatorship. Gradually, as the search for material and survivors of the 1930s brought me into contact with veteran Socialists and anarchists, and with younger Catholic, Communist and Socialist opponents of the regime, it was impossible not to develop a passionate interest in the daily political struggles going on around me.

The reality of it was brought home to me in innumerable ways. Many of the students whom I met in the University were active in the left-wing opposition. Police baton charges in the University campus were quite frequent. One day, returning home from an archive, I emerged from a metro station into a street in which a gun battle was raging between police and members of the terrorist organization FRAP. In May 1973, when a secret policeman was stabbed during a May Day demonstration, I was made quickly aware of the scale of the consequent repression. Students who used to work in the same archives as myself disappeared for several days. I later discovered that they had been arrested, beaten and questioned.

As far as my own writing was concerned, the first priority remained the Second Republic although my interest in the contemporary situation was growing. I began to collect newspapers, magazines and books with a view one day to writing the history of the anti-Franco resistance, a massive project which remains still to be finished. When I returned to England, I organized a seminar on contemporary Spain at the University of Reading which received frequent visitors from Spain and France. My own trips to Paris in search of research material and interviews with exiled republicans had already brought me numerous contacts. The most important was with the publishing house, bookshop and archive of Ruedo Ibérico, inspired and run by José Martínez Guerricabeitia, a difficult but remarkable man whose massive contribution to keeping alive the Spanish libertarian tradition has never been fully recognized. Out of the work of the seminar came the book *Spain in Crisis: Evolution and Decline of the Franco Regime*, which reflected the extent to which our work was focused on the victims of and the opponents to the Franco dictatorship rather than on the internal disintegration of the regime itself. By then, I was in London where my interest in the democratic opposition was intensified by close links with the great anti-Francoist fronts of the mid-1970s, the Junta Democrática, Coordinación Democrática and the Plataforma de Convergencia Democrática.

Inevitably, visiting Spain frequently I followed the political develop-ments of the period following Franco's death with great passion and, as the democratic regime was consolidated, with great satisfaction. Through living in Spain and through my work on the 1930s, I had come to understand something of the scale of suffering involved in the Civil War and the subsequent dictatorship. Moreover, I have always been treated with remarkable kindness and warmth by Spaniards. Accordingly, I could not feel anything less than joy at the re-establishment of democracy. Yet, looking back, as the fragility of the new regime was almost daily put to the test by its twin enemies, military subversion or *golpismo* and terrorism, I began to wonder how much of the process I had really understood. Like many commentators, I had believed that a transition process based on a consensus between the progressive forces of the old regime and the traditional democratic opposition would be as near stable as could be reasonably hoped. In a sense, Spanish democracy's survival of the daily bloodletting by ETA and the frequent efforts at a military coup has proved that to be the case. Nevertheless, although I had many more pressing commitments, I set out to make good the gaps in my own knowledge.

In the process, I learned much about ETA and much about the army to go alongside what I already knew about the democratic opposition. However, setting out to learn more of the aspects that I had tended to underestimate in my contributions to the *Spain in Crisis* volume, I also found myself fascinated by a gripping world of back-room negotiation and intrigue. This was one of the most remarkable legacies of Francoist politics. It was at the heart of the wheeling and dealing whereby moderate elements of the Franco regime peeled off to meet the opposition half way, prepared for their future by constructing new political vehicles like UCD and Alianza Popular, and dominated the politics of 1976 to 1982. Accordingly, the central theme of this book is often unrolled in smoke-filled rooms, while its two principal sub-plots take place in the military barracks where *golpismo* was fostered and on the streets where ETA went about its deadly business. It says rather less about the popular masses, the working class, strikes and social change than I had intended when I set out. None the less, it seems to me to go some way to capturing the essence of Spanish politics in the astonishing period from Franco's first intimations of mortality in 1969 to the realization of his worst nightmares with the coming to power of the PSOE in 1982.

Over the years in which the book was in the making, coterminous with the period covered, I learned much from my conversations with numerous protagonists. I would like to thank Felipe González, Alfonso Guerra, Javier Solana, Elena Flores, Gregorio Peces Barba, Narcis Serra, Carlos Zayas, Andrés García de la Riva, Antonio Masip, Alvaro Cuesta, Fernando Morán, Enrique Tierno Galván and Raul Morodo for their readiness to discuss the PSOE, the PSP and Coordinación Democrática; Nicolás Sartorius, Marcelino Camacho, Santiago Carrillo, Ignacio Gallego, Rafael Calvo Serer, José Vidal Beneyto and Manuel Azcárate for helping me to understand the PCE, the Workers' Commissions and the Junta Democrática; Félix Pastor Ridruejo, Rafael Cerezo and Manuel Fraga for talking to me about Alianza Popular; Juan Antonio García Díez, Javier Rupérez and Rodolfo Martín Villa for invaluable insights into UCD and its component parts; and General Manuel Prieto who helped me towards some understanding of the military mentality. I also learned a lot from brief conversations with Generals José Sáenz de Santamaría and Andrés Casinello.

Invaluable though such contacts were, my debt is even greater to those friends who over many years have discussed Spanish politics with me. Looking back over the ten years that this book has been brewing, I am awe-struck by the innumerable kindnesses that I have received from my friends. I would particularly like to thank for their hospitality, their insights and their encouragement Jerónimo Gonzalo Rubio, Joaquín Romero Maura, Angel Viñas, Manuel Arroyo Stephens, Miguel Angel

Aguilar, Juby Bustamante, Sheelagh Ellwood, Joan María and Susana Esteban, Kees van Bemmelen, Pepe Coll Comyn, Eduardo Sevilla Guzmán and Isidro López de la Nieta. I have learned an enormous amount over the years by both reading and talking to Juan Tomás de Salas. I would particularly like to express my appreciation for his kind invitation to take part in the *Jornadas sobre Violencia Política y terrorismo* organized in October 1984 by the Grupo 16 which gave me the priceless opportunity to meet and talk with Mario Onaindía and Txiki Benegas and to begin to understand more fully the Basque problem. I am immensely grateful to José Varela Ortega for giving me the opportunity to attend a magnificent seminar on the transition held in May 1984 in Toledo by the Fundación Ortega y Gasset which was addressed with great frankness by Adolfo Suárez and other prominent figures of the period.

I owe most to those friends who have not only discussed the issues of the book with me but also read and commented on the manuscript, Elías Díaz, Paul Heywood, Frances Lannon, Norman Cooper, Nicolás Belmonte and José Joaquín Puig de la Bellacasa. I have benefited enormously from their advice. It is not their fault but mine if what remains still contains errors of fact or interpretation. Once more, I am in the enviable position of being able to thank my editor at Methuen, Nancy Marten, for her patience, her calm good sense and her efficiency. I want also to record my gratitude to my colleague Dr Freda Harcourt, whose co-operation and solidarity at a time of ever-worsening academic cuts made it possible for me to carve out some time to work on this book. Most of all I would like to thank my wife Gabrielle for her forbearance while my mind was elsewhere among the political intrigues, the military plots and the terrorist conspiracies of another country.

Abbreviations

ACNP   Asociación Católica Nacional de Propagandistas (Catholic Association of Propagandists) – influential political pressure group.

BRIPAC   Brigada Paracaídista (Parachute Brigade) – key unit stationed at Alcalá de Henares just outside Madrid.

CCOO   Comisiones Obreras (Workers' Commissions) – Communist influenced trade union.

CEDA   Confederación Española de Derechas Autónomas (The Spanish Confederation of Autonomous Rightist Groups) – mass Catholic party in the Second Republic, led by José María Gil Robles.

CEOE   Confederación Española de Organizaciones Empresariales – Spanish Employers' Organization.

CESID   Centro Superior de la Información de la Defensa – Central Defence Intelligence Co-ordinating Agency, set up in 1977.

DAC   División Acorazada (Armoured Division) – crack army unit stationed at Brunete outside Madrid.

EIA   Euskal Iraultzako Alderdia (the Party of the Basque Revolution) – group linked to ETA-Político-Militar.

ETA   Euskadi ta Askatasuna (Basque homeland and liberty) – ultra-nationalist revolutionary terrorist organization.

FRAP   Frente Revolucionario Antifascista y Patriota – Maoist terrorist group linked to the Partido Comunista de España (Marxista Leninista).

GOE   Grupos de Operaciones Especiales – special operations forces, equivalent of SAS.

GRAPO   Grupos de Resistencia Antifascista Primero de Octubre – ostensibly ultra-left terrorist group, linked to the Partido Comunista de España (Reconstituido), but thought to be infiltrated by the police.

HASI   Herriko Alderdi Sozialista Iraultzailea (the People's Revolutionary Socialist Party) – Basque ultra-nationalist component of Herri Batasuna.

HOAC   Hermandad Obrera de Acción Católica (Workers' Brotherhood of Catholic Action).

JOC   Juventud Obrera Católica (Catholic Workers' Youth Movement).

KAS   Koordinadora Abertzale Sozialista (Basque Patriotic Socialist Liaison Committee) – Basque popular front of left nationalist groups, forerunner to Herri Batasuna.

LAIA   Langile Abertzale Iraultzaileen Alderdia (Patriotic Workers' Revolutionary Party) – political front of ETA-Militar, component of Herri Batasuna.

PCE   Partido Comunista de España (Communist Party).

PNV   Partido Nacionalista Vasco (Basque Nationalist Party).

POD   Plataforma de Organismos Democráticos – wide front of left, liberal, Catholic and regional opposition groups formed in late 1976.

PSC   Partit Socialista de Catalunya – Catalan branch of PSOE.

PSDE   Partido Social-Demócrata Español – tiny social democrat party led by Antonio García López after death of Dionisio Ridruejo.

PSOE   Partido Socialista Obrero Español (Socialist Party).

PSP   Partido Socialista Popular – small socialist group led by Enrique Tierno Galván.

PSUC   Partit Socialista Unificat de Catalunya (Catalan Communist Party).

RTVE   Radio-Televisión Española – Spanish state radio and television network.

SIPG   Servicio de Información de la Presidencia del Gobierno – Carrero Blanco's intelligence service.

UCD   Unión de Centro Democrático – centre–right coalition.

UDPE   Unión del Pueblo Español – political association started by Herrero Tejedor, carried on by Suárez and which formed the basis of Alianza Popular.

UGT   Unión General de Trabajadores – the trade union organization linked to the PSOE.

UMD   Unión Militar Democrática – clandestine organization of democratic army officers.

USDE   Unión Social Demócrata Española – small social democrat group led by Dionisio Ridruejo.

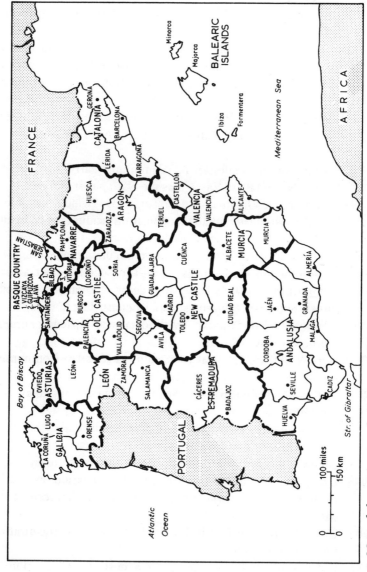

Map of the regions and provinces of Spain

1
The internal contradictions of Francoism 1939–69

When Franco died on 20 November 1975, few Spanish politicians of either right or left could have predicted with any precision the country's political development over the subsequent decade. Only the broad outlines were vaguely discernible. With their Caudillo gone, all but the most frenzied defenders of the Francoist fortress realized that concessions would have to be made to the democratic enemy at the gates. There was hope, but no certainty, that a passage to a pluralist regime might be managed bloodlessly through negotiation between the more liberal supporters of the dictatorship and the more moderate members of the opposition. Yet even the most reasonable men and women on both sides had widely differing views about what they expected from such dealings. Moreover, there existed powerful elements at the extremes of the spectrum who were unlikely to relinquish their maximalist positions. In the event, the skill and steadfastness of Adolfo Suárez, King Juan Carlos and the principal opposition leaders ensured a relatively tranquil transition. However, only the most percipient observer could have foreseen that their stumbling progress towards democracy would be through the ambushes laid by terrorists of right and left and across the minefields of military recalcitrance.

From the vantage point of 1969, the eventual scenario after the death of Franco in 1975 would have seemed unlikely in the extreme. Franco and his political advisers had by the late 1960s prepared the ground for a succession to a Francoist monarchy, to be personified in Juan Carlos and to be irrevocably tied to the principles of the military uprising of 18 July 1936. Those principles involved belligerent opposition to communism, socialism and liberalism, to democratic pluralism and to any form of regional devolution. Accordingly, the Prince was formally committed to take over a form of backward-looking centralist, authoritarian state which was already on a collision course with Spain's modern society and economy. It was not a prospect which boded well for the long-term survival of the monarchy in Spain. The transfer of power and the subsequent invigilation of the process was to be entrusted to Franco's faithful henchman, Admiral Luis Carrero Blanco. He had assumed the vice-presidency of the government in 1967 and was increasingly taking over the day-to-day running of the country from Franco. Contrary to the hopes of staunch Francoists, however, the rule of Carrero Blanco was to mark the disintegration rather than the consolidation of the regime. From 1969 until his assassination in 1973, Carrero witnessed the incessant penetration of the dictatorship's veneer of invulnerability by ETA terrorism. At the same time, faced with an inexorable rise in working-class and student dissent, he could find no more creative response than the traditional Francoist reflex of repression.

Gradually, Carrero's cabinets of technocrats and hard-liners found themselves forced to seek assistance even further to the right of the political spectrum. In the early 1970s, the government was seen to be permitting the squalid organizations of the extreme right to do its dirty work. In consequence, many Francoists were driven to wonder about the likely efficacy of Franco's plans to continue his regime after his death, a political option spoken about quite openly and seriously as *continuismo*. Supporters of Juan Carlos were beginning tentatively to wonder if his future was not being compromised by making it part of the *continuista* operation. The brutal incompetence which continued to poison relations with the Basques, the clergy and the workers caused growing disquiet among the more perceptive elements of Francoism.

A readiness to think beyond Francoist *continuismo* and to toy with the idea of an opening of the system (*aperturismo*) emerged very slowly. It was most common among the younger and almost apolitical functionaries who were more concerned with their own futures than with the shibboleths of the Civil War. An early trickle of defections under Carrero turned into a flood under his successor, Carlos Arias Navarro, once it became clear that his rhetorical commitment to reform could not withstand reactionary pressure. The cumulative effect of the Carrero and Arias periods was to demonstrate to moderates in both the regime and the opposition that only compromise could avoid bloodshed. This book is based on the premise, developed in chapters two and three, that the nature of the transition to democracy and of the subsequent period of crisis-torn politics can be properly understood only in terms of the deepening of the internal contradictions of the regime during these last six years of the dictator's life.

The most profound of those contradictions had arisen out of the economic growth over which the dictatorship had uneasily presided. The backward-looking rhetoric and authoritarian mechanisms of the regime were inappropriate to the needs of a modernizing state on the doorstep of the European Community. The Francoist incapacity to respond to the demands for liberalization coming from many sectors of a newly dynamic Spanish society was the most notable feature of the period 1969–75. The fact that the blind inflexibility of the regime drove its more liberal servants to consider dialogue with the opposition was, of course, only an inadvertent part of the Francoist legacy. The way in which the newly launched democracy nearly foundered between 1977 and 1981 must also be attributed in large measure to the problems bequeathed by the dictatorship. Franco's intransigent centralism and its heavy-handed application to the Basque Country were at the heart of ETA terrorism and the considerable popular backing which it enjoyed, at least until 1978.

Equally damaging was the deliberate and dogged maintenance of the Civil War division of Spaniards into the victorious and the defeated. The belief that democracy engendered chaos and national disunity was a central tenet of the regime's educational and cultural policy. Especially vehement in the military academies, it was behind the instinctive and violent rejection of democracy by the army and Franco's more extreme supporters after 1975. Until the Socialists came to power in October 1982, the issues of terrorism and military subversion remained intractable. Yet, as chapters four to seven argue, they were the central questions of the period during which Spanish democracy was being constructed. The problems faced by both UCD and the Socialists in government were similarly part of the Francoist burden. Unemployment and inflation may have been the consequence of the world situation but their resolution was rendered the more difficult by the serious economic imbalances left by the dictatorship.

Military interventionism, the virulence of the extreme right and the violence of the Basques, obsolete industries and uneven development have all conditioned Spain's political trajectory since 1975. What they have in common is that they are all symptoms of the fact that, under Franco, Spain was governed as if it were a conquered territory in the sway of an invading army. That is not to say that the military was the beneficiary of the dictatorship or the recipient of its plunder. The Spanish army was starved of modern equipment and turned into an instrument of social control rather than of national defence. In that sense, it could be argued that, in the distortions it suffered, the army was also a victim. It does, however, mean that despite its many advances and achievements Spanish democracy is, in both its birth and its formative development, a child of the Franco dictatorship.

The central function of the Franco regime was to institutionalize the Nationalist victory in the Spanish Civil War. The war had been provoked and fought by a coalition of right-wing forces in order to defend their sectional interests against a series of reforming challenges posed by the Second Republic. Landowners wished to preserve the existing structure of landed property; capitalists wished to safeguard their right to run industry and the banks without trade union interference; the army wished to defend the centralized organization of the Spanish State and the Church wished to conserve its ideological hegemony.[1] Each contributed as best it could to the Francoist war effort, financially, militarily or ideologically. Both their victory and its subsequent consolidation and defence were made possible by the co-option of a politico-military bureaucracy consisting of those members of the middle and working classes who might be denominated the 'service class' of Francoism. For various reasons, wartime geographical loyalty, conviction or opportunism, they threw in their lot with the regime.[2]

After the Civil War, these variegated forces of Francoism were united in various ways. There were networks of patronage and corruption and, above all, the so-called 'pact of blood' which linked them in complicity in the repression.[3] The triumph of Franco had divided Spain into the victors and the vanquished and the war between them smouldered on. This was apparent in the post-1939 repression. The regime admitted to 271,139 political prisoners in 1939. Prisons, concentration camps and labour camps remained full well into the 1940s. Until the tide turned against the Axis at the battle of Stalingrad and the Francoists began to fear for their own futures, executions continued on a large scale.[4] A sporadic guerrilla war took place all over Spain, reaching its peak between 1945 and 1947 and coming to an end only in 1951. It was hardly surprising therefore that the several 'families' or political groups which made up the Francoist alliance were held together by a fear that any relaxation of institutionalized repression might lead to renewed civil war and acts of revenge by their victims.

The unity of the victors was made to seem even more solid than it really was by the political dominance of the Falange. Unchallenged while Hitler was in the ascendant and still powerful thereafter, the Falange's youth and women's organizations, its rallies and its control of the regime propaganda apparatus, provided a totalitarian veneer to 1940s Francoism. Backed by a Gestapo-trained police force, that veneer seemed real enough to the vanquished. However, within the narrow circle of the victors, there was competition for power and influence.[5] The regime families, Catholics, monarchists, soldiers, clergymen, Falangists and technocrats, were formally united within the amalgamated single party known as the Movimiento. In practice, they were locked in a rivalry, the manipulation of which was to be General Franco's greatest achievement. At moments of special tension, the 'families' even committed acts of violence against one another.[6] For most of the time, however, their jockeying for pre-eminence took the form of intrigue and conspiracy within Franco's court. The Caudillo maintained his personal control in a number of ways. He used ministerial positions and state preferment with great skill. He exercised a blind eye where corruption was concerned. At the same time, his manipulation of the threat both of the exiled left and of international hostility to the regime caused most of the political élite to huddle around him. Moreover, the competing groups regularly appealed to Franco as arbiter in their conflicts.

The feuding forces of the right used their economic strength and their international connections in the internal competition for power and position. Ultimately, that struggle took place between two poles. On the one hand, there were the benefits, economic and social, of unity under Franco; on the other, the threats posed by the left, a potentially hostile population and the vagaries of the international situation. Accordingly, the socio-economic development of Spain was not merely the object of regime policies but it also in turn was to have a determining impact upon the internal dynamics of the regime. In 1939, the big landlords of the south were the paymasters of the regime, the Axis powers its main allies and the armed forces its greatest strength. By the 1960s, the economically dominant forces were multinational companies and indigenous banks, the main external influences the USA and the EEC, and the army reduced to being the regime's poor relation.[7] The relation of forces thus altered constantly, not only of one 'family' to another, but of all the Francoist 'families' to their democratic enemies. In consequence, rivalries grew more intense towards the end of the Franco period and even developed, or degenerated, into a barely concealed scramble for survival.[8] The forces which united in 1936 to save themselves were to split in 1976 in order to save themselves yet again, albeit this time with an accommodation to, rather than the destruction of, the forces of democracy. In death, as in birth, the legacy of Francoism was political opportunism.

The ultimate disintegration of the Francoist forces could barely have been foreseen in the 1940s. The main efforts of the regime were then devoted to eradicating the memory of the Second Republic, repressing its political cadres and harshly disciplining the working class and the peasantry. The traditional trade unions were destroyed, their funds and property seized by the state and the Falange. They were replaced by non-confrontational corporative or 'vertical' syndicates for various branches of trade and production. Within their confines, management, government and workers were theoretically represented although in practice they tended to be instruments for the elimination of strikes and the maintenance of low wages. A system of safe-conducts and certificates of political reliability made travel and the search for work extremely difficult. It thus turned those of the defeated who escaped prison or execution into second-class citizens.

The lower classes were thus forced to bear the cost of economic policies aimed at rewarding the regime's forces for their wartime support. Commitment to the southern *latifundistas* saw the maintenance of starvation wages and precluded the agrarian reform necessary for self-sustained growth. Autarkic tariff, currency and trade policies cut off the regime from the locomotive of Marshall Plan aid which contributed so much to the rebuilding of Europe's post-war economy. There was little about 1940s Francoism to justify later assertions that it was a developmental dictatorship. Indeed, by providing landowners with a passive and cheap labour force and with protection from foreign imports, the regime confirmed agricultural inefficiency and deprived industry of a peasant market. Autarky became a strait-jacket which confirmed the dominance of agriculture while simultaneously preventing it meeting any new demands placed upon it.[9]

By the end of the 1940s, the regime was to have increasing difficulty in containing the contradictions and imbalances of the economy. Inflation, rumblings of labour discontent and growing pressure for industrial development eventually forced the abandonment of autarky. Agricultural imbalances and inefficiency and the lack of coherent irrigation policies meant that Spain desperately needed to import food. Raw materials and energy were also in short supply. Deficiencies could not be made good without linking the country to the international economy or seeking American credit. In the deepening atmosphere of the Cold War, Franco's fierce anti-Communism made him an attractive ally. Similarly, his repressive labour legislation, fostering as it did high profit margins, made Spain equally attractive to investors. The link-up with the United States reduced pressure on Franco from inside and outside the regime, both by preventing further drops in living standards and by projecting the country into a worldwide anti-Communist crusade which helped to revive the spirit of the Civil War.[10] However, the first steps to economic liberalization caused resentment among some of the regime's 'families', notably the agrarians and the Falangists.

Some Francoist 'families' adapted to economic change, but others remained locked in a 1940s time-warp. The Falange maintained a vacuous rhetoric of social concern. It remained committed to the self-evidently hollow ideology of peasant sovereignty, despite evidence of the privileged position of the big landowners, and for long was oblivious to the massive social changes brought about by industrialization. Fundamental changes were to become widely visible in the 1960s, but as early as 1956 clashes occurred between progressive and backward forces within the Francoist camp.[11] In 1956, strikes and a violent university crisis saw Franco remove his most liberal minister, the social Catholic Joaquín Ruiz Giménez. He thus limited competition within the regime to the rivalry between Falangists and the technocrats of the immensely powerful Catholic pressure group, Opus Dei, known by its enemies as the 'holy mafia'. The logic of industrialization favoured the technocrats. Continued strikes and student unrest led Franco reluctantly to bring them into the cabinet in February 1957.

In a sense, the Caudillo was bringing the political superstructure into line with the social and economic changes already instituted. However, he was also acquiescing in a difficult gamble. Economic liberalization in a context of political authoritarianism implied a bid to create sufficient affluence to obviate strikes and deflect opposition. For a reactionary, agrarian regime like that of Franco, to make such a bid was to sow the seeds of its own disintegration. It signified acquiescence in the creation of a mass industrial proletariat whose political loyalty or apathy would depend on continuing prosperity. It also signified a gradual switch of power towards bankers and industrialists whose interests were far more internationally orientated and determined than those of the narrow Francoist élite.[12]

The post-1957 commitment to modern capitalist economic development ended the dominance of the Falange but did not alter the repressive nature of the regime. Economic liberalization was carried out behind the shield of reinforced army representation in the government. Most crucial in this regard was the appointment of General Camilo Alonso Vega as Minister of the Interior to provide swift and brutal repression when the social dislocation of liberalization led to rising discontent. The stringent austerity of the 1959 Stabilization Plan did in fact lead to an immediate plummeting of working-class living standards. By the early sixties, however, per capita income began to increase dramatically. The new working class was quick to flex its muscles and won a series of strikes in 1962 because, in the boom atmosphere, industrialists were loath to lose production.[13] Such consequences of the sprint for modernization caused great disquiet in many Francoist circles, especially the army and the Falange.

For the Opus Dei technocrats led by the Minister of Commerce, Alberto Ullastres, the solution to all Spain's problems lay in its full integration into Western capitalism. In pursuit of that goal, application was made in February 1962 for associate membership of the EEC, a development fiercely opposed by die-hard Falangists. Integration into a modern democratic Europe signified the end of their uniquely Spanish ideological concoction. For them the free interplay of political parties was a recipe for civil war. They preferred the safely authoritarian form of non-elective 'organic democracy' bestowed by Franco. Europe and democracy would expose the farce of the great paternalistic umbrella known as the Movimiento within which all the 'families' co-existed to the exclusion of the masses outside. Only after traumatic internal crises did the Falange withdraw its opposition to the capitalist expansion of the economy.

The Minister Secretary-General of the Movimiento, José Solís Ruiz, worked hard throughout the 1960s to prevent the single party being rendered entirely irrelevant by Francoism's new economic directions.[14] It was to be a futile effort. Cosmetic reform to modernize the Movimiento and thereby maintain its monopoly of political life was an unrealizable ambition. The Movimiento was incapable of keeping pace with the changing social reality of the country. The Franco regime had come into being to defend the interests of the victors in the Civil War. Precisely for that reason it prevented the free play of political parties and trade unions. The Movimiento was the institutional guarantee of that social and political exclusivism. It could only adjust to social change by ceasing to be what it was. As this became more apparent throughout the decade, tension among the regime families came increasingly to the fore. Each worked for the scenario which best suited their own future and many perceived that the future made more sense outside the Movimiento.

Stimulus for such activities had been provided by intimations of the Caudillo's own mortality. On 24 December 1961, Franco was accidentally shot in the left hand while pigeon-shooting at El Pardo. He was effectively incapacitated for the first months of 1962. His only provision for a diminished ability to govern was to ask General Alonso Vega, somewhat cryptically, to 'keep an eye on things' [*ten cuidado de lo que ocurra*].[15] Franco was justifiably confident that his Minister of the Interior, and his Director-General of Security, Carlos Arias Navarro, could maintain control. None the less, the incident seems to have impelled Franco himself, and many of his followers, to turn their attention to the succession. In the 1940s there had been fanatics ready to advocate that Franco declare himself King of Spain. That possibility had been discounted because of Franco's conviction that, to work well, monarchy had to have a tradition behind it. He was, however, committed to some eventual royal succession. Now, the closeness between the Caudillo and Camilo Alonso Vega raised the possibility of some kind of Francoist regency, with a hard-liner guaranteeing that the eventual monarch would not stray from the authoritarian path. That role was ultimately to be reserved for Carrero Blanco. In the meanwhile, there remained considerable room for speculation and manoeuvre with regard to the selection of a royal candidate.

Each of the regime families pinned their hopes on the pretender most likely to defend their interests. Liberals, like José María de Areilza, once Franco's Ambassador to Washington, pinned their hopes on the legitimate heir, Don Juan de Borbón; Carlists looked to Don Javier de Borbón-Parma. The most likely prospect was Prince Juan Carlos, the son of Don Juan, who had been groomed to be the Francoist monarch and whose cause was espoused by Carrero Blanco and the technocrats. The Falangist element in the Movimiento would have preferred a presidential succession. Since most of the regime families were monarchists, such an outcome was extremely improbable. Accordingly, the Falangists turned instead at the end of the decade to Don Alfonso de Borbón-Dampierre, son of Don Juan's brother and also fiancé of Franco's grand-daughter, María del Carmen Martínez-Bordiu. Franco himself probably gave little thought to the possibility of establishing a royal dynasty. However, Alfonso's cause was much favoured by the extreme right and especially by Franco's wife and his son-in-law Cristóbal Martínez-Bordiu, the Marqués de Villaverde. Alfonso de Borbón's existence served as a threat which could be used against Juan Carlos in the event of his being attracted by the democratic example of his father, Don Juan. Indeed, in general terms, the dynastic question provided a focus for the intrigues which increasingly occupied, and divided, the Francoist families.[16]

Discord over the succession was merely the most acute symptom of the tension arising from the dysfunction between the oppressively reactionary regime and the ever more dynamic society over which it ruled. Attempts were made to overcome this particular contradiction by the appointment of energetic new ministers. The commitment to economic liberalization, and the possibility of future political change, seemed to be embodied in the Opus Dei whiz-kid, Gregorio López Bravo, who was made Minister for Industry in the cabinet reshuffle of July 1962. Even more significant was the appointment of Manuel Fraga Iribarne as Minister of Information and Tourism. The hyperactive Fraga was to preside over, if not exactly attract, the tourist boom which contributed so much to economic growth. More crucially, he mounted a massive cosmetic effort to improve Spain's image abroad. Although Fraga and López Bravo were both loyal Francoists and untiring in the regime's cause, by the end of the decade they were to be bitter adversaries. The occasion was to be the notorious Matesa scandal when Opus Dei members were to be involved in the fraudulent use of government funds for the export of textile machinery. However, the cause was the abyss which separated the technocratic and the Falangist views of the Francoist future.

It was typical of the discords intrinsic to 1960s Francoism that economic progress was accompanied by continued repression. The regime's barbaric nature was unmasked in 1963. Despite pleas for clemency from ecclesiastical dignitaries around the world and from political leaders including Nikita Khruschev, Willy Brandt and Harold Wilson, Franco authorized the execution by firing squad of the Communist Julián Grimau. He had been horribly tortured before his trial. The consequent wave of international revulsion severely set back the regime's efforts to improve its image. The crudity with which Fraga reacted to the Grimau affair, authorizing the distribution before the trial of a pamphlet asserting Grimau's guilt, was especially counter-productive.[17] Four months later, after an indecently hurried trial, two anarchists, Francisco Granados Gata and Joaquín Delgado Martínez, were executed by the barbaric method of strangulation (*garrote vil*) for alleged implication in a bombing incident at Madrid police headquarters. Although not quite so clamorous as in the case of Grimau, the international outcry was considerable.[18] Inside the Francoist camp, there was some disquiet, most notably in the case of Joaquín Ruiz Giménez, the one-time Minister of Education, whose progress towards the opposition was somewhat hastened.

With a tightly censored press, the brutality of the dictatorship did less internal damage than might have been expected. Burgeoning prosperity and the football triumphs of Real Madrid and the Spanish national team made a far greater impact. The tourist industry, with an elaborate series of tax concessions, credits and building licences, generated economic growth as well as improving Spain's image abroad. Tourism helped attract foreign exchange but it also channelled investment away from productive industry. In fact, the Development Plans of the 1960s left vast areas of backwardness unresolved, not least by failing to tackle the two central problems of agrarian reform and overhaul of the fiscal system. Nevertheless, despite the unevenness of economic growth and the imbalances and dependencies which would have to be resolved in the future, growth was taking place. The increase of disposable income for large sections of Spanish society boded well for the survival of the regime. That was shown by the Francoist constitutional referendum of 14 December 1966 which sought popular endorsement of the arrangements for the succession to Franco. Fraga master-minded a gigantic propaganda campaign in which potential 'No' voters were described as 'criminals' and 'agents of Moscow'. Yet, for all the appalling pressures and the blatant manipulations, the famous 95.6 per cent 'Yes' vote did reflect something of the popular mood of 1966.[19]

Economic growth in the 1960s was something of a political time-bomb, creating as it did the structural problems which would eventually sweep away the Francoist political edifice. In the short term, however, despite the far-reaching deficiencies of the Development Plans, the immediate prosperity thereby generated brought respite to the regime. Sectional opposition continued to grow but there now existed a large middle segment of society, a depoliticized majority, which was willing to accept better food and clothing in lieu of those political liberties which could not in any case be remembered. In that limited sense, the results of the 1966 constitutional referendum provided the political élite with grounds for satisfaction. The overwhelming 'Yes' vote suggested that the carrot and stick policies of the Opus Dei had pulled the regime back from the abyss of the late 1950s. Then, the Communist Party was still able to point apocalyptically, but plausibly, to the appalling housing conditions and the derelict health and education services as evidence that a grasping and incompetent Francoist clique had brought Spain to the depths of economic ruin.[20] According to this analysis, the dictatorship was increasingly isolated and would be soon overthrown by a broadly based opposition front. Although officially sneered at, it was a view which caused some misgivings inside the Francoist stockade. However, the technocratic blend of prosperity, pseudo-liberalism and continued repression had been gradually undermining the Communist prediction, even to the extent of provoking a traumatic crisis within the PCE.[21]

The referendum result, however, obscured the reality of worker and student unrest. It also highlighted, for those prepared to look, the fact that the regime was mortgaging its future well-being to continued growth. The newly confident working class would not easily relinquish the improvements in living standards that took place in the 1960s. By moving away from autarky, the regime had made itself vulnerable to changes in the international economy. It would not be long before Spain's more perspicacious capitalists realized that the social strains attendant upon economic recession could be better absorbed within a more open political system. Even in the heady days of the mid-sixties, growth was driving a wedge between certain sectors of the economic élite and the regime. It was known that some businessmen were secretly dealing with the illegal Communist-dominated unions, the Workers' Commissions, rather than with the stultifying bureaucracy of the state-controlled *Sindicatos*. Wage and productivity agreements made with the genuine representatives of the workers had much more chance of being effective than the unrealistic deals fabricated by the corporative syndicates.

Those Francoists who perceived that prosperity's short-term political advantages could not last for ever were still a minority. Even the more far-sighted of them remained optimistic that it would be possible to adjust the Francoist system without root-and-branch change. Thus, although economic growth was creating profound dangers for the regime, the sixties were largely a decade of confidence for Francoists, however misplaced. The exiguous scale of defections was symptomatic of this. The crossing of the lines a decade earlier by the outstanding Falangist intellectual, Dionisio Ridruejo, was a relatively isolated gesture. It was matched only by the resignation in October 1964 of the Ambassador in Paris, José María de Areilza, and the withdrawal from the Francoist pseudo-parliament, the Cortes, in February 1964 of the ex-Minister of Education, Joaquín Ruiz Giménez. Areilza planned to work for the cause of the heir to the throne, Don Juan de Borbón. Since the university crisis of 1956, Ruiz Giménez had been moving towards the non-Francoist Christian Democrats. His journal, *Cuadernos para el Diálogo*, would soon become the focus for moderate socialist, and especially Catholic, opposition to the regime. Ridruejo's long process of disenchantment had led him eventually to a social-democrat stance where he was joined in the 1960s by a trickle of ex-Falangists, like Pedro Laín Entralgo, Antonio Tovar and José Antonio Maravall.[22] Ultimately, a flood of Francoist refugees would follow the lead of these pioneers. In the meanwhile, and in different ways, each was to serve as a bridge to the opposition.

Despite the growing scale and intensity of anti-regime feeling, the hope of the technocrats was that rising standards would gradually eliminate hostility to Francoism and that, in the meanwhile, its repressive mechanisms could stifle awkward problems. The irreconcilable contradictions between the antiquated political forms of the regime and the dynamics of a rapidly changing economy and society bubbled ever nearer the surface in the late 1960s. However, the point at which the pressure for change from workers, peasants, intellectuals and students would be matched by similar pressure from sectors once firmly Francoist would not come until after the crisis of 1973. Nevertheless, by 1969 it was increasingly obvious that the future of the regime was far from assured. The rising swell of unrest in factories and universities placed the question of the post-Franco succession firmly on the agenda. The naming of Juan Carlos as successor and the elaboration by José Solís Ruiz of a scheme for superficial political reform were responses to popular agitation. In their turn, these measures induced many hitherto insouciant Francoists to reconsider their options. Any illusions that it might be possible to contemplate the options in tranquillity were blown away in August 1969 by the outbreak of the Matesa textile machinery scandal. A bitter squabble exploded between the incriminated Opus Dei and a jubilant Falange. However, conflict between the regime families was fuelled by fears for the future as much as by rancours from the past.

The Opus Dei assertion that prosperity would permit painless liberalization and thereby guarantee the survival of the regime was hardly tenable in the face of strikes, demonstrations and the emergence of terrorism in the Basque Country. Many regime figures, especially in the armed forces and the Falange, concluded that modernization had been a mistake and that their safety lay in a return to the hard-line Francoism of the immediate post-Civil War period. Others, however, began to reflect that liberalization would have to go much further if a revolutionary deluge was to be avoided. The period from 1969 to 1973 would be characterized by a return to the unashamedly brutal strong-arm policies of the early days of Francoism. The consequent international outcry was considerable and would reach a crescendo at the time of the notorious

Burgos trials of ETA militants in December 1970. While hardly provoking a massive scramble for the lifeboats, the recrudescence of international hostility obliged many Francoists to reconsider their futures.

The emergence of the Basque revolutionary separatist organization ETA during the 1960s was merely the most spectacular of the problems facing the regime. The assassination of a well-known police torturer, Inspector Melitón Manzanas, in San Sebastián in August 1968, was the beginning of a long process whereby ETA began to destroy the myth of the regime's invulnerability.[23] With opposition apparently resurgent on various fronts, the dictator exposed the limitations of liberalization by declaring a 'state of exception' in the Basque Country. A state of exception gave the government emergency powers and relieved it of even token respect for the rhetorical guarantees of civil liberties enshrined in the Francoist constitution. This instinctive resort to blanket repression, an implicit admission of political bankruptcy, was repeated on 24 January 1969 when the Caudillo decreed a nationwide state of exception in response to student unrest.

Nothing more graphically underlined the contradictions of the effort to maintain an antiquated political structure at the same time as sponsoring a frantic economic boom than the situation in the universities. Student agitation had been intermittent since 1956 and virtually continuous since 1962. By the end of the decade, police occupation of campuses was almost permanent.[24] In the light of events elsewhere, especially in France and Italy, the regime regarded student demonstrations with intense concern. After all, not only were students in general being educated to be the future bureaucrats of the Spanish State and the managers of Spanish industry, but many of the individuals falling under police batons were the sons and daughters of the wealthy middle classes and even of senior Francoist functionaries. Already in April 1968 the gravity of the situation had been acknowledged by a feeble gesture consisting of the introduction of an Opus Dei member, José Luis Villar Palasí, as Minister of Education.[25]

The reverse for the Falangists was unmistakable. To have lost their grip on the student world was an indication of the creeping irrelevance of their political formulae. Unable to produce anything more substantial than vague rhetoric about the unfinished revolution, the Falange's incapacity to deal with the problems of a modernizing Spain obliged its senior members to make a choice between political reform and a retreat into the bunker. The direction of the wind had been clear since the government reshuffle of the summer of 1967. The removal on 22 July 1967 of pro-Falangist General Agustín Muñoz Grandes as Vice-President of the Government suggested that Franco wanted to keep his options open. On 22 September, the Caudillo's faithful Under-Secretary of the Presidency, Admiral Luis Carrero Blanco, filled the vacancy. Combining stolid Francoism with membership of the Opus Dei, Carrero believed that the regime could best survive in monarchical form.[26] The inexorable eclipse of the Falange was also visible in its rout in the universities and in its inability to control its other sphere of influence, the working class. Within the bland and mediocre uniformity of the Movimiento, the Falange held on to its last shred of political individuality by recourse to a tired leftist rhetoric. Accordingly, open recognition of the Falangist failure on the labour front was unequivocal evidence that the end was in sight.

The economic growth of the 1960s had brought increased prosperity to the workers but they received a disproportionately low share of the benefits of the boom. An intensification of class consciousness was reflected in the growth of various clandestine unions, especially the Comisiones Obreras, and the politicization of strikes. Solidarity stoppages, which had constituted only 4 per cent of labour disputes between 1963 and 1967, rose to over 45 per cent from 1967 to 1971.[27] The inadequacy of the official Organización Sindical, whose primordial function was to prevent strikes, was being exposed more starkly every day. Moreover, the problems of the working class were driving a wedge between Francoism and the Catholic Church. In the 1950s, organizations like the Hermandad Obrera de Acción Católica (Workers' Brotherhood of Catholic Action) and the Juventud Obrera Católica (Catholic Workers' Youth Movement) had been a refuge for working-class activists. In consequence, many young priests attached as chaplains to these branches of Acción Católica were radicalized. Moreover, in the 1960s, some members of the clergy, impelled to share the plight of their congregations, had become worker-priests. A survey of over 18,000 priests in 1969 revealed that 24.8 per cent considered themselves to be socialists, while only 2.4 per cent were Falangists.[28] Awareness of the conditions in which workers lived pushed increasing numbers of priests into anti-Francoism. In the same way, identification with persecuted regional minorities was driving many Basque and Catalan priests into the opposition.

The growth of progressive elements within the Church was not confined to the lower ranks of the clergy. In the aftermath of the Second Vatican Council, and especially as the Civil War generation dwindled, the Church adopted ever more liberal stances. On 24 July 1968 the Bishops' Conference had condemned the government-controlled corporative or vertical syndicates and issued a call for free trade unions. Moreover, the Vatican had put its weight behind the creation of a more liberal hierarchy. This was made clear during the course of the negotiations held in 1969 to renew the Concordat between Rome and Madrid. Progress was blocked by Franco's refusal to give up his right to nominate bishops, a recognition of the extent to which episcopal independence was becoming a political irritant. The Vatican and the Spanish hierarchy replied by exploiting the fact that, under the terms of the Concordat, the regime could not interfere in the appointment of auxiliary bishops or Apostolic administrators. To the chagrin of hard-line Francoists, more liberal nominations became the norm, although not without a fierce rearguard action by the regime and the reactionary members of the hierarchy. In a direct challenge to the regime's repressive policies towards the Basques and Catalans, the liberal Bishop of Santander, Monsignor José María Cirarda Lachiondo, was appointed Apostolic administrator of Bilbao and four Catalans as auxiliary bishops to Catalonian dioceses. Franco bitterly resented the 'ingratitude' of the Church and he regarded Bishop Cirarda as a dangerous subversive, especially after a secret report by the ultra-rightist fanatic, Blas Piñar López, had denounced him as a partisan of Basque separatism.[29]

This ferment in Spanish society and politics inevitably had repercussions within the Francoist camp. There were those within the élite, known as *aperturistas*, who were tentatively moving towards the conclusion that the dramatic social and economic changes of the decade between 1959 and 1969 had rendered the political structures of Francoism increasingly obsolete. The coded polemics about the future which proliferated after Fraga's partial reduction of censorship in his March 1966 Press Law reflected a growing awareness of the problems arising from modernization. The *aperturistas* wanted to adjust the political forms of the regime to at least one aspect of Spain's changing social reality – the emergence of large-scale capitalism, both indigenous and multinational, as the dominant economic force of the day. That reality carried with it the growing political irrelevance of large parts of the Francoist establishment. If the official *Sindicatos* and the weight of the forces of repression were an asset to the predominantly agrarian oligarchy dominant in the 1940s and early 1950s, by 1969 the economic development which they had partly facilitated was gradually removing the need for them.

Moreover, as the clandestine contacts between factory owners and the Workers' Commissions (*Comisiones Obreras*) showed, the new capitalism had altered the nature of the working-class threat to the oligarchy. The relationship between, on the one hand, workers paying hire-purchase instalments on a car, a flat or a television and, on the other, bankers and industrialists dependent on continued productivity, was clearly different from that between landless labourers and landlords in the 1930s and 1940s. The needs of a complex economy had created a new proletariat with relatively high levels of skill and income. With many of the larger and more competitive enterprises looking forward to integrating the working class into the capitalist system through reward-based productivity agreements and to expanding their operations into the EEC, the institutionalized social conflict of the Franco system was becoming a major obstacle to future growth.

Given Francoism's function as the defender of capitalism, it was inevitable that the dissatisfaction of the business class would eventually have its effect on the political structure. The backward agrarian capitalism of the 1930s had been replaced by the dynamic industrial and financial capitalism of the 1960s. It was inevitable that the political framework would have to be changed to adjust to that reality. The ultimate Francoist disintegration was hardly discernible in the incipient cracks of the late 1960s. Yet by the mid-1970s, the shrewder elements would be negotiating with the left and the more reactionary ones would become involved in desperate efforts to put the clock back by violence. It was to require six years of Basque terrorism and a rapidly deteriorating economy to create the conditions for the eventual transition to democracy by means of a negotiated break with the past, the so-called *ruptura pactada*. Lamentably, the same period was to see the consolidation of extremist positions among the groups who were to be the greatest enemies of the future democratic regime, ETA and the bunker. Thus, in the Carrero Blanco and Arias Navarro periods, the scene was set both for the triumph of moderation between 1976 and 1978 and for the growth of political violence between 1979 and 1981.

2
Holding back the tide:
the Carrero Blanco years 1969–73

1969 was a dramatic turning point in the history of the Franco regime. It was the year in which the most open and virulent case of inter-family rivalry erupted over the Matesa scandal. It was also the year in which ETA emerged as a daunting enemy of the regime. More importantly, it was the year in which Franco recognized his own growing incapacity, handed over the effective reins of government to Carrero Blanco and confirmed the succession of Prince Juan Carlos. The thoughts of the political élite inevitably turned to the future. They did so in an atmosphere of growing tension. Carrero Blanco was forced to deal with problems that had been no more than vague intimations three or four years earlier. The scale of the difficulties that he faced could be deduced from the fact that the regime would soon be seen to resort to ultra-rightist terrorism against its opponents. The confidence of the 1960s, symbolized by Fraga's 1966 referendum success, was crumbling in the face of the rising turmoil in universities and factories.

Given the links between Spanish business and the political élite, the consequent misgivings of industrialists and bankers found an echo within certain Francoist circles. However, it was in the nature of things that such doubts as were sown would be gradual in their effect. More dramatic, in terms of the crumbling of once-reliable loyalties, was the increasingly anti-regime attitude of parts of the Church. The liberal policies of the Vatican after the Second Council had had an important effect on the attitudes of many senior members of the hierarchy. That influence from above was matched by the radicalization of young chaplains associated with the JOC and the HOAC and of worker-priests. Many priests and religious experienced at first hand the privations of migrant workers living in the slums of the great industrial cities. In the Basque Country and Catalonia, a reaffirmation of the traditionally close relationship between the clergy and the faithful was reflected in a growing ecclesiastical sympathy with regionalist aspirations and even, in Euskadi, with ETA.

The sense that some regime elements were preparing an accommodation with the erstwhile enemy gave rise to a gnawing fear that the golden days of corruption and unpunished repression were drawing to a close. Between 1969 and 1975, anticipation of Franco's eventual demise affected different sectors of the regime forces in different ways. The younger functionaries, the politicians with directorships and consultancies in dynamic enterprises, the liberally inclined and the plain far-sighted began to toy with democratic notions. In contrast, the hard-line Falangists entrenched in the syndical bureaucracy, the police and the Civil Guard, and most army officers were determined to defend the dictatorship to the bitter end. This view was shared by those who had made enormous fortunes out of the regime, the so-called kleptocrats, and by many of the simple *serenos* (night-watchmen) and *porteros* (doormen) who saw their continued employment as consubstantial with the dictatorship. In such circles, there was a growing feeling that Francoism, abandoned even by the Church, would have to be defended as Hitlerism was defended in the last days of Berlin, from a bunker.

In the course of 1969, although a number of ultra-rightist bishops like Casimiro Morcillo González and José Guerra Campos remained fiercely Francoist, the Vatican continued to edge unmistakably into the ranks of the regime's enemies. In this sense, Pope Paul VI was continuing the change in perspectives inaugurated by John XXIII. The moderate Archbishop of Pamplona, Monsignor Tabera y Araoz, protested against the imposition of the state of exception declared in January 1969. Shortly afterwards, Tabera was elevated to the College of Cardinals. An even more dramatic symptom of Rome's determination to distance itself from Franco was the appointment in February of Monsignor Vicente Enrique y Tarancón as Primate of Spain. Committed to the spirit of the Second Vatican Council, Enrique y Tarancón was to be the instrument whereby Pope Paul VI was to express his distaste for the Franco regime.[1] The changing position of the Church, its increasing identification with regionalist and working-class protest, and its implicit denial of moral legitimacy to the regime were to have significant consequences within the corridors of power. Christian Democrat-inclined functionaries reinforced their commitment to a constitutional monarchy as the safest option. 'Liberal' Falangists began to toy gingerly with ideas of social democracy.[2] Equally, die-hard Francoists began for the first time to have intimations of isolation.

The state of exception declared in January 1969 was a reflex reaction to the early symptoms of beleaguerment. A resort to brutality was a tacit admission of helplessness before the growing clamour of workers, students and Basque activists. In fact, the declaration of the suspension of constitutional guarantees had provoked some opposition from Opus Dei ministers who wanted it confined to Madrid and Barcelona. Significantly, on 25 March, Fraga pressed successfully for an early end to the state of exception, claiming that it would damage the tourist trade. The Caudillo remained unconvinced, preferring public order to international goodwill. It was an ironic illustration of the contradictions between the new social and economic realities of Spain and the traditional political methods of the dictatorship.[3] The harshness of the regime's hard-liners, including Franco himself, inevitably placed the Opus Dei technocrats in a relatively favourable light. Their aim of fostering a capitalist economy integrated into the world market rendered them more progressive than some of the political troglodytes who found ministerial office under Franco.

None the less, it should not be forgotten that their efforts to promote growth were often characterized by inefficiency, corruption and high social cost. The Development Plans reflected the technocrats' belief that efforts to redistribute wealth, to diminish regional imbalances, or even to increase government investment would involve fiscal changes damaging to the privileged classes for whose protection the regime primarily existed. Accordingly, they presided over a growth that accepted and intensified the unequal distribution of wealth, regional inequality and technological dependence. Despite the self-congratulations of the technocrats, growth started before their plans came into being and often continued despite them. Once the economic impetus consequent upon the opening-up of Spain to world trade got under way, long-term planning was shelved in favour of stop–go policies which aimed no higher than the control of inflation and balance of payments deficits. Accordingly, when the boom of the 1960s began to slow down, the technocrats could respond only with austerity measures. Inevitably then, the social pressures against the regime were intensified. Growth had created a new working class whose militancy against poor working conditions and political repression could only be kept in check by rising living standards.[4]

Waves of social and political instability at the end of the 1960s impelled Carrero Blanco to urge Franco to hasten plans for the succession. The Caudillo had long been formally committed to the continuation of his regime in a monarchical form. He had delayed naming an heir not only because of his reluctance to relinquish power, but also because of the difficulty of finding a successor totally committed to the perpetuation of Francoism and acceptable to all the regime families. Such conditions excluded both the legitimate heir to the throne, Don Juan de Borbón, and the Carlist pretender, Carlos Hugo. In extremely complex circumstances and under threat from Franco to eliminate the monarchy for ever from Spain, Don Juan had agreed to his son, Prince Juan Carlos, being groomed for the job. His introduction into official life began during the 1960s. Juan Carlos enjoyed the support of an influential group of conservative Catholics within the regime, including Opus Dei members Laureano López Rodó and Admiral Carrero Blanco. The corollary of this was that the young Prince was regarded as a mere puppet of Franco by the democratic opposition. Nevertheless, Franco delayed making a final decision for as long as possible in order to retain the support of all the various monarchist factions and to avoid antagonizing the Falangists. The deteriorating political situation added a certain urgency to the question and lengthy constitutional preparations finally culminated in the official proclamation of Juan Carlos as successor on 22 July 1969. On the following day, the Prince took an oath of loyalty to Franco, to the principles of the Movimiento and to the Fundamental Laws of the Francoist State.[5]

In Francoist constitutional terms, there was no continuity with the Borbón monarchy of Alfonso XIII which had ended in 1931. Instead, a new Francoist monarchy, coincidentally personified by a Borbón, was being 'installed'. In the turgid expression of one of the Prince's tutors, the Falangist constitutional lawyer, Torcuato Fernández Miranda, the new monarchy would be 'the personification of the historico-national legitimacy incarnated in the Spanish State born of the rebellion of 18 July 1936'.[6] Partly out of habits of obedience and partly in the confidence that the constitutional bonds would prevent Juan Carlos ever changing anything, the bulk of the Falange accepted the nomination. Indeed, there was general satisfaction in Francoist circles that definite provision had finally been made for the regime's continuation. Liberal monarchists who supported Don Juan and had advocated a policy of evolution from within were disappointed to see their hopes dashed. Some, notably the president of the newspaper, *Madrid*, the Opus Dei reformist, Rafael Calvo Serer, and the ex-ambassador, José María de Areilza, began to move nearer to the opposition. The left was outraged. The Socialists denounced the attempt 'to impose, in a grotesque piece of medieval play-acting, a future cardboard king'. The Communists rejected Franco's determination to continue ruling from the grave by institutionalizing *inmovilismo*.[7] Neither they, nor the Francoists who welcomed the announcement of a successor, could foresee the role that would be played by Juan Carlos in the transition to democracy from 1976 onwards.

The elevation of Juan Carlos was accompanied by another effort to adjust to the future. The Minister Secretary-General of the Movimiento, José Solís Ruiz, presented a Statute of Associations to the Consejo Nacional in July. This empty formalization of the regime's 'limited pluralism' permitted the creation, not of political parties, but of associations which could 'formulate and contrast legitimate opinion'. The so-called *Estatuto Solís* was a meaningless varnish for the Movimiento. Associations would have no electoral life, would have to have a minimum membership of 25,000 and could only be legalized by the Consejo Nacional del Movimiento. Totally rejected by the democratic opposition, the associations were limited to Francoist factions. The most ultra-reactionary was Blas Piñar's Fuerza Nueva. More liberal were Acción Política under Pío Cabanillas Gallas and Reforma Social Española under the progressive Falangist Manuel Cantarero del Castillo.[8] Franco had never been averse to efforts to provide a cosmetic veneer of liberalism if only to impress foreigners. However, his obsessive hatred of political parties ensured that reform would never alter the dictatorial essence of his regime.

Any doubts on that score were wiped out by the activities of the police and the courts during the summer of 1969. While the nomination of the Prince and the Statute of Associations were being orchestrated as evidence of the regime's liberalization, barely a day went by without arrests or trials of workers, students or Basque militants. Sentences ranged from one year for painting slogans on walls to sixteen years for membership of ETA. The harshest treatment seemed to be reserved for priests. Military judges bitterly resented what they saw as the betrayal of the clerics. Their determination to stamp it out merely intensified the identification of the Church with the opposition, especially in the Basque Country. Distribution of ETA propaganda brought sentences of ten years. Perhaps the most representative case was that of Father Bericiartua, accused of 'military rebellion'. His crime was the possession of large stocks of leaflets denouncing the imprisonment of Basque priests in the gaol at Zamora. Although Bishop Cirarda Lachiondo invoked his powers under the Concordat to deny permission for the trial, the military tribunal at Burgos delivered a sentence of eight years.[9]

The perpetual readiness of the regime to lash out against its enemies was to be exercised with ever greater frequency but in 1969 it was overshadowed by a major internal dispute. This arose out of the collapse on 10 August 1969 of Maquinaria Textil del Norte S.A. (Matesa). Matesa was a company directed by an Opus Dei member, Juan Vila Reyes, a close friend of Laureano López Rodó, the Minister for the Development Plan. A huge misappropriation of state funds in the region of 10,000 million pesetas had been used to finance Opus Dei ventures abroad as well as to line the pockets of Vila Reyes. Apart from López Rodó, the most directly implicated ministers were Faustino García Monco (Commerce), Juan José Espinosa San Martín (Finance), and Gregorio López Bravo (Industry), together with the Governor of the Bank of Spain, Mariano Navarro Rubio. All were members of Opus Dei. However, López Rodó enjoyed the favour of Carrero Blanco and López Bravo was a friend of the Franco family. None the less, Falangists who had long resented the growing dominance of the technocrats, particularly Fraga and Solís, thought that they could use the situation to benefit their own brand of *apertura*. The Ministry of Information permitted the press to unleash a violent campaign against the Opus. It was a serious miscalculation.

A resurgence of the Falange would not have favoured Carrero's plans for a smooth transition to a Francoist monarchy. Moreover, while the Caudillo had always discreetly permitted competition between the regime factions, he had never permitted untrammelled power struggles. Fraga and Solís had overreached themselves in their attack on the Opus. Even before the Matesa affair, the stifling puritanism which characterized Franco, Carrero Blanco, their wives and the dictator's immediate entourage had already been outraged by the liberalization of the press sponsored by Fraga at the Ministry of Information. The blatant attempt to reverse the Opus Dei scenario for a Francoist monarchy deeply offended Franco. It was thus relatively easy for Carrero Blanco and López Rodó to turn the potentially damaging Matesa crisis to their advantage. A report by Carrero Blanco, handed to the Caudillo on 16 October 1969, passed lightly over the 'lamentable negligence' of the ministers responsible for Matesa's activities, but stressed that the subsequent press campaign had severely damaged Spain's international credibility. Pointing a finger directly at the Minister of Information, Carrero's report helped to sink Fraga.

A major cabinet reshuffle, for which Carrero had been pushing for over eighteen months, was announced on 29 October. Carrero's own pre-eminence was enshrined in the fact that, although he had been Vice-President of the Council of Ministers since 1967, he now for the first time played a role in the selection of the cabinet. Franco's presidency was little more than nominal. It was to be Carrero Blanco's own team. Fraga was replaced at the Ministry of Information by the Opus Deista Alfredo Sánchez Bella. At the Movimiento, Solís was substituted by the sinuous Torcuato Fernández Miranda, the Falangist most committed to the monarchy of Juan Carlos. While García Monco and Espinosa San Martín were made sacrificial victims, López Rodó remained as a key figure and López Bravo was promoted to Foreign Minister. The Opus now controlled Education, Information, Foreign Affairs and the four economic ministries of Finance, Commerce, Industry and the Development Plan. The heavy-handed Minister of the Interior, General Camilo Alonso Vega, on reaching his eightieth birthday, was replaced by a bureaucratic military lawyer, Tomás Garicano Goñi.[10]

Conscious of his own dwindling vitality, Franco increasingly delegated responsibility on his Vice-President and Carrero Blanco was effective Prime Minister. The dour dry-land Admiral was the best guarantor of the policy of *continuismo*. Although reputed to have used his influence with Franco to have autarky abandoned and the technocratic experiment launched, Carrero was eminently acceptable to the *inmovilistas*. A living embodiment of hard-line Francoism, he had been the Caudillo's closest adviser since 1940. His first political assignment had been to represent Spain at the 1939 celebrations in Rome of the twentieth anniversary of the Fascist movement. From May 1941 he acted as Under-Secretary of the Presidency, in effect as Cabinet Secretary. In July 1951, Franco promoted him to ministerial rank 'to save having to repeat what happened in cabinet'.[11] Even the most inflexible reactionary had reason to be confident of Carrero's capacity to prevent Juan Carlos deviating from the norms laid down by Franco. With his powerful group of Opus Dei technocrats, he was aiming to build a post-Franco Francoism on a basis not of political liberalization but of continued prosperity. It was hardly surprising that before the end of 1969 the new Minister Secretary-General of the Movimiento, Torcuato Fernández Miranda, was obliged to put an end to the Solís project of political associations presumably for fear that they would spawn real parties.

Ultimately, Carrero's scheme was to end with his own assassination and massive economic crisis. The combination of worldwide recession and the structural weaknesses of the Spanish economy would ensure that, within a year of his death, there would be one-time Francoists attempting to manipulate political liberalization as a substitute for continued prosperity. In 1970, however, three years before the outbreak of the energy crisis, there were even hopes that the Opus Dei group could consolidate economic growth by securing Spanish entry into the EEC. The new Minister for Foreign Affairs, Gregorio López Bravo, began a frenetic programme of refurbishing the regime's external relations. However, he constantly ran into the barrier that entry into Europe required political liberalization which the regime could not contemplate. The problem had been underlined when 131 members of the moderate opposition, Socialists, Christian Democrats and Liberals, had sent an open letter to Franco on 23 December 1969. Widely publicized throughout Europe, the letter underlined the distance between Spain and the EEC. Its demands for basic human and political rights were reiterated when the West German Foreign Minister, Walter Scheel, visited Madrid and on 24 April 1970 met Joaquín Ruiz Giménez, José María de Areilza, Joaquín Satrústegui and Enrique Tierno Galván. To the chagrin of Franco himself and the Spanish press, which denounced their treachery, the four had managed to publicize yet again the regime's unsuitability for integration into Europe.[12]

Further evidence of the ultimate inability of the Carrero team to resolve the contradictions between the regime and society was provided by a deterioration of labour relations throughout 1970. The year began with 20,000 miners on strike in Asturias and there were major disputes involving shipyard and agricultural workers.[13] The government was forced to import coal to keep the iron and steel industries going. This constituted something of a triumph for López Bravo since a significant proportion of the imports came from the Eastern Bloc. It also reflected Soviet readiness to punish the Spanish Communists for their condemnation of the invasion of Czechoslovakia.[14] Industrial tension mounted throughout the spring and early summer. After months of conflict in the Asturian mines, the strike wave reached a climax when construction workers in Granada and Madrid metro workers came out. On 21 July the police opened fire on more than 2000 building workers in Granada killing three and wounding several others.[15] The ready recourse to violence was indicative of the regime's crisis of authority. This was confirmed by the hysterical reaction of the Movimiento press which accused the local clergy of provoking the strike. On 28 July Archbishop Benavent Escuín of Granada, previously regarded as a conservative, issued a pastoral letter condemning police brutality against the workers and defending worker-priests from the accusations of the Falangist press.[16]

Jealously, albeit vainly, trying to keep syndical territory as its exclusive preserve, the Falange bitterly resented the Church's intervention. During the Asturian miners' strike, the Archbishop of Oviedo, Monsignor Díaz Merchán had issued a pastoral letter supporting the miners and condemning government reprisals against them. Now Granada Cathedral had provided sanctuary for striking building workers, and use of Church buildings for meetings and as a refuge from the police became increasingly common. Since the police could not be seen to attack the clergy, there began to emerge parallel terror squads. Extremists of Fuerza Nueva, using names like the Guerrilleros de Cristo Rey (the Warriors of Christ the King), entered churches and perpetrated vicious attacks on priests. Such activities merely drove the Church even further away from the regime. Frequent trials of priests for propaganda offences involving support for working-class or regionalist aspirations also drove wedges between Catholics and the Francoist state apparatus.[17]

With the intensification of working-class opposition, the regime returned ever more openly to its authoritarian habits. On 26 July the Comisiones Obreras held a secret national congress in a convent outside Madrid. Many Catholic labour leaders were present but Communist influence was visible in the decision to step up actions until a general strike could be co-ordinated nationally. This perpetual Communist ambition was never to be fully realized but the build-up of conflict throughout 1970 accentuated the siege mentality of the regime's forces. On 29 July, for the first time since the Civil War, the Madrid metro was brought to a standstill by a strike which was the unexpected culmination of a three-month dispute over wages. An emergency meeting of the cabinet decreed the military mobilization of the 3800 workers who were thereby subjected to the threat of court martial for mutiny. The strikers had no choice but to return to work. The impression that the regime could maintain control only by means of repressive brutality persuaded large numbers of workers and middle-class professionals that action to bring about political change was of the greatest urgency.

After a short respite during the summer, the regime was faced in the autumn by a renewed strike wave. The Madrid metro workers refused to do overtime. In Seville, railway workers downed tools. In Asturias, a mining accident which killed three workers was the occasion of a strike of 3500 miners. The nationalized coal company, Hunosa, replied with a lock-out affecting 15,000 workers. Ultimately, these were economic strikes. Prices were rocketing – meat by 40 per cent since 1968, fruit by 30 per cent. Transport, heating, clothing and most food products were rising to a point at which the average two-child family needed a monthly income of 12,000 pesetas in order to survive. The legal minimum wage was 120 pesetas per day and many workers received less. The most precarious situation was to be found among unskilled and casual labour. Accordingly, one of the largest and most bitter strikes of the autumn took place in the Madrid construction industry. 20,000 workers were involved, although the Communist Party claimed that there were five times that many.

For the Communists, the strikes were proof that large numbers of people supported their strategy of a broad alliance of anti-regime forces, known as the 'Pact for Liberty'. They were now encouraged to believe that they could soon put the 'Pact' into practice through a great national strike action.[18] The Comisiones Obreras called a day of struggle on 3 November to demand amnesty for political prisoners. Because of police repression and the lack of an immediate economic motivation, the popular response was patchy. The greatest impact was among Madrid and Barcelona metallurgical workers, shipyard workers in the Basque Country and El Ferrol and building workers in Seville. Even the exaggeratedly low official estimate acknowledged 25,000 strikers across the country. The public support given openly for the first time by many intellectuals, artists, students and housewives was evidence of the widening solidarity of opposition forces.[19]

In contrast, there were deepening cracks within the coalition of Francoist forces as, under pressure, the government of Carrero Blanco reverted to its most basic instincts. Thus, the intensification of repression seemed merely to provoke greater defiance from the opposition. The number of people tried for political offences in the first nine months of September 1970 was 1101. A disproportionate number of those charged were Basques. To draw attention to this fact, Joseba Elósegi, a Basque nationalist, set fire to himself while Franco presided over the world jai-alai championships in San Sebastián on 18 September. Elósegi had been in command of the only Basque military unit present in Guernica on 26 April 1937 when it was destroyed by Franco's German allies. By his action, Elósegi implicitly related the struggle to defend Euskadi against Francoist troops during the Civil War to the battle being fought by the young nationalists of ETA in the 1960s.[20] Franco remained impassive as the badly burned Elósegi was taken away. However, at a time when the *continuismo* of Carrero Blanco's cabinet of technocrats required integration into Europe, the incident drew international attention to the persecution of the Basques. Entirely insensitive to the worldwide revulsion that it was provoking, the government announced its intention to hold a great show trial of sixteen ETA activists. The consequent explosion of marches, protest demonstrations and violent clashes with the police underlined the contrast between a regime that was losing its way and an opposition which demonstrated ever greater cohesion and resolve.[21]

With Franco sinking into senility and the economic situation deteriorating, the confidence that had characterized the technocrats in the summer of 1969 had dissipated. The conflict over Matesa had eliminated reformist Falangism as an option and even such an unrepentant Francoist as Manuel Fraga began to take his first tottering steps towards a progressive or 'centrist' position. Carrero Blanco's cabinet was known as the *'monocolor'* because, from the regime families who had peopled earlier governments, he had selected primarily the now dominant technocrats and the military men. Behind them, the only other remaining option was the bunker. In fact, Carrero Blanco was to demonstrate a growing sympathy with the ultra reactionaries associated with Blas Piñar and José Antonio Girón de Velasco. Once Minister of Labour and a man who had made a fortune out of the regime, Girón was to be the backbone of the extreme right over the next twelve years. Carrero's sympathy with nostalgic hard-liners did not, however, mean that he was out of step with his cabinet colleagues. The technocrats were not averse to harsh measures. Indeed, it was rumoured that they acquiesced in the existence of ultra-rightist squads because these thugs not only did the regime's dirty work for it but also, by establishing an extreme pole even further to the right, allowed the government to present itself as belonging to the centre of the political spectrum.[22]

While ultra-rightist squads assaulted liberal and leftist priests and lawyers, the government occupied itself throughout 1970 with silencing even the moderate opposition as well as locking the door definitively on reform. In March, the monarchist José María de Areilza wrote an article on 'the Spanish road to democracy' in *ABC*. He pointed out that the regime's objective of integration into Europe was unlikely to be fulfilled until Spain had real democracy complete with political parties. On 1 April, the Catholic daily *Ya* called for the democratization of Spanish life. Carrero Blanco himself replied, under his pseudonym of Ginés de Buitrago, in the crudest terms. *ABC* was obliged to print his article. In it, he likened efforts to democratize Spain to attempts to get a reformed alcoholic to take a drink. Not only did he reiterate adamantly that the principles of the Movimiento were unchangeable but he also declared that rather than Spain having to adapt to Europe, Europe would do well to imitate Francoism.[23] That liberalization was less likely under this cabinet than its predecessor was confirmed when the new project for political associations was unveiled by Torcuato Fernández Miranda in late May. Associations would not be allowed to press causes 'outside or against the principles of the Movimiento'.[24]

The turn even further to the right under Carrero was pushing many one-time regime stalwarts into the opposition. Since the social and political standing of such people gave them access to the press, the '*monocolor*' cabinet found itself subject to more vocal criticism inside Spain than any previous Francoist government. The greatest thorns in its collective flesh were *Ya*, the daily associated with the Catholic pressure group, the Asociación Católica Nacional de Propagandistas, *Cuadernos para el Diálogo* in which Christian Democrats and moderate socialists worked under the auspices of Joaquín Ruiz Giménez, and, perhaps most of all, the evening newspaper *Madrid*. *Ya*, although conservative, had followed the Church hierarchy in establishing some distance between itself and the regime. Simultaneously, many important regime functionaries who belonged to the ACNP were beginning to become critical as liberalization seemed ever more unlikely. Given its political and ecclesiastical connections, *Ya* was almost immune to regime pressure.

Cuadernos para el Diálogo, like other liberal magazines, was subjected to constant harassment in the form of fines and the banning of individual issues. Indeed, on 13 March 1970, the Tribunal Supremo confirmed a fine of 50,000 pesetas imposed on Ruiz Giménez on the grounds that the press had no right to try to change the system.[25] *Madrid*, however, posed more intractable problems. The paper had been bought in 1961 by the Opus Dei cultural organization FACES (Fomento de Actividades Culturales, Económicas y Sociales) as part of the technocratic operation to prepare for the post-Franco future. Various prominent Opus Deistas were involved, including López Rodó. However, the paper was not a success and in 1966 it was taken over by the Opus Dei intellectual, Rafael Calvo Serer. In the 1950s, he had launched the idea of a 'third force' of Don Juan supporters and Opus Deistas to work with the Falangists and Christian Democrat conservatives who made up the bulk of the civilian element in Franco's governments. Since then he had evolved towards a more constitutional monarchist position. Under his presidency, *Madrid* was opened up to a wide spectrum of liberal and democratic opinion. A team of outstanding journalists, including Miguel Angel Aguilar, José Oneto and Francisco Cerecedo, made it the most exciting newspaper published in Spain.

Madrid soon roused the hostility of Fraga, although Calvo Serer's connections with the regime protected him for some time. A four-month suspension was the regime's reply to a celebrated article by Calvo, ostensibly calling for De Gaulle to retire but widely understood to be a hint to the Caudillo. The paper thereafter survived various court cases but its days were numbered. Its pro-Don Juan line was anathema to Carrero Blanco and the technocrats who were committed to building a Francoist monarchy around Juan Carlos. From February 1970 it was made clear that the regime was out to get the paper. During the orchestrated build-up to the Burgos trials, *Madrid* failed to adopt the required tone of patriotic hysteria. Within a year, the paper was closed on flimsy charges of 'administrative irregularities' and Calvo Serer went into exile. He was to be greeted as a great prize by the opposition, especially the Communists who welcomed him for his contacts with Don Juan and because, as a conservative, a Catholic and a monarchist, he could add credibility to their claim to be building the widest front of anti-regime forces.[26]

In the meanwhile, the task of the opposition had been rendered considerably easier by the waves of revulsion provoked by the Burgos trials held from 3 to 28 December 1970. Normally, the regime's judicial farces were held in secret. However, since two Basque priests were among the accused, Monsignor Cirarda Lachiondo, as Apostolic administrator of Bilbao, had interceded with the Vatican to press for the trial to be held in public. In the event, the trials of the sixteen accused were amongst the longest ever held by the dictatorship and the clumsiness with which they were conducted turned them into a trial of the regime itself both by the ETA defendants and by the world's press. Moreover, the rift between the regime and the Church became almost total. On 22 November, Monsignor Cirarda and Bishop Argaya Goicoechea of San Sebastián issued a joint pastoral letter condemning the procedures of the trial and the application of the recently reintroduced Law on Banditry and Terrorism and demanding pardons for anyone sentenced to death. The government-orchestrated press reacted hysterically especially in response to the Bishops' condemnation of all violence regardless of its perpetrators.[27]

A furious press campaign accused the clergy of temporalism, an offence which had not ruffled the regime's conscience when Francoism was preached from the pulpit in the 1940s. A statement by the Ministry of Justice on 21 November in reply to the joint pastoral letter made reference to the violence and murders committed by the accused. The

Church was appalled at the easy assumption of the defendants' guilt before the trials were held. The clear implication that the Church's duty to the regime was to provide moral sanction for institutionalized violence against its Basque enemies was unacceptable to the hierarchy, not least in the light of the presence of priests among those about to be tried. Accordingly, when the XIII Assembly of the Episcopal Conference opened on 1 December near Madrid, a pro-government statement by a group of ultra-reactionary bishops was shelved. Instead, the liberal line of Cardinal Enrique y Tarancón prevailed and the Conference expressed its solidarity with Bishops Argaya and Cirarda and called on the government to show clemency.[28]

The attitude of the Church gave a tremendous moral boost to the anti-Franco opposition. The clandestine unions and the left parties were already mounting a massive propaganda operation against the regime. Nineteen prominent opposition leaders, including the socialist Enrique Tierno Galván and the Comisiones Obreras lawyer Nicolás Sartorius, were arrested while preparing a public letter of protest against the trials. One hundred lawyers responded to the arrests with a sit-in at the Madrid Palacio de Justicia. Three thousand students and workers clashed with the armed police in Barcelona. The Universities of Madrid and Barcelona were on strike. The regime was unable to comprehend that the Basque cause had enormous sympathy throughout Spain. When the trial opened, it was against a background of street demonstrations organized by ETA and the rest of the left. Barricades went up in many Basque towns and massed battles were fought with the police and Civil Guard. Even official sources admitted that there were 180,000 on strike in Euskadi.[29]

To draw attention to the plight of the accused, for six of whom the prosecution was demanding death sentences, on 1 December 1970 a section of ETA kidnapped the West German Honorary Consul, Eugen Beihl, in San Sebastián. Before the trials had started a conflict had arisen within ETA between those who thought that the organization should be part of a wide working-class struggle against the dictatorship and those who were more committed to violent 'military' or terrorist means and narrowly nationalist ends. Such divisions were to be a constant feature of the history of ETA. Invariably, the more socialist fraction would be expelled and the line of 'legitimacy' would be that pursued by the more violent, nationalist section. With age and experience, ETA militants would come to despair of the endless cycle of violence, seeing progress in political methods and links with other leftist groups. A new genera-tion of young and unsophisticated activists would replace them and put their hopes in violence. Accordingly, the Burgos prisoners who belonged to the more socialist ETA-Sexta Asamblea (Sixth Assembly) would move into more conventional politics.

The kidnappers of Eugen Beihl belonged to the more nationalist ETA-Quinta Asamblea (Fifth Assembly). ETA-V kidnapped Beihl as an act of self-assertion and to establish the fact that the Basque struggle did not need the help of liberals and leftists from elsewhere in Spain. As well as bringing pressure on the government, the kidnapping was meant to show that ETA-V's 'military' methods were more efficacious than the wide popular mobilizations being organized throughout Spain. It was announced that Beihl's fate would depend on whether death sentences were implemented. While frenzied searches were being carried out, the West German government began to exert pressure to ensure that clemency would be exercised. As Germany was Spain's second most important supplier, second most important customer and third largest foreign investor, threats of economic sanctions carried enormous weight. In a sense, this ensured that the trial had had its teeth drawn even before it began.[30] In the event, Herr Beihl was freed on Christmas Day 1970 before the sentences were announced. This gesture, with its implication that ETA was not frightened of Francoist 'justice', infuriated the more reactionary elements within the regime. Curiously, the Beihl kidnapping demonstrated the extraordinary identification between ETA and the Basque people. While being held in a Basque village, almost certainly on the French side of the border, Herr Beihl took advantage of his captors' carelessness to escape. He was recaptured by villagers and turned over once more to ETA-V.[31]

The trials began on 3 December. Both the behaviour of the army officers in charge and of the accused made it clear that this was meant to be a judgement on and a punishment of the entire Basque people. By making a collective prosecution, the military lawyers focused world attention on the nationalist aspirations shared, and the Francoist brutality suffered, by all sixteen defendants and many other Basques. The alleged terrorist crimes of some of the defendants received considerably less attention. In any case, constant demonstrations in the capitals of Europe and parts of Latin America, together with the agitation in Euskadi and other areas of Spain, ensured that the specifics of the trial were less prominent than its more generalized repressive function. The cabinet guaranteed that this would be the case when it met on 4 December in extraordinary session to decree a three-month state of exception in Guipúzcoa. House searches, unlimited detention, banishment and censorship of mail were to be even more unrestrained than usual. The link between the trial and the wider persecution of the Basque people could hardly have been established more graphically.[32]

On 6 December, the first of the accused, Jesús Abrisqueta Corta, made his statement. To the astonishment of both public and press, the President of the Tribunal, Colonel Manuel Ordovas, permitted him to give a detailed account of the torture to which he had been subjected by the police. The next three defendants did the same, as well as discussing the oppression of the Basque people by the Francoist state. It is possible that Ordovas's forbearance reflected a distaste for the repressive function being attributed to the army as well as a readiness to embarrass the police. On 7 December, the trial was adjourned and, when it was resumed, it was clear that Ordovas had been ordered to put a stop to further revelations. Both the accused and their lawyers were constantly interrupted and threatened. The session of 9 December ended in chaos. Mario Onaindía Nachiondo, after giving a detailed defence of ETA's position within the Basque struggle, was ordered to be silent. He jumped from the witness box and began to sing the hymn of the Basque Warrior, the *Eusko Gudariak*. The other fifteen accused, chained together, joined in, as did many members of the public. Two officers of the tribunal drew their swords in an ineffectual effort to restore order. After the court had been cleared, the trial was resumed in camera.[33]

In the days that followed, it became clear that the trial had brought to the surface enormous reserves of anti-regime feeling. A long wait began for the announcement of the sentences. Violence continued with clashes between police and demonstrators in Madrid, Barcelona, Bilbao, Oviedo, Seville and Pamplona. On 12 December, 300 Catalan artists, writers and intellectuals shut themselves in the Abbey of Montserrat and issued a manifesto in solidarity with the Basque people, calling for political amnesty, democratic freedoms and the right to regional self-determination. The Abbot, Dom Cassia Just, expressed his approval and *L'Osservatore Romano* published the manifesto. However, with the Civil Guard besieging the monastery, the demonstrators ended their occupation on 14 December for fear of reprisals against the Abbot and his monks. Nevertheless, the Abbot declared to *Le Monde* that the Church should not be associated with a regime that sentenced people, including Catholics, for no other crime than opposition to Franco. The Communist Party saw the events in Montserrat, the strikes in Euskadi and the demonstrations in the rest of Spain as evidence that an enormous opposition front was being built.[34]

Inevitably, the clamour of condemnation drove the regime and its most frenetic supporters to lash out. On 14 December, in the absence of López Rodó and López Bravo, the cabinet suspended *habeas corpus* in the entire country. Within the armed forces, there was intense resentment at having been made the target for popular discontent as a result of being given the role of cleaning up a mess which was regarded by officers as the consequence of political weakness. Mutterings among the officer corps led to petitions being sent to leading generals in protest at the interference of world opinion in Spanish matters. On 14 December, a group of senior officers gathered near Madrid, at the Carabanchel shooting range, under the conservative Captain-General of the Madrid military region, Joaquín Fernández de Córdoba. After agreeing that opposition should be silenced, they sent a delegation to see Franco. It was in response to the message delivered by Fernández de Córdoba and hard-line generals, Tomás García Rebull, Captain-General of Burgos, Alfonso Pérez Viñeta, Captain-General of Barcelona and Manuel Chamorro, that Franco called the emergency session of the cabinet which suspended constitutional guarantees.[35]

This victory for the ultras heralded the start of a massive counter-offensive by the regime. Since such an operation could be mounted convincingly only by unleashing the ultra masses, it inevitably deepened the cracks within the cabinet. Those members of the regime's service classes, from police torturers to the lowliest pen-pushers of the syndical bureaucracy, who saw their privileges challenged by the opposition blamed the Opus Dei as much as they did the 'reds' and 'separatists' who were their direct enemies. On 16 and 17 December, there were enormous pro-Franco demonstrations organized in Burgos and Madrid. Demonstrators were bussed into the capital from rural Castile, given a day's pay and a packed lunch. Government employees were given the day off to attend. The organization of the day of 'national affirmation' was carried out by a hastily assembled committee of regime hard-liners, senior army officers and ex-ministers who had been supplanted by technocrats.

Anti-Opus banners could be seen in profusion, ranging from 'Franco si, Opus no!' to 'God save us from weak governments!'. Just as, three days before, Franco had been pushed by senior generals, now he was again under pressure. That he could be manipulated by those who wanted revenge for the Opus victory after the Matesa scandal was indicative of his waning health. It had not originally been his intention to attend the rally. He arrived in civilian clothes, having been urged to attend at the last minute by his wife who in turn had been persuaded by the fervour of Franco's personal physician, Vicente Gil. An excitable reactionary, Dr Gil nearly came to blows with the Opus Deista Minister of Information, Alfredo Sánchez Bella. Infuriated because Sánchez Bella failed to give the fascist salute, Dr Gil screamed at him that the technocrats were inept and called him 'a capon'. In the course of the following week, there was a series of stage-managed demonstrations and a hysterical press offensive.[36] Given the renewed weight of repression, the opposition withdrew into silence.

However, despite the apparent reinforcement of the regime, the public self-assertion of the bunker was in fact a symptom of its isolation. Reduced in October 1969 to the technocrats and the hard-liners, the cabinet was pushed nearer to the ultras by the aftermath of the Burgos trials. Carrero Blanco was quick to demonstrate that he was untainted by Opus Dei 'liberalism'. He was due to speak to the Cortes on 21 December. Flushed with the success of the fascist rally five days earlier, the ultras were prepared to give him a rough ride. Their resentment of his links with the Opus technocrats was shown when they stamped their feet and booed his arrival. However, a virtuoso display of 1940s anti-Communist rhetoric soon brought the *procuradores* over to Carrero's side. He presented ETA, the international campaign during the trials and domestic opposition as interlocking parts of a great Communist conspiracy against the regime. He denounced calls for political liberalization as nostalgia for 'the rancid manifesto of Marx and Engels'. With the Burgos trial judges still deliberating, Carrero took for granted the guilt of the defendants, which delighted his listeners even if it stressed once more the extent to which the entire process was an operation to teach the Basques a lesson. He drew applause by announcing the decision taken seven days earlier to suspend for six months Article 18, *habeas corpus,* of the Francoist Constitution, El Fuero de los Españoles.[37]

There was a strong element of bluster in this, just as there had been in the various ultra rallies. None the less, the determination to win back the ground lost during the trial was reflected in the verdicts which were finally announced on 28 December. Colonel Ordovas had been in contact, in contravention of judicial procedures, with General Joaquín Fernández de Córdoba. General García Rebull, who, as Captain-General of the Sixth Military Region (Burgos), would be responsible for signing any death sentences, was under great pressure from brother officers to ensure a tough line. In consequence, the six death sentences asked for by the prosecution were confirmed. Three of the accused were found guilty of two capital charges each and were thus sentenced to death twice. It now lay with Franco to implement or commute the sentences. While the ultras howled for blood, the Caudillo was aware that the international and national agitation provoked by the trials would be magnified tenfold by executions. It is likely that West German pressure had determined clemency some weeks before. In addition, the bulk of the cabinet was in favour of pardons. The trial of strength with the Basques at Burgos had been lost. World opinion and the courage of the rest of the Spanish opposition had ensured that. However, the week of fascist demonstrations and what Franco, in his end-of-year message, called the 'plebiscite' on 17 December helped save the regime's face. More crucially, it permitted him to be shrewdly magnanimous and grant pardons from a position of apparent strength.[38] In contrast, his failure to do the same five years later was to be symbolic of the total degeneration of his rule.

Before the Burgos trials, the tide had been turning against the regime. Worker and student opposition, and even the violent resistance of the Basques, found ecclesiastical support. The fact that, despite economic modernization, the government was forced to rely ever more on repression drove increasing numbers of Francoists into the opposition. The attitude of the Church accelerated this process. After the Burgos trials, the trickle of defectors became steady, although it was not to become a flood until 1974. The trials had altered the balance of forces within Spain. The opposition was more unified than at any time since the Civil War. ETA had boosted the morale of the entire left and it had united the Basque Country around its cause. Henceforth, Euskadi was to become a redoubt of defiance against the regime. The frantic violence to which Carrero Blanco and his successor Arias Navarro were forced to resort built up reserves of hatred which were to place the Basques in the vanguard of the struggle against Franco and, after his death, of the battles to establish democracy.

In the short term, the trials had starkly underlined the rivalry between Opus Dei and the ultras. The fact that, when under pressure, Carrero's reflexes led him to rely on the ultras indicated the way in which the regime's options were running out. For the moment, Franco had arbitrated well, appeasing the bunker with ferocious sentences, the technocrats with the pardons. However, surrounded by an ultra clique in his residence at El Pardo, including his wife, his son-in-law, the Marqués de Villaverde, and the irascible Dr Vicente Gil, and subject to the pressures of old guard stalwarts like José Antonio Girón, the Caudillo was gradually losing control. His moments of lucidity were becoming less and less frequent. The capacity for calculated arbitration between the regime families was replaced by a reversion to earlier instincts which gave even greater weight to the inhabitants of the bunker. On 3 February 1971, the Marqués de Villaverde brought the hostility between the bunker and the Opus out into the open with a speech delivered in Guadalajara. His audience chanted slogans against the Opus Dei. The process whereby the entourage at El Pardo worked to turn the dictator against the technocrats was severely to limit the flexibility with which the cabinet could respond to its mounting political problems.[39]

At times, the bunker went too far. On 8 January 1971, the Captain-General of the Ninth Military Region (Granada), Fernando Rodrigo Cifuentes, addressed a gathering of Civil War veterans. Reminding them of their victory against 'red freemasonry' then, he called on them to combat the Opus Dei's 'white freemasonry which, under the pretext of pursuing noble ends tries to introduce discord among noble elements of the nation'. In consequence, he was put on the reserve list. However, the army remained a bastion of reactionary political attitudes. Rodrigo Cifuentes had committed the sin of bringing regime conflicts out into the open. More discreet hard-liners continued to find preferment. Tomás García Rebull was rewarded for his firmness during the trials with promotion to the First Military Region, Madrid. One of the most unwavering military ultras, General Carlos Iniesta Cano, was made Director-General of the Civil Guard. These promotions reflected the extent to which the resurgence of opposition placed the onus for the defence of the regime on to the army. One of the central tasks would be the control of Madrid. The military governor of the capital was General Angel Campano López. He had endeared himself to the ultra camp during the Burgos trial agitation with a much-quoted remark about the need 'to impose martial law for a week and shoot a hundred thousand'.[40]

The consolidation of the ultras within the military hierarchy optimized the regime's defensive armoury. However, the triumph of *inmovilismo* did little to facilitate the resolution of the enormous social problems facing the government. This was highlighted by the inadequacies of the new Ley Sindical introduced on 16 February 1971. Its admission of limited professional and trade associations did nothing to provide workers with greater participation or representation. The Communist Party pronounced it to be 'a fascist abortion'. With the notable exceptions of the reactionary Archbishop Cantero Cuadrado and Bishop Guerra Campos, the majority of the Church hierarchy condemned the new law. The reality of labour relations was to be found not in Falangist jurisprudence but in the police stations where workers were tortured.

In Seville, protests against the continued suspension of article 18 of the Fuero de los Españoles had culminated in strikes. The police had entered factories and carried off workers. A broad spectrum of lawyers, professors, doctors, architects and workers presented the Cardinal-Archbishop of Seville, José María Bueno Monreal, with a detailed denunciation of police brutality. In Pamplona, a strike in the metallurgical sector throughout January had been contested by police violence. On Holy Thursday, 8 April 1971, a document denouncing the torture of workers, signed by 200 Navarrese priests, was read out in 80 per cent of the churches of Navarra. In Pamplona Cathedral, in the presence of the local authorities, the auxiliary bishop stated, 'I have seen with my own eyes here in Pamplona the tortures, the arbitrary interrogations and the unjustifiable and inexplicable arrests. Those who practise, order, tolerate or ignore them cut themselves off from the Church.'[41]

Just as the continued repression of the working class exposed the emptiness of the syndical law, so too the cabinet's swing to the right emphasized the meaninglessness of the project for political associations which was still being discussed. After the orgy of extremism unchained in late December 1970, the technocrats had been obliged to re-establish their credibility by being more Francoist than Franco. Carrero Blanco had once more slammed the door on political parties in his speech of 21 December. The cosmetic reform now floating around regime circles would permit a pluralism, within the Movimiento, not of parties but of 'the legitimate contrasting of opinions'. As Joaquín Ruiz Giménez commented sadly, far from opening the windows of the system, the new project simply dug deeper the internal labyrinths of the Movimiento. José María de Areilza saw it as merely a mask for *inmovilismo*. Even within the regime, a number of distinguished Francoists began to make public their disappointment at the lack of progress towards political evolution. In July 1971, Ramon Serrano Suñer, the architect of the Francoist state, spoke in Burgos about the need for a controlled return to a party system. Juan Manuel Fanjul Sedeño, one-time Vice-Secretary-General of the Movimiento, a monarchist member of Opus Dei, claimed in November that a democratic opening was necessary for the survival of the system. Despair at the fossilization of the system led him to declare six months later that 'the only thing that happens when you retreat to the cellars of the Chancellery is that you provoke the collapse of the Chancellery on top of you'.[42] Fanjul Sedeño, who was later to be an *éminence grise* of Adolfo Suárez's UCD after the death of Franco, was thereby inadvertently instrumental in coining the expression 'the bunker' to denote the intransigent extreme right.

Intelligent Francoists could not help but be alarmed at the blindness of the government. Unable to stop the rising waves of opposition, Carrero simply introduced tougher measures, making more offences, hitherto under civil jurisdiction, subject to military law. Fines and suspensions were imposed upon the press with greater strictness. On 25 June 1971, the country's most progressive magazine, *Triunfo*, was suspended for four months and fined 250,000 pesetas. On 25 November, *Madrid* was closed down. It was further evidence, if any were needed, that the government of neo-Francoist technocrats was incapable of sponsoring any kind of political evolution.[43] Moreover, the identification of the technocrats with undiluted Francoism had been graphically illustrated on 1 October 1971. The same ultras who had organized the demonstration in Madrid's Plaza del Oriente on 17 December 1970 had planned to repeat the operation in Burgos. However, the technocratic ministers found out and took it over. The Ministry of the Interior was used to mobilize the local structures of the Movimiento. Hundreds of trains and buses provided free transport. Thousands of soldiers attended in civilian clothes. It was rumoured that the Movimiento had issued cassocks to make it appear that many priests were with Franco and against the hierarchy. About 200,000 of the regime's servants assembled to cheer Franco. They almost certainly missed the point that they had been used by the technocrats. A partial amnesty granted by Franco reached few political prisoners but it did reach those former ministers and officials who had been fined as a result of Matesa. It was hardly surprising that the technocrats were anxious to silence the liberal press.[44]

The rumours about Falangists disguised as priests reflected the fact that Movimiento propagandists were rattled by the accelerating liberalization of the Church. A number of appointments in 1971 showed that the regime was indeed being systematically isolated from an ever more progressive Church. In June 1971, the reactionary Archbishop of Madrid-Alcalá, Casimiro Morcillo González, died. Recognizing the immense importance of the Madrid diocese, the Vatican appointed as Apostolic Administrator no less a figure than the Primate himself, Cardinal Vicente Enrique y Tarancón. He did not wait long before showing the extent of his determination to dissociate the Church from the regime. On 13 September 1971, he inaugurated an Asamblea Conjunta de Obispos y Sacerdotes (joint assembly of bishops and priests) which issued a declaration which dramatically rejected the triumphant Civil War ideology of the dictatorship. In it, there figured the words

'We recognize humbly and we ask forgiveness because we were not able when it was necessary to be true ministers of reconciliation in the heart of the people divided by a war among brothers.' (*'Reconocemos humildemente y pedimos por ello perdón, por no haber sabido ser, cuando fue necesario, verdaderos ministros de la reconciliación.'*) In December 1971 the Vatican underlined the fact that Madrid-Alcalá was the real seat of Church power by confirming Cardinal Enrique y Tarancón in the post. He was replaced as Primate by Archbishop González Martín, whose centralist views had caused much friction when he was Archbishop of Barcelona. This solved a problem for the regime but it also permitted the appointment to Barcelona of the liberal Catalan Archbishop Narcis Jubany Arnau.[45]

In the meanwhile, working class protest was becoming more persistent than ever. Wage rises were well below the rate of inflation. Moreover, the much vaunted growth in GDP simply hid the reality of working-class social conditions. Access to certain consumer goods was feeble compensation for an inadequate level of social services. The planners had failed to solve the housing problems created by massive urbanization. The gap was filled to the lowest standards conceivable by speculative builders. The consequent problems of poor sanitation and deficient provision of educational and medical facilities contributed to the politicization of working-class consciousness. The Communist Party, for instance, put immense effort into helping resolve the daily problems of working-class *barrios* through ostensibly non-political neighbourhood associations. The regime was not prepared to make any concessions. Despite the rhetoric of the new syndical law, the Ministry of Labour was meeting strikes with preventative arrests and limits on the reporting of labour disputes in the press.

Strikes became more bitterly contested and solidarity actions in response to police brutality raised Communist hopes of a general strike. On 13 September the building workers went on strike in Madrid. A Communist labour leader, Pedro Patiño Toledo, was shot dead by the Civil Guard while he distributed leaflets. 70,000 workers refused to return to the sites for five days as a mark of solidarity and mourning. In October there were fierce confrontations in the Asturian mines and the SEAT (Sociedad Española de Automoviles de Turismo) car works in Barcelona. Both strikes had their origins in protests against appalling working conditions but were quickly politicized by the intervention of the police. Since both the Asturian mines and SEAT were state-owned, the strikes were treated as direct challenges to the regime. The SEAT factory was occupied by 7000 workers in protest at the sacking of twenty-three strikers including nine shop-stewards. The Civil Governor sent in the police who were fought off with hosepipes.[46] Many employers were increasingly disturbed by the way in which labour disputes were aggravated by government intervention. In the more advanced industrial regions, Madrid, Barcelona and the Basque Country, they were coming to see the regime's repressive mechanisms as a positive obstacle to workable labour relations. Many of them were by-passing the official syndical structures and negotiating directly with representatives of the clandestine unions.

The inflexibility of the regime was giving substance to the Communist Party strategy of the so-called Pact for Liberty, particularly in Catalonia. During 1971, a series of preparatory meetings had been held by delegates of all the principal Catalan opposition forces, the Communist Partit Socialista Unificat de Catalunya, many socialist groups, the Comisiones Obreras, liberal monarchists, Catholics, professional organizations and women's groups. On 7 November, about 300 delegates gathered secretly in Barcelona for the first Assemblea de Catalunya, inspired in part by the experience of the previous year in Montserrat. The most remarkable feature of the Assemblea and its programme for political amnesty and liberty was the width of the political spectrum that it spanned. The signatories included several prominent members of the Catalan industrial and banking bourgeoisie. It was rumoured that the Assemblea had received a telegram of solidarity from a Catalan bishop.[47] There could hardly have been stronger evidence of the fact that, in the face of the retrogression of the regime, influential sectors of Spain's economic oligarchies were making alternative arrangements for their own survival. The example of the Assemblea was soon to be followed elsewhere, especially in Madrid and Seville.

It does not seem to have occurred to the Carrero Blanco cabinet that its hard line was merely serving to widen the opposition. Moreover, it could devise no more creative response to dissent than to acquiesce in ever greater violence. Throughout 1971 and thereafter, numerous neo-fascist terrorist squads made their appearance and began to carry out violence against all those who could be considered the enemies of the regime. Gelling around the magazine *Fuerza Nueva* and its editor, Blas Piñar, who was a friend of Carrero, groups like the Guerrilleros de Cristo Rey, the neo-Nazi Partido Español Nacional-Socialista, the Comandos de Lucha Antimarxista and many others carried out assaults on workers, priests and intellectuals. Made up of hired thugs, the sons of ultras and sometimes off-duty policemen, they acted with sufficient impunity to suggest official connivance. After all, they did work which the technocratic cabinet, anxious for integration into Europe and ostensibly Catholic, would have found embarrassing to have done officially.

In the universities, liberals and leftists were subjected to sporadic terror. The churches of progressive priests were invaded and clergy and congregations attacked. In working-class *barrios*, raids were made against known union leaders. Art galleries and bookshops were destroyed. The apartment of a neo-fascist sympathizer exploded in Barcelona on 6 February 1972 wrecking the building and killing six people. It was popularly supposed that what had exploded was an arms dump despite the official explanation of a faulty gas fitting.[48] The activities of the ultra squads were an effort to repair leaks in the dam of Francoism. Some of the more unimaginative supporters of the regime who had lived well off it for so long now recognized that society was changing beyond the capacity of institutionalized Francoism to contain it. Accordingly, to protect their privileges, and those of their masters, they were trying to terrorize the clock back.

That terror squads were thought necessary was testimony to the heightened morale and courage of the opposition. The 'legal' mechanisms of the regime were less able to silence workers, students or regionalists. The successes of ETA and the catalyst of the Burgos trials were partly responsible for this change in the balance of power between regime and opposition. The trials had also affected ETA. Bombings, robberies and attacks on the forces of order continued to be carried out by the militants of ETA-V. The lesson of Burgos and the great popular mobilizations which it had provoked was that ETA must unite the nationalist and labour struggles. On 19 January 1972, a spectacular tactic was employed to reinforce the demands of striking Basque workers. The industrialist, Lorenzo Zabala, was kidnapped in Durango and released only after his company, Precicontrol, announced that 183 sacked strikers would be reinstated and pay increased. The clandestine unions had mixed feelings about this intervention, and over the years would come to resent interference in the labour struggle. At this time, such Robin Hood-style actions were meant to back up the ETA assertion that its military front was a complement to the mass struggle of the workers.

In those days before its murderous post-1975 degeneration, ETA was admired by some sections of the left both in Spain and abroad as an efficacious instrument of opposition against the dictatorship. Now, in addition to its regular activities of stealing money, explosives and printing equipment and attacking the security forces, ETA began to assault the local headquarters of the vertical syndicates. At the same time, known meeting-places of the wealthy oligarchy, casinos and yacht clubs, were blown up. On 12 January 1973, another industrialist, Felix Huarte, was kidnapped in support of workers on strike at one of his companies in Pamplona, Torfinasa. It was a clever propaganda stunt since it was impossible at that time to walk the streets of any town in Spain without seeing the name Huarte emblazoned on a construction site. Just as in the case of Zabala, the desired wage increases were conceded.[49]

Whatever the effect on the morale of the striking workers of Torfinasa, the real significance of the kidnapping of Huarte lay in its long-term impact on ETA itself. Huarte was one of Spain's more progressive industrialists. Like others of his kind, he had begun to by-pass the official Sindicatos and to negotiate directly with the Comisiones Obreras. For this reason, the chorus of protest at the kidnapping was broken by a discordant voice from within the Movimiento. In a demagogic attack on Huarte, Emilio Romero wrote in the daily linked to the Sindicatos, *Pueblo*, that if the company would pay up under threat of violence it should have done so in normal negotiations through the syndical mechanism. Romero's article reflected the anguish of Falangists that economic and social changes were rendering the Movimiento and the Sindicatos increasingly irrelevant. However, the polemic which ensued with the more establishment-orientated evening newspaper *Informaciones* alerted the theorists of ETA to the possibilities of divisions within the Francoist clans.

Hitherto, the strategy of ETA, postulated on the assumption that Francoism was a monolithic block, tended to see armed struggle in relatively crude terms. The traditional ETA view, like that of the nineteenth-century Russian terrorist, Nechayev, favoured a dynamic of action–repression–action whereby violence against servants of the state would provoke a level of repression which would mobilize popular militancy against the regime. In the 1970s, however, a determination to link up with the labour movement had led to armed struggle being seen as something which would come into operation after strikes had reached deadlock. This had been the case with the kidnapping of Lorenzo Zabala. In 1973, the repercussions to the Huarte case led ETA's theorists to see the contradictions between the interests of the Francoists of the syndical and repressive apparatuses and those of the advanced sectors of the economic oligarchy. This point had been perceived fifteen years earlier by the Communist theorist, Fernando Claudín, an insight which had led to his expulsion from the PCE. In fact, neither then nor subsequently was ETA, with its rapid turnover of militants, notable for theoretical sophistication. None the less, it was decided to concentrate on actions which would accentuate the divisions within Francoism. To this end, plans began for the kidnapping of the Vice-President, Carrero Blanco.[50]

Perhaps inevitably, ETA activities were not received with universal acclaim by the left in the rest of Spain. Both the Comisiones Obreras and the Socialist UGT preferred to build up working-class strength by gradual development of mass solidarity rather than by violence. Central to the action–repression–action cycle of ETA's plans were the blanket reprisals which hit the left and the working class in general. The Communists in particular, having adopted a policy of seeking alliances with the 'dynamic sectors of Spanish capitalism' as part of their Pact for Liberty policy, were hostile to ETA. However, that did little to diminish the regime's sense of being under siege nor to dissuade it from reacting violently against both strikers and terrorists. Indeed, by 1973, operations against ETA were taking the form of direct military confrontations between large contingents of Civil Guards and small ETA *comandos*. ETA claimed that the regime had decided to face no more Burgos trials and was set upon the physical elimination of its members. The most effective blow struck against ETA was the killing in Algorta on 19 April 1973 of Eustakio Mendizabal, 'Txikia', perhaps the one leader capable of holding together its military and labour fronts. His death allowed the tensions within the movement to come to the surface. Within eighteen months, the workers' front would split off, leaving ETA more committed than ever to armed violence.[51]

In 1972 and 1973, the Basque Country had not yet assumed the vanguard role that it was to have in the mid-1970s. The confrontations which seemed most likely to bring down the regime were in the factories and the universities. The Communist conviction that Francoism would be overthrown by a revolutionary general strike seemed to be justified by the scale and intensity of strikes in the first years of the decade. In March 1972 a strike at the state-owned Bazán shipyards in El Ferrol was treated with such brutality that the entire town was politicized. On 10 March the police fired on a demonstration of 3000 strikers, killing two and wounding another fifteen. When the government threatened to militarize the workers and apply martial law to them, there were solidarity strikes all over Galicia, in the Asturian mines, in Catalonia and in the Basque Country.[52] Clashes between police and students reached similar intensity. From 13 to 18 January, more than fifty people were hurt in fighting at

Madrid University. Students marched through the streets of the capital and by the end of the month most of the University had been closed by the authorities.[53] Further violence in the University of Valladolid led to the promotion of hard-liners within the Ministry of Education as the first step towards a purge of subversive teachers and students from the universities. This did nothing to stop student unrest and the first quarter of 1973 witnessed even more violent clashes.

The cabinet of technocrat modernizers whose job had been to guarantee Francoism after Franco by creating the prosperity to draw the sting from political opposition was virtually bankrupt. The morale of the opposition was high, the situation in the Basque Country could hardly have been more explosive and the Church had effectively joined the enemy. The anti-Francoism of many bishops had been clear for some years, but the regime had played with the fiction that criticism emanated only from a handful of hotheads. The reality became unavoidable after Franco's end-of-the-year message in 1971. In a warning to the bishops, he had declared that 'a State cannot fold its arms in the face of certain temporal positions taken up by some ecclesiastics'. Far from being cowed, the Church hardened its position. On the following day, Monsignor Suquia Goicoechea, Bishop of Malaga, issued a pastoral in which he declared that the hierarchy would not be silenced by threats. The ACNP daily, *Ya*, normally respectful towards the regime, commented daringly that 'we should think twice, when the ecclesiastical hierarchy speaks, before accusing it of invading the temporal sphere'.[54] Thereafter, the outspoken criticism of the regime's brutality by the Church's Pax et Justitia commission constituted the most damning evidence of the failure of the fanatically pious Catholics of Carrero Blanco's cabinet.

The Carrero Blanco–López Rodó scheme of neo-Francoist *continuismo* had found no solution, other than a hardening of official oppressive violence and a furtive reliance on ultra-rightist terrorism, to the profound social and political unrest that it had inherited. The consequences of this failure were, broadly speaking, twofold: the intensification of divisions within the regime forces and the clarification of options within the opposition. The steady build-up of strikes and their extension as repression provoked solidarity actions were confirming the Communist Party in its view that the transition from dictatorship to democracy would be carried out by a combination of the Pact for Liberty and a national general strike. With the regime brought to its knees by the strike, the forces united by the Pact would establish a provisional government and then call constituent elections.[55] The Partido Socialista

Obrero Español was less specific, and certainly less *triunfalista*, about how it proposed to conquer democracy. After years of impotence, the PSOE was experiencing a process of revival. Its XII Congress in exile, held in Toulouse from 13 to 15 August 1972, had seen the emergence of an influential group of militants, led by Felipe González from Seville and Nicolás Redondo from Bilbao, who supplanted the obsolete exiled leadership. Their main concerns were with rebuilding the PSOE. Their project for overthrowing Franco was vague but not unsimilar to that of the PCE, which after all resembled the scenario by which the PSOE had come to power in 1931. The Socialists too were sure that the working class would be in the forefront of the battle and that the PSOE's political task was to seek unity with other opposition forces.[56] Groups to the left of the PCE, most of them relatively small, had roughly similar programmes for the replacement of the dictatorship.

The moderate opposition, made up of and increasingly swelled by defectors from the regime, had an altogether less conflictive view of the future. For many years, important conservatives, like Joaquín Satrústegui and José María de Areilza, had hoped for a non-violent transition to a democratic monarchy under Don Juan de Borbón. Others, like Dionisio Ridruejo or Joaquín Ruiz Giménez, were stronger in their hostility to the regime yet still maintained hopes of a peaceful evolution to democracy by means of an ever greater isolation of the Francoist residue. The rigidity of Carrero's rule, together with the emergence of ultra-rightist violence, not only accelerated the growth of the moderate opposition but also spread the conviction that the Carrero option consisted of little more than a determination to go down fighting.

Accordingly, a search began for a way that would permit a transition without bloodshed. The idea began to emerge, among academic theorists and politicians, that the Francoist constitution's own rhetoric could be exploited to permit a real evolution. Areilza, Antonio Garrigues y Díaz Cañabate who resigned as Ambassador to the Holy See, and other leading figures of the moderate opposition, came around to the idea that to have any chance of success in bringing off a 'legal' evolution to democracy they must recapture Juan Carlos from the technocrats.[57] In the event, that was to be easier than they expected. By comparison with the support enjoyed by the Communist Party among the working class and that the Socialists would soon find behind them, the moderate opposition had little in the way of active militants. However, when in 1976 there seemed every possibility of a bloody confrontation between the immobilism of the regime and the forces of the left, the legalist and evolutionary project, fully backed by Juan Carlos, was to come into its own.

For Carrero Blanco, evolution meant at most political associations. Franco's 1972 end-of-year message spoke of the 'legitimacy of the disparity of ideas and tendencies'. On 1 March 1973, Carrero addressed the Movimiento's consultative assembly, the Consejo Nacional, and proposed measures which were to increase the participation of the Spanish people in political life. However, what he was proposing amounted to little more than a three-group associationism, as always within the Movimiento, to consist of a Falangist right, a technocratic centre and a conservative Christian Democrat 'left'. A political spectrum consisting of Girón, López Rodó and Federico Silva Muñoz, who had been Minister of Public Works until 1970, was hardly a revolutionary prospect. However, for hard-liners like Blas Piñar or General Carlos Iniesta Cano, such liberalizing talk was responsible for the break-up of the country's social and political stability. In early April there were solidarity strikes all over Catalonia after a striker was killed by the police in San Adrián de Besós.[58] The ultra-right was determined that the rot must be stopped.

Their opportunity came on 1 May. During the traditional working-class demonstrations in Madrid, a secret police inspector, Juan Antonio Fernández Gutiérrez, was stabbed to death by a member of the ultra-leftist FRAP. Two other secret policemen were also wounded. It was rumoured that the stabbing had been an act of revenge for the death of the striker. Years later, it was revealed that FRAP was riddled with police *agents provocateurs*. At the time, the incident provided the perfect excuse for a massive offensive by the hard-liners of the regime. There were mass arrests and leftists were tortured. However, the most significant events began with the funeral of Fernández Gutiérrez. The cortège was led by General Iniesta. Members of the police demonstrated in demand of repressive measures while 3000 Falangist war veterans screamed for vengeance. Their placards praised the neo-Nazi ultras and called for the shooting of 'red archbishops'. Effectively, a police mutiny in the presence of Carrero Blanco was being tolerated, a clear indication that the tide was running in favour of the ultras. The entourage at El Pardo easily managed to convince Franco that the government had failed in its task of keeping order.

On 8 June, Carrero was promoted to President of the Council of Ministers and on the 11th announced the formation of a cabinet which finally brought down the curtain on liberalization. López Bravo was dropped; López Rodó exiled to the Ministry of Foreign Affairs and the thankless task of representing a dour cabinet in the wider world. The few technocrats who managed to remain, like José María López de Letona at Industry and Tomás Allende y García Baxter at Agriculture, or to come aboard, like Fernando de Liñán at Information, were strictly Carrero's own men. The Falange was back with a vengeance with Francisco Ruiz Jarabo at Justice, José Utrera Molina at Housing, Licinio de la Fuente at Labour and Enrique García Ramal at Sindicatos. There were significant concessions to the ultras in the appointments of Carlos Arias Navarro, once strong-arm Director-General of Security and later *Alcalde* (mayor) of Madrid, at the Ministry of the Interior, and of Julio Rodríguez Martínez, a wildly belligerent hard-liner, at Education. The Minister Secretary-General of the Movimiento, Torcuato Fernández Miranda, survived and was promoted to become Vice-President. On 23 June, Fernández Miranda denounced the 'ideological pluralism on which party democracy is based'. If the '*monocolor*' cabinet had been grey, its successor sported the blue of the Falange.[59] Everything about the new government suggested the preparation of a holding operation to cover the succession. Madrid wags called it 'the funeral cabinet'. It was a team fitted to stifle reform and crush opposition. On the sinking ship of Francoism, the crew could think of no better tactic than to put on diving suits.

Franco's much quoted remark that everything was 'well tied down' (*atado y bien atado*) could hardly have been more misplaced. After a short respite during the summer, the working class was as militant as ever. In November, the government introduced a series of stabilizing measures in response to rampant inflation. Almost immediately there were major strikes in Catalonia, the Asturian mines and the Basque steel industry as well as in less traditionally conflictive areas. Since workers needed two jobs or long overtime in order to give their families a reasonable standard of living, social conflict was the greatest problem faced by the Carrero government. The energy crisis was on the horizon and, for a country as dependent on imported energy as Spain was, recession was inevitable and with it further labour problems. The only response of which the cabinet was capable was renewed repression. That much was made clear by the preparation of the *proceso 1.001*, a show trial of ten members of the Comisiones Obreras charged with illegal association. It was to be a public demonstration of the cabinet's determination to crush the underground unions, a kind of Burgos trial of the workers.[60]

In the event, the trial was held in an atmosphere of terror with the accused and the lawyers being threatened with lynching by hysterical rightist mobs surrounding the Palace of Justice.[61] This was the first consequence of the fact that, fifteen minutes before the proceedings were due to open, Carrero Blanco was assassinated by an ETA *comando*. A bomb placed under the street blew his car right over the Church that he had just attended. The earlier scheme to kidnap Carrero had been dropped when he became Prime Minister and subject to more thorough security measures than before.[62] The assassination had been timed to coincide with the beginning of the *1.001* trial in order to boost the morale of the workers by demonstrating the vulnerability of their enemies. However, in line with the theoretical discussions which had followed the kidnapping of Huarte, it was also hoped that the murder of Carrero Blanco would affect the internal politics of the regime. The calculation was that the regime would either swing to the right and therefore be even further isolated from the people or else begin a process of *apertura* which would provoke the rage of the ultras. It was a blow calculated to smash Franco's plans for the continuation of his regime.

ETA's communiqué accepting responsibility for the assassination was unequivocal. The operation was meant to avenge the deaths of ETA militants like 'Txikia' but it was also intended to intensify divisions among regime forces: 'Luis Carrero Blanco, a hard man, violent in his repressive attitudes, was the key which guaranteed the continuity and stability of the Francoist system. It is certain that, without him, the tensions between the different tendencies loyal to General Franco's fascist regime – Opus Dei, Falange, etc. – will be dangerously sharpened. We therefore consider our action against the president of the Spanish government to be indisputably an advance of the most fundamental kind in the struggle against national oppression and for the cause of socialism in Euskadi and for the freedom of all those who are exploited and oppressed within the Spanish state.'[63]

A year later, *Le Monde* quoted 'an ex-ambassador of Franco, one of the most subtle and Cartesian analysts in Madrid', almost certainly José María de Areilza, to the effect that Carrero's death had shortened the process of the post-Franco succession by at least five years.[64] In fact, it is unlikely that Carrero Blanco could long have averted the clash within the regime between the advocates of reactionary politics and the champions of modern economics, let alone have silenced the rising clamour of popular militancy. On the other hand, his background gave ample reason to speculate that he would have been more intransigent than his successor when faced with demands for reform. It is certainly the case that tensions emerged rapidly after his death. However, in view of the deteriorating economic situation, they would anyway have come to the surface soon after.

One crumb of comfort for the *continuistas* was the relatively smooth way in which the regime's constitutional mechanisms functioned in overcoming the problems of administrative continuity and general confidence. The Vice-President of the Government, Torcuato Fernández Miranda, took over as interim Prime Minister until a successor could be named. Yet, behind the scenes, there was evidence of positions being taken up for the forthcoming power struggle. The most dramatic events concerned the attitude of the ultras who reacted as ETA had foreseen. They were not placated by the fact that the 'Carabanchel Ten' leaders of the Comisiones Obreras were given sentences in the *1.001* trial totalling 162 years.[65] There was posturing and threatening behaviour by ultra-rightists sufficient to convince many on the left, wrongly as it happened, that a night of the long knives was imminent. In the hospital where the Admiral's body was taken, infuriated members of the ultra establishment talked of a *razzia* (punitive raid) against the enemies of the regime. Most prominent leftists went into hiding. The Admiral's funeral was turned into a neo-fascist rally at which the Archbishop of Madrid was insulted and strident calls were heard for a return to strong government.

The most disturbing incident came about as a result of the emotional reaction to the assassination shown by General Carlos Iniesta Cano, the Director-General of the Civil Guard. Iniesta, a close friend of José Antonio Girón de Velasco and one of the more extreme military ultras, issued an order to his local commanders to shoot subversives and demonstrators. However, the most senior military minister Admiral Gabriel Pita da Veiga, the interim Prime Minister, Torcuato Fernández Miranda and the Minister of the Interior, Carlos Arias Navarro, backed up by the head of Carrero's private intelligence service, Lieutenant-Colonel José Ignacio San Martín, acted together to prevent a bloodbath. Iniesta was forced to rescind his telegram and placed briefly under house arrest. The leader of Fuerza Nueva, Blas Piñar López, was ordered to keep his men under control. When he tried to harangue a crowd at the scene of the crime, a police helicopter hovered above drowning his speech. The American Ambassador and leaders of the moderate opposition were informed that the situation was under control. Two of Carrero's ministers, Julio Rodríguez (Education) and José Utrera Molina (Housing) presented themselves in an emotional state at the office of the chief of the Madrid police, Colonel Federico Quintero Morente, and offered to join a revenge squad to seek out and kill the assassins.[66]

The clash between prudent and irresponsibly reactionary elements over the Iniesta incident was repeated in the scramble to find a successor to Carrero. The logical choice seemed to be the interim Prime Minister, Torcuato Fernández Miranda, not least because of his close relations with Prince Juan Carlos. However, he was not favoured by the bunker precisely because of that relationship, because he was by their standards something of an *aperturista* and his bleakly taciturn manner hardly meshed with their style of bluff camaraderie. To an extent, he was a victim of the machinations of a number of ultras who were able to exploit Franco's increasing infirmity in order to push a retrogressive line. The same fate was suffered by another remote 'liberal' possibility, the Chief of the General Staff, General Díez Alegría. With the Madrid political élite alive with speculation, the real decisions were taking place in the squabbling inner circle of the senile dictator. Franco himself was thought to favour another military figure, either Admiral Nieto Antúnez or General Castañón de Mena. Middle-of-the-road opinion within the Movimiento was betting on 'progressive' figures like the conservative Catholic Federico Silva Muñoz, the Opus Deistas Gregorio López Bravo or Laureano López Rodó, or even Manuel Fraga. However, none of these names was to the liking of the bunker. A joint campaign to influence the Caudillo was mounted by his wife, Doña Carmen, by his frenetically reactionary medical advisor, Dr Vicente Gil, and by Girón. Under this assault, and suffering from a heavy dose of influenza, Franco made a decision which, perhaps for the first time in his dictatorship, was not his own and appointed Carlos Arias Navarro.[67] This was further indication that the disintegration of the regime anticipated by ETA had already begun.

As well as being a close friend of the Franco family, there was ample reason for Arias to be an acceptable candidate as far as the bunker was concerned. He had been nominated by the Barcelona daily *La Vanguardia* as the hardest man in Carrero's cabinet. An expert in questions of internal security, he had been a long-serving Director-General of Security under the hard-line General Camilo Alonso Vega. During his six months as Minister of the Interior, there had been major offensives against ETA, with nine militants shot, against the PCE, with several regional networks broken up, and against the Comisiones Obreras.[68] However, lingering doubts about Carrero's death remained. After all, Arias was the minister ultimately responsible for the astonishing security failures at the time. No controls were imposed at Barajas airport or on roads out of Madrid for five hours after the explosion. There was widespread scepticism about the ease with which the complex preparations for the operation were carried out in an area containing the US embassy and many official buildings. It was odd that security searches prior to Henry Kissinger's visit the previous day had revealed nothing of the elaborate preparations made by the ETA *comando* which had tunnelled under the Calle Claudio Coello. Arias was partly redeemed by the fact that Carrero had ignored his warnings to change his rigidly regular daily route.[69]

In any case, his previous track record as a prosecutor during the Civil War, as a provincial governor active in the repression of the 1940s *guerrilla* and as a policeman was enough to reassure the Francoist élite that there would be an iron fist to deal with any threats to the established order. He kept on eight of Carrero's ministers in his new cabinet and added, or reintroduced, a number of tough Falangist bureaucrats. The team announced on 3 January 1974 could not have been more backward-looking.[70] To outside observers, it seemed that Arias constituted the swing to the right anticipated by ETA. However, all was not entirely as it seemed.

3
A necessary evil: the Arias Navarro experience 1974–6

It would be wrong to see the assassination of Carrero Blanco as itself provoking the final crisis of the Franco regime. After all, the problems which were to be central to that crisis – labour militancy, Basque terrorism and divisions among the Francoist families – had been present when Franco first promoted Carrero from Under-Secretary to the Presidency to Vice-President of the Council of Ministers in September 1967. Those problems had grown even more acute by the end of the 1960s when the Caudillo, after thirty years at the helm, began to place ever more weight on the shoulders of his dry-land admiral. The creeping historical obsolescence of Francoism was emphasized by the fact that the dwindling of the dictator's own energies coincided with the rising tide of working-class and regionalist opposition and a less sympathetic international context.

During the period of Carrero Blanco's pre-eminence, it was almost inevitable that existing rivalries within the Francoist camp would sharpen as domestic and international pressures caused various groups to reconsider their political options. Carrero's mission had been to stop this happening by clamping down on the opposition and by permitting the most minimal *apertura*. It was in this sense that Carrero Blanco was to have acted as a bridge between hard-liners and progressives within the regime. However, the resolution of the contradictions between a developing society and a retrograde polity required more dramatic changes than Carrero could have offered without betraying either himself or his master. That was made clear by the events of the summer of 1973 and the reversion to a tough cabinet, whose most representative figure had been Arias Navarro. At the moment of his death, Carrero's government was already running into serious difficulties. Thus, ETA's action came to accelerate the potential centrifugal tendencies among the regime forces. When the debris and dust cleared after the explosion in the Calle Claudio Coello, the more perceptive began to intensify their own plans for post-Franco survival.

Arias Navarro had been picked by Franco, and was favoured by the ultras, as a man capable of continuing Carrero Blanco's holding operation. There was little about his new cabinet to disconcert either the Caudillo or his old guard. The inclusion of three vice-presidents – the Ministers of the Interior, Finance and Labour – indicated that the government's main preoccupations would be the closely linked issues of public order, inflation and working-class unrest. One of Carrero's last measures had been the stabilization package introduced in November 1973. Almost immediately, there were strikes in the Asturian coal mines and the Basque steel industry. The Catalan textile sector also had labour problems and there were fierce conflicts in normally quiet towns like Zaragoza, Valladolid and Alcoy. The combination of uncontrolled inflation and a wage freeze had explosive political implications.[1] Spain's almost total energy dependence made her especially vulnerable to the sharp contemporary rises in crude oil prices.[2] Moreover, two of her main sources of foreign currency, tourism and remittances from emigrant workers, were about to be dramatically diminished by the impact of the energy crisis on northern Europe. The assassination of Carrero Blanco slowed down the rhythm of strikes for only the briefest of intervals since energy costs were passed on virtually indiscriminately to the consumer. In the first quarter of 1974, electricity prices rose by 15 per cent, petrol by 70 per cent, butane gas, the most widely used fuel for heating and cooking, by 60 per cent and transport costs by 33 per cent. Already at the beginning of the year, inflation was running at an annual rate of over 25 per cent at the same time as wage increases were held to 15 per cent.[3] The consequent drop in the spending power of the working classes was reflected in the quickening pace of strikes.

Even the narrow reactionary clique within which Franco increasingly isolated himself had been acutely aware of the problem of labour militancy during the process of selecting a successor to Carrero.[4] Arias revealed his own orthodox Francoist instincts with the appointment of a hard-liner as Minister of the Interior. The new cabinet Vice-President in charge of internal security, José García Hernández, had been, like Arias, an ex-assistant to the notorious General Camilo Alonso Vega. Carrero's Minister of Labour, Licinio de la Fuente, was retained. De la Fuente was a Falangist with a reputation within the regime for social concern. However, the working-class movement was not appeased. Its leaders were only too aware that the rest of the cabinet was hardly likely to permit Licinio de la Fuente to exercise the flexibility so urgently needed on the labour front.

The case of the third Vice-President was, however, notably different. Antonio Barrera de Irimo, one-time president of the Spanish telephone company, could reasonably be seen as a representative figure of the more dynamic sectors of Spanish capitalism. His retention from Carrero's cabinet seemed to be an unexpected concession to modernity by Arias Navarro. Indeed, it underlined the ambiguity, not to say schizophrenia, which was to characterize Arias's period in power. Arias's instinctive inclinations were Francoist but he accepted grudgingly that some effort must be made to streamline the system. In fact, Barrera de Irimo had shown some reluctance to accept a portfolio and had done so only at the insistence of Prince Juan Carlos. His initial reticence permitted him to exact a price from Arias. This consisted of the right to nominate the Ministers of Commerce and of Industry and thus to create a coherent economic team.[5] He thereby established a relatively progressive bridge-head within the cabinet.

In fact, whatever Arias's own ideological tendencies, and despite the determination of the ultras that his cabinet would make the last stand of undiluted Francoism, the lesson of Carrero Blanco's death had been learnt in certain crucial areas of the political élite. Barrera de Irimo's appointment was not the only hint of changes to come. Arias had tried to introduce as Minister Secretary-General of the Movimiento one of its more forward-looking bureaucrats, the Opus Deista, Fernando Herrero Tejedor. The significance of this lay in the fact that any reform of the existing political system within Francoist 'legality' would have to pass through the institutions of the Movimiento. Earlier, and extremely timid, attempts to reform the Movimiento by the previous Minister Secretary, Torcuato Fernández Miranda, had already alerted the ultras to such a possibility. Indeed, Fernández Miranda had been excluded from the presidency precisely because of this. Now, clearly suspecting that Herrero Tejedor might have been selected to oversee just such a reforming operation, the bunker went into action. José Antonio Girón de Velasco, its most prominent figure, used his enormous influence with Franco to block the appointment of Herrero and to ensure the inclusion in the cabinet of a reliable ultra. The preferred candidate was José Utrera Molina who, after the death of Carrero, had proposed forming part of a revenge squad.[6]

This initial reverse for Arias foreshadowed the difficulties that were to beset his time in government.

In fact, Arias Navarro's cabinet was not entirely devoid of reformists who had already accepted that change was inevitable if disaster were to be avoided. Apart from Barrera de Irimo, there was also the one-time protégé of Manuel Fraga, Pío Cabanillas, as Minister of Information. At the Ministry of Education, there was Cruz Martínez Esteruelas, a Movimiento figure with a reputation for dynamism and friendship with Fraga. Although he was later to revert to his Francoist origins, the universities breathed a sigh of relief at his appointment. This was hardly surprising given that his predecessor, the brutish Julio Rodríguez Martínez, who had also offered to join a revenge squad to track down the killers of Carrero Blanco, had nearly wrecked the entire education system with his aggressiveness and bizarre schemes. Somewhat more incons-picuous, but also significant, was the appointment as Minister of the Presidency, and effectively head of the civil service, of Antonio Carro Martínez. The new Minister was closely linked to the reformist group known as *Tácito*.

Antonio Carro's influence lay behind the fact that Arias introduced into the secondary level of his government members of the *Tácito* group as under-secretaries. Within the Francoist civil service, many of the best-educated and talented functionaries belonged to *Tácito*. They were conservative Christian Democrats committed to peaceful reform of the system from within. Closely linked to the Catholic pressure group, the Asociación Católica Nacional de Propagandistas, they derived their collective identity from newspaper articles signed by *'Tácito'*. Written sometimes by individuals and other times by a team, these influential articles advocating legal reform were published from 1972 in the Catholic daily, *Ya*. Their most prominent representatives within the new government were Marcelino Oreja Aguirre, Under-Secretary of Information, and Landelino Lavilla, Under-Secretary of Industry. With immensely powerful ramifications in the banking and industrial world, and as faithful interpreters of the policies of the ecclesiastical hierarchy, the ACNP and the *Tácitos* constituted a pressure group that Arias would find hard to ignore.[7]

Throughout 1974, Arias walked a tight-rope between the wishes of the reformists and those of the bunker while all the time the problems of opposition pressure, labour militancy and terrorism grew unchecked. The leading *Tácito*, Alfonso Osorio García, made it clear to Arias that the backing of his group would be available for a cabinet committed to change. That this was not an offer to be disdained was shown by an extension of *Tácito*'s public activities to include political dinners and public lectures which encompassed a remarkably wide and influential section of the economic, social and political establishments. On the other hand, there was the bunker, with its ready access to Franco and with whom Arias Navarro sympathized. On balance, however, the Prime Minister decided to go against his own inclinations and with the Christian Democrat reformists. Thus, Carro Martínez and the *Tácitos* helped Arias produce his first, surprisingly liberal, declarations of intent.[8]

The celebrated speech of 12 February 1974 put forward a programme for a controlled opening-up of the system, an *apertura*. The so-called 'spirit of 12 February' proposed wider political participation albeit within the limits of the strictest Francoist order. A restricted reform provided for the election, as opposed to the government appointment, of mayors and local officials. There was to be an increase from 17 per cent to 35 per cent of the total in the number of the deputies in the Cortes not simply appointed (*nombrados a dedo*) but elected through the strictly limited suffrage of the Sindicatos or of 'heads of families'. The vertical syndicates were promised greater bargaining power. Political associations, but not political parties, were promised. Praise for Franco was followed by the astonishing statement that the responsibility for political innovation could no longer lie only on the Caudillo's shoulders.[9] However, the rigid commitment to Francoist thinking and the loudly expressed determi- nation to stamp out 'subversion' ensured that reform as conceived by Arias amounted to little of real substance. Moreover, in the following two years, even that was to be whittled down to nothing by the bunker. Yet, it still remained the most liberal declaration ever made by a minister of Franco. The opposition remained unimpressed, believing that reformist speeches or the promotion of individuals from *Tácito* was merely a façade.

At first, however, some credibility was given to the 'spirit of 12 February' by the less repressive approach to the press and publishers adopted by Pío Cabanillas at the Ministry of Information. That, together with a widening of toleration for the most moderate sections of the opposition, gave rise to some optimism. In fact, Arias's rule was to oscillate between these tantalizing promises of liberalization and the most violent repression. The *Tácitos* may have brought Arias to open his eyes to the growing power of the opposition and to acknowledge that, if they were to survive, reform had to be attempted. Nevertheless, he continued to react to social unrest with unflinching harshness. In part instinctive, this was also a reflection of the success that the bunker had in triggering the reflex reactions of the dying dictator. As long as the Caudillo lived, the old guard was still powerful and could mobilize him against reform. This was done by the simple device of assembling dossiers about the descent into pornography and disorder allegedly brought about by liberal weakness.

The bunker's readiness to play this card rendered Arias Navarro's position impossible. His task was to adjust the regime's political structures to the changed economic and social situations. The increased unemployment and the diminished living standards brought about by the energy crisis made this a dauntingly difficult job. As the progressive *Tácitos* argued, a limited political reform was a reasonable concession in order to ensure that rising popular militancy did not sweep away the entire edifice of power and them along with it. Unfortunately for Arias, the need constantly to mollify the bunker obliged him to adopt policies which had the contrary effect. Such policies coincided with his own inclinations but they rapidly exhausted his exiguous reserves of credibility as a reformer.

Within two weeks of the 12 February speech, Arias felt himself obliged to prove that the new spirit would not prevent his defending fundamental Francoist values. After the death of Carrero Blanco, the conciliatory gestures of Cardinal Vicente Enrique y Tarancón paved the way for a short-lived truce between the regime and the Church.[10] After a visit from the Primate in mid-January, Arias had spoken of a new understanding between Church and State. A delegation had been dispatched to the Vatican in an attempt to improve relations. Difficulties hinged above all on the continued imprisonment in Zamora of clergy associated with the regionalist and working-class organizations. The 'betrayal' of the regime by left-wing priests drove the ultras to paroxysms of fury and *El Alcázar* had even urged its readers to use violence to make the Church hierarchy mend its ways.[11] The rage of the ultras derived in part from the high number of Basques among the offending clergy. Indeed, the traditionally close relationship between the Basque clergy and their flock ensured that they could not stay aloof from the problems arising from ETA's war against the regime. Thus, the bishopric of Bilbao found itself in the front line of the conflict between Church and State.[12]

Tension came to a head on 24 February 1974. Monsignor Antonio Añoveros Ataún, the Bishop of Bilbao, authorized the issue of four homilies drawn up by the Pastoral Commission of his diocese which quoted the words of Pope John XXIII, 'everything that is done to repress the vitality of ethnic minorities seriously violates the requisites of justice'. The texts, which were photocopied and widely distributed, ended with an appeal for the Basque people, and other national minorities in Spain, to be allowed to conserve their separate identities 'within a socio-political structure which would recognize their right to do so'. Although not a Basque, Añoveros was a convinced social Catholic, as his activities as Bishop of Cadiz had shown. Now he believed himself to be acting within the 'spirit of 12 February' and was in fact its first test. However, in the aftermath of the assassination of Carrero Blanco by ETA, this moderate defence of Basque aspirations was more than the extreme right would tolerate. The ultra press denounced the pastoral as a subversive attack on national unity and Arias, always something of an anti-clerical,[13] bowed to the pressure. The Minister of the Interior, José García Hernández, placed both Añoveros and his Vicar-General, Monsignor José Angel Ubieta López, under house arrest. Any remaining hopes of reconciliation were dashed when a clumsy effort was made to expel Añoveros to Lisbon or Rome.

The Bishop refused to leave, saying that he could do so only on direct orders from the Pope. He pointed out that forcible expulsion would be a violation of the Concordat and would involve the excommunication of any Catholic who laid hands on him. The Bishops' Conference, meeting in Madrid under the presidency of Cardinal Enrique y Tarancón, confirmed this and gave whole-hearted support to Añoveros. Pope Paul VI, who had long regarded the Franco regime with distaste, also backed the Bishop. The affair attracted immense publicity both inside and outside Spain and became a source of profound embarrassment to the Spanish government. Newspaper editors who printed extracts from the homily were called before the Tribunal de Orden Público. There was a heated confrontation in the cabinet between Pío Cabanillas, Antonio Barrera de Irimo and Antonio Carro on the one hand, and Arias and his dour entourage on the other. Eventually, Franco himself took a hand. Desperate not to see the destruction of the Concordat, which was one of his greatest early triumphs, the Caudillo obliged Arias to back down. While the ultra press raged because Monsignor Añoveros arrived in Madrid for consultations with Tarancón wearing a Basque beret and Blas Piñar harangued crowds of his followers with denunciations of the clerical corrupters of the regime, the Prime Minister was making a humiliating retreat. By that time, relations with the Vatican had been brought to the brink of total breakdown and Arias had succeeded in accelerating the Church's withdrawal from the orbit of the regime's forces.[14]

This blow to the credibility of the 'spirit of 12 February' was compounded almost immediately by further proof that Franco and the bunker were in no mood to make any more concessions that might be interpreted as weakness. Already, in the first two months of 1974, the police had arrested over 150 members of working-class organizations, ETA and leftist fractions such as FRAP, the Liga Comunista and the Movimiento Comunista.[15] On 1 March, Franco refused to commute the death sentences passed on the Catalan anarchist Salvador Puig Antich and the Pole Heinz Chez, both accused of killing members of the forces of order. Despite an international outcry, and protests from the Vatican, the EEC and several heads of state, the executions were carried out, by *garrote vil*, on 2 March. This defiant flouting of humanitarian norms was symptomatic of the intensification of the bunker's siege mentality. The ultras had every reason to feel isolated. In response to the growing strength of the anti-Francoist opposition, increasing numbers of businessmen and regime functionaries were opting for change. That was in itself a reflection of the increasingly hostile international climate. On 14 March the European Parliament reacted to the executions and the harassment of Añoveros with a condemnation of the Franco regime and a declaration that 'the Spanish government's repeated violation of basic human and civil rights and its lack of respect for the rights of minorities in a Europe that is seeking its free and democratic way to unity, prevent Spain's admission to the European Community.'[16]

Such a reaction from the 'corrupt' democracies can barely have surprised the bunker. In contrast, increasing signs that the regime of the Greek colonels was tottering and the collapse of the Portuguese dictatorship on 25 April 1974 had an altogether more traumatic effect. The fact that forty-five years of authoritarianism could disappear overnight in Portugal came as a profound shock to the Spanish bunker and as a great morale booster to the opposition. The fact that the poor relation could manage democracy could only intensify demands for change in Spain. Aware that the progressive elements within the regime would be impelled to hasten their plans for reform and that waverers would go over to the reformist camp, the ultras reacted swiftly. José Antonio Girón de Velasco, in cahoots with Antonio Izquierdo Feriguela, editor of the Movimiento's official newspaper, *Arriba*, launched a bitter attack on the liberals within the government. The so-called *Gironazo* of 28 April reflected the ultras' fear of the impact of external events on ordinary Spaniards through the partially liberalized media. 'We live in difficult times', wrote Girón, 'but we will not be defeated by the confusion orchestrated within Spain and from abroad.' The *Tácitos* and the reformist ministers were denounced as 'false liberals infiltrated into the administration and the high offices of State'. A few weeks later, at a pre-publication promotion of a book of Carrero Blanco's speeches, Blas Piñar took up the theme. Condemning the 'abject freedom of the press', he described Spanish political life as being under the sway of 'dwarves, cowards and the spoilt brats of the regime'. Declaring war on Arias's *apertura* as 'an opening to subversion', Piñar announced that 'the hour of caudillos and warriors has struck'.[17]

Implicit in the words of both Girón and Blas Piñar was the threat that, in the last resort, whatever the growing impetus of reformism, the bunker could always appeal to the armed forces. That was broadly true although the military was perhaps not quite as monolithically ultra-rightist as Girón might have supposed from his friendships with reactionary Generals like Iniesta Cano or García Rebull. On the same day as the *Gironazo*, General García Rebull stated in *Nuevo Diario* that he viewed 'parties as the opium of the people' and politicians as 'vampires'. Behind the scenes, however, ultra generals were not entirely confident that they could control events. Fearing that the liberals in the cabinet were paralleled by open-minded Generals like Díez Alegría, they began to conspire to consolidate their power. Iniesta Cano had been smarting ever since his rebuff by Arias over the belligerent telegram that he had sent to Civil Guard units during the aftermath of the Carrero assassination. In collusion with a number of retired Generals, including García Rebull, and the Captains-General of Valladolid, Pedro Merry Gordón, and of Madrid, Angel Campano López, Iniesta planned to avoid his own imminent retirement and instead to replace Díez Alegría in the key post of Chief of the General Staff. Campano was to take over from Iniesta as head of the Civil Guard and there was to be a purge of officers suspected of liberalism.

The plot apparently enjoyed the support of Franco's immediate family circle, while the Caudillo himself was kept in ignorance. However, when the plan was put to the Minister for the Army, General Francisco Coloma Gallegos, Arias came to hear of it. He threatened to resign. Since the conspirators were hardly ready to seize power, he thereby put a stop to the implementation of their plans. Iniesta was forced to retire on schedule on 12 May and was replaced by the relatively liberal General José Vega Rodríguez.[18] However, in recognition of the need to appease the bunker, Arias dismissed Díez Alegría and replaced him with the tough Captain-General of the Eighth Military Region of La Coruña, Carlos Fernández

Vallespín. It was widely rumoured that Díez Alegría was being punished for a visit to Rumania during which he met President Ceaucescu and for the fact that Santiago Carrillo had claimed to be in contact with him. Carrillo had been in Rumania at the time, but they did not meet since General Díez Alegría declined to do so without authorization from Arias. The Communists maintained, however, that Díez Alegría had contacted them on the day of the Carrero Blanco assassination. The bunker was in fact frightened that Díez Alegría could turn out to be the Spanish Spinola. Indeed, ever since the Portuguese revolution, he was reported to have received hundreds of monocles in the post. It was understandable that Carrillo's references to Díez Alegría in his press conferences and his confidence in the early 'Portugalization' of Spain should provoke anxiety on the Spanish right.[19] However, there was an element of hysteria in this since opposition leaders, including the Communists, knew only too well that a pro-democratic military intervention was inconceivable.

The government continued to totter along the disputed frontier between the ultras and the regime liberals. The total of arrested leftists for the first half of 1974 came to over 500. Arias Navarro's responses as a tough ex-Director-General of Security remained intact. At the end of May, he submitted to the Cortes his limited project for political associations. On 15 June, in a speech in Barcelona, he presented the package to the nation. Although well received by the newspapers associated with the regime's reformists, *ABC* and *Ya*, the speech merely underlined the restricted nature of the changes on offer. As well as affirming that the 'spirit of 12 February' was indistinguishable from the 'permanent spirit of the Franco regime', Arias made it clear that associations would never be more than legalized tendencies deriving exclusively from within the Movimiento. In other words, without being sufficiently *inmovilista* to pacify the bunker, the project was also unlikely to draw the teeth of the opposition, newly resurgent after the Portuguese events.[20] This was made clear within a week of Arias's speech. On Saturday 22 June in Estoril, a large number of the more moderate opponents of Franco met to celebrate the saint's day of Don Juan de Borbón, the legitimate heir to the throne. Numerous declarations were made in condemnation of the Francoist imposition of the succession of Juan Carlos, most notably by Joaquín Satrústegui, leader of the liberal monarchists, and by Fernando Alvarez de Miranda, a prominent Christian Democrat. On the following day, 20,000 Spanish workers from all over Europe gathered in Geneva to hear Dolores Ibárruri and Santiago Carrillo announce confidently that they would soon be in Madrid as part of a provisional government.[21]

The fortress of Francoism was shakier than it had been for nearly thirty years. When Franco fell ill with phlebitis and was taken to hospital on 9 July, hopes of real change flared. Optimism in the *Tácito* group that the Caudillo might resign in favour of Juan Carlos was stimulated by the provisional delegation of powers to the Prince on 19 July. It turned out to be a humiliating experience for him. Franco showed remarkable tenacity and was able to leave hospital on 30 July. His entourage at El Pardo, frantic at the prospect of losing their grip on power, encouraged him to waste no time in resuming his powers. The febrile atmosphere in which the palace clique lived was revealed by the circumstances surrounding the dismissal of Franco's personal physician, Dr Vicente Gil, on 29 July. It was Dr Gil who had urged that, to prolong his life, Franco should renounce political power. In consequence, he was subjected to the anger of an outraged Sra Franco and was the victim of an attempted beating by the Caudillo's son-in-law, the Marqués de Villaverde, who had belatedly arrived to take charge of treatment. Dr Gil claimed that while Franco lay dying, Villaverde had been attending the Miss World contest in Manila.[22] It came as no surprise when the Prince's apprenticeship was formally ended on 2 September. The short-lived transfer of powers and the antics of the El Pardo courtiers can have done little to foster his enthusiasm for the Francoist cause.[23]

The main consequence of Franco's illness was its boost to the morale of the opposition. At last there was evidence that Franco would die soon. Coming so soon after the Portuguese revolution, it accelerated the movement towards unity on the left. The Communist Party's policy of the 'Pact for Liberty' had had its first major success with the foundation in November 1971 of the Assemblea de Catalunya. The Assembly movement included a wide range of left-wing parties, of which the most important was the Catalan Communist Party PSUC (Partit Socialista Unificat de Catalunya); a number of working-class organizations of which the Comisiones Obreras was the most dominant; and a broad span of legal associations. The Assembly was represented all over Catalonia and, apart from its wide spectrum of popular support, included bankers and industrialists among its leaders. In subsequent years, similar democratic juntas and round tables (*mesas*) sprang up all over Spain.[24]

When Franco's illness was announced, Santiago Carrillo had tried to force the pace by launching, in Paris on 30 July 1974, the Junta Democrática. It consisted of the Comisiones Obreras, the miniscule

Partido Socialista Popular of Enrique Tierno Galván, various regionalist groups including Alejandro Rojas Marcos's Andalusian Socialist Alliance, the Carlists and numerous individual independents of whom the most prominent was the monarchist Rafael Calvo Serer. The links with Tierno Galván, Rojas Marcos and other significant individual participants had been provided in Madrid by Calvo Serer's lawyer Antonio García Trevijano. Efforts were made to persuade Felipe González and Joaquín Ruiz Giménez to join in and conversations were held with representatives of the Partido Nacionalista Vasco. Carrillo claimed later that García Trevijano had even had promising talks with an important member of the military high command. Through Calvo Serer, attempts were made to persuade Don Juan de Borbón to endorse the operation. From his Portuguese exile in Estoril, Don Juan declined. Since the Junta's programme proposed to leave to a future referendum the issue of whether Spain should be a monarchy or a republic, Don Juan's refusal was hardly surprising.[25]

The rest of the Junta's programme called for a take-over of power by a provisional government; a total political amnesty; the legalization of all political parties; trade union freedom and the return to the unions of the property seized from them after the Civil War; the freedom to strike, to meet and to demonstrate pacifically; freedom of speech, of the press and the media; independence of the judiciary; the political neutrality of the armed forces; regional autonomy; the separation of Church and State; free elections within eighteen months of the establishment of the provisional government; and membership of the EEC. Despite the ultimate non-participation of crucial individuals and groups such as the Christian Democrat fractions or the Partido Socialista Obrero Español, the Junta and its programme of *ruptura democrática* remained a very considerable publicity coup for the Communists. Opposition circles in Madrid and Barcelona buzzed with excitement and the bunker's sense of being beleaguered reached panic proportions.[26]

Meanwhile, after years of lethargy, the PSOE was undergoing a process of revitalization. The weary exiled leadership of Rodolfo Llopis had for years been locked in a tense rivalry with Enrique Tierno Galván's tiny Socialist Party of the Interior (later to become the Partido Socialista Popular) and with a Madrid-based section of the PSOE led by Pablo Castellano and Luis Gómez Llorente. All three were now being elbowed aside by a dynamic alliance of Enrique Múgica and Nicolás Redondo from Bilbao and Felipe González and Alfonso Guerra from Seville. The leadership of Felipe González was confirmed at the XIII Congress-in-exile of the PSOE held at Suresnes near Paris in mid-October 1974. At this stage, the PSOE leadership had a more realistic sense than did the PCE of the possibilities for a *ruptura* with the past. Aware that violent overthrow of Francoism was impossible, González and his companions were coming to the reluctant conclusion that some kind of negotiation with regime reformists would probably be necessary. This was one of the reasons for the PSOE's not joining the Junta Democrática. For such negotiations to have a chance of success, the PSOE would need to have avoided taking up a position on the dynastic issue of Juan Carlos versus Don Juan. Accordingly, by steering clear of Carrillo, Calvo Serer and the Junta, Felipe González was ensuring that he would be neither used by the Communists nor embroiled in conspiracy with Estoril.[27]

Also in the autumn of 1974, as a challenge to Arias's law of associations, a new timidly left-of-centre political party was announced. Known as the USDE (Unión Social-Demócrata Española), it was the brain-child of the one-time Falangist but widely respected opponent of the regime, Dionisio Ridruejo, and of the economist, Antonio García López.[28] The USDE, like the PSOE, did not become part of the Junta Democrática, despite the efforts of García Trevijano and the Communists to persuade Ridruejo to join them. None the less, the Junta's success as a publicity coup galvanized the PSOE, along with the USDE and Ruiz Giménez's Christian Democrats, into greater efforts to organize their own anti-Francoist front.

The Communists entertained hopes that a Junta-inspired nationwide strike would bring down Francoism and lead to the establishment of a provisional government, rather along the lines of the transition from the Primo de Rivera dictatorship to the Second Republic in 1931. Their optimism was misplaced, albeit understandable in the absence of other historical models. None the less, the resurgence of leftist confidence confirmed the bunker in its belief in the necessity of last-ditch defensive tactics. Accordingly, when, on 10 September, Arias Navarro announced that he was still determined to carry out the 12 February programme and introduce political associations before January 1975, he ran into fierce opposition. The opportunity for frenzied attacks by the ultras on the 'weakness' of the government was provided by a bloody terrorist incident in Madrid. On 13 September, the Cafetería Rolando in the Calle del Correo near police headquarters in the Puerta del Sol was destroyed by a bomb explosion. The bar was a police haunt and there were several policemen among the eleven dead and over seventy wounded. An air of mystery was added to the incident by reports that an internal circular in the Dirección General de Seguridad on the day of the explosion had suggested that officers not eat at Rolando.

Originally attributed by the authorities to both the PCE and ETA, responsibility was energetically denied by the Communists and only belatedly claimed by ETA. The delay was the consequence of a bitter internal debate provoked within ETA by the bombing which hastened the eventual division of the organization into ETA-Militar and ETA-Político-Militar. In fact, the bombing was almost certainly carried out by an ETA squad and some Madrid sympathizers. There was an immediate round-up of leftists known to sympathize with the Basque cause, including Eva Forest, a well-known Madrid psychologist and wife of the Communist playwright, Alfonso Sastre, and a Barcelona lawyer, Lidia Falcón. Curiously, none of the accused was ever brought to trial. Some years later, however, Lidia Falcón published a vehement, and uncontested, denunciation of Eva Forest which suggested that her influence in the Rolando attack was considerable.[29] It was understandable that the police would want to saddle the Communist Party with some of the moral opprobrium attached to ETA violence. However, the person of Eva Forest provided, as it had in the case of the Carrero Blanco assassination, a plausible connection. The links between Eva Forest and ETA remain mysterious.

The political backlash of the Rolando bomb followed quickly. It began with an assault on Arias by Blas Piñar in the pages of *Fuerza Nueva*. The entire cover of the issue of 26 September was taken up with the words 'Everything has a limit'. Blas Piñar's editorial dissociated his movement from Arias on the grounds that his reforms were sowing 'fields of corpses'. Then, the ultras at El Pardo, led by the Marqués de Villaverde, went into action. Two Movimiento newspaper editors, Antonio Izquierdo of *Arriba* and Emilio Romero of *Pueblo*, prepared a dossier for Franco allegedly revealing the scale of 'pornography' permitted by the Ministry of Information. Advertisements for camping furniture featuring women in bikinis were inter-collated with clippings from *Playboy*, which remained illegal in Spain, in such a way as to scandalize the puritanical dictator. He was easily convinced that the Minister of Information was opening up Spain to a deadly combination of Marxist and erotic subversion.

Franco was even more irritated by evidence in the dossier to the effect that Pío Cabanillas was permitting the press to air the 'oil of Redondela' scandal in which his brother, Nicolás, was implicated. A company specializing in the refining and warehousing of vegetable oils, REACE, in which Nicolás Franco had substantial interests, had apparently for some years been speculating with its clients' oil. In 1972, over four million kilos of olive oil were discovered to be missing. In the course of the police investigation, numerous witnesses 'lost their memories' and six died in mysterious circumstances. Nicolás Franco's name had been assiduously kept out of the proceedings. The case finally came to trial in Pontevedra on 21 October 1974 and was avidly covered by the press. José María Gil Robles, acting as lawyer for one of the accused, skilfully brought out the links with the Caudillo's brother. When Arias next spoke to Franco, he was told that Pío Cabanillas must be dismissed. The departure of the Minister of Information on 29 October seemed to be the beginning of a series of triumphs for the bunker. On the same day, the anniversary of the foundation of the Falange, the Consejo Nacional del Movimiento had been addressed by Francisco Labadié Otermín in the presence of the Caudillo himself. His declaration that the Nationalist victory in the Civil War would be 'defended tooth and nail' brought the ritual chants of '¡Franco! ¡Franco! ¡Franco!'. In the meanwhile, police round-ups of leftists and striking workers continued at a steady pace.[30]

In fact, the ultras' triumph merely exposed as never before the internal crisis of the regime. With the stock market dropping, it confirmed the views of many reformists and brought many ditherers into their camp. The exposure of the regime's bankruptcy led to a wave of significant resignations. One of the most important was that of the Minister of Finance, Antonio Barrera de Irimo, whose business links made him an excellent barometer of opinion within the Spanish and multinational industrial élite. Other resignations came from rising figures who would later be ministers under Juan Carlos. Francisco Fernández Ordóñez abandoned the presidency of the government holding corporation INI, the Instituto Nacional de Industria. Juan José Rosón resigned as Director-General of RTVE. Pío Cabanillas's Under-Secretary, Marcelino Oreja, led a protest resignation by numerous highly placed functionaries belonging to the *Tácito* group. Their joint verdict on Arias's 12 February reform project, 'a political line died yesterday', emphasized the Prime Minister's isolation.[31]

The crisis had left the bunker far from content and efforts to mobilize its forces more effectively had resulted in the establishment of a massive organization of nationalist Civil War veterans (Confederación Nacional de Ex-Combatientes) under the leadership of José Antonio Girón de Velasco. As if to emphasize the extent to which events were running away from Arias's control, the police, apparently without his authorization, arrested the leaders of the moderate opposition at the end of

November. They were meeting at the Madrid offices of Antonio García López of the USDE to discuss the establishment of a rival front to the Junta Democrática. The incident caused an international scandal akin to that provoked by the Añoveros case. Among those arrested were Felipe González, García López, Dionisio Ridruejo and several Christian Democrats. Joaquín Ruiz Giménez, who had left the meeting before the police arrived, presented himself for arrest at the Dirección General de Seguridad. After a few days, they were released.[32] By then, Arias Navarro's position had deteriorated even further.

The Prime Minister's continuing efforts at reform seemed ever more futile. The Statute of Associations presented on 2 December and approved by the Consejo Nacional on 16 December offered nothing. Only within the orbit of the Movimiento would associations have any electoral existence. They were required to have at least 25,000 members distributed over a minimum of fifteen provinces, thereby excluding regionalist associations. The admission procedures were to be of the most labyrinthine nature. For the opposition, it offered absolutely nothing apart from proof of Arias's commitment to the Francoist past. Even the *Tácito* group pronounced the Statute to be little improvement on the efforts made by Solís in 1969.[33] The reaction of *Tácito* was a reflection of the way in which influential sectors of the Spanish oligarchy were finally coming to echo the opposition's demands for democracy.

In the course of 1974, there had been virtually open meetings between prominent industrialists and financiers on the one hand and members of the moderate opposition on the other. Among the most celebrated were those which took place at the Hotel Ritz and at the home of Joaquín Garrigues Walker in Aravaca, just outside Madrid. Garrigues, apart from being Areilza's son-in-law, was one of the most significant figures in the Spanish business world. For many years, his family's legal practice had represented several important multinational corporations. He made no secret of his conviction that political liberalization had to be risked in order to avoid cataclysmic confrontation. Now he resigned his many company directorships to be able to devote his energies to the creation of the Partido Demócrata which was eventually to become the nucleus of the Federación de Partidos Demócratas y Liberales.[34] This, together with efforts made by Francisco Fernández Ordóñez to organize a Social Democrat Party and evidence of frenzied activity across the entire spectrum of the civilized right, coincided with the seemingly inexorable progress towards unity being made by the two left-wing fronts.

In contrast, Arias's government was increasingly adrift in a sea of popular militancy. Throughout late 1974, ETA had carried out a renewed offensive against the forces of order and in December began to throw its efforts into gaining amnesty for its imprisoned members. A strike on 11 December, called by ETA and other local leftist forces, saw 200,000 workers down tools in the Basque Country. The universities were in a state of constant turmoil which was not calmed by the Minister of Education, Cruz Martínez Esteruelas, when he closed down the University of Valladolid in January. Strikes spread across the country, partly in response to the deteriorating economic situation, but with an increasingly political dimension. The biggest strikes were in the Madrid construction industry and in Catalan metallurgical plants. The most political and most widely publicized were of actors in Madrid theatres and of senior functionaries who held a one-day stoppage on 6 February 1975.[35]

The democratic ferment had reached even into the armed forces. In his new year message, the Minister for the Army, General Francisco Coloma Gallegos, spoke of the need to avoid dissension in the ranks. Behind his cryptic remarks was knowledge of the fact that, in the course of 1974, military intelligence services had discovered the existence of clandestine assemblies of young officers which seemed potentially comparable to those who had organized the Portuguese Armed Forces Movement. The officers concerned were politically unaligned. However, the reaction of the military authorities was to treat them as if they were part of the Communist Party's efforts to infiltrate the forces with democratic juntas. The intelligence services stepped up their vigilance in order to expose the full ramifications of the dissident officers' activities. Within days of Coloma Gallegos's speech, they published their manifesto under the title of the Unión Militar Democrática. Never very large, the UMD caused panic because of the Portuguese example. The first arrests, of Major Julio Busquets Bragulat, Spain's foremost military sociologist, and of Captain José Júlvez, occurred in February 1975. Not until the summer did the intelligence services accumulate sufficient information to permit sweeping arrests of UMD leaders.[36]

In the context of the rising popular clamour for democracy and of the preparations for the future being made by the left and the civilized right, Arias Navarro's feeble efforts at reform and his battle with the bunker seemed increasingly irrelevant. However, he continued to fight on an increasingly narrow front. Frustrated by the way in which his timidly *aperturista* plans were being sabotaged by the official media of the Movimiento, he was provoked into decisive action when the anniversary of his 12 February speech was ignored. For once decisive, he sacked

Antonio Izquierdo Feriguela, the director of *Arriba*, and Antonio Castro Villacañas, director of the Movimiento's press and radio networks. The ultras were not dismayed. Led by Alejandro Fernández Sordo, the Minister of the Vertical Syndicates, the hard-line rightists in the cabinet blocked legislation to introduce a limited right to strike. On 24 February, Licinio de la Fuente, Minister of Labour since 1969, and a Francoist beyond suspicion of liberal tendencies, resigned in frustration.[37]

On 4 March, Arias announced a reshuffled cabinet which suggested a determination to break free of the restrictions imposed by the ultras. The Minister of Justice, Francisco Ruiz Jarabo, a close ally of Girón, was replaced by the somewhat more liberal ACNP member, José María Sánchez Ventura. Even more significantly, the Minister Secretary-General of the Movimiento, José Utrera Molina, one of the bunker's links to Franco himself and a powerful obstacle to Arias's plans, was replaced by the more reformist Fernando Herrero Tejedor.[38] Combining shrewd intelligence with a good relationship with Franco, Herrero Tejedor was an Opus Deista with irreproachable Movimiento credentials. A flexible opportunist, he was widely tipped by Francoist *cognoscenti* to be the ultimate successor to Arias and the man to organize the transition to the monarchy. He provoked much comment in regime circles by symbolically moving his office from the Yoke-and-Arrows-emblazoned Movimiento building in the Calle Alcalá to the Palace which housed the Consejo Nacional. Thereafter, he was to work hard to give credibility to the idea of political associations although it was already too late to give vitality to a lifeless fraud. He established contacts within the tolerated moderate opposition of the Christian Democrats and Ridruejo's social democrats, as well as creating his own association, the Unión del Pueblo Español. However, Herrero Tejedor was killed in a car crash on 12 June 1975. Franco seems to have regarded the accident as a providential sign that he should effectively close the door on experiments with associations. He insisted that Arias replace Herrero by José Solís, the arch-conjurer of empty cosmetic reform.[39]

While Herrero's death put an end to progress with associations, it opened the way to the emergence of the man who was to preside over the transition period, Adolfo Suárez González. Having become Herrero Tejedor's secretary in the mid-1950s, Suárez had risen on his coat-tails to become an archetypal Movimiento bureaucrat. Driven by a powerful ambition, Suárez joined the Opus Dei and made friends with important regime figures during the period of the early 1960s when Herrero was Vice-Secretary-General of the Movimiento under Solís. Thereafter, by carefully cultivating the then Minister of the Interior, General Camilo Alonso Vega, he became civil governor of Segovia in 1968. As he neared the top, Suárez used his friendship with Herrero Tejedor both to attract the attention of Franco and to become friendly with Prince Juan Carlos.

Suárez was made Director-General of Spanish Television, RTVE, in 1969 at the suggestion of Carrero Blanco who had, in turn, been given his name by Juan Carlos. He used his control of the media to promote Juan Carlos who at that time was the subject of popular jokes portraying him as Franco's puppet. He also worked to foster the image of ministers with whom he wanted to curry favour. In his period in television, he began to build a reputation as a man who enjoyed a special relationship with the army. He established a close friendship with Andrés Casinello Pérez, second-in-command of Carrero Blanco's intelligence service, and ingratiated himself with senior generals by making television time available to them and by sending flowers to their wives. In consequence, when he became Vice-Secretary-General of the Movimiento himself in February 1975, the Minister Secretary-General, Herrero Tejedor, had asked him to prepare a report on the armed forces and their attitudes to political change. He made use of the undertaking to consolidate his links with senior officers and with the Prince, who was impressed by the report and its conclusion that the army would acquiesce in a mild political reform.[40]

On the death of his protector, Suárez resigned as Vice-Secretary to take over Herrero's political association, the Unión del Pueblo Español, his inexorable rise apparently cut short. In fact, the trend was such as to suggest that Herrero Tejedor himself would have been overtaken by events. Increasing numbers of once unshakeable Francoists were preparing their future by admitting to a conviction that some kind of change was inevitable. One right-wing commentator, Luis María Ansón, wrote maliciously: 'the rats are leaving the regime's ship .... The cowardice of the Spanish ruling class is truly suffocating.... Already it has reached the beginnings of the *sauve qui peut*, of the unconditional surrender.' However, the same commentator named Suárez politician of the month in the magazine *Blanco y Negro* on 2 July. At that time, Ansón was one of the few political observers to see Suárez as a possible figure in a future *aperturista* reform. Yet, given that Juan Carlos had been obliged by Franco to swear fidelity to the principles of the Movimiento, it was clear that, to avoid bloodshed, attempts at real change would have to be carried out by someone who knew how to manipulate the structure of the regime. The most appropriate person, in terms of knowledge of the constitutional system, would be Torcuato Fernández Miranda. However, Suárez's dynamic and youthful image, and his experience of all levels of the Movimiento, fitted him for the part too.[41] In any case, in early 1975, their plans went no further than remodelling the Francoist structure. It was to be the sheer weight of working-class, regionalist, student and opposition pressure over the next eighteen months which was to force them to contemplate democratic change.

Suárez was certainly still unaware that he might play any such role. On the contrary, he was involved with Solís and Emilio Romero in pushing the Unión del Pueblo Español as the *continuista* option within the arena of political associations. The UDPE would be able to mobilize the entire press and radio network of the Movimiento. There was every likelihood that such an enterprise would swamp the more reformist associations being planned by Fraga, Pío Cabanillas, Federico Silva Muñoz, José María de Areilza, Francisco Fernández Ordóñez and the *Tácitos*. When they realized that the UDPE was likely to be as all-embracing as the Movimiento itself, they pulled out of the associations project, forming instead private companies, FEDISA and GODSA, for the study of political options for the future. Without such representatives of 'respectable' Francoism, the whole associations project was left in ruins. However, one of the more senior and conservative *Tácitos*, Alfonso Osorio, continued with attempts to create a reformist association, the Unión Democrática Española, with Federico Silva. The personnel that Osorio gathered together were later to play a significant part in the creation of Adolfo Suárez's UCD.[42]

In relation to the turmoil of the country as a whole, plans for associations and *continuismo* could hardly have seemed more irrelevant in 1975. Attacks on left-wing lawyers and clergymen, on bookshops and workers were carried out by rightist terror squads. These assaults intensified the critical position of powerful sectors of the Church. A statement from the Pax et Justitia Commission on 26 May called for an end to indiscriminate police action and demanded that the authorities take action against ultra-rightist terrorist groups.[43] These had been unleashed under the cover of the three-month state of exception declared on 26 April in Vizcaya and Guipúzcoa. In immediate terms, this measure was a response to the continuing success of ETA's terror campaign. However, it also represented a last-ditch effort by ultra-rightist elements to hold back political change. Its ferocity was counter-productive: opposition unity was strengthened. Catholic liberal Francoists were confirmed in their determination to dissociate themselves from the regime. More dramatically, a wave of militancy was provoked in the Basque Country which was to hasten Spain towards democracy.

The state of exception launched a massive operation of police terror against the populations of the two provinces. The homes and offices of suspects were vandalized. Arrests were made on such a scale that the Bilbao bull-ring had to be used briefly as a detention centre. Torture and beatings were commonplace. The wives and girlfriends of wanted men were seized as hostages and subjected to inhuman treatment. The mass intimidation of the population was intensified by the activities of ultra-rightist terror squads. Using names like Antiterrorismo ETA or the Batallón Vasco-Español, they machine-gunned and bombed the bars frequented by nationalists, the offices of lawyers, publishing houses and the businesses of ETA sympathizers. The entire operation was a collective reprisal by the forces of the bunker against the most militant provinces in Spain. Far from cowing the population, however, it gave rise to a massive popular reaction in the Basque Country backed by solidarity actions all over Spain. Generalized resentment was focused by the killing of several innocent bystanders whose funerals were then turned into gigantic solidarity demonstrations.[44]

The scope of the militancy was widened immeasurably by the regime's most extreme attempts to terrorize the Basque people. Death sentences passed on Juan Paredes Manotas 'Txiki', José Garmendía Artola and Angel Otaegi Etxeberría did as much to politicize the Basque Country as the Burgos trials had done in 1970. Doubts about the specific guilt of 'Txiki' Paredes and Angel Otaegi, together with outrage at the way the badly wounded Garmendía had been treated, fuelled the widespread conviction that the bunker was lashing out wildly in order to teach Basques a lesson. Despite the blanket repression to which the area was subject, a huge solidarity demonstration was held on 11 June 1975 and general strikes paralysed the region on 28–29 August and 11–12 September.[45]

When the state of exception came to an end on 26 July 1975, barely a month had passed before it was effectively reintroduced and extended to all of Spain by means of a draconian anti-terrorist law.[46] This came on top of a renewed censorship which had seen many newspapers and weekly magazines seized. This was a tribute to the immense influence enjoyed by such champions of democratic ideals as *Cuadernos para el Diálogo* and *Triunfo*. Now, even academic journals, such as the highly prestigious *Sistema* directed by the Socialist intellectual Elías Díaz, were prosecuted for 'under-hand incitement of rebellion' (*solapada incitación a la rebelión*).

The regime's attempt to resolve its crisis by a return to the situation of untrammelled repression which it had enjoyed in the 1940s was unable to hold back the surging waves of strikes. Initially economic strikes assumed a wider political significance. Liberal elements in the Francoist administration were appalled at the savagery displayed by the bunker. FEDISA, the political 'study society' founded by Fraga, Areilza and Cabanillas, issued an unequivocal demand for progress from authoritarianism to democracy.[47] They were in fact expressing the alarm which was gripping bankers and industrialists. The possibility of a bloodbath that would destroy Spain's chance of entering the EEC sent shares plummeting during the tense period from the passing of the anti-terrorist law to the executions carried out in late September.[48]

The last spasm of Francoism so besmirched Spain's international image that it seriously split Arias Navarro's cabinet. The three Basques already under sentence of death were joined on 12 September by three members of FRAP, accused of terrorist murders. Then, on 18 September, a further five FRAP activists were given capital sentences. On 26 September Franco chaired a cabinet meeting to discuss the possible reprieve of the eleven people awaiting execution, two of them pregnant women. Almost simultaneously, the European Parliament, in emergency session, called for all to be reprieved. In the event, the two women and four of the men, including the badly handicapped Garmendía, had their sentences commuted. Those on 'Txiki' Paredes, Angel Otaegi and three FRAP members, José Humberto Baena, José Luis Sánchez Bravo and Ramón García Sanz, were upheld. The international outcry was deafening. Harsh criticism from the Pope brought Spain's relations with the Vatican once more to breaking point. In defiance of the international and domestic revulsion that had been generated, the executions took place on 27 September. Thirteen countries withdrew their ambassadors from Spain. Four Spanish embassies were set on fire. The Mexican president called for Spain's expulsion from the United Nations. The European Commission called for a suspension of trade with Spain on 6 October.[49]

The fear and distaste provoked by the brutality of the dying Franco was matched by the consolidation of the prestige of the opposition. The Junta Democrática had been followed in June 1975 by the Plataforma de Convergencia Democrática which united the PSOE with Dionisio Ridruejo's Unión Social-Demócrata Española, the left Christian Democrats of Joaquín Ruiz Giménez's Izquierda Demócrata Cristiana and a number of regionalist groups, including the Partido Nacionalista Vasco. Dominated by the PSOE, the Plataforma was somewhat more open to the notion of dialogue with the regime reformists than the Junta Democrática which remained committed to a strategy of strikes and mass demonstrations. However, the regime's blood-lust helped overcome the Socialists' residual suspicions of the PCE to such an extent that both opposition fronts began negotiations for their ultimate unification. The foundation of the Plataforma had been announced at a meeting of the moderate opposition held at Estoril on 14 June. Over one hundred prominent liberal opponents of the regime, seated at tables decorated with Spanish flags and red carnations, were addressed by Don Juan de Borbón. His statement re-asserted his position as legitimate heir to the throne, accepted the need for popular endorsement of the monarchy and asserted his commitment to human rights. By questioning the Francoist succession to Prince Juan Carlos, Don Juan provoked an outburst of panic among the regime reformists and no doubt caused them to reflect on the need to make a more serious commitment to democracy if they were to survive.[50]

Meanwhile, Franco's last days were lived out in an orgy of confrontation. On 1 October, the Caudillo addressed his Falangist hordes in the Plaza de Oriente in a ritualistic rejection of change which recalled his previous performances in the 1940s and after the Burgos trials. Exposure to the chill autumn winds of Madrid probably contributed to Franco's final illness. On the same day, in revenge for the executions, four policemen were shot by a new terrorist organization, calling itself the Grupos de Resistencia Antifascista Primero de Octubre (GRAPO). Over the next five years GRAPO was to act as a dangerous *agent provocateur* and it was eventually revealed to have curious connections with the police. In the meanwhile, demonstrations, strikes and shootings punctuated Franco's death agony.[51] Assassinations carried out by FRAP and ETA were quickly followed by reprisals from ultra-rightist terrorists. There were widespread fears that, ostracized by the civilized world, Franco would unleash an outburst of rightist violence. There were rumours that Morocco was about to launch a 'green march' against the Spanish Sahara. The Francoist world order was crumbling rapidly. Accordingly, the announcement of the Caudillo's heart attack on 21 October provoked a collective sigh of relief. In the month up to his death on 20 November, the value of shares on the Madrid stock exchange rose substantially.

Liberal Francoists flooded to the Zarzuela Palace, residence of Prince Juan Carlos. The *inmovilista* solution to Francoism after Franco had died with Carrero Blanco. The slightly *aperturista continuismo* of Arias

Navarro had been negated by the machinations of the bunker and by Franco himself. The violence of September 1975 underlined more than ever that the political obsolescence of the regime's structures had created a powerful coincidence of interest in change which spanned the democratic opposition and large areas of the economic oligarchy, the middle classes and the administration. Hopes were now centred on Juan Carlos. His silences during the final excesses of Franco caused disquiet on the left, but in the three weeks before the Caudillo's death, his contacts with European emissaries and with liberals inside Spain suggested that he was likely to attempt to steer Spain towards democracy.[52]

When Franco's death was announced, people danced in the streets of Basque towns. Although there was considerable apprehension in the air, Madrid and Barcelona were quietly drunk dry of champagne. It was a dramatic rebuff to the hopes of those of the Caudillo's immediate entourage who had dreamed of holding back the clock. It was widely rumoured that he had been kept alive on life-support machines long after the hope of his recovery had gone.[53] This was allegedly in order to permit the announcement of his death on 20 November, the anniversary of the death of José Antonio Primo de Rivera. Nothing could more starkly illustrate the extent to which Franco's 'courtiers' lived detached from the real world of Spain in the 1970s than their readiness to believe that the mystical association of the deaths of the dictator and of the founder of the Falange could somehow facilitate the survival of Francoism.

No significant head of state, other than the Chilean dictator General Pinochet, attended the Caudillo's funeral. In dramatic contrast, Giscard D'Estaing, the Duke of Edinburgh, the US Vice-President and the President of the Federal Republic of Germany attended Juan Carlos's coronation.[54] Enormous goodwill, both inside and outside Spain, greeted the beginnings of Juan Carlos's reign. Yet the obstacles awaiting his efforts to democratize the country were enormous. The legacy of bitterness and hatred which had politicized – some would say revolutionized – the Basque people would bedevil Spanish politics for years to come. Moreover, for all that history seemed to be on the side of the progressive forces who wished to advance towards democracy, the bunker remained powerful, entrenched in the army, the police and the Civil Guard. Over 100,000 Falangists were still authorized to carry guns. The problem was illustrated starkly on 22 November when Juan Carlos addressed the Francoist Cortes. His mildly progressive speech, which ostentatiously omitted references to 18 July 1936, was received coldly by the *procuradores* who then gave an ecstatic ovation to Franco's daughter.

To a large extent, the resolution of the crisis without large-scale bloodshed depended on the skill of Juan Carlos, of the ministers that he chose and of the leaders of the opposition. The King faced a very considerable dilemma. There was much to be said for democratization. His advisers had kept him fully aware that important sectors of Spanish capitalism were anxious to ditch the political mechanisms of Francoism. He was equally conscious of the consequences of the Greek royal family's failure to go with the tide of popular democratic sentiment. The declarations of his father must also have influenced him. By opting boldly for progress, he would be assured of mass support for the monarchy. However, he was equally aware of the strength, determination and ill will of the bunker. More importantly than was perhaps perceived at the time, he was also tightly bound by the same Francoist Constitution to which he owed his accession. Accordingly, in the early days of his reign, he stepped cautiously.

Extreme leftists continued to be rounded up and the bunker remained optimistic. After all, as they perceived things, for Juan Carlos to preside over the introduction of democracy into Spain would be to deny the purpose of his inheritance and his training. As Blas Piñar blustered hopefully, 'this is no monarchical restoration but the installation of a new Francoist monarchy which has no other thought behind it than the Nationalist victory in the Civil War'.[55] By excluding the monarchy from Spain for forty years and by his arrogance in nominating his own royal successor, Franco seemed to have destroyed any political neutrality that Juan Carlos might have enjoyed, just as he had undermined the monarchy's other two central attributes of continuity and legitimacy.[56] The bunker hoped that Franco's influence would still be felt from his tomb in the Valle de los Caídos. It was hardly surprising that the left greeted the coronation with headlines in its clandestine press that proclaimed 'No to an imposed King!' and 'No to the Francoist King'.[57] The fact that Juan Carlos's first acts were aimed at consolidating his position within the army did little to endear him to the opposition. Already on 2 November, in a brilliant public relations coup *vis-à-vis* the army, he had made a lightning visit to Spanish garrisons in Morocco. Indeed, his sensitivity to military feelings was to form the basis of a relationship on which a future democratic Spain would lean heavily. On 22 November, he sent a message to the armed forces, renewing his oath of fidelity to the flag and acknowledging their position as defenders of Franco's Fundamental Laws. A few days later, a royal decree made the late Caudillo senior officer in perpetuity of the army, navy and air force.[58]

The obligatory placation of the bunker was matched by the most minimal concessions to the left. A limited pardon reached common criminals but released few political prisoners. Thus, at the very moment that the King and Queen drove down streets lined with cheering crowds, riot police were using baton charges, tear-gas and water-cannons to break up demonstrations outside the country's prisons. Many organizations, including *Colegios de Abogados* (Bar Associations), Pax et Justitia, and the parties of the left protested at the limitations of the pardon and called for a full amnesty. Disappointment turned to anger when several released prisoners, including the Comisiones Obreras leader, Marcelino Camacho, were re-arrested. Huge amnesty demonstrations were held in Seville, Valladolid, Vigo, Barcelona and Madrid. Felipe González was harassed by police at Madrid's civil cemetery where he attended a tribute on the fiftieth anniversary of the death of the PSOE founder, Pablo Iglesias.[59]

Juan Carlos's long-term survival depended on his coming to terms with the overwhelming popular urge for democracy. However, Franco had rigged the constitutional cards in such a way as to make it extremely difficult for him to do so. The regime's institutions, the Consejo del Reino, the Consejo Nacional del Movimiento and the Cortes were in the hands of committed Francoists and behind them stood the army and the Civil Guard. On the other hand, there was international support for a move towards democratization. Moreover, at the coronation mass, Cardinal Enrique y Tarancón had made the King aware of popular expectations when he appealed to him to become 'King of all Spaniards'.[60]

His first government was, almost inevitably, disappointing to those who hoped for reform. Juan Carlos would have preferred to dispense with Arias and appoint some more sympathetic figure. There was already some friction between them in part because of Arias's tendency to treat the young King in the same patronizing and dismissive way as Franco had. Now, on 13 November, Juan Carlos had, without Arias's knowledge, met various members of the military high command to discuss the future. Arias was furious when he found out. To assert his authority, he resigned, in the confident knowledge that, with Franco in his death agony, Juan Carlos would find it difficult to cope with an additional crisis. As he expected, the King was forced to ask him to stay on. However, to carry out the political modernization that he knew was essential to the survival of the monarchy, the King needed someone more open to change. At one stage, he toyed with the idea of appointing his one-time tutor, the expert in Francoist constitutional law, Torcuato Fernández Miranda. Fernández Miranda was hardly a liberal but his expertise would be essential for any projected change. However, the Prince was advised, perhaps not entirely impartially, by the secretary of the royal household, General Alfonso Armada Comyn, another ex-tutor, that the hostility of the bunker would make this dangerous. In any case, Fernández Miranda told the King that he would be more use as President of the Cortes and of the Consejo del Reino from which positions he could facilitate a 'legal' reform. Another possible candidate to be Juan Carlos's first Prime Minister was José María López de Letona. As Minister for Industry between 1969 and 1973 he had acquired a reputation as a dynamic technocrat with excellent business contacts. In the event, to guarantee support in the Consejo del Reino for the dual nomination of Torcuato Fernández Miranda, the King was obliged to seek the help of Arias. Accordingly, he shelved for the moment the idea of replacing his Prime Minister.[61]

Arias was confirmed in his post on 4 December after agreeing only reluctantly to submit the token resignation demanded by protocol. In the main, Arias's cabinet reflected his Francoist inclinations. However, although it contained a high proportion of hard-liners, he had been persuaded by the King and Torcuato Fernández Miranda of the need for different, if not exactly new, blood. Accordingly, in the list announced on 10 December, there were a number of significant innovations. Manuel Fraga as Minister of the Interior, the Conde de Motrico, José María de Areilza, as Foreign Minister and Antonio Garrigues as Minister of Justice were all known to be committed to reform to greater or lesser degrees. They and several other ministers had at one time or another represented the interests of prominent Spanish companies and of important multi-national corporations like United States Steel, IBM, Rank Xerox and General Electric. As Areilza noted in his diary, the survival of capitalism would require some political sacrifices.[62]

Another crucial appointment was of the Christian Democrat Alfonso Osorio as Minister of the Presidency. Since this ministry gave him responsibility for the national patrimony, it permitted him to hold regular meetings with the King. Indeed, the appointment almost certainly reflected the wishes of Juan Carlos himself. The make-up of the cabinet suggested that, despite the wishes of the bunker, some sort of change was in the offing. In this respect, the dual appointment of Torcuato Fernández

Miranda as President of the Cortes and of the Consejo del Reino was paramount. His capacity for political intrigue, his knowledge of Francoist constitutional law and his acquaintance with the entire Francoist political élite made him the perfect guide to the labyrinth in which Juan Carlos was trapped. He quickly ensured that he would have a mole in the cabinet by persuading Arias to accept his new protégé, Adolfo Suárez, in the key post of Minister Secretary-General of the Movimiento.[63]

The possible long-term repercussions of such appointments or indeed of the Byzantine, and at this stage still limited, operation being plotted by Fernández Miranda could hardly have been foreseen. Inevitably, the reaction of the ever-widening opposition coalitions was to denounce what they saw as a poorly camouflaged exercise in continuity. It was difficult to draw any other conclusion from Arias's speech to the Consejo Nacional del Movimiento on 19 January 1976 which announced his firm decision to be faithful to his origins. He assured his listeners that he accepted 'with honour the entire past of our regime from its first heroic and painful moments right up to yesterday' and that he harboured 'neither murky desires of revisionism nor suicidal aims of stirring up our institutional system'. These remarks emphasized how little had been offered by Arias in his vague intimations that he hoped eventually to see some kind of elected parliament with four or five legal parties. The most that could be hoped from Arias was that he might try to bestow upon Spain, in a paternalistic fashion, the mildest democratization which could defuse the crisis without provoking the bunker. This task was entrusted to a joint commission, or Comisión Mixta, of the senior cabinet minsters and members of the Consejo Nacional. At its first meeting, on 11 February 1976, Arias starkly reiterated his position when he declared that 'what I want to do is continue Francoism. And as long as I'm here or still in political life, I'll never be anything other than a strict perpetuator of Francoism in all its aspects and I will fight against the enemies of Spain who have begun to dare to raise their heads.' Symbolically, the Prime Minister's office was dominated by an easel supporting a large portrait of Franco in belligerent contrast to a diminutive photograph of the King.[64]

Even if Arias was in part attempting to pacify the bunker, there was little here to dissuade the opposition from its commitment to the swift and complete demolition of the Francoist system, the so-called *ruptura democrática*. The left's minimum demands of full political amnesty, legalization of all political parties, free trade unions, the dismantling of the Movimiento and the Sindicatos, and free elections were hardly negotiable with Arias. The first half of 1976 would see a trial of strength between the two options. Eventually, Arias's intransigence would make way for the more flexible approach of Torcuato Fernández Miranda and Adolfo Suárez. It was the threat of popular militancy throughout Spain, and of violence in the Basque Country, which persuaded the more liberal members of the government, and especially those close to Juan Carlos, that only a more positive commitment to democratic change could prevent a serious challenge to the existing order.

Mass demonstrations in favour of amnesty for political prisoners and large-scale industrial strikes spread during the first months of 1976. In part, the strikes were not unconnected with the fact that about two thirds of the country's *convenios colectivos*, or wage agreements, were due for renegotiation in the first three months of the year.[65] In this regard, labour unrest was intensified by the government's imposition of a wage freeze. Nevertheless, strikes everywhere were politically motivated. In some cases they were a response to Communist calls for a 'national democratic action' to overthrow the regime. They were much more a reflection of a general popular urge for political reform. In the Basque Country, strike action and mass demonstrations were inextricably linked and reached a fever pitch unknown elsewhere. The special frenzy of popular militancy there was a legacy of the violence used by the forces of order during the state of exception of 1975.

For obvious reasons, the strikes with greatest political impact were in the public services. At the beginning of the year, Madrid was the scene of intense pressure on the government. Successive actions by metro workers and postmen brought threats that their theoretical military status would be activated rendering them liable, under military law, to charges of mutiny if they did not return to work. The army was brought in to run the underground trains. Stoppages in the metal and construction industries virtually paralysed the capital's outer suburbs. The use of police charges to break up groups of strikers reflected the Francoist instincts of both Arias and his Minister of the Interior, Manuel Fraga. Later strikes by postmen and the workers of the national railway RENFE were met by militarization.[66]

The industrial unrest served to convince the more liberal ministers of the urgency of dialogue with the opposition. Arias himself remained intransigent and the only contacts were unofficial. The most important were those between Areilza and the left Christian Democrat, Joaquín

Ruiz Giménez. An ex-Minister of Education under Franco, Ruiz Giménez was an idealistic social Catholic. He had maintained close contacts with the Socialists through *Cuadernos para el Diálogo*, the journal which he had founded in 1963. Universally respected, he had emerged as the opposition's most suitable interlocutor with the government. The scale of Ruiz Giménez's task was indicated by Areilza's remark that he was 'like a sister of charity preaching chastity in a whorehouse'.[67] Areilza himself as Foreign Minister was undertaking a complex operation to secure the support of the Western democracies for a political reform under the auspices of Juan Carlos. He was thus as convinced of the need to reach a compromise with the opposition as he was appalled by the rigidity of Arias Navarro. For the opposition, the attitude of Areilza and the few cabinet liberals did not mitigate the overall picture of the government's dogged inflexibility. Accordingly, the pressure was stepped up.

After the Madrid strikes of January, February was punctuated by 80,000-strong amnesty demonstrations on successive Sundays in Barcelona.[68] However, the greatest militancy was reached in the Basque Country. The pardon issued on coronation day had affected fewer than 10 per cent of the 750 Basque prisoners. Rather than defusing the tension bequeathed by Franco, the pardon's inadequacy had provoked a feeling of popular rage. The bulk of the Basque population believed that ETA violence was a justifiable response to the institutional violence of Francoism and disappointment with the pardon was quickly converted into an intensive amnesty campaign. In scope and intensity, Basque amnesty actions exceeded similar movements in the rest of Spain. Frequent demonstrations were backed by labour disputes, sit-ins, hunger strikes and mass resignations by municipal officals. Demands for freedom for prisoners were combined with calls for the legalization of the Basque flag, the *Ikurriña*.

The campaign was irremediably complicated by the fact that ETA had not laid down it arms on the death of the dictator. In the first three months of 1976, several Civil Guards were killed trying to take down booby-trapped *Ikurriñas*, a number of alleged informers were shot and an industrialist was kidnapped and murdered. This not only enraged the bunker, but it also provoked the Minister of the Interior, Manuel Fraga, into declaring war on ETA on 8 April.[69] Relations between Fraga and the Basques had been stretched to the limit already at the beginning of March. A two-month-long strike in the town of Vitoria culminated in a massive demonstration on 3 March. As the workers left the Church of

San Francisco, they were charged by riot police. Three were killed and over seventy badly hurt. Two more workers died as a result of their injuries some days later. In reply, a general strike was called throughout the Basque Country. Fraga had been abroad at the time but returned quickly. The subsequent atmosphere was illustrated during a visit made to the local hospital by Fraga and Rodolfo Martín Villa, the Minister for the Sindicatos. A relative of one of the wounded asked them if they had come to finish him off. The events of Vitoria destroyed any credibility that the government had had in the region, reinforced popular support for ETA and intensified the militancy of the Basque working class. Fraga's declaration of war, which signified a stepping-up of police activity and was accompanied by the re-emergence of the ultra-rightist hit-squads, immeasurably worsened the situation.[70]

While the opposition in the rest of Spain was committed totally to the struggle for democracy, popular aspirations in the Basque Country were becoming increasingly much more far-reaching. The area had been radicalized to such a degree that there was considerable mass backing for the revolutionary separatist aspirations of ETA. Whilst militancy elsewhere in Spain could be expected to diminish once democracy was established, Euskadi was at a point from which pacification and a return to normal were already near to impossible. ETA's theorists were anxious to capitalize on the militancy which had been engendered by their struggle and its repression. The polemic about how best to combine military and political activities had raged in the movement ever since the assassination of Carrero Blanco had put political change on the agenda. For some hard-liners of the ETA Military Front, terrorist activism had become virtually an end in itself. More thoughtful members of the Political Front felt that preparations should be made for the post-Franco future lest the bourgeois Partido Nacionalista Vasco hog the political capital accumulated during ETA's struggle. The increasingly bitter debate within ETA had come to a head after the Cafetería Rolando bombing of 13 September 1974. That senseless act had emphasized the extent to which the Military Front was running out of control. Rejecting the efforts of cooler heads to tie terrorist actions to majority decisions, the 'milis' broke away to form ETA-Militar. The bulk of the organization became ETA-Político-Militar.

The differences between the two organizations had been slight at that stage although they were to widen rapidly over the next three years. ETA-M was the more exclusively nationalist and was committed to the rigid separation of political and military activities. In the wake of its formation, an extreme nationalist political party had been founded, LAIA (Langile Abertzale Iraultzaileen Alderdia or the Patriotic Workers' Revolutionary Party). ETA-PM, in addition to nationalism, retained wider socialist objectives, and its leaders believed that political and military actions were compatible. ETA-PM's activist units were known as the *Comandos Bereziak*. They were eventually to be at the heart of a further crisis arising out of the on-going contradictions between terrorism and more conventional political activities. It began with the kidnapping by ETA-PM *Comandos Bereziak* on 17 March 1976 of Angel Berazadi Urbe, an industrialist from San Sebastián and a sympathizer of the PNV. When his family refused to pay the full ransom demanded, he was murdered. This non-political crime provoked a firm condemnation of ETA-PM by the PNV-dominated Basque government-in-exile.

The murder of Berazadi dissipated some of the popular sympathy enjoyed by ETA and hastened the thinking of ETA-PM's foremost theorist, Eduardo Moreno Bergareche 'Pertur', on the problems arising from the continued use of violence in the changing political situation. 'Pertur' produced an influential report, the *Ponencia Otsagabía*, in which he advocated that ETA-PM abandon military activities in favour of political ones. The *Ponencia Otsagabía* was to form the basis of the philosophy behind the establishment of ETA-PM's own political party EIA (Euskal Iraultzako Alderdia or the Party of the Basque Revolution). Led by ex-*Etarras*, both LAIA and EIA, and other small parties of the so-called patriotic or *abertzale* left, were to become the dynamic leadership of a popular movement whose aims were beyond solution by any Madrid government. It was perhaps for this reason that 'Pertur' was kidnapped and murdered at the end of April. At the time, his death was attributed to right-wing terror squads but later investigations pointed to ETA-PM's own *Comandos Bereziak* and particularly to their leader Miguel Angel Apalátegui 'Apala'. He was apparently determined to prevent at any cost the drift towards orthodox politics advocated by 'Pertur'.[71]

The internal conflicts of ETA did little to diminish the growth of left nationalism in 1976, stimulated as it was by the violence of the forces of order. In a way that was not true of other sectors of the democratic opposition, the legacy of bitterness left by the dictatorship was intensified under Arias Navarro. The democratic fronts which were established in the rest of Spain, and which were constantly being widened to include moderates, never took root in the Basque Country. The Communist Party's Asamblea Democrática de Guernica was a failure. Instead, the *abertzale* left organized in 1975 its own front, known as KAS, the Koordinadora Abertzale Sozialista. Its far-reaching nationalist aspirations became known as the 'Alternativa KAS' and were to remain the core of *abertzale* ambitions well into the 1980s.[72]

To a very large extent, the remainder of the Spanish left was slow to appreciate what was happening in Euskadi. However, the Communist Party gradually came to terms with the fact that possibilities for its strategy of 'national democratic action' to overthrow the Francoist establishment were effectively limited to Madrid and Barcelona. The PCE leadership was forced to accept that the situation in the Basque Country was beyond its control. In consequence, behind his continuing triumphalist rhetoric, Santiago Carrillo came to perceive the potential weakness of the PCE's position. The strategy based on the conviction that a nationwide strike would bring about the *ruptura democrática* was quietly acknowledged to be erroneous. If working-class militancy was to be incapable of defeating the Francoist establishment then the *ruptura* could only come from some process of negotiation between government and opposition.

Carrillo was quick to see that the immediate danger facing the PCE was marginalization from such a process. Despite the greater militancy and discipline of the PCE's rank and file and its numerical superiority, in terms of activists, over the rest of the opposition, negotiations would favour the more obviously 'respectable' Socialists and Christian Democrats. Accordingly, the PCE Secretary-General recognized the urgent need for closer unity between the Junta Democrática and the Plataforma de Convergencia Democrática. By dropping the PCE's insistence on the *ruptura democrática*, the total break with the Francoist system and the departure of Juan Carlos, Carrillo facilitated the fusion of the two organizations. At the end of March, they became Coordinación Democrática, popularly known as the 'Platajunta'. Although the unwieldy width of the coalition was to soften the opposition's capacity for decisive action, its formation paved the way for negotiation with the reformists within the system and thus exposed divisions inside the cabinet.[73] The extent to which meaningful political debate was being limited to that between the opposition and the regime reformists was illustrated by a curious side-effect of the creation of the Platajunta.

Alarmed at the prospect of co-operation with the Communists, the more conservative wing of Ruiz Giménez's Christian Democrats broke away under the leadership of Fernando Alvarez de Miranda. After lengthy heart-searching, Ruiz Giménez's group had changed its name from Izquierda Demócrata Cristiana to the more progressive and less obviously confessional Izquierda Democrática. For some time, Ruiz Giménez had been urging Alvarez de Miranda to use his influence with the *Tácitos* to impel them to abandon their ambiguity and to condemn Arias's *continuismo*. Alvarez de Miranda hoped to persuade the *Tácitos* to come over to the Izquierda Democrática and help it become the basis of a future large-scale Christian Democrat party. The *Tácitos*, however, were suspicious of Ruiz Giménez's left-wing contacts, as indeed was Alvarez de Miranda. Ruiz Giménez was not prepared to break his links with the labour leaders he had defended over many years. The consequent split in Izquierda Democrática was formalized in April 1976. Together with Oscar Alzaga and Iñigo Cavero, Alvarez de Miranda broke away and formed a group, under the resuscitated title of Izquierda Demócrata Cristiana, whose positions were extremely close to those of the *Tácitos*. Alvarez de Miranda and his companions were eventually to end up in UCD. In the meanwhile, however, they served as a useful bridge between their erstwhile friends in the opposition and the *Tácitos*.[74] Alvarez de Miranda's abandonment of Ruiz Giménez was an indication of the changing atmosphere. The generalized struggle for democracy was already giving way in some circles to the staking out of precise positions for a possible democratic future.

Arias remained unmoved by all the activity within the opposition. He was tied to the past, his responses ever more dictated by his instincts as a Francoist policeman. More realistic and flexible ministers, like Adolfo Suárez and Alfonso Osorio, came round to Areilza's position on dialogue. Manuel Fraga, on the other hand, reacted violently. Against the advice of the growing liberal camp in the cabinet, Fraga arrested the various opposition leaders who met on 29 March to announce the formation of the Platajunta.[75] As Minister of the Interior, Fraga had been originally considered as one of the more reformist members of the cabinet. However, the events in Vitoria, which severely damaged the credibility of the government as a whole, particularly undermined that of Fraga. In fact, Fraga had already begun a concerted policy of currying favour with the old Francoist élite, especially within the army.

Shortly after the Vitoria events, Fraga was visited by the Valencian Christian Democrat Emilio Attard who asked him to ensure that the police would be careful in controlling an impending amnesty demonstration in Valencia in which some of his followers would be involved. To the alarm of Attard, Fraga informed him that it was the demonstrators in Valencia who would have to be careful, 'because I'm going to smash them to pulp' (*porque los voy a moler a palos*). Further evidence of Fraga's return to bellicose authoritarianism came a month later, on the eve of a projected PSOE May Day ceremony at the grave of the Party's founder, Pablo Iglesias, in the Madrid civil cemetery. At a dinner held at the home of Miguel Boyer, who was later to be Minister of the Economy in Felipe González's first cabinet, Fraga was outlining his plans for the future, unaware that he would not be playing the central role therein. In a threatening manner, he told Felipe González that the Socialists might be legalized in eight years and the Communists never. 'Remember', he said with typical Fraga bluster, 'I represent power and you're nothing' (*recuerde que yo soy el Poder y Vd. no es nada*). The dropping of the liberal veneer was a miscalculation from whose effects Fraga was not to recover until the elections of October 1982. In the spring of 1976, the re-adoption of an impetuously authoritarian style effectively eliminated him as a possible successor to Arias.[76]

In contrast, the crisis of Vitoria, which so united the left, was to be a considerable boost to the career of the as yet unfancied Adolfo Suárez. Fraga being absent in Germany when the news broke, the Minister Secretary-General of the Movimiento had assumed control of the Ministry of the Interior. General Prada Canillas, Captain-General of the Burgos military region, within which Vitoria lay, was urging the declaration of a state of exception. Suárez opted instead for a more discreet introduction of police reinforcements from neighbouring provinces. Subsequently, with the aid of Alfonso Osorio, Suárez convinced the King that his firm handling of events had prevented more bloodshed.[77] The rise in Suárez's stock was curious. Areilza did not consider his young rival to be a convinced democrat because of his apparent readiness to use the apparatus of the Movimiento to fabricate a merely cosmetic democratic change. The view that Suárez was fundamentally reactionary was shared by other Movimiento stalwarts.[78] However, contacts with the King's advisers, especially Torcuato Fernández Miranda, were convincing Suárez that the future lay in the direction of more commitment to democracy. He was already establishing contacts with the 'tolerated opposition' of the Unión Social-Demócrata Española and with the Christian Democrats linked to Fernando Alvarez de Miranda. Since this latter group was close to the King, Suárez became ever more the focus of royal hopes as a man who might be able to link disparate sectors of Spanish politics. Suárez himself got a hint of this at the 1975 cup final when, as the Minister in charge of the Delegación Nacional de Deportes, he sat next to the King. Indicating the young president of Real Zaragoza, who contrasted markedly with the ageing president of their opponents, Real Madrid, Juan Carlos asked him if he had ever noticed how good young presidents were (*qué majos son los presidentes jóvenes*).[79]

In the meanwhile, Arias's cabinet persisted in tinkering with a new law of political associations in the gradually dawning knowledge that his scheme for tightly limited reform had run aground. At the suggestion of Torcuato Fernández Miranda, Suárez was chosen to present the new law to the Francoist Cortes and did so with great style. The King was delighted and praised his eloquence by calling him '*pico de oro*' (literally golden beak, but with the sense of silver-tongued). As a future candidate for political power, however, Suárez suffered from his lack of contacts in the illegal opposition.[80] His more obviously liberal colleagues were already coming to see the urgent need for dialogue with the left. The opposition had long since come to terms with the fact that a revolutionary attempt to overthrow Francoism would only lead to civil war. Even the PCE now dropped its rhetorical demand for a full-scale *ruptura demo-crática* and accepted, along with the PSOE and the more progressive Christian Democrats, the idea of a negotiated break with the dictatorship, the so-called *ruptura pactada*. The creation of Coordinación Democrática had implied a realistic assessment of the limits of mass action. Now there would be a turn towards a more moderate programme. It aimed at widening the opposition front to include centre and even right-of-centre groups while simultaneously isolating the government.[81]

The King was kept informed of this process by his advisers. From March, if not earlier, he became increasingly dissatisfied with Arias's inability to react other than with repressive violence to the growing strength of the opposition. The royal intentions were signalled when he allowed himself to be quoted in *Newsweek* to the effect that his Prime Minister was 'an unmitigated disaster'. On 9 June 1976, after Suárez's charismatic speech, the Cortes passed the new law of political associations but refused to make the necessary amendments to the penal code to permit the legalization of political parties as envisaged by the law. Arias was exposed as being as unable or unwilling to deal with the bunker as he was incapable of controlling the opposition. Juan Carlos was already convinced that the transition to democracy necessary for his own survival had to be placed in the hands of someone able to handle both bunker and opposition. Aware that dissatisfaction with Arias was also rife among senior army officers, the King felt that he must act before the military asked him to do so. In such an event, the preservation of his own authority would oblige him to keep on Arias.[82] The situation was thus urgent. Accordingly, after he had received assurances of American support during his triumphal visit to the USA in early June, Juan Carlos asked for Arias's resignation. Suggestions of American influence were played down. However, Areilza believed that the replacement of Arias by Suárez had been planned since Easter and perhaps even since Henry Kissinger's visit to Madrid in January.[83]

At the time, the King's delay in replacing Arias Navarro raised doubts about his commitment to democratization. Convinced that the adjustment of Spain's political structure to the changed economic and social realities of the 1970s was inevitable, many observers tended to interpret hesitation as bad faith. However, such a view underestimated the residual power of the bunker in general and of the armed forces in particular. The subsequent emergence of what became known as *golpismo* puts Juan Carlos's slowness in a different perspective. The delicacy of his dealings with the military establishment was an invaluable contribution to the coming of democracy. Similarly, the entire Arias experience was of crucial importance in a number of ways. His timid and restricted reforms had the merit of drawing the fire of the bunker and thereby allowed the ultra-right to discredit itself in the eyes of the remainder of the Francoist élite. The corollary of that process was that the very inadequacy of Arias's schemes impelled a large number of Francoist bureaucrats and businessmen into the reformist camp. Joaquín Garrigues Walker, Francisco Fernández Ordóñez, the *Tácitos* and others were thus to find themselves in the position of intermediaries between the right and the opposition.

This was perhaps the central factor in ensuring a bloodless transition to democracy. Equally, the flimsiness of Arias's reforms and the heavy-handed repression which accompanied them drove the left towards unity. That unity, and the popular militancy behind it, was the key to the democratization process. Without it, even the most flexible and reformist functionaries would never have been obliged to think about the future. The fact that Arias was unable to control the bloodlust of the bunker, notably in the Basque Country, immeasurably boosted the strength of the popular forces. The opprobrium generated by the extreme right in the Arias period also ensured that the weight of international opinion would swing behind the democratic left. A glance back at the Spain of Carrero Blanco underlines the importance of the Arias years, painful though they were, in bringing the country nearer to its goal of democracy.

4
Reconciling the irreconcilable: the political reform of Adolfo Suárez 1976–7

The thirty months from the death of Carrero Blanco to the resignation of Arias Navarro had witnessed cataclysmic changes in Spain. In 1973, despite the impact of economic modernization, despite the rising tides of labour, student and regionalist militancy, the stark outline of Franco's Spain remained as discernible as it had been thirty years before. The divisions among the Francoist families were beginning to rumble beneath the surface but were still far from suggesting that the fortress might one day be betrayed. The besieging army of Communists and Socialists, workers and students, Basques and Catalans still seemed a long way from victory. The death of Carrero Blanco smashed the myth of Francoist invulnerability, ignited the squabbles within the walls and roused the opposition to seek the unity which had always eluded it. Two and a half years later, the opposition was making the pace; many of the regime's brightest and best had gone over to the democratic enemy and the ultras were being reduced to a narrow, resentful, albeit still powerful, minority. Yet formally, Spain was no nearer to being a democratic country than she had been on 12 February 1974. For all that the Arias years had paved the way, for all the growing confidence of the opposition, the ostensible power of the Francoist establishment and, above all, of the armed forces remained undiminished. If a catastrophic clash between the irresistible force of the left and the immovable object of the right was to be avoided, it was essential that rapid progress be made to the introduction of democracy and in such a way as to meet with the approval of the armed forces and the bulk of the old guard.

The views of the Francoist establishment eliminated Areilza as the man to work the miracle. He was damned by his liberalism. Fraga had ruled himself out by his belligerent style. In any case, both were more dominant personalities than Juan Carlos wished. On the recent royal visit to the United States, Areilza had apparently imposed himself on the proceedings with a certain arrogance and certainly with less deference than was strictly proper.[1] Moreover, in his years as a fervent supporter of Don Juan, he had often been critical of Juan Carlos. The ideal candidate now would be both younger and more acceptable to the Francoist élite. Thus it was that Torcuato Fernández Miranda stage-managed the 3 July meeting of the Consejo del Reino which was to choose the *terna*, or three-man short-list, from which the King would select his new Prime Minister. Since it was widely expected that Fernández Miranda would be fighting to include Fraga and/or Areilza, the prior decision not to choose either made his task easier. They were 'sacrificed' and the majority of the Consejo members were so pleased to have eliminated them that they seemed not to notice how Fernández Miranda used all his skill to ensure that the name of Adolfo Suárez appeared.

After lengthy debate and successive rounds of voting, his name stayed in the ring. For most Consejeros he was not so much a serious candidate but rather a safe Movimiento figure to vote for in order to keep others out. One Movimiento right-winger who did not vote for Suárez, Joaquín Viola Sauret, one-time *Alcalde* (mayor) of Barcelona, commented dismissively, 'I may live in Barcelona, but I'm from Cebreros and I know this lad only too well.' Cebreros in the province of Avila was Suárez's home town. In the end, the *terna* consisted of Adolfo Suárez, Gregorio López Bravo, once the most glamorous of Franco's technocrats, and Federico Silva Muñoz, the dourly conservative Christian Democrat. The Consejo presented the list in the confidence that the choice would be between the two senior candidates. Indeed, one Consejero even commented to Fernández Miranda that the inclusion of Suárez was a terrible waste since he had no chance of being picked and so his place could have been used to flatter a more important member of the establishment.[2] Only Areilza and Fraga can have been more surprised by the appointment on 3 July of Adolfo Suárez since both they themselves and the press had been confident about their own chances.[3]

For the King, Suárez signified someone who, as a Movimiento *apparatchik*, would be able, especially under the guidance of Fernández Miranda, to use the system against itself and so initiate reform. That asset was not widely appreciated in mid-1976. Arias told Suárez that he was delighted with his appointment if only because it meant that neither Areilza nor Fraga would be President of the Council of Ministers. Indeed, Suárez's Francoist credentials delighted the bunker as much as they horrified the opposition. Massive demonstrations in favour of political liberties and amnesty were thus called by the left in the second week of July. Their success left Suárez in little doubt that speedy and thorough reform was necessary if the crisis was to be resolved without violence.[4]

In fact, Suárez's most difficult immediate task was the formation of a cabinet team. Both Areilza and Fraga had written to him to express their refusal to continue in the government. They, like many others in the political élite and in the opposition, believed that Suárez's stay in power would be short. The new Prime Minister, in order to avoid the fatal step of forming a cabinet composed entirely of his cronies from the Movimiento, looked for assistance to Torcuato Fernández Miranda and to Alfonso Osorio. A prominent member of the *Tácito* group, Osorio became Vice-President of the Cabinet and Minister of the Presidency. At the request of the King, he threw his considerable influence into persuading other *Tácitos* to accept posts. He also tried to recruit the Christian Democrat followers of Fernando Alvarez de Miranda, who was offered the portfolio of Education. Alvarez de Miranda refused to join a non-elected government and thereby showed that, for the moment at least, the liberal right would keep its distance.[5]

The final cabinet list was sneered at as a 'cabinet of assistant lecturers' (*penenes* or *profesores non-numerarios*), a witticism attributed to Francisco Fernández Ordóñez. None the less, the unchanged military ministers aside, Suárez's ensuing team of conservative Catholics like Marcelino Oreja, at Foreign Affairs, and Landelino Lavilla, at Justice, gave him a better chance to carry out reform than his critics had believed possible.[6] Paradoxically, the dropping of Areilza helped the transition process. In power, he would certainly have faced greater right-wing intransigence than awaited Suárez. Out of it, he was able to devote his not inconsiderable prestige and his silver tongue to the task of fostering dialogue between the civilized right and the opposition.[7]

With a government made up of men linked in various ways to the more progressive sectors of Spanish capitalism, Suárez set about introducing plans for a more meaningful democratization. He informed his new cabinet that his strategy would be based essentially on speed. He would keep ahead of the game by introducing specific measures faster than the *continuistas* of the Francoist establishment could respond to them.[8] His programme, announced on television, recognized popular sovereignty, promised a referendum on political reform and elections before 30 June 1977. It was accompanied by a limited royal pardon for political offences which was well received in most of Spain but did little for Suárez's credibility in the Basque Country. For the bulk of non-politicized Spaniards, however, fearful of losing the material benefits of the previous fifteen years, but receptive to political liberalization, the combination of Juan Carlos and Adolfo Suárez was an attractive option. It seemed to offer the chance of both protecting the economic and social advances of recent times and of advancing peacefully and gradually towards democracy.

The skill with which Suárez projected his television image of modernity and charm helped consolidate political support among the silent majority. Elsewhere, a dynamic and polemical press quickly became the arena for debate about political reform. Indeed, the press in general, and *El País* and *Cambio 16* in particular, virtually became a protagonist in the transition process by acting as a constant source of pressure on Suárez. Despite his advantages, he faced a difficult situation just as Arias had done. On the one side, there was the bunker and the army, strong and suspicious. On the other, there was the opposition with its clamouring masses. At first, Suárez seems to have conceived his task as one of sharing out power between the opposition and the *aperturistas* of his cabinet. However, the opposition quickly made it clear that it was not looking for a back-stairs deal but rather conceived of the *ruptura pactada* as consisting of negotiations for the opening of a constituent period. Bringing the opposition to collaborate in a process of democratization within Francoist 'legality' was to be one of Suárez's greatest tasks and consequently greatest triumphs.

Carrillo in particular was keeping up the pressure by a calculated policy of bringing the PCE back to the surface, challenging the cabinet either to tolerate his party's existence or else to reveal its true colours by reverting to repressive action. He began by holding an open meeting of the PCE Central Committee in Rome at the end of July. Amply publicized by the media, it had considerable impact, revealing to the Spanish public for the first time that a significant number of intellectuals and labour leaders were Communists. Then, in the autumn, the Party began the distribution of carnets to its members inside Spain. Carrillo, who was living clandestinely in Madrid, informed Suárez through intermediaries that, if he did not receive a passport, he would hold a press conference in Madrid in the presence of Oriana Fallacci, Marcel Niedergang and other influential foreign correspondents. The reason for such tactics derived from a small incident in late July. Carrillo had applied formally for a passport at the Spanish embassy in Paris. He was received by the ambassador, Miguel María de Lojendio, and revealed to him that he had been inside Spain clandestinely. Shortly after getting Lojendio's report, Suárez had reacted in classic Francoist style and relieved him of his post for receiving Carrillo without instructions. It was hardly surprising that the PCE had little or no faith in Suárez's proclaimed reformist intentions.[9]

A struggle was thus developing between Suárez and the opposition for control of the transition process. As an excuse for delay, Suárez could point to the army; as an incentive to hurry, the opposition could point to the rising swell of popular pressures. Strikes had increased tenfold in relation to the previous year.[10] For a man who had worked in 1971 on a television campaign to get public collaboration in the military repression of strikes, negotiations with Communists and Socialists did not come easy. However, since the fate of the monarchy was in the balance, Suárez was being helped by Juan Carlos's advisers. While Torcuato Fernández Miranda master-minded dealings with the Francoist establishment, the professor of constitutional law, Carlos Ollero, counselled realistic dealings with the opposition.[11] It was clear that, to ensure a bloodless transition without economic or social dislocation, Suárez had to take the initiative away from the left. That could only be done by a skilful combination of substantial concessions and efforts to split the united front of the opposition. A prime objective was to force back the Communists from setting the pace of opposition demands to a more defensive position of trying to prevent their own isolation.

Throughout August, Suárez had interviews with a wide range of opposition personalities, including Felipe González, and made a favourable impression on them. The PSOE leadership was already convinced that the Francoist system was unlikely to be overthrown by popular action. There would be no Portuguese-style revolution of the carnations. By early 1976 the Socialists had come to the conclusion that, given the relation of forces, their ideal of totally sweeping away Francoism with a provisional government and a constituent Cortes to decide on the form of regime was utopian. When Suárez met Felipe González on 10 August, the PSOE leader had already reached the conclusion that a constitution elaborated by a freely elected Cortes would in itself constitute a *ruptura*. He knew that, to get to that point, it would be necessary to negotiate with 'the forces that occupy the apparatus of the State'. Accordingly, he was greatly impressed by the president's humility and readiness to listen *'como una esponja'* (like a sponge). Their relationship was to remain cordial throughout the transition period. The PSOE's communiqué after the meeting recognized that Suárez was 'well-disposed to the creation of a genuinely democratic regime'.[12] It constituted an important step on the way to a negotiated change.

Suárez also made contact with Carrillo through the lawyer and director of the Europa Press Agency, José Mario Armero. He urged the PCE leader not to make the transition impossible.[13] By this, of course, he meant the sort of peaceful transition that would leave as much of the existing social, economic and political structure intact as possible. In fact, having spent time in Madrid talking to José María de Areilza and Joaquín Ruiz Giménez, Carrillo was fully aware that some kind of compromise with the reformist right was inevitable. Accordingly, knowing that the idea of a provisional government imposed by popular force was an unlikely outcome, he assured Suárez of his commitment to pacific change.[14]

The new president was walking a tightrope. Any reform had to be steered past the army and the Francoist establishment and at the same time exposed to the suspicious scrutiny of the opposition. On 4 September, a wide range of liberal, social democrat and Christian Democrat groups gathered at the Eurobuilding in Madrid to discuss with Coordinación Democrática and with other regional opposition fronts a series of questions concerning the elaboration of a united strategy.[15] Chaired by Joaquín Ruiz Giménez, and widely reported by the media, the meeting signified that opposition unity now reached even some *aperturista* refugees from the Franco regime. In practical terms, all that came out of the meeting was the creation of a liaison committee, but that was sufficient to oblige Suárez to hasten his preparations for the presentation of his project of political reform.

Inevitably, there were constant rumours of military subversion. Indeed, faced by the surging waves of opposition confidence, the army and the bunker huddled together ever more defiantly. The military capacity to invigilate the political process had been maintained by the continued presence of ultra generals at the head of the service ministries. In the first government of the monarchy, Juan Carlos had hoped to introduce the liberal General Manuel Gutiérrez Mellado into the cabinet. As a friend of Díez Alegría, and by his opposition to severe punishment for the moderate officers involved in the Unión Militar Democrática, he had earned the dislike of the military bunker. To keep him out of the cabinet, a prominent ultra general, almost certainly Jaime Milans del Bosch, had assembled a critical dossier in which it was insinuated that Gutiérrez Mellado was really the head of the UMD. Thus, overall responsibility for defence affairs passed, in both the Arias and Suárez cabinets, to the reactionary General Fernando de Santiago y Díaz de Mendívil.[16] Under his influence, relations between senior military figures and the civilian bunker were extremely close despite regular declarations of the armed forces' apoliticism. Such statements were probably sincere in so far as loyalty to the principles of Francoism did not signify a political stance to the hard-liners but merely an unavoidable patriotic duty. Throughout 1976 there had been contacts between leading generals and Francoist ultras like José Antonio Girón de Velasco, President of the Confederation of Nationalist Ex-Combatants, Blas Piñar, head of *Fuerza Nueva*, and the retired head of the Civil Guard, Carlos Iniesta Cano. Their meetings aimed to bolster military doctrinal intransigence in the face of democratic reform.[17]

Juan Carlos was aware of the extent to which the ultras were trying to block the transition. Accordingly, the appointment of Suárez had been matched by the naming of General Gutiérrez Mellado as Chief of the General Staff. The determined progress towards dialogue with the opposition caused first friction then rage among the ultras. The trend of the conflict was symbolized by General de Santiago's furious response to the fact that Suárez had removed Arias's life-size portrait of Franco from his office. More substantively, they had clashed bitterly in the presence of the King over the initial amnesty granted on 30 July 1976 and Suárez had declared that he would not tolerate such outbursts. Behind the amnesty, to the intense chagrin of some of the Captains-General, there was a secret arrangement for the deportation of some imprisoned *Etarras*.[18] Inevitably the atmosphere was tense on 8 September 1976, when Suárez submitted his reform project to a group of senior officers and appealed for their 'patriotic support'. Those invited to the meeting included the military ministers, the nine Captains-General and the Chiefs of Staff of the three services. Since they enjoyed the backing of Juan Carlos, Suárez's persuasively expounded plans were accepted with reluctance and with a demand that the Communist Party be excluded from any future reform. Suárez placated them with an assurance that the international loyalties enshrined in the PCE's statutes would preclude its legalization. He did not tell them that through his secret contacts with Carrillo, he was working towards a change in those statutes and an eventual legalization of the Communist Party. Curiously, eight years later, Suárez remained convinced that he had 'never deceived any officer'. The confusion of sophistry and truth was a central part of Suárez's armoury. Occasionally, it would backfire. In the case of the legalization of the PCE, what the army saw as the breaking of his word earned

Suárez a bitter hatred which was to dog him until his departure from the political scene in 1981.

Nevertheless, two days after the meeting with the high command, the cabinet approved the law for political reform without any opposition from the four military ministers. A few days later, matters took a different turn when the Minister for Syndical Relations, Enrique de la Mata, introduced a draft project for trade union reform. This provoked the determined opposition of General de Santiago y Díaz de Mendívil, who believed that the disorder of the 1930s had emanated from the trade unions. So energetic was his protest on 21 September that Suárez obliged him to resign. The Prime Minister was asserting himself because he knew that he could not afford to have the reform programme slowed down. He was also happy to seize the opportunity to replace Santiago with Gutiérrez Mellado. However, his firmness worried the Minister of the Presidency, Alfonso Osorio. Ever shrewd and cautious, and essentially very conservative, Osorio believed that General de Santiago should have been brought around by persuasion because of his immense influence among the right-wing opponents of reform. Suárez, on the other hand, was confident that he understood the armed forces sufficiently well to permit himself such firmness. He cannot have foreseen the immediate consequences which heralded the progressive deterioration of his relations with the military.

General de Santiago circularized his senior colleagues with a letter explaining his position:

The political evolution of our fatherland is running along channels, and is based on premises, with which I have not felt myself identified. My deep conviction that a political intervention by the armed forces could only produce undesirable situations in the short term led me to eschew intransigent positions. However, I also consider, personally as well as in my capacity as the spokesman of the armed forces inside the government, that such restraint and understanding are ultimately limited by the mistaken interpretations that have been placed upon them. The government is preparing a measure, which I have opposed in vain, authorizing trade union freedom. This means, in my opinion, the legalization of the CNT, UGT and FAI trade unions, responsible for atrocities committed in the red zone during the Civil War, and of the Workers Commissions, trade union organization of the Communist Party. I am convinced that the consequences of this measure will be immediate, and since neither my conscience nor my honour permit me to take responsibility for, nor implicate the armed forces in, such a measure, I decided to present my irrevocable resignation.

This text, apart from masking the fact that General de Santiago had effectively been dismissed, implied that any other officer who accepted a ministry in Suárez's cabinet was both immoral and dishonourable. Santiago's stance, and perhaps also his distorted vision of Spanish history, gave rise to declarations of solidarity from other officers and expressions of delight from the bunker press. *El Alcázar*, the ultra-rightist newspaper whose board of directors was headed by General Jaime Milans del Bosch, published a letter from the irrepressible General Iniesta Cano thanking Santiago for his 'priceless lesson'. Iniesta had been enraged by café rumours that Santiago had not resigned of his own free will. Under the headline 'A Lesson In Honour', Iniesta built on Santiago's own circular by stating that his example had to be followed by any officer committed to the service of the fatherland. This was effectively a declaration of war against General Manuel Gutiérrez Mellado, Santiago's successor. The implications were discussed at a cabinet meeting on 1 October at which it was decided that both Santiago and Iniesta would be punished by being relegated to the reserve list.

Understandably, Suárez wished to assert his authority over the army. In this case, however, he acted precipitately in that such action was contrary to the tenets of Spanish military law. Prominent bunker figures like Juan García Carrés, Jaime Milans del Bosch and José Antonio Girón de Velasco rallied around Iniesta and encouraged him to oppose the punishment. After vigorous protest from Iniesta and frantic consultations with military juridical experts, the case was given to General Joaquín Fernández de Córdoba for adjudication. General Fernández de Córdoba was a traditionalist and a close friend of Iniesta. Not only did he declare the government's decree improper but he also judged the conduct of both generals to have been blameless. In the full glare of publicity, the cabinet had been made to look ridiculous and vindictive. General Gutiérrez Mellado was placed in an appalling position, having to suffer the contempt of his comrades-in-arms and the hostility of General de Santiago, perhaps the most influential officer in the entire army. The bunker was delighted.[19] It had found two paladins of its ideas and their articles in *El Alcázar* over the next five years were to reflect and promote the growth of anti-democratic sentiment, or *golpismo*, within the armed forces. None the less, Santiago's removal deprived the bunker of a strategic position. Despite the hostile atmosphere in which he had to work, Gutiérrez Mellado was able to begin the urgent task of promoting a new generation of officers loyal to the coming democratic regime.

In the short, and indeed middle, term, basic fidelity to Juan Carlos rather than any deep-rooted commitment to democracy was the most that the Defence Minister could hope for from senior officers. At the end of 1976, the ultra Director-General of the Civil Guard, Angel Campano López, was replaced by General Antonio Ibáñez Freire, a man close to Gutiérrez Mellado. The fact that he had to be promoted expressly to Lieutenant-General provoked fury in reactionary segments of the military hierarchy devoted as they were to the most rigid seniority in promotions. The most vociferous critic was General Jaime Milans del Bosch. The policy of replacements continued after anti-government demonstrations by groups of policemen and civil guards. The Director-General of Security, Emilio Rodríguez Román, was replaced by Mariano Nicolás García and the Inspector-General de la Policía Armada (Head of the Police), General Aguilar Carmona, by General José Timón de Lara.[20] At a time when the government and the opposition were creeping towards agreement, Gutiérrez Mellado and Suárez were aware that efforts had to be made to keep the function of maintaining public order in a nascent democracy out of the hands of bloodthirsty reactionaries.

In the meanwhile, however, the task of steering the reform project through the labyrinths of the Francoist establishment occupied most of Suárez's time. The text approved by the cabinet on 10 September was made public shortly afterwards. The reaction of the opposition was mixed. Given that the project allowed for the elections promised before mid-1977 to be presided over by the existing government and that there was no question of Suárez resigning in favour of a provisional government, a declaration of the executive committee of the Communist Party on 15 September vehemently denounced the text as an 'anti-democratic fraud'.[21] Other groups within the opposition were, however, pleasantly surprised by the extent to which daily life was being liberalized, thereby giving substance to Suárez's claims. The press was functioning normally, political groups to the right of the PCE were unhindered and the PSOE was preparing to hold its XXVII Congress. The Minister of the Interior, Rodolfo Martín Villa, had issued provincial civil governors with instructions to prohibit all public activities by the Communists.[22] Yet, to a certain degree, even the PCE was unofficially allowed to go about its business. The initiative was swinging Suárez's way. He insinuated to the Socialists and the left Christian Democrats that he could make even greater concessions provided that they did not rock the boat and provoke the army by prematurely insisting on the legalization of the PCE. With typical skill and cunning, Suárez was trying to use the issue to drive a wedge into the opposition and to impose caution on Carrillo. Thus, in late September, Felipe González was adamant that legalization of the Communist Party was a non-negotiable pre-requisite of democracy. Yet by the end of November, he was arguing that it was unrealistic to insist on it.[23] Faced with the self-evident impossibility of imposing changes against the will of the army and with the substantial indications that things were progressing steadily under Suárez's guidance, the opposition could do little but acquiesce.[24]

In fact, with the aid of Torcuato Fernández Miranda, Suárez was having considerable success in steering his reform project through the Francoist institutions, although he was constantly worried that the obstacles could at any moment prove too great. Votes were nervously counted in advance and many were secured by promises of positions of influence in the post-election democratic regime.[25] On 8 October, in an atmosphere of some tension, the project was approved with minor amendments by the Consejo Nacional by 80 votes to 13 with 6 abstentions. In mid-November, when it was discussed in the Cortes, Blas Piñar assumed the defence of the bunker's positions and Miguel Primo de Rivera that of the reform project. Virtuoso displays of sophistry using the entire panoply of Francoist political theories came from both sides. The prior back-stage manoeuvres of Suárez and Fernández Miranda bore fruit when the reform was approved by 425 votes against 15, with 13 abstentions.

The likely outcome had been carefully calculated. Some possibly recalcitrant *procuradores*, as the Francoist Cortes members were called, were packed off on an official junket to Panama, via the Caribbean. Others were promised seats in the future Senate. Much was made of the fact that the proposed democratic Cortes and Senate had the same number of seats combined as the Francoist Cortes. This influenced many *procuradores* who had come to believe that they genuinely 'represented' the areas on which they had been imposed and therefore assumed that they would simply be elected by their grateful constituents. In general, the vote in favour of the political reform project was a collective suicide based on the ingrained habits of obedience to authority, an inflated sense of patriotism and, above all, tempting promises whispered in the ears of those whom Suárez later referred to as the '*procuradores del harakiri*'.[26] The wisdom of the Suárez–Fernández Miranda route to democracy was confirmed after the vote when the Minister for the Navy, the extreme rightist Admiral Gabriel Pita da Veiga, a personal friend of Franco, remarked 'my conscience is clear because the democratic reforms will be carried out through Francoist legality'. With Franco's institutions in voluntary liquidation, the road was open to the elections. Suárez now had good reason to be confident that the left would be obliged to accept his version of reform bestowed from above.[27]

In fact, the opposition remained distrustful, which was understandable after the empty efforts of reform witnessed successively from Solís, Carrero Blanco and Arias Navarro. On 23 October, Coordinación Democrática had united with five regional fronts from Valencia, Catalonia, the Balearic Islands, the Canary Islands and Galicia, to form the Plataforma de Organismos Democráticos. Meeting on 4 November in Las Palmas, the new organization rejected Suárez's plans for a referendum on his political reform project. Arguing that the referendum would be meaningless while political parties were still illegal, while the government still maintained monopolistic control over radio and television, while there were still political prisoners, and while the huge apparatus of the Movimiento still existed as a mechanism of electoral pressure, the POD called for abstention.[28] However, despite the apparent strength and firmness of the opposition stance, the pace was increasingly being dictated by Suárez.

Indeed, the strike wave reached its peak in November without seriously disrupting the government's timetable for gradual reform. Thereafter, it tended to lose steam. Committed political or trade union activists aside, the broad mass of the people welcomed the changes introduced by Suárez and were likely to vote in favour of his project. In addition, the incorporation into the opposition of centrist elements had led to a softening of militant attitudes. Accordingly, the great general strike called for 12 November was posed in economic rather than political terms. Its slogans were protests against the wage freeze and redundancies, although the political implications were clear enough. In the event, more than a million workers were involved, but the strike never spilled over into the great national action against the Suárez reform that the Communists had hoped for. That was in large part because of the elaborate precautions taken by the Minister of the Interior. As soon as he received intelligence reports about the strike's preparation, Martín Villa organized a committee to elaborate a counter-strategy. It was composed of senior public-order, telecommunications, traffic and intelligence experts. The police arrested workers' leaders in Madrid, Barcelona, Valencia, Bilbao and Seville. They thereby neutralized the nerve centres of the movement and so appreciably limited its impact.[29]

It was also an indication of the fact that Suárez was succeeding in persuading the mass of the population that his reform programme was genuine. Moreover, taking place only three days before the project was to be submitted to the Cortes, the relative failure of the strike strengthened his hand. It contributed to his success in the Cortes from 16 to 19 November. Furthermore, it confirmed the tendency of many opposition groups to acknowledge the validity of dealing with Suárez in order to liquidate Francoism. The president's many conversations with moderate opposition figures were paying dividends. With more liberal and social-democrat groups joining the Plataforma de Organismos Democráticos, the readiness to negotiate displayed by Joaquín Ruiz Giménez prevailed over the more maximalist positions of the Communists and the Socialists. A summit meeting of the POD and other groups held on 27 November reaffirmed many of the demands of the Plataforma's inaugural declaration of 4 November. However, the crucial condition of a provisional government of 'democratic consensus' to oversee the forthcoming elections was dropped.[30] The way was now open for a 'committee of personalities' from the opposition to negotiate with the government.

The extent to which Suárez's option had established itself was indicated by the pre-electoral tone of the XXVII Congress of the PSOE held in Madrid at the beginning of December. The PSOE leaders were clearly aware of the popular impact of Suárez's progress so far and they were also anxious to prevent the president exploiting a weakness on their flank. Suárez had astutely permitted the emergence of a number of other pretenders to the socialist mantle. There was the Federación de Partidos Socialistas, a collection of small provincial groupings of vaguely socialist independents. More influential was the tiny Partido Socialista Popular, a group of significant intellectuals and professionals. They were led by two political scientists, the opposition veteran, known as the 'old professor' (*el viejo profesor*), Enrique Tierno Galván, and his assistant Raul Morodo. Finally, and potentially the most dangerous, were the returned exiles and old militants of the so-called PSOE-Histórico, who had not recognized the fact that Felipe González had replaced the Toulouse-based émigré leaders. They might be able to mount an irritating challenge to the PSOE's legitimacy.

In consequence, the PSOE leadership feared that, if they refused to participate in the elections out of a reluctant solidarity with the Communists, people would go to the polls anyway and PSOE votes would go to the rival socialist parties. In retrospect, these parties appear inconsequential but, at the time, they were perceived within the PSOE as potential rivals. A crucial task for the party was thus to establish the PSOE's authenticity. Alfonso Guerra skilfully orchestrated the presence of Willy Brandt, Michael Foot, Mario Soares and other major European Socialist leaders in such a way as to demonstrate the PSOE's exclusive membership of the international socialist family. Then, Felipe González not only imposed an unequivocally moderate line on his party, but he also made it clear that the PSOE would participate in the coming elections even if all parties had not been legalized beforehand.[31] This approach reflected the advice of the German Socialist leadership whose influence on the PSOE was considerable.

The wisdom of the Socialists' moderation was confirmed on 15 December when, despite the abstention calls of the opposition, the referendum on political reform saw the project approved by 94 per cent of the vote. The abstention calls were certainly a tactical error. However, without more guarantees from Suárez regarding the legalization of political parties, neither the PSOE nor the PCE leaderships felt able to endorse his line publicly. There was an unreal air about their declarations on abstention calls and they were not taken as binding by the left-wing rank and file. Indeed, both Carrillo and González knew that the referendum would be a success for Suárez. They certainly did not perceive the result as a defeat for themselves. Indeed, given that opposition pressure throughout 1976 had pushed the government towards democratization, the referendum result was in a sense a victory for the left as well as for Suárez. None the less, the boost to the president's position was immeasurable.[32]

Flushed with success and on the verge of negotiations in which he held most of the cards, Suárez still faced two problems either of which could have upset the delicate balancing act that he was performing. The unresolved questions of the legalization of the Communist Party and of terrorism, particularly that of ETA, were always likely to destroy Suárez's uneasy truce with the army. The Communist problem lent itself to his personal brand of back-stage wheeling and dealing. It would eventually be solved, albeit not without leaving a residue of festering resentment in military circles. Basque terror, in contrast, was to prove intractable and, in the long run, was to be Suárez's undoing. Osorio wrote in his diary that Suárez simply did not understand the Basques.[33] After all, immersed in the gargantuan task of creating a democratic polity, consumed by the problems of placating both bunker and opposition, Suárez could hardly be expected to sympathize with the revolutionary nationalist aspirations of the *abertzale* left, let alone understand why ETA continued its guerrilla war. The turbulent months between July 1976 and June 1977 hardly permitted him to dedicate sufficient time to comprehending or resolving the Basque question. In any case, influenced by the Francoist reflexes of his confidant, the Minister of Agriculture, Fernando Abril Martorell, Suárez regarded the Basque problem as one of public order. He never appreciated its roots in the excesses and atrocities of Francoism. Accordingly, he left the 'technical' question of dealing with terrorism to his extremely competent Minister of the Interior, Rodolfo Martín Villa. It was unfortunate that he did so. Martín Villa's unequivocally Falangist background tended to arouse the suspicion of the left in general. The fact that he had been civil governor of Barcelona in September 1975 when 'Txiki' Paredes was executed there ensured that he provoked intense hostility in Euskadi.[34]

In fact, when Suárez came to power, he inherited a virtually impossible Basque situation, certainly one that could not be solved by police action or by the use of ultra-rightist terror squads. What was required was a dramatic conciliatory gesture which could have isolated ETA from its mass support. However, total amnesty and the legalization of the Basque flag, the *Ikurriña*, were beyond what the bunker would tolerate, and, for that matter, beyond what Suárez himself could yet countenance. With civil guards and policemen dying regularly in clashes with ETA, such short-sightedness was understandable. On the other hand, amnesty demonstrations, with 60,000 participants in San Sebastián on 3 July and with 100,000 in Bilbao on 8 July, revealed the scale of popular commitment. It was obvious that without a major token of conciliation, support for ETA and the *abertzales* could only grow. The first partial amnesty conceded on 30 July 1976 was insufficient to calm the Basque situation. Not encompassing crimes of blood, it left 145 *Etarras* still in custody. Thus, the amnesty campaign continued throughout 1976 and, as demonstrators were killed in clashes with the police, the bitterness of the confrontation was heightened. Industrial strikes followed in rapid succession.

Eventually, ETA broke the self-imposed ceasefire which it had observed during the summer and, on 4 October 1976, murdered the president of the Guipúzcoa Diputación Provincial (provincial council), Juan María Araluce Villar, along with his four escorts. With the bunker screaming for the declaration of a state of exception, Suárez was in an intolerable position. Progress towards amnesty seemed impossible without provoking the right. Accordingly, efforts were made to contact ETA. Highly secret preliminary talks with ETA-PM were held in Geneva in November. At first, ETA-Militar ignored an invitation to attend but, a few days later, sent an observer to a second meeting. The ETA-PM representatives demanded the gradual release of all prisoners before the elections, limits on the activities of the forces of order and legalization, or at least toleration, of all the *abertzale* parties. In return, they offered a suspension of armed struggle. Note was taken by the government agents but, for the moment, little more. It was the beginning of an extremely risky gamble, the outcome and consequences of which were not to be apparent until the summer of 1977.[35]

By comparison with ETA, Suárez's other outstanding problem on the left, the legalization of the Communist Party, was relatively uncomplicated. The popular endorsement of his programme in the December referendum and the PSOE's decision to take part in elections even without the legalization of the PCE gave Suárez most of the cards in the coming contest with Carrillo. Nevertheless, aware that the rest of the opposition was unlikely to risk its own gains in order to help the Communists, Carrillo played his own hand with skill and daring. Already in contact with Suárez through intermediaries, Carrillo's clandestine presence in Madrid was an open secret among the political élite. He now decided to force the pace by coming out into the open. On 10 December, he called a press conference with over seventy Spanish and foreign journalists. It was a provocation which deeply embarrassed the Ministry of the Interior.[36] However, Carrillo's words to the assembled reporters were conciliatory. He insinuated that, provided the PCE was allowed to take part in the elections, the Communists would co-operate in the elaboration of a social contract to deal with the economic crisis.

In the light of Communist influence in the Comisiones Obreras, and given that working-class unrest was one of the main reasons why Francoists had ever contemplated reform in the first place, this was a significant offer. Indeed, it foreshadowed the extent to which Carrillo would be a useful parliamentary ally to Suárez in years to come. At the time, the government was furious and ordered Carrillo's detention, although it took the police until 22 December to find him. The PCE executive committee used the time before his inevitable arrest to prepare a massive campaign in favour of his release. Detained for eight days, Carrillo posed a dilemma for the government and no matter what they did he stood to gain. Suárez wanted to avoid the issue by deporting him to France until Martín Villa pointed out that to do so would merely postpone the problem since Carrillo would certainly be back within a few weeks. Not to have released him, or to have staged a trial, would have damaged the Prime Minister's reforming credibility. By freeing Carrillo, as he realized that he had to, Suárez was taking a substantial step towards legalizing the PCE.[37]

However, the slightest hint that Communism might acquire legal status in Spain once more was guaranteed to intensify the problem of the bunker. Within the army, Gutiérrez Mellado was committed to a policy of promoting liberal officers. This had to be balanced by exaggerated rhetorical acquiescence in the traditional values of the armed forces as the guardian of national integrity and by the promotion of some ultras in the empty hope of thereby neutralizing them. The removal of a few committed Francoists infuriated the ultras, particularly as continued terrorist activity was keeping military nerves on edge. In fact, as soon as Suárez had made his first announcement of his commitment to change, there had begun a highly orchestrated effort to destabilize Spain along the lines practised by the extreme right in South America and Italy. The allegedly Marxist-Leninist splinter group, GRAPO, suspected by Gutiérrez Mellado of being infiltrated or manipulated by the right and elements of the police, began first a bombing campaign. Then, with two further actions, intended apparently 'to lift up the hearts of the people' and expose the falsity of the political reform, GRAPO terrorists managed to galvanize the ultra-right. Significantly, just before the referendum, they kidnapped Antonio María de Oriol y Urquijo, president of the Consejo del Estado, on 11 December 1976. The massive referendum vote in favour of change on 15 December suggested that the operation had not had the desired effect. Accordingly, on 24 January 1977, they seized General Emilio Villaescusa Quilis, president of the Consejo Superior de Justicia Militar.[38] The bunker was able to assert that Suárez's government was throwing away the achievements of the Civil War. A concerted campaign was launched against the reform process in general and against General Gutiérrez Mellado in particular.

As part of the rightist strategy of tension, on the same day as the kidnapping of Villaescusa, ultra terrorists murdered five people, four of whom were Communist labour lawyers, in an office in the Atocha district of Madrid. The PCE refused to be provoked and instead issued appeals for serenity. At the funeral of the victims, the Party organized a gigantic display of silent solidarity. Not only was Suárez personally impressed by the demonstration of Communist strength and discipline, but much popular hostility to the legalization of the PCE was dissolved by the restraint of its response to the tragedy. A delegation of opposition leaders negotiated with Suárez and, in return for promises of action against the bunker's violence, they offered him a joint government-opposition declaration denouncing terrorism and calling for national support for the government. It was a significant advance for Suárez. His popular backing was substantially reinforced and he was publicly endorsed by the left as belonging to the democratic forces in Spain.[39]

Thus, the poisonous situation in the Basque Country aside, Suárez was advancing along the path towards controlled democracy in the rest of Spain, dealing adequately with both the bunker and the Communists. None the less, the ultimate objective was not merely to proceed to elections which the better-organized left-wing parties might win. The entire point of the operation was to guarantee the political and economic survival of that broad spectrum of the Francoist establishment which, unlike the bunker, had thrown in its lot with the monarchy. In that respect, the Suárez option was the last card of *aperturismo*. Accordingly, the vision of Suárez and his closest collaborators went far beyond the projected elections. Regular public opinion polls carried out by the government convinced them that a centre-right party, not too tainted by Francoism, and backed by Suárez's control both of the apparatus of the Movimiento and of the media, would have a healthy electoral future. In fact, throughout the autumn of 1976, the various progressive ex-Francoists who had swelled the ranks of the moderate opposition in increasing numbers over the previous decade joined with more recent converts to democracy in frantic preparation for political life under a democratic regime.[40]

One of the first off the mark was Manuel Fraga. He was sure that forty years of dictatorship had left the majority of Spaniards as convinced rightists. Accordingly, he linked up with six other ex-Francoist dignitaries, Laureano López Rodó, Licinio de la Fuente, Federico Silva Muñoz, Cruz Martínez Esteruelas, Enrique Thomas de Carranza and Gonzalo Fernández de la Mora. Known collectively as the '*siete magníficos*' (the magnificent seven), they hoped to capture this imagined majority of what was called 'sociological Francoism'. Although Fraga underestimated the popular urge for change, he was successful in attracting large sectors of Suárez's political association, the Unión del Pueblo Español. It was to become eventually the focus of the ambitions of many optimistic Francoist veterans including Gregorio López Bravo and Carlos Arias Navarro. With substantial backing from the banks, Fraga's party Alianza Popular was created with breathtaking speed in the second half of September 1976, although its electoral impact lay in the distant future.[41] To some extent, the forging of Alianza Popular, together with the evidence of the opinion polls, confirmed Suárez's growing conviction that the most appropriate territory for his own political future was the centre. There existed centre–right parties and grupuscules by the score. The process whereby they coalesced to become the Unión de Centro Democrático under the leadership of Adolfo Suárez was kaleidoscopic, confusing and highly unedifying.

One of the extraordinary features of the political manoeuvring of the autumn and winter of 1976 had been the elimination of the more liberal and anti-Francoist Catholics led by Joaquín Ruiz Giménez and José María Gil Robles. This was especially ironic since Ruiz Giménez had been the first politician to perceive the possibilities of a great union of the centre. United in the so-called Equipo de la Democracia Cristiana, Ruiz Giménez's Izquierda Democrática and Gil Robles's Federación Popular Democrática were widely expected to have a significant presence in the coming democratic regime. In fact, they were to be excluded from the great political operation of the centre and were thus condemned to electoral annihilation. They had already been abandoned by the more conservative Fernando Alvarez de Miranda who was uneasy about their contacts with the left. His breakaway group from Ruiz Giménez, the Izquierda Demócrata Cristiana, was already involved in the process that would first unite it with some of the *Tácitos* in a conservative Christian Democrat party, the Partido Popular Demócrata Cristiano, and then take it into UCD.

The isolation of the Equipo de la Democracia Cristiana was also partly the consequence of Gil Robles's scarcely concealed distaste for the Francoist background of many of the more conservative Christian Democrats. Franco had loathed Gil Robles despite his services to the 1936 uprising because, it was said, he resented the ex-Jefe of the pre-war CEDA having once, as Minister of War, exercised authority over him. Ostentatiously spurned by the Caudillo in 1937 as insufficiently authoritarian, Gil Robles had an especially long history of anti-Francoist monarchism. He was consistently uncooperative in negotiations during 1976, regarding his interlocutors as barely redeemable political juvenile delinquents. Gil Robles refused to join in the great 'operation of the centre' and Ruiz Giménez, ever loyal and honest, kept faith with him despite being aware that, electorally isolated, disaster would await them. In addition to his distaste for the ex-Francoists, Gil Robles had been mistakenly confident that he had the backing of the Church. His error was exposed in the spring of 1977 by a series of articles published in *El País* by José María Martín Patino, the close confidant of Cardinal Vicente Enrique y Tarancón. In fact, in reaction to the damage that the Church had suffered from too close an identification with Francoism, Cardinal Enrique y Tarancón, was determined to maintain its political independence. By refusing to support confessional parties but expressing sympathy for 'parties of Christian inspiration', Tarancón was effectively dropping Ruiz Giménez and Gil Robles in favour of the formations which were to become UCD. In so doing, the Church was probably backing the safer options in terms of the future defence of its own interests.[42]

The demise of the Christian Democrat left, rather as the creation of Alianza Popular had done at the other end of the spectrum, helped demarcate the political centre which was to be occupied by the UCD. The Unión de Centro Democrático was the result, in the broadest terms, of an electoral alliance of five main groups, each in its turn composed of several others. The most numerous segment of the future party was constituted by a broad spectrum of conservative Christian Democrats, many of whom had attained senior positions in the Francoist civil service, while others had maintained their distance from the dictatorship. In the autumn of 1976, an important group of the former, Alfonso Osorio's political association, the Unión Democrática Española, together with some *Tácitos*, combined with a group of the latter, Fernando Alvarez de Miranda's Izquierda Demócrata Cristiana. The resulting party was called the Partido Popular Demócrata Cristiano. A similar group composed of other *Tácito* functionaries and a variety of Christian Democrats was launched on 1 December 1977. Known as the Partido Popular, its early sponsors, who included the Valencian lawyer, Emilio Attard, and the liberal Catholic, José Antonio Ortega y Díaz-Ambrona, were rather overshadowed when the need for well-known figureheads led to the late inclusion of Pío Cabanillas and José María de Areilza. These two barely distinguishable parties, united as Centro Democrático in mid-January 1977, became the basis of UCD.[43] At this stage, neither could count on much popular support. Indeed, it was suggested that the prominence of the hitherto obscure Emilio Attard was due to the fact that he had appeared at one of the foundational meetings with a bus-load of his supporters from Valencia. In a party with more chiefs than indians, a coach full of rank-and-file militants counted for much.[44]

Complex negotiations added two further, but small, groups to Centro Democrático in early 1977 – the various social democrats led by Francisco Fernández Ordóñez and the several liberal parties under Joaquín Garrigues. Garrigues was quoted as remarking that his rank and file fitted comfortably into one taxi. Neither social democrats nor liberals were entirely natural partners for the Christian Democrats and both were eventually to be crucial to the fragmentation of UCD. However, with elections on the horizon, the central requirement shared by all these groups was the speedy creation of an electorally viable party. Accordingly, the ruthless quest for profitable alliances, which had so repelled Joaquín Ruiz Giménez, rode rough-shod over ideological, personal or moral considerations. The most revealing light on this aspect of the process was shed during February and March 1977. Suárez was impressed by the success of the nascent coalition and, with his own Unión de Pueblo Español drifting into the orbit of Manuel Fraga, was anxious to take it over as his own electoral vehicle. Given the government's control of Radio-Televisión Española and of local administrative machinery, he was confident of being an acceptable leader.

However, he was worried by, and not a little envious of, the considerable success being enjoyed by Areilza in his public appearances. There would not be room for two leaders in the new grouping. Suárez felt, as the King had before him in 1976, that Areilza would try to dominate him. Accordingly, he requested Alfonso Osorio to clear the way. At a dinner held on 19 March at the home of an ex-*Tácito*, José María Ruiz Navarro, to which all the major centre leaders except Areilza were invited, Osorio made it clear that the government's electoral weight would be thrown behind the centre only if the undisputed leadership of Suárez were accepted and a solution found to 'the problem of José María de Areilza'. A few sibylline words of regret aside, Pío Cabanillas and the rest of the Centro Democrático leaders had few qualms about opting for the certainty of power under Suárez. Aware of the weakness of Centro Democrático, with its exiguous organizational and publicity apparatus, they barely hesitated in dumping Areilza. Any doubts that they might have felt were soothed by the dignified manner in which the Count bowed to the inevitable and resigned on 24 March.[45]

Similarly, practical rather than ethical considerations dictated the inclusion into UCD of its fifth and crucial component group, the Movimiento bureaucrats, rather like Suárez himself, who were coalescing around Rodolfo Martín Villa. Various provincial governors, town mayors and top syndical officials had been encouraged to resign and dedicate themselves to the new grouping in return for promises that there would be places for them in the future regime. They were known as the *Azules*, because of the blue shirts of the Falange which they had once worn. Many of them found it difficult to shake off the rhetorical habits of Franco's single party. Emilio Attard claimed to be astonished, at a meeting of UCD parliamentary candidates, when one, on being approached by Suárez, threw back his shoulders, clicked his heels and, in a revealing display of jocular camaraderie, barked the old Falangist greeting *a tus órdenes, jefe'* ('I await your orders, chief'). The *Azules* had been sufficiently carried away by the empty pseudo-leftist social rhetoric of the Movimiento to make an abortive attempt in 1976 to build a pseudo-socialist party, the Federación Social Independiente. In contrast, another legacy of the Movimiento, their skill in handling the levers of local power, was their highest card when it came to negotiating their incorporation into Centro Democrático. That was the key to their future rather than their short-lived attempts to create a party with the veterans and exiles from the PSOE-Histórico, with the miniscule Reforma Social Española of the dissident Falangist Manuel Cantarero del Castillo and with Antonio García López's PSDE, the heir to Ridruejo's USDE.[46]

The final negotiations which brought all these, and many lesser, component groups together consisted of tough and sordid horse-trading. The formal agreement for the electoral coalition to be known as the Unión de Centro Democrático was signed on 3 May 1977 and, since the candidate lists had to be submitted by 9 May, frantic deals were made in the following five days. Ultimately, however, Suárez's control of the state electoral machinery gave him enormous power. Having eliminated Areilza, he now made it clear that he had prior commitments to a large number of *Azules*. Many of these commitments were, of course, debts incurred by Suárez in the autumn of 1976 in the process of securing sufficient votes to ensure that the Francoist Cortes would approve his project of political reform. In consequence, and also because of the origins of many other centrists, the final lists were dominated by men who, under Franco, had been *procuradores* in the Cortes, mayors, civil governors, directors of state industries or of the state television network RTVE, syndical officials, leaders of the Movimiento's student organization SEU (Sindicato Español Universitario), top ministerial functionaries and so on. Many Christian Democrat opponents of Francoism were simply pushed to one side. After the 1977 elections, about twenty-five successful UCD deputies were to be men who had also served in Franco's Cortes. When the legislature of 1979 is added, a total of about fifty UCD deputies emerge as ex-Francoist *procuradores*. Moreover, about one third of UCD parliamentary deputies were members of Opus Dei.[47]

Aware of the weakness of the Centre without Suárez's muscle, Members of Centro Democrático who at least had some tepid anti-Francoist history had to accept the arrival of what they christened *'la nueva división azul'* ('the new Blue Division', a reference to the legion of

Falangist volunteers who fought for Hitler in Russia).[48] Over the years, they would grow more embittered as they realized that real power in the party would lie with Suárez and his cronies and, to a lesser extent, with the 'barons' of the component groups. Collectively, Suárez's inner circle came to be known as '*la empresa*' ('the firm'). The essential nature of the new centre conglomeration was perceived by Areilza when he informed his colleagues of the Partido Popular that he was prepared to withdraw: 'Suárez has demanded my head. You must get a good price for it. In exchange, there could be ministries, under-secretaryships and other senior posts. On the bus that goes from the Moncloa [the presidential palace] to the Carrera de San Jerónimo [the site of the Cortes], there should be seats for everyone.'[49] The bus metaphor was inadvertently prophetic. Until the party's disappearance in 1982, the members of UCD, like those of the Radical Party during the Second Republic, were to resemble the passengers on a bus, united not by ideology or ideals but by the coincidence of the journey.

As an electoral coalition, UCD was united around Suárez because of his access to state funds and his control of government patronage and the radio and television networks. Once those assets had contributed to electoral victory, he was to be able to dissolve the component elements of the coalition into a party united around himself as the fount of patronage. Without a coherent ideology, UCD would inevitably suffer from its clientelist nature. In 1977, however, it was the natural home of those lesser Francoists who had foreseen in time the obsolescence of the dictatorship. It was also the fruit of the dissatisfaction with Francoism manifested by the more enlightened members of the economic establishment since the late 1960s. Thus, UCD was composed of junior Francoists uncompromised by the worst crimes of the regime. Many had held the post of ministerial under-secretary or director-general under Franco and most had worked for the government in some way, especially in state-run enterprises. Except for the *Azules*, they could not be defined as committed Francoists, although pro-Franco declarations littered their early careers. Rather they were ambitious men launched by the competitive state examination system of *oposiciones* into the world of public administration and committed to little except their own careers. The bulk of them had close relations with business, industry and especially the banks. In this regard, the Catalan Socialist, Ernest Lluch, made the *bon mot* that the UCD front bench (or *banco azul*), always upholstered in blue leather in the Spanish Cortes, was the '*bancoazul*' that is to say the blue, or Falangist, bank. In other words, UCD was the ideal instrument to ensure that in the transition from a dictatorial to a democratic regime, real government power would remain in the hands, if not of the same people as before, at least of sufficiently conservative individuals to guarantee the existing structure of economic and social power.[50]

While UCD was still in the process of being forged, Suárez had still to steer his reform project to its culmination. The process of legalizing political parties had begun in February 1977. The stumbling block was the PCE. For the bunker and the army, to legalize the Communists meant throwing away everything that they had fought for in 1936. General Gutiérrez Mellado's plans to liberalize the army had already led to unrestrained verbal attacks on him. On 24 January 1977, the same day as the Atocha massacre, a large number of senior officers met at the Casino Militar in Madrid and called for the resignation of the government. Then the first of an escalating series of incidents took place at the funeral of two policemen killed by GRAPO. Ultra slogans were chanted and Gutiérrez Mellado was publicly insulted by the naval captain, Camilo Menéndez Vives, who went virtually unpunished and was to become something of a fixture of rightist subversion.[51]. It was obvious that the rage of the ultras would be pushed on to an altogether higher plane when Suárez legalized the PCE. He had little choice. Democracy would simply be incomplete if it excluded a party of the significance of the PCE. In any case, Suárez was confident that, by delaying the PCE's entry into the game, he would diminish Communist electoral support. Accordingly, by 27 February, the President was prepared to meet Carrillo, although his decision to do so was the death blow to his already deteriorating relations with Torcuato Fernández Miranda.[52]

After a marathon eight-hour meeting at the home of José Mario Armero, Carrillo and Suárez reached a basic agreement. In return for legal status, Carrillo undertook to recognize the monarchy, adopt the red-yellow-red monarchist flag of Spain and offer his support for a future social contract. There was a strange mutual infatuation between Suárez and Carrillo which was to be the basis of future political co-operation throughout the entire transition period. In the meanwhile, however, the PCE sharply reminded the government of its capacity to cause an international scandal if it were excluded from the elections. It did so on 2 March by playing host at the Hotel Melià-Castilla in Madrid to a Eurocommunist summit meeting of Carrillo, Berlinguer and Marchais. On 9 April, with most of the Madrid political and military élite out of town for the Easter weekend, Suárez, mistakenly confident of army acquiescence, announced the legalization of the PCE. Its statutes had been especially altered to maintain the spirit of his autumn promise to the military hierarchy.[53]

The sophistry did not save Suárez from the unrelenting hatred of the bunker, although he was never to understand why. In 1984, he was still affirming that he had not deceived the military. The attempted coup of 23 February 1981 was eventually to be the most graphic consequence of the army's conviction that he had. Fury in the bunker was compounded by the fact that, while jubilant Communists celebrated their legalization, the gigantic red Yoke-and-Arrows symbol was being removed by workmen from the façade of the Movimiento headquarters at Calle Alcalá 44.[54] By legalizing the Communists, Suárez became guilty in the eyes of the ultras of a vile betrayal of the cause for which the Civil War had been fought. The immediate result was the indignant resignation of the Minister of the Navy, Admiral Pita da Veiga. A number of civilian ministers, headed by the Finance Minister Eduardo Carriles, were also ready to resign, but were dissuaded by Alfonso Osorio.[55] The Army Minister, General Félix Alvarez Arenas, drew back from resignation only because his senior colleagues made it clear that no one would replace him. Allegedly egged on by Fraga and the other '*magníficos*', no senior officer would agree to replace Pita. Only after much embarrassment was Suárez able to persuade the retired Admiral Pascual Pery Junquera to take over as Minister for the Navy.

Suárez met the high command on 11 April to justify to them what he had done. He even played them a tape-recording of the proceedings of their meeting on 8 September 1976. It was to little avail. The depth of feeling within the army was made public after a meeting on 12 April of the Consejo Superior del Ejército chaired by General José Vega Rodríguez. Its communiqué referred to the general revulsion that the measure had caused, although it also accepted the *fait accompli* in disciplined form. A more extensive statement, strongly critical of both Suárez and Gutiérrez Mellado, was sent privately to the King. It was claimed several years later by Suárez that he had orchestrated the issue of the communiqué in order to take the edge off military discontent. General Ibáñez Freire, the Director of the Civil Guard, allegedly in collusion with the President, drew up a note which was specifically designed to defuse some of the tension. As a further safety precaution, efforts had been made to keep key military units short of petrol in the preceding weeks.[56]

Even so, the legalization of the PCE, inevitable and necessary part of the transition as it was, nevertheless constituted a gift for the ultras.

Propaganda was stepped up in military barracks to drive home the extent of Suárez's 'treachery'. A series of straw organizations, the Juntas Patrióticas, the Unión Patriótica Militar and the Movimiento Patriótico Militar, were invented to cover the flooding of military housing estates with cyclostyled propaganda. It consisted of virulent diatribes against both the military reforms of General Gutiérrez Mellado, insultingly referred to as Señor Gutiérrez, and a government which permitted the deterioration of patriotic values, outrages against the flag and ETA terrorism. This blanket propaganda gave the impression that sectors of the army had reached the conclusion that an intervention in politics was essential.[57] Its impact was consolidated almost daily by incitements to military subversion by the bunker press, *El Alcázar*, *El Imparcial* and *Fuerza Nueva*.

Inevitably, in the eyes of its devotees at least, stridently centralist ultra-rightism derived immense plausibility from the apparent separatism inherent in Basque aspirations. Fortunately for Suárez, the fact that his government had started to negotiate with ETA in November 1976 was not known to the bunker. Those earlier talks were taken up again in February 1977 through the mediation of the journalist, José María Portell. A sporadic truce worked out in French Euskadi was rewarded by a trickle of released prisioners and a further partial amnesty on 14 March 1977 which left twenty-seven *Etarras* behind bars. At that point, the various *abertzale* parties declared that they would boycott the June elections unless all prisoners were released. With barricades going up in many Basque towns and clashes between *abertzales* and the forces of order a daily occurrence, the two wings of ETA renewed their terrorist activities. Alarmed at the prospect of the imminent elections being disrupted, the government then negotiated a ceasefire with both ETA fractions and conceded total amnesty on 20 May. The slowness of Suárez to grasp the gravity of the Basque problem had thus led him to give both ETA and the bunker the clear impression that amnesty had been a capitulation in the face of armed violence.[58]

Since October 1975, the *abertzale* groups had been united into a loose popular front known as KAS or the Koordinadora Abertzale Sozialista. Its programme, known as the Alternativa KAS, called for total amnesty, the removal of the army from Euskadi, the dissolution of the government-controlled forces of order and self-determination for Euskadi, as well as a number of other demands which could equally never be accepted by any Madrid government. Both before and after the negotiated ceasefire of 20 May, there had been heated debate within the KAS liaison committee over the question of electoral participation. Broadly speaking, ETA-Político-Militar, and the political party associated with it, EIA or Euskal Iraultzako Alderdia (the Party of the Basque Revolution), favoured taking part in order to give a parliamentary voice to popular left nationalism. ETA-Militar, and its own political front, LAIA or Langile Abertzale Iraultzaileen Alderdia (the Patriotic Workers' Revolutionary Party), came out against participation after some agonized contortions.

The split among the *abertzales* was consolidated shortly after when EIA undertook electoral negotiations with the Trotskyist Movimiento Comunista, itself the product of an earlier 'political' schism from ETA in 1966. The resulting coalition, Euskadiko Eskerra or the Basque Left, was to suffer electorally from the confusion generated during the *abertzale* debate over abstention although it did gain both a Cortes deputy and a senator in the June elections. Those members of EIA who did not approve of the new line, together with a militant section of LAIA and some other extreme nationalists, decided to form a new party after the elections. It was called Herriko Alderdi Sozialista Iraultzailea or HASI (The People's Revolutionary Socialist Party) and was founded on 3 July 1977. Unlike Euskadiko Eskerra, HASI, LAIA and the other *abertzale* groups would remain bitterly hostile to the new democratic polity. The deficiencies of Suárez's Basque policy had ensured that the same armed violence and popular militancy which had sustained the amnesty campaign would later be put at the service of the Alternativa KAS.[59] This was to be the greatest blot on Suárez's record during the transition.

Nevertheless, it would be churlish not to recognize the astonishing advances achieved by Suárez. In addition to gaining Francoist acceptance of his political reform and gaining control of a major electoral coalition, he had reached agreement with the moderate opposition, legalized the PCE, and secured ETA's agreement not to disrupt the elections. Still, the louring presence of the army ensured that the joint commission of the opposition and the government had elaborated an electoral law in a spirit of some trepidation. However, the campaign was carried out in an atmosphere of popular fiesta which recalled for many the coming of the Second Republic in 1931. The best-attended meetings were those of the PSOE, followed by those of the PCE. UCD's campaign tended to concentrate on television, press and radio where its resources were virtually unlimited.[60] Eighteen million people voted, nearly 80 per cent of the total electorate, and 90 per cent of them voted clearly for change.

In fact, Spaniards wanted change but not confrontation and this favoured Suárez and Felipe González. In contrast, Carrillo and Fraga awakened memories of the conflicts of the past. Despite plentiful financing, Alianza Popular's line-up of prominent Francoists did not help its cause, all the more so after an astonishing interview given by Arias Navarro to the journalist Pedro J. Ramírez. Arias claimed to make regular visits to the Valle de los Caídos in order to commune with Franco and to request the Caudillo's immediate miraculous return to sort things out. His meetings during the campaign were openly reactionary and nostalgic, provoking chants of 'Franco, Franco, Franco'. By giving one of Alianza Popular's three television spots to Arias, who struck an unrepentantly Francoist note, Fraga almost certainly lost many votes. Curiously, the AP figure with the most modern and liberal image, Gregorio López Bravo, played virtually no part in the campaign. Fraga, on the other hand, was his usual whirlwind of energy and patriotism. Constant use of the slogan 'Spain, the only thing that matters' provided the patriotic tone. He also ostentatiously sported a pair of MCC braces, purchased while Ambassador in London, whose red and yellow colours passed for those of the Spanish flag. The effect of dynamism was spoiled, however, by the occasions on which his notorious temper got the better of him. In Lugo (Galicia), on 6 May, he responded to hecklers chanting references to the killings in Vitoria by tearing off his jacket and jumping down into the audience in order to pursue them.[61]

The Communists were especially disadvantaged by memories of the Civil War. This was perhaps inevitable since the post-Franco liberalization had unleashed a publishing boom in popular history and thereby revived awareness of the PCE's past Stalinist crimes. The Communists themselves did not help matters by giving prominence in their lists to wartime figures like Carrillo or Dolores Ibárruri. The Socialists, on the other hand, derived benefit from their Civil War record and from a hidden continuity of PSOE tradition in many families. Equally, the image of honesty and competence generated by Felipe González and the prestige conferred by the support of European Socialist leaders made him a serious rival to Suárez. However, one error made by both the Socialists and Communists was to believe, on the basis of opinion poll predictions, that Fraga's Alianza Popular would constitute a more serious danger than it eventually did. Thus, they tended to concentrate too much of their electoral fire in his direction.[62]

In consequence, neither the PSOE nor the PCE made direct attacks on the UCD during the campaign. The most telling assault on UCD actually came from José María de Areilza campaigning on behalf of a group of liberal, Socialist and Christian Democrat candidates for the Senate, known as the Senadores para la Democracia. On 28 May, in the Rayo Vallecano football stadium on the outskirts of Madrid, Areilza declared that UCD and Alianza Popular were 'two wings of Francoism who are in agreement beneath the surface of their apparent battles and who will do everything possible to ensure that the next Cortes will be neither constituent nor sovereign'. Suárez himself avoided confrontation by the simple device of refusing to take part in any debate with other party leaders, usually on the most specious grounds. His advantages were overwhelming. In addition to UCD's exploitation of government control of the media, massive funding from the banks permitted a huge advertising campaign. Hoardings which had been set aside for government appeals to vote aimed at the population at large carried UCD posters. Every housewife in the country was sent a letter from Suárez outlining his plans to improve living standards. Indeed, the UCD propaganda machine worked especially hard to appeal to women. The press built on Suárez's film-star looks to create an image of the devoted family man and practising Catholic. Sixty per cent of UCD voters were to be women. As might have been expected, in the light of its privileged position, UCD won the elections, with 34.3 per cent of the vote; but the Socialists were not far behind with 28.5 per cent. Alianza Popular polled only 8.4 per cent behind the PCE with 9.3 per cent.[63]

The Franco regime had been laid to rest on 15 June 1977. The end had been nigh for many years, but the method had been lacking. The growing decrepitude of the Caudillo's system had been obvious for years. From the late 1960s, an increasing number of one-time Francoists had come to see this. A two-way process began. On the one hand, various efforts were made to adapt Francoism without fundamentally changing it. One after another, Solís, Carrero and Arias tried, and, one after another, they were shipwrecked on the intransigence of the bunker and on their own irretrievably Francoist instincts. On the other hand, these successive failures of reform convinced larger and larger sections of the economic oligarchy, liberal monarchists and, eventually, the more far-sighted Francoists, that their survival depended on change. Thus, the ideals of the opposition, nurtured since 1939, came to be shared by its erstwhile enemies, albeit in a restricted and often little more than rhetorical form. What had hitherto been missing was both the will and the formula whereby the transition from dictatorship would be carried out without violence or substantial loss of privileges. The polarization provoked by bunker extremism, the inefficacy of Arias Navarro and, above all, the death of Franco, provided intelligent Francoists with the necessary political will. Torcuato Fernández Miranda and Suárez provided the formula.

In the summer of 1976, however, bloody confrontation had still seemed possible. That it did not come about was a tribute to the skill of Adolfo Suárez and his advisers, to the courage and determination of King Juan Carlos but, especially, to the reason and moderation displayed by Felipe González, Santiago Carrillo and the other leaders of the opposition. It is extremely difficult to exaggerate the sacrifices made by the opposition. The terrorist outrages of early 1977 inclined the left to moderate its aspirations. Hopes of significant social change were shelved in order that the urgent immediate goal of political democracy might be secured. The exuberance, joy and sheer spectacle of the election campaign rather obscured this as well as creating expectations which were to be badly dented over the following four years. Formal political democracy was a towering achievement after thirty-eight years of Francoism but, in many respects, it was only a timid beginning. The left had abandoned any thoughts of a settling of accounts with the jailers, torturers and thieves who had enjoyed the fruits of victory since 1939. The fate of the Portuguese PIDE at the hands of an enraged populace was not repeated in Spain. Less dramatically, large numbers of Francoist cadres remained in positions of power by means of a simple transfer from the Movimiento to UCD. For them, the transition constituted less a fundamental change than a political re-adaptation of certain élite forces.[64]

Having kept alive the ideals and ideas of democracy for nearly forty years, the opposition was fully aware of this. Perhaps its greatest sacrifice was to accept the legality of the Francoist constitutional system which was the basic premise of Suárez's project of political reform. When it had been a question of prisoners being tortured or striking workers being shot, the Francoist establishment had never balked at violations of the human rights supposedly enshrined in the Fundamental Laws. The legal delicacy that had to be observed during the autumn and winter of 1976 was the object of private scorn on the left. On the other hand, negotiations with Suárez had dwelled on the power of the armed forces and the continuing strength and malevolence of the bunker. Hopes of a thoroughgoing change of the social fabric, agrarian reform, redistribution of wealth, the most minimal aims of the left, were thus quietly dropped in order to guarantee the crucial political reform. The leadership of the opposition and its politically aware cadres knew this but the broad popular masses did not. Accordingly, while the Suárez reform was ample for the conservative middle classes, the great popular hunger for change went unsatisfied. In a context of rising inflation and increasing unemployment, there was little chance of popular expectations being fulfilled by a government whose *raison d'être* lay in the belief, generated in the wake of the energy crisis, that political reforms could avoid the need for social change. Under Suárez, popular enthusiasm was to turn to popular disenchantment. To recognize this should not diminish the scale of his achievement in leading Spain during the transition process. Nevertheless, awareness of the role played by the opposition not only explains the bloodless nature of the political changes of 1976–7. It also clarifies the difficulties that Suárez was to face in power.

5
Building a new world with the bricks of the old: the democratic pact 1977–9

The popular mood after the elections of 15 June 1977 was one of justifiable optimism, although there were ominous clouds of unfinished business on the horizon. Only a minority of ordinary Spaniards, and indeed perhaps only the more cautious professional politicians, understood the scale of the problems which lay ahead. To bring both the army and the Basque extremists into the democratic fold and at the same time to confront the economic problems left by the dictatorship were tasks fraught with danger. The prevailing euphoria of mid-1977 was based on the fact that the transition had been carried through by a broad consensus of right and left and then ratified by a remarkably mature electorate. The pre-electoral confusion of over 300 political parties had been reduced on 15 June to a four-party system and the voters had opted overwhelmingly for moderation. In opinion polls, four out of every five Spaniards described themselves as belonging to the area between right and left of centre.[1] After decades of being told by Franco and his minions that they were incapable of ruling themselves democratically, the majority of Spaniards were justifiably proud of the way things were turning out.

Nevertheless, the problems which were to undermine their new democracy over the next four years – military subversion, terrorism and economic stagnation – could not be resolved merely by the existence of a moderate electorate. Indeed, the near total absorption of the political class in such problems would eventually provoke a certain disillusionment in the mass of voters who had expected that 15 June 1977 had heralded the birth of a new Spain. This should not, however, obscure the many positive features of life in democratic Spain. To an observer familiar with the Spain of General Franco, cultural and educational resurgence, a high level of parliamentary co-existence and, above all, popular enthusiasm for the new regime were palpable signs that democracy was tapping energies long suppressed. A short-lived pornography boom at cinemas and newspaper kiosks was the symptom of change which most infuriated the bunker. However, the transitoriness of the boom did not prevent bunker propaganda doggedly continuing to identify democracy with pornography.

It was in the nature of things that the UCD would be reluctant to carry the banner of structural reform. A fragmented coalition whose components represented elements of the financial and industrial élite and the more progressive segments of the Francoist bureaucracy was hardly fitted to undertake major fiscal and agrarian reform. Indeed, over the next three years, the upper ranks of UCD were to demonstrate a much deeper commitment to the scramble for highly paid official posts. The component groups of the UCD electoral coalition had planned to go their separate ways after the elections and agreed to unification not out of ideological affinity but only to guarantee their proximity to the fount of power. The agreement to unite was rewarded by ministerial and other posts and reflected in the composition of the new cabinet. Suárez's personal friends were well represented, most dramatically in the case of his new Vice-President for Political Affairs, the unknown Fernando Abril Martorell, an agronomist whom he had befriended in Segovia when Civil Governor there.

The *Azules* under Rodolfo Martín Villa also had their 'parcel of power' in and around the Ministry of the Interior. The social democrats were given several 'economic' ministries from which they hoped to carry out fiscal reform. The Christian Democrats kept, in the person of Landelino Lavilla, the Ministry of Justice. Their spiritual leader, Fernando Alvarez de Miranda, refused a ministry and became President of the Cortes. Alvarez de Miranda, who wanted to see UCD develop into a Christian Democrat party within the European CD Union, was always to be a thorn in the side of Suárez. He had been reluctant to see the dissolution of the component parties into UCD without a full debate to clarify its ideological position. His opposition to Suárez's amoral pragmatism and social democrat aspirations led to the President's remark to him, 'Fernando, you're too good. When you go to heaven, you'll end up with a restricted view seat and you won't see God' (*'Fernando, tu eres demasiado bueno. Cuando vayas al cielo te va a tocar columna y no vas a ver a Dios'*).[2] The Christian Democrats were to be a constant source of preoccupation for the President and would play a key role in his eventual downfall. In general, the need to placate all these various groups was always to be a major political handicap for Suárez when it came to composing a cabinet. The most conservative of the Christian Democrats, Alfonso Osorio, stayed out of the operation altogether. Instead, he linked up with José María de Areilza and Manuel Fraga's Alianza Popular to make the so-called Aravaca Pact. Out of these talks, the unequivocally rightist Coalición Democrática emerged.[3]

The struggle to keep the disparate UCD together; the handicap of not having an overall parliamentary majority; the problems of constructing a widely acceptable constitutional framework; the incessant need to resolve disputes over both the new Constitution and the rights of autonomous nationalities; and above all the daily erosion of energy and vision by the anti-democratic violence of right and left; all these things conspired to diminish Suárez's ability to deliver a brave new world. Prior deals both within UCD and with other parties were always required before major Cortes votes. Accordingly, natural inclination and the essence of the problems facing him accelerated the President's withdrawal into smoke-filled rooms. His secretive style of backstairs dealing and a generalized sense of helplessness in the face of ETA and the army were, by 1980, to convert the optimism of 1977 into disenchantment with Suárez and UCD. In the course of four years, a spiral of terrorism and military interventionism carried apprehension and fear into daily life.

Yet the creation of a democratic regime and the probability of wide concessions of regional autonomy had seemed to constitute adequate grounds for expecting that ETA violence might come to an end. That this was not to be the case was in large measure the consequence of Suárez's earlier slowness in conceding political amnesty. That failure, under-standable perhaps in the light of the President's need to take note of the wishes of the army, had compounded the Francoist legacy of bitterness in the Basque Country. The more extreme nationalist factions were quick to exploit that inheritance in order to further their own sectarian vision of a future Euskadi independent of both Spain and France. This was not an aspiration shared by all Basques and was one that could only be achieved at the cost of provoking an intervention by the Spanish army. That would in turn mean a return to authoritarianism in the rest of Spain and civil war in the Basque Country.

The fact that Suárez had eventually capitulated before the June elections, and granted a total amnesty on 20 May, apparently in response to terrorist actions, was seen as merely a vindication of armed action by some sections of the *abertzale* left. The only left Basque nationalist group to respond to Suárez's concession had been Euskadiko Eskerra. Led by ex-*Etarras* and associated with ETA-PM, Euskadiko Eskerra had been formed from the fusion of EIA with the Movimiento Comunista before the elections. It had been rewarded in the elections with a parliamentary deputy, Francisco Letamendía, and a senator, Juan María Bandrés Molet, both for the province of Guipúzcoa. The remainder of the groups loosely united in the Koordinadora Abertzale Sozialista remained unremittingly hostile to Madrid. Indeed, their activities were soon to suggest that, far from being prepared to come to terms with the new democratic regime, they were committed to a strategy which was likely to risk its destruction.[4]

The two wings of ETA reacted differently to the election results of 15 June 1977. ETA-PM's response was to conclude that Euskadiko Eskerra's success justified the strategy of combining legal and illegal methods. The belief that the changing political situation would require armed struggle to be relegated to an ever more secondary role had originated with 'Pertur' and his seminal report, the *Ponencia Otsagabía*. The adoption of his line was to lead eventually to Euskadiko Eskerra's fusion with the Euro-communist wing of the Basque Communist Party and incorporation into conventional parliamentary activity. In the short term, the abandonment of violence was to cause internal division, schisms and a nostalgic longing for armed action. The older heads of ETA-PM, ex-prisoners like Mario Onaindía, had moved away from violent activism and concentrated their energies in EIA and Euskadiko Eskerra. ETA-PM itself, as a clandestine military organization, remained in the hands of young men and women always prepared to return to terrorism. Accordingly, although it continued to respect the ceasefire negotiated in May, ETA-PM was still part of the violent *abertzale* opposition to the democratic regime.

Nevertheless, ETA-PM was considered by ETA-Militar to be a traitor to the cause of an independent Euskadi. This view was shared by an important dissident fragment within ETA-PM. Led by the cold-blooded fanatic Miguel Angel Apalátegui, 'Apala', who had opposed the line of 'Pertur' and was suspected of having murdered him, the opponents of negotiation with the government had formed the so-called *Comandos Bereziak*. In an effort to break the truce of 20 May 1977, they had been responsible for the kidnapping of the Basque industrialist Javier de Ibarra y Berge on the same day. After the elections, and throughout the summer of 1977, the *Comandos Bereziak* negotiated their merger with ETA-M. Both groups were united in accepting Apalátegui's sectarian view that the elections were a stunt 'to legitimize fascism'. ETA's existence only made sense as opposition against a dictatorship. Accordingly, the leadership of the *Milis* simply closed their eyes to the fact that democracy had been established in Spain.[5] Popular electoral abstention in the Basque Country of about 22 per cent was myopically assumed to be a gesture of *abertzale* support for ETA-Militar. The fact that published levels of abstention were not higher was taken as further evidence that the election results were a fraud.

In the xenophobic view of the newly augmented ETA-Militar, therefore, nothing had changed since the dictatorship. The centralist forces which had always oppressed Euskadi continued to do so and their police were as brutal as ever. The only difference, in the eyes of the left *abertzales*, was that Spanish tyranny was now masked by the trappings of a fraudulent democracy. This partisan vision was shared by appreciable numbers of Basques, especially young ones, and curiously by immigrants who converted to *abertzalismo* out of a desire to prove that they 'belonged' in the host community. It was carried by the *abertzale* newspapers, the weekly *Punto y Hora* and the daily *Egin* which had a circulation of 80,000.[6] More significantly, it was vindicated for many by the behaviour of the government and the Spanish right throughout the summer of 1977. Once again, the battleground was the amnesty issue. At this stage, the few ETA prisoners still remaining in Spanish gaols were convicted of crimes of blood committed since the death of Franco. Accordingly, demands for their amnesty could only provoke fury in Spanish right-wing circles.

On 10 July, five columns set out from different points of Euskadi on a 'Marcha de la Libertad' which was scheduled to end in Pamplona on 28 August. The initiative was backed by LAIA, HASI, EIA and most *abertzale* groups but not by the PNV or the Basque sections of the PSOE or the PCE. As the march gathered supporters along the route, generalized chants for amnesty were turned into attacks on the government for two reasons. First, on 29 July, the Minister of the Interior, Rodolfo Martín Villa, authorized the arrest of exiled *Etarras* who had been openly returning to Euskadi. Then this challenge to the *abertzales* was strengthened by the Spanish government's request for the extradition of 'Apala' who had been detained in France. The march of liberty became a march against the extradition on which the most common chants were *Apala askatu* (liberty for 'Apala') and *presoak etxera* (prisoners home). ETA-Militar threatened to take up arms again if the French acceded to Madrid's petition. Throughout August, there were demonstrations of up to 30,000 people at a time right across the Basque Country, as well as smaller ones in the South of France. Many individuals began hunger strikes in solidarity with that begun by Apalátegui. When the march reached Pamplona, it was refused entry by the Civil Governor. The columns stopped on the outskirts of the city. After incendiary speeches by the veteran *abertzale* leader, Telesforo Monzón, it was dispersed with some brutality by the police.[7]

The impact on Basque public opinion was considerable. It was compounded by the activities of *agents provocateurs*. In late August, groups of *incontrolados*, armed with clubs, chains and pistols, disrupted summer festivals in several small Basque towns. The authorities rejected accusations made by the Euskadiko Eskerra deputy, Francisco Letamendía, that the police were involved. However, at Amorabieta in the province of Vizcaya, the local people organized vigilante groups who captured and disarmed a gang which included a police officer. The continued anti-Basque and anti-democratic sentiments of the forces of order, together with the continued amnesty demonstrations, gave credibility to the *abertzale* claim that the elections had changed nothing.[8] Young policemen from poorer parts of Spain were posted to the Basque Country. Even if they were apolitical on arrival, the ostracism of their wives and children by the local population and the general atmosphere of bitter hostility soon turned them into determined enemies of the Basque cause. The Basque problem required the greatest delicacy and courage from the central government. Both Suárez and Martín Villa were to be found wanting, perhaps understandably, given the weight of opinion within the armed forces and the police. None the less, they consistently resisted pressure for the army to be sent into Euskadi. The right wanted to see no concessions made to Basque aspirations and stood to gain political capital from the existence of ETA terrorism. It came as no surprise, when the summer 1977 truce in Euskadi was finally broken, that the detonator was ultra-rightist terrorism.

On 5 October the offices in Pamplona of the *abertzale* weekly, *Punto y Hora*, were bombed by a fascist organization calling itself the Alianza Apostólica Anticomunista. It was the excuse that the restless adolescents of ETA-Militar needed to unleash a terrorist offensive against the government. On the following day, the President of the Diputación Provincial de Vizcaya (the provincial council), Augusto Unceta Barrenechea, was murdered by an ETA-M commando along with his two Civil Guard escorts.[9] It was almost a year to the day since the assassination of Juan María Araluce. The death of Unceta constituted the beginning of a massive escalation of the dialectic of terror and repression. It was a process which favoured both ETA-M and the ultra-right to the detriment of the democratic regime. In the following months, alleged informers and rank-and-file policemen were shot down in steady succession. While the government groped towards a formula for the establishment of Basque autonomy, ETA-M worked for all-out confrontation between Spain and Euskadi.

Out of such conflict, the *abertzale* extremists hoped to forge an independent revolutionary state. Accordingly, the last thing that the ETA-Militar leadership wanted was compromise by Madrid. Thus, in order to provoke an intensification of repression and thereby build popular support, attacks were made on senior military officers. A policy which was to bear fruit in the proliferation of army interventionism, or *golpismo*, began with the assassination of the Pamplona Police Chief, Major Joaquín Imaz Martínez, in late November.[10] Although it was never to provoke the desired military invasion of Euskadi, ETA-M's strategy did ensure that police methods continued to be dominated by indiscriminate brutality. Protest demonstrations, punctuated by the chant '*Gora ETA! ETA herria zurekin!*', ('Long live ETA! ETA the people is with you!'), were evidence of the popular support for the activists generated by police repression.

That smouldering hatred engendered under Franco remained intense was partly the consequence of mistakes made by the government in 1976 and 1977 over the amnesty issue. However, it owed more to the behaviour of the unreformed forces of order. All over Spain, people were prepared to believe that, despite the Francoist background of their new UCD rulers, real change was under way. In contrast, substantial numbers of Basques believed that fascist oppression continued to exist under another name. Habits of police violence died hard and, even outside Euskadi, there were several scandals in 1977. On 27 August, the Socialist parliamentary deputy for Santander, Jaime Blanco, was beaten up by policemen at a political meeting. Expressions of outrage at this incident were described by the ultra magazine *Fuerza Nueva* as a smear campaign against the armed forces. In the heated parliamentary debate of the consequent PSOE censure motion on 13 and 14 September, the Socialist deputy leader, Alfonso Guerra, told Martín Villa that, if he wanted to see democracy in Spain, he should resign. In December, at a gathering of Andalusian nationalists in Malaga, the police opened fire, killing one man and wounding six others. A few days later, a student was shot at the University of Lalaguna in Tenerife. Far from taking action against those responsible, Rodolfo Martín Villa supported the police and was denounced again in the Cortes by Alfonso Guerra as 'the last redoubt of Francoism'.[11] To a large extent, Martín Villa faced within the police the same problem being confronted in the army by Gutiérrez Mellado. Necessary reforms were shirked at first because of the fear of mutiny. Not until 1979 did Martín Villa begin to succeed with his plans to introduce a substantial reform of the police.[12]

Ever since the legalization of the PCE, the propensity to anti-democratic conspiracy in the higher echelons of the armed forces had been intensifying. The door-to-door distribution of propaganda in the name of straw organizations like the Unión Patriótica or the Juntas Patrióticas, backed by the daily message of the ultra press, had given wide currency in military circles to the notion that army intervention was both desirable and necessary. The relative ease with which the duplicated diatribes against the Minister of Defence, General Gutiérrez Mellado, were distributed and the failure to clamp down on its sources raised the question of the political loyalty of the intelligence services. In fact, the actively negative role played by military intelligence, in preventing information about conspiracies reaching the government and in terms of providing information for the preparations for coup attempts, was a crucial element of *golpismo* after 1977. Originally created to eradicate any signs of liberalism in the armed forces, the intelligence services were hard-line Francoist in their composition, objectives and methods. After the death of Franco, they were subjected only to the merest cosmetic reorganization. In consequence, the sworn enemies of the democratic regime were provided with an invaluable instrument with which to co-ordinate military plotting and to provide an alternative chain of command during a coup. At the same time as the bunker press was inciting officers to intervention, the intelligence services were failing to report on the success of this propaganda within the ranks. Indeed, as far as the government was concerned, the problem with the intelligence services seemed to be inefficiency rather than disloyalty. Suárez once complained that two intelligence service captains had their jobs described on their visiting cards.[13]

When Franco died, there were eleven competing intelligence services, most of which were controlled by the military. The principal ones were administered independently by the Presidencia del Gobierno, or the cabinet office, by the General Staff, by each of the three armed service ministries, and even by the fascist veterans' organization, the Hermandad de Alfereces Provisionales. The most powerful was the Servicio de

Información de la Presidencia del Gobierno (SIPG) set up by Carrero Blanco and run until early 1974 by Lieutenant-Colonel José Ignacio San Martín López. San Martín was later to be involved in the Tejero coup attempt of 23 February 1981. The SIPG was originally created to maintain vigilance of the universities, the Church and the Labour Movement but, after the Portuguese revolution, its activities were extended to include, and indeed concentrate on, the armed forces. In addition to rooting out subversion, the SIPG was rumoured to be involved in directing and subsidizing the violence of ultra-rightist groups against liberal and leftist priests, lawyers, trade unionists and booksellers.

Under the first democratic government of Suárez, a vain attempt was made to break the power of the SIPG. It was subsumed on 2 November 1977, together with the independent services run by each branch of the forces, into the Centro Superior de la Información de la Defensa (CESID). Since the CESID, on its creation, inherited the personnel of its various predecessors, the dominance of Carrero's trusted servants, the so-called 'hombres de Carrero', was unaffected. They were thus able to build up a parallel power structure virtually independent of the military hierarchy which was more or less loyal to the King and therefore to Gutiérrez Mellado. The Suárez government turned a blind eye to this and regularly issued statements praising the loyalty of its intelligence services despite evidence that the CESID was devoting its energies to spying on ministers and other politicians while failing to investigate military subversion.[14]

As early as the autumn of 1977 there were signs of anti-democratic ferment in the army. Resentment of the legalization of the PCE and of government weakness in the face of the Basques was exacerbated by rumours throughout the summer that the cabinet intended to purge older officers and thereby prevent them fulfilling their career and pension prospects. Optimism in political circles that loyalty to the King would keep the military in check was brusquely disabused in mid-September. A meeting of senior generals was held at the home of General Fernando de Santiago y Díaz de Mendívil in Játiva in the province of Valencia. Bringing together three ex-Ministers for the army, Antonio Barroso Sánchez Guerra, Francisco Coloma Gallegos and Félix Alvarez Arenas, the ex-Minister for the Navy, Admiral Pita da Veiga, and the ultra Generals Carlos Iniesta Cano, Angel Campano López and Jaime Milans del Bosch, it was presided over by General Santiago. Between 13 and 16 September, they discussed the military situation and drew up a memorandum calling upon the King to appoint a government of national salvation to be presided over by Santiago. In the event of the King refusing, he was to be asked to sack Suárez and suspend parliament for two years. Despite widespread rumours about the meeting, Ministry of Defence spokesmen denied unofficially that any such memorandum had been presented. Nevertheless, behind these requests for what amounted to a bloodless *coup d'état*, there was the clear threat of outright military intervention.[15]

Disturbing rumours suggested that civilian support for such subversion went beyond the incitements of the bunker press and consisted of the organization of civic support networks. The same ultra politicians, José Antonio Girón de Velasco, Blas Piñar, Juan García Carrés and José Utrera Molina, who were thought to be behind the propaganda campaigns of the 'patriotic juntas', were allegedly arranging for their followers to take over the civil service, local government and communications in the event of a coup. Such activities were to be stepped up over the next three years.[16] In the light of this, and given the enormous prestige within the army of the generals involved in the Játiva meeting, the government was understandably loath to take dramatic measures which might have precipitated events. Nothing was done to punish the implicitly mutinous meeting. With major developments imminent in terms of the negotiation of a social contract, the Pacto de la Moncloa, and of relations with the Basque Country and Catalonia, the cabinet wanted to play for time.

Thus, General Gutiérrez Mellado persisted with a policy of trying to bring the armed forces under control by means of strategic postings and promotions. The most important was the removal of Milans del Bosch from the crucial post of Commander of the Brunete Armoured Division. The División Acorazada, or DAC as it was known, was the key to any coup attempt. It was put under the command of General Antonio Pascual Galmés. An effort was made to soften the blow by the promotion of Milans to be Captain-General of the Third Military Region, centred on Valencia. In fact, this merely placed a determined enemy of the regime in a powerful position without breaking his influence over the DAC at Brunete. Other changes were even less positive and just nourished military suspicions that the government was weak, indecisive, meddlesome and vindictive.

Evidence of weakness was provided by the official reaction to an incident on 8 October 1977 in which Lieutenant-Colonel Antonio Tejero of the Civil Guard came near to provoking a massacre in Malaga. Infuriated by ETA-M's assassination of Augusto Unceta Barrenechea and his Civil Guard escorts two days previously, Tejero broke up a legally authorized demonstration by local youth organizations in favour of a reduction in the voting age to eighteen. His men were fully armed with live ammunition rather than with riot control gear and only the pacific response of the young demonstrators prevented bloodshed. Tejero was punished only by being confined to barracks for one month during which time he was visited by enthusiastic ultras.

The treatment accorded Tejero contrasted dramatically with three important sackings. In the first, General Alvarez Arenas was removed from his post as Director of the Escuela Superior del Ejército (the higher military college). Like Milans, he was being punished for his presence at Játiva but the effect was botched by the announcement that he was being disciplined for extremist declarations made by one of his subordinates. Since Alvarez Arenas had already severely reprimanded the culprit, his removal seemed to be an act of high-handed pettiness by General Gutiérrez Mellado. On 31 October, General Alfonso Armada Comyn was relieved of his post in the secretariat of the King's Household for reasons that remain obscure. It was rumoured that he had used palace notepaper to write letters in support of his son who had run as an Alianza Popular candidate, an accusation which he always denied. Armada later claimed that he had requested a transfer but it appeared that his barely concealed political views had led to pressure from Suárez for his removal. On 16 December the eccentric and irrepressible General Manuel Prieto López was dismissed as Commander of the VI Zone of the Civil Guard for a speech condemning the use of its units in inappropriate circumstances. All three sackings could be seen as ill-advised over-reactions and they caused intense ill-feeling within the Forces.[17]

The failure of the cabinet to eliminate military subversion or Basque terrorism did not mean that it was entirely ineffectual or inactive. In the case of Catalonia, the special relationship established between Suárez and the seventy-seven-year-old exiled President of the Generalitat de Catalunya, Josep Tarradellas, enabled the Prime Minister to carry off a spectacular political coup. While not so conflictive as the Basque Country, Catalonia still constituted a significant problem for the government. Pressure for concessions to the area's nationalist aspirations was growing but could not be met without the cabinet appearing to lose the initiative and without provoking the resentment of the armed forces. A way out had emerged as early as October 1976. A prominent Catalan banker with important political connections in Madrid, Manuel Ortínez, suggested to Alfonso Osorio that Tarradellas could be the key to a peaceful resolution of the Catalan question.

At the time, Tarradellas seemed to be merely an eccentric anachronism.

Yet, as Ortínez made clear to Osorio, the majority of Catalans accepted him as the legitimate embodiment of Catalanism. Tarradellas had never been properly elected as successor to the wartime President of the Generalitat, Lluis Companys. Nevertheless, he had proudly borne the standard of the Generalitat during a lonely and austere exile. He considered himself to be above parties and to be the spiritual leader of Catalonia. Accordingly, Osorio came to believe that, if the co-operation of Tarradellas could be secured, tension in Catalonia would be defused. In addition, a propitious context for the future development in Catalonia of a government-sponsored party might be created. Suárez was persuaded to send an emissary, his intelligence chief, Colonel Andrés Casinello, to speak to '*El Honorable*' Tarradellas in France. Although Casinello's report was sympathetic, Suárez decided that the Catalan leader's age made him a bad bet. He was also rather narrow-mindedly put off by what he saw as the air of operetta surrounding Tarradella's determination to be received in Barcelona by a traditional guard of honour of Mozos d'Escuadra. It was typical of a Castilian ex-Francoist that he should misunderstand the importance to the Catalans of the symbolism of the Generalitat.[18]

Suárez's reluctance lost him valuable time. The swift introduction of devolutionary legislation similar to the Catalan Autonomy Statute of 1932 could have given the UCD much greater control over the autonomy process. It would certainly have paved the way to a similar procedure in the Basque autonomy process, kept control of the pace of regional devolution in the hands of government and perhaps limited the subsequent Babel of demands for autonomy from regions without any historic tradition of local nationalism. However, such a determined course of action would inevitably have provoked immense hostility on the right given that the Civil War had been fought in part to destroy such legislation. Accordingly, the necessary will and vision was lacking and Suárez, true to his Movimiento origins, was never particularly sensitive where the nationalities were concerned. What finally galvanized him into action was the outcome of the 15 June elections in Catalonia. The UCD had been swamped by the so-called *partidos sucursalistas*, the PSC and PSUC, the Catalan branches of nationwide parties, the Socialists and the Communists. With his unparalleled instinct for political advantage, Suárez began to realize that he could use the powerful emotional symbol of the Generalitat to recapture the lost initiative.

On 27 June 1977, Tarradellas went to Madrid and engaged in arduous negotiations with the Prime Minister. Effectively, in return for the re-establishment of the Generalitat, through an adaptation of the 1932

Statute, Tarradellas would pledge Catalan loyalty to the monarchy, acceptance of the unity of Spain and respect for the armed forces. Suárez commented later that, during the meeting, Tarradellas's central preoccupation had been to ensure that he would be accorded full military honours. This suggested not just the stubborn pride of '*El Honorable*' but also his shrewd perception that it was essential for the army to be seen to acquiesce in the process of devolution. None the less, the meeting was a major theatrical gesture which somewhat undermined the electoral victory of the Catalan left-wing parties as well as re-affirming Suárez's penchant for government by private negotiation. The re-establishment of the Generalitat was also an immense popular success although a price had to be paid in terms of resentment within the army. The Captain-General of Catalonia, Francisco Coloma Gallegos, protested at the reception of Tarradellas by Juan Carlos. Both the King and General Gutiérrez Mellado had to work hard to placate him and thus ensure that Tarradellas would receive the desired military honours when he returned in triumph to Barcelona on 23 October.[19]

Suárez's deal with Tarradellas was announced to the cabinet on 29 September. Progress with the Basques was to be altogether slower in large part because of the amnesty question. By the beginning of October 1977, there was an intensification of united opposition pressure for a wide-ranging amnesty to include not just *Etarras* but also army officers who had fought for the Republic during the Civil War and even terrorists of the ultra-right responsible for the Atocha massacre. Amnesty was a crucial item on the agenda when Suárez arranged to meet representatives of all the political parties. In the course of lengthy sessions held at the Palacio de la Moncloa over the weekend of 8–9 October, he struck an ominous note. After a week of rising tension in the Basque Country which had seen the murder of Augusto Unceta Barrenechea, he began to talk of the need to take into account the views of what he called the *poderes fácticos*. These *de facto* powers invigilating the democratic regime – the army, the banks and, to a lesser extent, the Church – were to become an ever more frequent point of reference throughout the late 1970s and early 1980s. The most powerful and least reticent of them was clearly the army, a fact reflected in the exclusion from the amnesty passed in the Cortes on 14 October of both the Republican officers and those involved in the Unión Militar Democrática. Nevertheless, the amnesty, backed by a nearly unanimous vote, like the restoration of the Generalitat before it, was a potent symbol of reconciliation and co-existence.[20]

In the starkest possible contrast, the spectre of military resentment continued to hover in the background to negotiations over Basque autonomy. The Basque government-in-exile, unlike the merely symbolic Generalitat personified in Tarradellas, was a substantial reality. Moreover, it was by no means above parties, composed as it was by representatives of the Partido Nacionalista Vasco and of the PSOE. Accordingly, Suárez was not prepared to contemplate an arrangement with the Basque president, or *Lendakari*, Jesús María de Leizaola, like that concluded with Tarradellas. Instead, the Minister for the Regions, the Andalusian Manuel Clavero Arévalo, negotiated with parliamentary representatives of the PNV (Juan de Ajuriaguerra) and of the Basque branches of the PSOE (José María 'Txiki' Benegas) and of UCD (Juan de Echeverría) the creation of a body to be called the Consejo General Vasco. Discussions about autonomy would then take place between the government and the Consejo General.

Debate over who should be the President of the Consejo General led to a deadlock between the PNV and the PSOE. To avoid having to tolerate a nationalist, Juan de Ajuriaguerra, at the head of the new body, the UCD representatives put their weight behind the PSOE candidate, Ramón Rubial. Inevitably, these developments excluded the *abertzales* and generated their hostility and suspicion. They denounced the Consejo, with its bureaucratic structure and its formal relations with the central government, as far removed from the spontaneous will of the people which they believed themselves to represent. In fact, the groups close to ETA-M, particularly HASI and LAIA, seemed worried that the Consejo would become a pacific channel for the wishes of the people and thereby interrupt the dynamic of an ETA activism backed by popular assemblies and demonstrations.[21]

The most conflictive issue as far as Basque autonomy was concerned hinged on the position of Navarre. In the eyes of the *abertzales* and some of the northern Navarrese, the province was part of Euskadi. For the army, the UCD and the Spanish right in general and the Navarrese right in particular, it was a bulwark of Spanish unity. Moreover, neither the PSOE nor the PCE were in favour of including Navarre within the Basque Country. After bitter anti-Basque demonstrations organized by the ultra-right in Navarre throughout December, the jurisdiction of the Consejo General Vasco was limited to the three indisputably Basque provinces of Vizcaya, Guipúzcoa and Alava.[22] It came into being on 4 January 1978. In itself it was a positive step in the direction of peace in the Basque Country but the scarcely concealed animosity of both the army and the *abertzales* boded ill for the future.

UCD's policy on autonomy was destined to infuriate the military and ETA in equal degrees. In the jaundiced view of the *abertzales*, the UCD was master-minding an elaborate operation to render Basque self-government innocuous by first swamping it in a sea of autonomies and then conditioning it to the lowest common denominator. For most army officers, UCD's autonomy concessions were a wild orgy at which the debauched victim was Spanish unity. In fact, the government was dealing with a complex situation in which the PSOE and the PCE were committed to some form of federal state while the extreme right remained as obsessively tied as ever to rigid centralism. At the same time, in the political ferment of 1977, autonomy demands were emerging from the most unlikely parts of Spain. It was an inevitable reaction both to the corruption and inefficiency of local government under Franco and to the economic imbalances bequeathed by his regime. The compromise solution encharged to Manuel Clavero Arévalo had to take the steam out of local aspirations without enraging the sensibilities of the military. Throughout the period from October 1977 to October 1978, Clavero tried to create a two-tier system. The three historic nationalities, Catalonia, Euskadi and Galicia, were permitted to elaborate an autonomy statute which had then to be submitted to local referendum. Thirteen other regions, some small like Cantabria, others large like Andalusia, were subjected to much vaguer arrangements.[23] It was a solution which, in the short term at least, satisfied no one. Moreover, by seeming to be hastening Spain quietly towards a federal structure, it was to be at the heart of growing military disaffection with the democratic regime.

The antipathy of the military and the *abertzales* excepted, however, the autumn and winter of 1977 were marked by a remarkable spirit of co-operation and sacrifice among the main political parties. This reached its apogee in the agreements signed by thirty-one representatives of virtually all parties and known as the Pacto de la Moncloa. Arising from the meeting held on 8–9 October and another on 13 October, the Pact aimed to establish a common response to the problems of terrorism, inflation, unemployment and the growing trade deficit. The meetings and the Pact were another triumph for Suárez's style of private wheeling and dealing. Just as he had exploited Tarradellas to control the Catalan situation, now he exploited Santiago Carrillo equally skilfully. The Communist leader had spent the summer of 1977 frenetically trying to make good the PCE's disappointing showing in the elections by pushing for a government of 'democratic concentration'. Carrillo argued that the strength of anti-democratic forces in Spain called for an Italian-style 'historic compromise' among the parliamentary parties to help build a strong framework for democracy. Suárez was not prepared to share power but he was happy to take advantage of Communist influence in the workers' movement. Secret negotiations with Carrillo played on the PCE leader's anxiety to be near the levers of power and secured his backing for an austerity package. Armed with the virtual agreement of the Workers' Commissions, Suárez was able to exert considerable pressure on the PSOE to accept the package. In any case, with the death of Augusto Unceta fresh in their minds, the politicians were anxious to make a success of the Moncloa meetings.[24]

The Moncloa Pact was in many respects the culmination of the policies of moderation and self-sacrifice pursued by both the Socialists and Communists throughout the transition period. The left accepted wage ceilings of 20–22 per cent, at a time when inflation was 29 per cent, together with a series of monetarist measures to restrict credit and public spending. In return, the government made promises of major structural reform, especially in agriculture and the tax system, undertook to reorganize the police and pledged the return of the *patrimonio sindical* – the buildings, newspapers and funds of the trade unions confiscated by the Francoists after the Civil War. In fact, the government fulfilled few of its promises and, in consequence, the Spanish working class bore the brunt of the economic crisis. Over the next three years, inflation dropped to 15 per cent, although remaining nearly twice the OECD average, and unemployment soared from 7 per cent to nearly 13 per cent. UCD's monetarist policies led to a flood of bankruptcies and plant closures.[25] This was to be exploited by ultra-rightist propaganda. Conveniently forgetting the extent to which the world context was as responsible for the economic down-turn in the 1970s as it had been for the boom years of the 1960s, the press network of the extreme right began to make simplistic and unjustified comparisons with the prosperity attributed to Franco.[26]

The Moncloa Pact was claimed as a colossal victory by Carrillo at the PCE's great carnival, the *Fiesta de Mundo Obrero*.[27] In fact, as Suárez knew, the PCE and even the PSOE would be unable to oblige the government to fulfil its side of the bargain. The Pact was a necessary evil, virtually the only way, short of revolutionary measures, of confronting the inextricably linked problems of the burden of Francoist economic imbalance and the unfavourable international situation. An austerity programme was hardly likely to generate popular enthusiasm. The subsequent increase in unemployment, together with the failure of the government to keep its promises, provoked instead considerable popular disappointment, which was eventually picked up by the press and elevated into the *desencanto* of 1980. Given the exaggerated expectations that democracy would be a panacea for all of Spain's ills, this was perhaps inevitable. After the political excitement of the previous year, the need to deal with painful problems like terrorism and economic stagnation was bound to be anticlimactic. Similarly, the elaboration of complex juridical texts such as the Constitution, autonomy legislation and a new penal code could ill compare with the intoxication and novelty of the election campaign. Throughout the next two years, the government was to appear to be adrift in contrast to the purposeful dynamism which had characterized Suárez's first year in power. Yet, while both the extreme right and ETA were to exploit the image of a government bogged down in intractable problems, considerable achievements were being forged behind closed doors.

Such had been the case with the social contract hammered out at the Moncloa and it was even more so with the creation of the Constitution. A political truce between the parties, the so-called *Pacto constitucional*, considerably facilitated this momentous task. An all-party drafting committee, the *Ponencia*, consisting of seven parliamentary deputies, was elected by the Constitutional Committee of the Cortes at the beginning of August 1977.[28] The seven carried out their labours in a spirit of compromise and co-operation and by mid-November they had produced a draft text. At the beginning of 1978, a somewhat more refined draft was placed before the thirty-six members of the parliamentary Constitutional Committee. Despite inevitable friction over such issues as abortion, autonomies, private education and the death penalty, a steady pace of progress was maintained under the witty and flexible chairmanship of Emilio Attard. Attard became the darling of the press because of his droll interventions and the members of the Committee were known as '*los locos de Attard*' (a pun on *locos de atar*, whose equivalent would be something like 'mad as Attards').[29]

A crisis was reached in May 1978 when it became known that one of the main reasons for the smooth functioning of the Committee was that many clauses were being agreed beforehand between the UCD and the PSOE behind the backs of the chairman and the other Committee members. Secret deals on various clauses of the draft were being concluded by Fernando Abril Martorell of the UCD and Alfonso Guerra of the PSOE in late-night sessions in private apartments and occasionally in Madrid restaurants. This provoked the withdrawal from the

Committee of both Alianza Popular and the Partido Nacionalista Vasco. The Committee, with Alianza Popular restored to its ranks, finished its deliberations on 20 June. The text was then put before the full Chamber of Deputies and the Senate and was ratified on 31 October 1978. Apart from the failure to satisfy the Basques, it was a text whose moderation and guarantee of basic liberties was broadly acceptable to all but the extremes of left and right.[30]

In general terms, the positive achievements of the Constitution were appreciated by the population at large, despite its concern with problems of unemployment and terrorism. Lacking the sensational aspects of assassinations or street crime, the Constitution inevitably received less media coverage. None the less, university experts in constitutional law were in constant demand to give lectures explaining the text and its implications in the small towns and villages of Spain. In Euskadi, however, the continuing tension between the forces of order and large sectors of the population made the nascent Constitution seem an empty irrelevance. Random brutality by the police and Civil Guard, together with the Francoist past of the Minister of the Interior, Rodolfo Martín Villa, fuelled popular support for ETA. The widespread belief in the Basque Country that the relentless harshness of the police had the support of the Minister gave credibility to the ETA contention that the fight against Madrid must go on. On 11 January 1978, a policeman and two *Etarras* were killed in a shoot-out in Pamplona. Astonishingly, it was reported that, when asked for comment by journalists, Martín Villa unwisely remarked '2–1 to us'.[31] Wall slogans and banners focused increasingly on Martín Villa as the heir to Francoist oppression. His repeated declarations to the effect that the problems of Euskadi were police matters rather than political ones left many Basques convinced that nothing could be expected from UCD. This was a view shared by influential figures within the army.

Indeed, after his succession of triumphs during the autumn of 1977, the tide turned against Suárez in the course of 1978. In addition to the issue of political terrorism, the ultra press was able to exploit a rise in the crime rate to generate middle-class panic about a collapse of law and order. On 25 January 1978, the ex-mayor of Barcelona and one-time Movimiento hard-liner, Joaquín Viola Sauret, and his wife were horribly murdered with explosives by a gang of extortionists. Coming after a wave of kidnappings and muggings, the appalling deaths of the Violas unleashed a storm of protest. The increase of street crime was a reflection of spiralling unemployment. The ultra-right preferred the explanation that delinquency was being perpetrated by leftists released from prison by amnesty measures. On the left, the view gained currency that the police were trying to undermine democracy be simply letting crime get out of hand. There was certainly a remarkable contrast between the brutal efficacy of the police under Franco and its apparent helplessness in the democratic regime. As *El Alcázar* explained the crime wave, 'What is happening in Spain? The answer is simple and hardly complex: Francisco Franco died.'[32] In fact, the Spanish crime rate was not unusual by European standards. None the less, the law and order issue contributed significantly to the erosion of the public credibility of the Suárez government.

It was, however, ETA terrorism and the military reactions provoked by it which were eventually to destroy Suárez. Nevertheless, there were other reasons for the immediate deterioration of his image. Although the wage restraint agreed in the Pacto de la Moncloa had helped to reduce inflation by almost half, businesses continued to close at an alarming rate and unemployment to rise. The Minister for the Economy, Enrique Fuentes Quintana, aimed to fulfil some of the government promises of structural reform made in the Pact. However, his plans for cut-backs in steel production and for the nationalization of electricity production offended the conservative backers of UCD. Aware of his growing isolation, Fuentes Quintana resigned on 22 February. The fall of Fuentes represented a blow to the social democratic pretensions of some sectors of UCD and a boost to the Christian Democrat wing and their supporters in the banking world. The consequent cabinet reshuffle saw a significant turn to the right. The powerful Ministry of the Economy, and with it a deputy premiership, was assumed by Suárez's Movimiento crony, Fernando Abril Martorell. Another friend from Suárez's days as Civil Governor of Segovia, Salvador Sánchez Terán, became Minister of Transport. The press began to talk of the 'Segovia mafia'. The Ministry of Industry was taken over by Agustín Rodríguez Sahagún, who was related to Suárez by marriage (concuñado) and was also the Vice-President of the right-wing employers' organization, the Confederación Española de Organizaciones Empresariales (CEOE).[33]

Abril Martorell's declarations to the effect that he favoured monetarist policies provoked fears on the left that the government was not going to fulfil its side of the Pact. The entire parliamentary opposition, from Alianza Popular/Coalición Democrática to the Communist Party, was united by a conviction that the new UCD cabinet had little or no respect for the Cortes. This was provoked in part by a statement by the UCD

Secretary for Relations with the Cortes, Rafael Arias Salgado, to the effect that the government had no obligation to explain the reshuffle to parliament. The mordant deputy leader of the PSOE, Alfonso Guerra, was quoted as remarking that 'there are those like Manuel Fraga who evolve from Francoism to democracy but Arias Salgado is the clearest example of the opposite – he is evolving from democracy to Francoism'.[34] A major debate was called for 1 March and took place in the absence of Suárez. Abril offered an unconvincing account of Fuentes Quintana's resignation and the opposition united to back a motion condemning the inadequacy of his explanation. The impression that Suárez was simply not governing was reflected in a dramatic fall in his opinion poll ratings.[35]

Nowhere was his popularity as low as among the senior ranks of the army. The hope of many politicians that the passage of time would reconcile the armed forces to the democratic regime was simply not being fulfilled. Indeed, throughout 1978, Suárez and Gutiérrez Mellado seemed to be skating on ever thinner ice. The precariousness of the situation was underlined on 17 May by the resignation of the Chief of the General Staff, General José Vega Rodríguez, hitherto regarded as a reliable moderate. In fact, contacts with Blas Piñar and a growing anxiety about the terrorist problem had undermined his loyalty. He took his stand on the issue of the promotion out of turn of General Antonio Ibáñez Freire from Director-General of the Civil Guard to Captain-General of the Fourth Military Region, Barcelona. General Gutiérrez Mellado was obliged to flout the rigid seniority system of promotions in order to favour the careers of loyal officers. An earlier promotion of Ibáñez Freire to Lieutenant-General in December 1976 in order to permit his taking over the Civil Guard had provoked expressions of outrage among reactionary generals. Gutiérrez Mellado believed that political security should take precedence over seniority where key appointments were concerned. Vega Rodríguez, and many other officers, disagreed violently. This was not necessarily as a result of rightist sympathies but was equally likely to stem from attachment to entrenched and cherished traditions. It was, however, an issue which was seized upon eagerly by the ultra-right.

The resignation of Vega Rodríguez was a bitter blow for Gutiérrez Mellado at the same time as it provided a focus for discontent within the army. As Vega's successor, the apparently apolitical General Tomás Liniers Pidal was appointed Chief of the General Staff. The nature of his apoliticism was swiftly revealed when, in a speech delivered in Buenos Aires on 15 June 1978, Liniers praised the Argentine military's 'legitimate' use of violence in their 'dirty war' against the opposition. He implied that similar methods would be appropriate in Spain. No action was taken against him.[36] In fact, in the test of strength between the ultras and the government, the initiative seemed to be passing to the bunker. Large increases were being decreed in military budgets, with salaries raised by 21 per cent, but this seemed to do little to deepen military loyalty to the new regime. Increasingly, senior officers were informing the government that the process of regional devolution would have to be slowed down. Not to do so could only intensify their hostility to the democratic regime. To do so could only provoke further ETA terrorism, if provocation were needed.

Throughout the two preceding years, the number of terrorist victims had remained steady: twenty-six in 1976 and twenty-eight in 1977. From the beginning of 1978, however, there began a massive escalation for which ETA was primarily, if not exclusively, responsible. Throughout 1978, the year of the Constitution, eighty-five people were to die as a result of terrorist activities and the forces of order gave every appearance of being unable to do anything about it. Hopes that the democratization of Spain would lead to the withering-away of ETA could no longer be entertained. It was becoming increasingly clear that ETA-M was not only unconcerned by the fate of democracy in Spain but was actively hostile to its consolidation. The elaboration and eventual putting into practice of its constitutional framework would eventually marginalize ETA-M's sectarian option. An intensification of violence against policemen and soldiers would, however, provoke the brutality which would keep support at boiling point. It would also persuade many generals that a firmer, more decisive, hand was necessary.

In the on-going spiral of repression and terror, ETA-M and the extreme right fed off each other's blood-lust. The maintenance of a climate of violence actually benefited the *abertzale* groups close to ETA-M such as HASI and LAIA by obscuring and postponing the complex issue of the future Basque state for which in theory they were fighting. The inevitable popular resentment of the forces of occupation was electorally more potent. In fact, there is reason to believe that the police were partially out of government control in the summer and autumn of 1978.[37] This was especially clear in the case of Navarre. On 1 May the trade union demonstration in Pamplona was attacked by police under the command of an ultra-rightist, Comandante Avila. When a Spanish flag was pulled down, rubber bullets and smoke bombs were used on the crowd. Ten days later, on 11 May, off-duty Civil Guards ran amok in the town.[38]

The build-up of tension culminated at the traditional bull-running festival of San Fermín on 8 July. In contravention of specific orders from the Civil Governor of the province of Navarre, a local officer, Comandante Rubio, unleashed an especially violent intervention by riot squads against a small amnesty demonstration in the Pamplona bull-ring. The subsequent wave of terror, apparently master-minded by Comandante Avila, left one civilian dead and forty wounded, as well as putting an end to the San Fermines. Both the Civil Governor and Comandante Avila were dismissed but no other disciplinary proceedings were taken. A series of strikes and demonstrations began to spread across the Basque Country in protest against the events of Pamplona. On 11 July a march by bank employees in San Sebastián was fired on by the police. One man was shot dead and several others wounded. The Basque Country was paralysed by a general strike similar to those which had accompanied the amnesty campaign of 1976 and 1977. The response of the police starkly exposed the reasons why ETA could rely on widespread support for its war. A company of armed police went berserk in the Rentería suburb of San Sebastián, looting shops and vandalizing apartment buildings. Martín Villa announced to the Cortes that there would be no purges of the police and made it clear that fear of serious acts of indiscipline inhibited any attempt at reform. He was quoted during the summer to the effect that he could only trust twenty officers.[39] The declarations of the Minister gave heart to the ultra-right and spread despondency in democratic circles.

The UCD government would never be able to find a political solution to the problem of ETA while it remained incapable of controlling police officers actively hostile to democracy and to Basque aspirations, many of whom belonged to ultra-rightist organizations. Just as Suárez and General Gutiérrez Mellado tried to capture the loyalty of recalcitrant army officers by reacting mildly to signs of indiscipline and by loudly asserting their faith in the military, Martín Villa backed his men in the hope of eventually securing their acceptance of the new regime. Gradually, his policy paid off but the vehemence of many of his declarations severely undermined prospects for peace in the Basque Country. When he was quoted after the Rentería incidents as saying that 'we make mistakes; they commit murder', he was effectively confirming to *abertzales* the ETA claims that Francoist oppression of Euskadi lived on and making it easier for armed resistance to find popular support. Rentería consolidated the common Basque perception of the Spanish forces of order as a rapacious foreign army of occupation.

To *abertzale* eyes, ETA's actions were legitimate self-defence. Ulti- mately, far more than the drab cabinet crisis of March, it was the inexorable wave of terrorism which fed the government's image of paralysis and incapacity. Until after Suárez's resignation in early 1981 and the subsequent military coup, barely a week went by without ETA killing a policeman or a Civil Guard. The lead in indiscriminate terrorism was taken by ETA-Militar. In fact, the crudity and cruelty of some of its political decisions began to diminish its popular support, although hardly enough to help Suárez. On 17 March two innocent workmen were killed during an attack on the construction site of the nuclear power plant at Lemoniz. A generalized outrage spread even to some of the *abertzale* faithful when, on 28 June, ETA-M murdered the journalist José María Portell. The author of two important books on ETA, at the time of his death he was working on an investigation of the death of 'Pertur'. It was speculated that he was murdered to prevent revelations about ETA-M's part in that killing. Even if true, this was not the only motive behind his assassination.

The wave of killings had led the government to attempt a negotiated truce with ETA. Peace efforts had been made by the Catalan President, Tarradellas, by the Basque Socialist, José María 'Txiki' Benegas, and by Portell, who had earlier acted as go-between in the talks held before the 1977 elections. He had worked out a scheme for ETA's viewpoints to be made public and debated in the Monday newspaper *Hoja del Lunes*. This progress towards dialogue seems paradoxically to have been one of the motives for his murder. A feeble ETA-M communiqué issued to justify the assassination accused Portell of confusing issues and being 'an instrument of intoxication'.[40] This led to speculation that he had been eliminated by elements of ETA-M precisely because they did not want a truce but wished instead to push the army into invading Euskadi and thereby setting off a national revolutionary rising. ETA's lack of interest in a negotiated truce was revealed later in November 1978 when Martín Villa went secretly to meet ETA-M representatives in Geneva. Their talks broke down on the deliberately provocative demand that they be crowned with a press photograph session and the issue of a joint communiqué as if each side represented a sovereign nation state.[41]

Military intervention was, in fact, a much more likely consequence of ETA violence than the popular revolutionary action which ETA-M hoped to provoke. In fact, sympathy for ETA was maintained only because of the continued activities of rightist terror squads and the outbursts of police indiscipline such as that which was to destroy the July 1978 San Fermines in Pamplona. The exaction of a 'revolutionary tax' from Basque businessmen was rapidly undermining the tolerance of the

PNV and there was mounting evidence of funds being withdrawn from the Basque Country.[42] Holding the Basque bourgeoisie in contempt, ETA-M was hardly deterred from its objective. The determination to detonate a military intervention was starkly illustrated on 21 July, the day on which the Cortes was to finish its deliberations about the new Constitution. At 8.30 a.m. General Juan Manuel Sánchez-Ramos Izquierdo and his ADC, Lieutenant-Colonel José Antonio Pérez Rodríguez, were machine-gunned down in a Madrid street. Originally claimed by GRAPO, the killings were later and authoritatively attributed to ETA-M. The fact that neither officer was notably significant within the military structure was ETA-M's way of announcing that all ranks were at risk in a democratic Spain. Adopting an air of scandalized horror, the ultra-rightist press drew comparisons with the situation prior to the military uprising of 1936.[43]

The following five months were marked by an incesssant counterpoint of terrorism and rightist reaction. Both ETA-M and the ultras shared a determination to prevent the new Constitution being put into practice. *El Alcázar* had followed the elaboration of the text with great hostility, describing it as Communist-inspired and opening the way to drugs, abortion and the dismemberment of Spain. The paper's stance over the forthcoming constitutional referendum had given rise to an acrimonious meeting of the leadership of the Junta Nacional de la Confederación de Ex-Combatientes. Girón and the senior leadership had advocated an appeal for a No-vote. The *El Alcázar* editor, Antonio Izquierdo, had felt that since a government victory was inevitable, a call for abstention would be less likely to open the bunker to ridicule. Accordingly, the official line was abstention although, throughout the campaign, the paper carried advertisements from various ultra organizations in favour of a negative vote. One of the curious features of 1978 was the fourfold increase in the sales of *El Alcázar* which, as the electoral fortunes of the bunker showed, probably was more of a tribute to its provocative style than to any resurgence of the extreme right.[44]

As if determined to give credence to the doom-laden prophecies of *El Alcázar*, ETA-Militar embarked in late August 1978 on a wave of killings of members of the security forces. The immediate objective was to prevent both the parliamentary ratification of the Constitution and the organization of the referendum to give it popular endorsement. On 13 October, *Etarras* attacked a police jeep in Basauri (Vizcaya), killing two policemen and seriously wounding a third. At the following day's funeral service, the Civil Governor of Vizcaya, Luis Alberto Salazar Simpson, a close friend of Suárez, the Director-General of Security, Mariano Nicolás García, and the head of the police, General José Timón de Lara, together with other senior officials, were barricaded in the Basauri barracks by enraged policemen who chanted insults against them and the democratic regime. This mutiny led to 344 police officers being posted outside Euskadi and a further 25 being expelled from the force.[45]

It was thus in an atmosphere of great tension that the Cortes gave its overwhelming approval for the Constitution, voting on 31 October 1978 by 363 votes for, to 6 against, with 13 abstentions. In the Senate, similar results were announced: 226 votes for, 5 against and 8 abstentions. The general mood of optimism was diminished only by the ominous abstention of the PNV. As so often before, the Partido Nacionalista Vasco was playing an ambiguous game. There was little doubt that the bulk of its leadership approved of the Constitution. However, in the fevered atmosphere generated by the extreme *abertzales*, the PNV did not want to be seen to be in agreement with the government. Accordingly, it called for abstention in the constitutional referendum.[46] Inevitably, an intensification of the ETA offensive destroyed the euphoria inspired by the parliamentary unanimity of support for the Constitution. After the thirteen victims of October, ETA-M was to claim another thirteen in the course of November. Determined to smash the referendum campaign, ETA-M stepped up the violence within Euskadi itself. On 15 November, at Mondragón, in a clash with Civil Guards, two ETA gunmen were killed along with an innocent woman bystander. ETA-M struck back on the following day by assassinating a magistrate, José Francisco Mateu Cánovas, one-time hard-line president of the Francoist Tribunal de Orden Público. Right-wing circles seethed with angry resentment. With the crime wave on the increase, a debate on law and order in the Cortes saw Martín Villa savaged by Manuel Fraga.[47] The descent into violence could hardly have served the interests of the ultra-right more directly.

The deteriorating political situation had already swung many neutral officers over to the ultra camp. However, although the context favoured their plans, the shrewder heads among the ultras realized that Gutiérrez Mellado's policy of strategic promotions, timid though it seemed, was gradually undermining their positions. They had tried to counter his efforts by a tactic of progressively applying for transfers to key operational and intelligence units. However, by the autumn of 1978, they felt that it was necessary to exploit their strength before the reformist efforts of Suárez and Gutiérrez Mellado received further legitimation in the constitutional referendum fixed for 6 December. The date chosen for the projected coup was 17 November. 'Operación Galaxia', as it came to be known having been plotted in the Cafetería Galaxia in Madrid, envisaged the seizing at the Moncloa of Suárez and the entire cabinet. It constituted an attempt to add force to the plans first mooted at the previous year's meeting of Generals at Játiva. By kidnapping the government, the plotters hoped to create a power vacuum which would convince other units of the need to intervene, first to uphold law and order, and then to impose a government of 'national salvation' to suspend parliament and launch a 'dirty war' against ETA.

17 November was selected because the King was scheduled to be on a state visit to Mexico, the Minister of Defence and the Joint Chiefs of Staff to be out of Madrid, and a large number of senior generals to be on promotion courses in Ceuta and the Canary Islands. Furthermore, large contingents of fascists, some of them armed and many in paramilitary uniform, were expected in the capital for the commemoration on 20 November of the third anniversary of Franco's death. The planned coup was preceded by an orchestrated campaign of propaganda in army barracks. On the morning of 17 November, there took place an incident which seems to have been part of the pre-coup strategy of tension. General Gutiérrez Mellado, on a tour of garrisons to explain the Constitution, was encountering considerable hostility from officers who had been encouraged by the ultra press to regard such an initiative as the imposition of politics on the army. In Cartagena, the impetuous head of the Levante region of the Civil Guard, General Atarés Peña, shouted out that the Constitution was a lie. General Gutiérrez Mellado ordered him, and anyone who agreed with him, to leave. Atarés left accompanied significantly by Jaime Milans del Bosch, Captain-General of the Third Military Region. On returning to the room to hear Gutiérrez Mellado remark that 'a general must know how to wear his stars with honour', Atarés could not control his indignation and insulted the Minister of Defence, calling him 'freemason, traitor, pig, coward and spy' to the applause of many officers present. Curiously, General Atarés had been Colonel Tejero's commanding officer in the Basque Country in 1976.

In fact, whether Atarés Peña's outburst was aimed to provoke a local rising or not hardly mattered, for the plot had been discovered earlier. One of the conspirators, an infantry major attached to the Police Academy, informed the head of the police, General Timón de Lara, and an investigation was undertaken. On 16 November, Adolfo Suárez was given a full report by the chief of the Intelligence Service of the Civil Guard, Colonel Andrés Casinello Pérez. The two prime movers, Lieutenant-

Colonel Antonio Tejero Molina of the Civil Guard and Captain Ricardo Sáenz de Ynestrillas of the police, were arrested. In general, however, the government showed alarming signs of wanting to brush the affair, and its more disturbing implications, under the carpet. Thus, nothing was done to prevent a series of events almost certainly linked with the projected coup. These included the attendance by 500 officers at a fascist ceremony at Franco's tomb in the Valle de los Caídos on 20 November and the celebration of an international fascist gathering in Madrid two days earlier at which Blas Piñar called for a military uprising. Indeed, the way in which both the Atarés Peña incident and the Galaxia conspiracy were handled did little to diminish the growing conviction in military circles that the democratic regime could be attacked with virtual impunity.

The low-key response of the government was paradoxically a reflection of the profound anxiety instilled by the Galaxia operation. It emerged, for instance, that nearly 200 officers had been contacted by Tejero and Ynestrillas. With the excuse that they did not take the matter seriously, they failed, almost without exception, to report on the planned mutiny. It is difficult to avoid the conclusion that many of them were simply waiting on events. In particular, the intelligence services had played a disturbingly ambiguous role. They had failed to discover the conspiracy or, if they had, to inform the government. One senior intelligence and counter-insurgency expert, Lieutenant-Colonel Federico Quintero Morente, who was on a posting to the Operations Division of the General Staff, did find out about the plot. He informed the head of the Division, General Luis Sáez Larumbe. On the grounds that it was 'a mad fantasy', Sáez Larumbe chose not to take the matter further. Subsequent investigations gave no grounds for complacency. It appears that units in Burgos, Valladolid, Seville and Valencia were involved and on the alert the night before Galaxia was due to take place. Apparently, it was only the energetic intervention of the liberal General Antonio Pascual Galmés which prevented the crack División Acorazada de Brunete (DAC) joining in. The Armoured Division was the key to control of Madrid.[48]

Perhaps the most remarkable feature of the Galaxia business was the fact that Tejero had been able to go about conspiring so freely. He was already notorious as an hysterical opponent of the democratic regime. He had been pushed to extremist positions by his period of service in the Basque Country. Renowned for theatrically embracing the bloody corpses of Civil Guards killed in bomb and sniper attacks by ETA, he developed a bitter hatred of the politicians whom he blamed for failing to smash terrorism. Accordingly, he encouraged his men in the sort of blanket brutality which itself provoked popular support for ETA. At the same time, he began to mix with the ultra-rightists who persuaded him that he could be Spain's saviour. In September 1976 he had gained notoriety and a certain popularity in the more reactionary circles of the military hierarchy for an impertinent telegram that he sent to the Minister of the Interior, Rodolfo Martín Villa. Tejero was incensed at the legalization of the Basque flag after so many civil guards had died taking down *Ikurriñas* which had been booby-trapped. His telegram sarcastic-ally requested instructions about the honours to be rendered to the newly authorized flag.[49] After being briefly confined to barracks, he was posted to Malaga. There too he provided ample proof of his inability to refrain from meddling in political matters. Outraged by ETA's assassi-nation of Augusto Unceta, he came near to provoking a blood-bath on 8 October 1977 when he suppressed a legally permitted demonstration. It was typical of the kid-glove treatment given to rebellious army and Civil Guard officers in the post-Franco period that Tejero was punished for his persistently mutinous attitudes merely by relegation to a desk job. At the Agrupación de Destinos, or postings section, of the Civil Guard, he had ample opportunity to mix with ultras eager to encourage his nascent *golpismo*.[50]

After Galaxia, Tejero was made to serve only seven months' detention before being given another post in Madrid at the head of a transport unit, where he was able to bask in the adulation of civilian ultras for whom the plot had made him a hero. General Atarés Peña was court-martialled by General Luis Caruana Gómez, the Military Governor of Valencia, who was later to play a significant role in Tejero's 1981 coup attempt. Caruana absolved Atarés of the charge of indiscipline. Galaxia was in most respects a rehearsal for what was to become the conspiracy of 23 February 1981. That its failure should be followed less than two and a half years later by a more thoroughly planned repeat performance may be attributed to the weakness of the government's response in 1978. The minimal punishment was meted out only to those whose involvement was too conspicuous to be ignored. The bunker line was that the Galaxia plot had in reality just been a hypothetical chat in a bar, and official statements presented the events of November 1978 as the wild schemes of an unrepresentative minority, '*cuatro locos*'. Nor was the policy of appease-ment confined to the government. All sides of the political spectrum, including the Socialists and Communists, were accomplices in rhetorical wishful thinking about military loyalty.[51] In the following months, however, despite all the confident bluster, the government was to find itself increasingly making concessions to the military hierarchy and turning a blind eye to insubordination.

ETA-M's leadership gave no indication that it was in any way disconcerted by Galaxia's exposure of the effects within the army of its violence. On the contrary, the number of attacks on policemen and Civil Guards in Euskadi increased. In consequence, the constitutional referendum was held on 6 December in an atmosphere of intense nervousness. The result was a clear popular ratification of the Constitution. However, both the low general turnout and the comparatively high proportion of negative votes in the Basque Country gave cause for concern. Over Spain as a whole, the average abstention rate was 32.3 per cent. The abstentions were some indication of the creeping apathy which was to characterize the last two years of Suárez's period in office, although they were not dramatically high by European standards. Of those who did vote, 87.79 per cent did so affirmatively. The highest levels of abstention, 51.46 per cent were recorded in the Celtic mists of Galicia. The area is renowned for its low indices of politicization and its distrust of Madrid. To make matters worse, polling day was marked by torrential rain. On the other hand, negative votes in Galicia were among the lowest in Spain.[52]

Altogether more worrying were the Basque results, with 51.1 per cent abstentions. Of those Basques who did vote, 23.54 per cent cast negative votes. The level of abstention reflected, at least in small villages, an element of fear. Effectively, abstention calls had destroyed in rural areas the secrecy of the ballot since to vote at all implied a rejection of the *abertzale* parties' instructions. Suspicion of enthusiasm for the Constitution could incur the displeasure of ETA-M with extremely dangerous consequences. Those who voted could be easily watched by the more extremist *abertzales* and reprisals taken against those deemed to be 'collaborators'. The scale of affirmative votes cast, 76.46 per cent, hardly sustains the *abertzale* claim used to justify continued violence from ETA that Euskadi had rejected the Constitution.[53] None the less, the fact that Basques did vote in relatively substantial numbers against the Constitution dramatically underlined the need to elaborate a satisfactory autonomy statute for Euskadi. In order to get parliamentary authority for such a course, Suárez called general elections for 1 March 1979.

The twin tasks of winning the elections and negotiating with the Basques took place against the interminable counterpoint of terrorism and *golpismo*. The rate of ETA-M attacks on policemen and civil guards was higher even than in 1978. It was, however, the attacks on senior officers which drove the ultras to apoplexy. On 2 January, ETA-M murdered Major José María Herrera Hernández, ADC to the Military Governor of Vizcaya. On the following day in the capital itself, they assassinated the Military Governor of Madrid, General Constantino Ortín Gil. His funeral was interrupted by chants of '¡*El Ejército al Poder!*' ('Power to the army'), and frenzied insults directed at Rodolfo Martín Villa and General Gutiérrez Mellado. With tension in military barracks at boiling point, the ultra press became more explicit in its calls for military government. Martín Villa's public statement that 'if we do not finish off ETA, ETA will finish us', was an ill-advised, albeit unintentional acknowledgement of the ultra accusation that Spain was experiencing *desgobierno*, 'disgovernment' or lack of government.

The provocation of the right was stepped up on 9 January 1979 when GRAPO murdered a judge of the supreme court, Miguel Cruz Cuenca, giving rise to renewed speculation about the activities of *agents provocateurs*.[54] Infiltrated by the police or not, GRAPO, in comparison with ETA-M, was a mere side-show.[55] The virulence of ETA's offensive was perhaps partly a response to the successes of under-cover anti-terrorist hit squads which had killed a number of *Etarras*, including the ETA-M leader, José Miguel Beñarán Ordeñana, 'Argala'. Much more so, however, it was related to the negotiations over the Basque autonomy statute. The aim was to push the government into accepting a text which was as near as possible to the maximalist demands of the Koordinadora Abertzale Sozialista, the so-called Alternativa KAS.

The loose KAS coalition had been diminished somewhat by EIA's inclusion in Euskadiko Eskerra and the gradual evolutionary process of that party to moderation. The remaining *abertzale* groups had gathered in late 1977 at Alsasua in Navarre under the leadership of the wildly messianic *abertzale*, Telesforo Monzón. The Mesa de Alsasua (Alsasua Round Table), organized by the 'Ayatollah Telesforo', as Monzón was nicknamed, was converted on 28 April 1978 into Herri Batasuna (Popular Unity). An *abertzale* coalition made up of HASI, LAIA and numerous small left nationalist groups, Herri Batasuna was the fruit of the years of popular demonstrations in favour of amnesty for ETA prisoners. It considered itself to be the antithesis of conventionally organized parties and its radicalism was enshrined in its reliance on the rhetoric of popular assemblies (*asamblearismo*) for decision-making.

Herri Batasuna was closely linked to ETA-Militar and was devoted to the political implementation of the Alternativa KAS. With its demands for the expulsion of the army and the Civil Guard from Euskadi, for the unification of the French and Spanish Basque provinces and for an independent Basque State, the Alternativa KAS was never going to be negotiable with Madrid. Nevertheless, it was an indication of the hatred engendered by the forces of order and the rightist terror squads that, by 1980, Herri Batasuna was to be the second most important group in Basque politics. Linked as it was to a powerful terrorist organization, Herri Batasuna had a magnetic appeal for many ultra-leftist and ultra-nationalist groups. Moreoever, commitment to the Alternativa KAS guaranteed a constant ferment of militancy. Since ETA-M would continue the armed struggle for the Alternativa KAS, there would always be, no matter how many amnesties were granted, a fresh supply of ETA prisoners as a focus to rally the HB rank and file through amnesty mobilizations.[56]

In the elections of 1 March 1979, the impact of Herri Batasuna surpassed all expectations. Indeed, the very fact that there was a lull in ETA-M terrorist activities would be directly attributed to the emergence of the new coalition. A voluntary truce was observed in order to permit an electoral demonstration of ETA-M's popular support. A communiqué was issued by the leadership calling upon their supporters to vote for Herri Batasuna as an 'active abstention'. Since the HB candidates had declared their intention of not taking up their parliamentary duties if elected, a vote for the coalition was to be a positive rejection of Madrid and its policies. The fact that the patriarchal Monzón was arrested early on in the campaign for 'apologia of terrorism' generated significant *abertzale* support. At the polls, Monzón was elected to the Cortes for Guipúzcoa and the ETA lawyer, Miguel Castells, to the Senate. Herri Batasuna gained a further two Cortes seats in Vizcaya, one of which was won by Francisco Letamendía who had abandoned Euskadiko Eskerra. This *abertzale* success indicated the extent to which the government faced real difficulties in the negotiation of the Basque statute.[57]

The emergence of Herri Batasuna was not the only surprising thing about the results. During the two months of the campaign, the opinion polls had placed the PSOE slightly in the lead.[58] It was widely assumed that the PSOE would derive considerable benefit from its merger in April 1978 with the Partido Socialista Popular of Enrique Tierno Galván. Despite his greatly inflated academic reputation, the '*viejo profesor*', as he was known, enjoyed great popularity as well as influence among generations of Socialist intellectuals. Even leaving aside the additional votes that Tierno and the PSP might bring, the UCD was believed to have suffered irremediable attrition in the endless battles against terrorism, unemployment and inflation. Nevertheless, the UCD won the elections, increasing the number of its seats in the Cortes from 165 to 168, while the PSOE rose only from 118 to 121.[59] A number of factors had tipped the balance in UCD's favour.

During the campaign, a statement by the standing committee of the Bishops' Conference condemning 'materialist ideologies' was widely taken to be the Church's endorsement of UCD. In the PSOE's southern strongholds, votes were lost to the recently created Partido Socialista de Andalucía, which was rumoured to receive money from UCD's slush fund or 'fondo de reptiles' despite its advocacy of Andalusian nationalism. In the Basque Country, the Socialists' condemnations of ETA lost them 70,000 votes and three parliamentary seats. So great was *abertzale* hostility to the PSOE that its campaign meetings were regularly disrupted and, at one in Eibar, Molotov cocktails were thrown. Yet, most crucial of all was the intervention of Suárez. After his silence and isolation during the previous months, he used his television charisma to dazzling effect. This was particularly true of his final speech on the eve of the elections in which he launched a devastating attack on the PSOE as the Marxist party of abortion and divorce. It was a blatant appeal for the '*voto de miedo*' or the fear vote which was calculated to have swayed over one million undecided voters.[60]

The election campaign generated far less popular enthusiasm than had been witnessed during the euphoric scenes of 1977. It was understandable that, after two referendums and now the second general election in just two years, the abstention rate should rise to 33.6 per cent. The voting age had been lowered to eighteen, increasing the electorate by three and a half million, yet the number of votes cast was down on the 1977 figure by over 300,000. After the boom years of student militancy, this was now the period of the *pasotas*, an other-worldly cross between punks and hippies who rejected politics altogether. All the parties experienced a drop in militant fervour. Members of the Communist Youth complained that the only political activity left for them was to stick posters on walls or sweep out party headquarters. Veterans of the anti-Franco struggle joked nostalgically that '*Contra Franco vivíamos mejor*' ('Against Franco, we lived better'), a pun on the rightist catch-phrase '*Con Franco, vivíamos mejor*'. In the case of the PCE, a dramatic fall in membership was largely a reaction to the sclerotic leadership team brought back from exile by Carrillo. Bit by bit, the Stalinist habits of these 'Parisians' repelled many of the party's best and brightest young militants.[61]

However, the PSOE too was to experience a serious internal crisis after its ebullient doubling of membership over the previous two years. As the PSOE came nearer to gaining power, its leadership became progressively more embarrassed by the party's official definition of itself as Marxist. At the same time, the consolidation of a social democrat image, which was shown by opinion polls to be electorally successful, was resented by a radical section of the party.[62] Throughout the 1979 election campaign, Felipe González worked hard to project moderation and statesmanship and to dampen the extremism of some of the unskilled and unemployed workers who thronged his meetings. The electoral benefit derived by Suárez's last-minute attack on PSOE Marxism intensified the Secretary-General's determination to resolve the contradictions within his party. Given the Socialists' pre-election expectations, defeat was traumatic. There was no shortage of cautious voices to suggest that it was all for the best and to express a rhetorical relief at not having to take on the mantle of power yet. Whether merely a way of diminishing the pain of defeat or genuine, such remarks implied a belief that it was still too soon after the death of Franco for the right to tolerate peacefully a transition to a Socialist government. That the electorate or sections of the PSOE really believed this to be the case is difficult to say with certainty. The leadership, however, was convinced that it was the party's radical image which made such speculation possible.

In fact, difficulties had been brewing in the PSOE for some time. Felipe González was almost universally admired, both within and without the PSOE, for his honesty, common sense and warm humanity. Behind the scenes, the day-to-day tasks of running the party were left to his lifelong crony, the acerbic Alfonso Guerra, once hysterically described by Abril Martorell as 'the Spanish Josef Goebbels'. Guerra ruled the PSOE's local federations with an iron hand. However, after the party's vertiginous growth throughout 1977 and 1978, even Guerra with his legendary capacity for work found it difficult to impose homogeneity over ideological and generational disparities. In early 1978 the PSOE had absorbed the Federación de Partidos Socialistas, a disparate collection of regional groupings whose leadership included a number of technocrats who were later to be ministers in the first Socialist government – Enrique Barón, Eduardo Barrionuevo and Julián Campo. In May of the same year, the small but prestigious Partido Socialista Popular of Tierno Galván had been taken over. A similar process led to the fusion in July of the various Catalan Socialist parties with the PSOE.[63]

The incorporation of these new groups swamped the PSOE with senior cadres much to the chagrin of those who had been longer in the party.

The new arrivals had negotiated their insertion directly into the higher ranks of the PSOE with the Seville–Basque axis which had led the party since 1974. Inevitably, they consolidated the strength of the Felipe González–Alfonso Guerra leadership. This was especially galling for the Madrid-based group of Pablo Castellano, Luis Gómez Llorente, Francisco Bustelo and others who had kept the PSOE alive in the capital during the late fifties and throughout the sixties. They regarded the parachute landing of the new technocrats as leading the party in an unacceptably social democrat direction. Their suspicions were aroused on 8 May 1978 when Felipe González announced to a group of journalists in Barcelona that, at the next PSOE Congress, he would propose the elimination of the party's definition as exclusively Marxist. In fact, Felipe González's shrewd attempt to contest the middle ground between the PSOE and the UCD bore fruit in Socialist victories in the Senate by-election held on 17 May 1978 in Asturias and Alicante.[64]

The ideological misgivings of the Madrid group were compounded by resentment in the provinces of Alfonso Guerra's high-handed manipulation of the party apparatus. This became particularly acute during the compilation of lists of candidates for the March 1979 elections. The imposition of candidates from party headquarters in Madrid, together with the rigid discipline and personal loyalty that Guerra demanded – and usually inspired – from the PSOE's paid officials, led to considerable discontent in Extremadura, Valencia, Aragon and, above all, in Galicia. There were numerous resignations in protest, of which the most notable was that of Modesto Seara Vázquez, the ambitious Secretary-General of the party in Galicia, who accused Guerra of Stalinism.[65] The various resentments of González's ideological moderation and Guerra's tough administrative centralism came to a head at the PSOE's XXVIII Congress held in Madrid from 17 to 20 May 1979. The dramatic events there ultimately hinged on the relationship between the PSOE's ideological stances and its electoral ambitions. One crucial factor was the extent to which, during the previous two years, Suárez had taken the UCD into social democrat territory felt by many PSOE leaders more properly to correspond to the Socialists. Moreover, by the time that the XXVIII Congress assembled, victory for the PSOE in the municipal elections held on 3 April had convinced the Socialist leadership that only fear of the party's Marxism had prevented similar success in the general elections.[66]

The delegates to the XXVIII Congress were predominantly activists elected by local provincial PSOE groups. Only 30 per cent of them were paid party bureaucrats controllable by the apparatus. The remainder felt free to give vent to their dissatisfaction with the rightward electoralist trend of the party. Felipe González, however, refused to play to the gallery. In his opening speech in defence of the outgoing executive, he accepted the usefulness of Marxism as an analytical tool without acknowledging it as the party's absolute and exclusive value system. He recommended to the delegates that their efforts at the Congress be directed towards the elaboration of 'a project capable of mobilizing the different sectors of society'. On the following day, 18 May, the committee encharged with the party's ideological definition (the *ponencia ideológica*) produced a text which reaffirmed the PSOE's character as a Marxist, class party. When this was accepted by the plenary session of 19 May, the corridors seethed with conspiracy. It was widely assumed that Felipe González would seek a compromise with the *críticos*. However, in a moving and historic speech, he announced to a shocked assembly on 20 May his determination not to stand again for the post of Secretary-General, a decision seconded by the entire executive.

The critics of Felipe González found themselves in the position of the sorcerer's apprentice. Although Pablo Castellano was reported in the press as having told Luis Gómez Llorente that he was to be the next Secretary-General, the *críticos* recoiled from picking up the crown. There were a number of reasons for this. They were taken rather by surprise and had not had time to concoct a full candidacy for all the leadership positions. They were also taken aback by the panic with which the bereft delegates had reacted to Felipe González's gesture. More practically, it was intimated to them that Guerra's loyal party functionaries would simply not work for them if they tried to take over. Moreover, they knew that the bulk of the parliamentary party was solidly 'Felipista'. Finally, Enrique Tierno Galván, who had played an ambiguous and opportunistic role in the schemes of the *críticos* now pulled back and began to talk of the negative way in which the Church, the army and the banks would react to an ultra-leftist PSOE. Accordingly, with the *críticos* paralysed, a steering committee, the *comisión gestora*, was set up to arrange an extraordinary congress at which efforts would be made to resolve the split.[67]

With the extraordinary congress scheduled for late September, Felipe González spent the summer of 1979 touring the provinces and explaining his stance to the rank-and-file militants. At the same time, Alfonso Guerra tightened his control of the party apparatus. He was immensely helped by a change in party regulations as a result of which the individual election of delegates by each town was replaced by the elaboration of provincial or regional block delegations.[68] At the extraordinary congress, which was held in Madrid on 28 and 29 September, there were fifty as opposed to the one thousand delegations of the XXVIII Congress. Moreover, the delegation chairmen more or less exercised a block vote. Guerra himself had total control of the largest delegation, the Andalusian, with 25 per cent of the total votes. With the entire national press and the television supporting Felipe González, it was perhaps inevitable that the *críticos* would suffer a humiliating rout. The moderates were victorious all along the line, with the *críticos* relegated to a marginal position. Henceforth, the establishment of socialism would take a back seat to the immediate task of winning elections and completing the democratic transformation of the country. The Secretary-General himself had increased his stature sevenfold and was acclaimed across the political spectrum as a future national leader.[69]

By contrast, Suárez's star was on the wane. One symptom of this was UCD's disappointing performance in the municipal elections of 3 April 1979. They were a crucial stage of the transition to democracy. Despite the dramatic progress made in Spain, local administration remained unreformed. It was, of course, an area in which people felt better able to express their political preferences than they did in national elections where the fear factor remained potent after forty years of Francoism and the subsequent rumblings of the army. Accordingly, the PSOE and the PCE between them gained control of twenty-seven provincial capitals, representing 10,500,000 people. In contrast, the UCD, although gaining many rural municipalities, won only twenty-three provincial capitals, representing just 2,500,000 people. Herri Batasuna captured 15 per cent of the Basque vote and control of a number of small towns.[70]

More significant was the negative impression rapidly inspired by Suárez's new post-election cabinet announced on 5 April after a month's deliberation. A week previously, Suárez had been badly mauled in the Cortes when he presented himself for investiture and presented his new programme of government. The PSOE was already smarting from Suárez's pre-election speech in which he had raised the spectre of the party's Marxism. Now, on the advice of Abril Martorell, the UCD proposed to proceed to a vote on the investiture and the programme without a proper debate. The opposition was furious and Felipe González quoted speeches by Suárez from his days in the Movimiento in praise of General Franco. With support from Alianza Popular/Coalición Democrática and the suspect Partido Socialista de Andalucía, Suárez won the vote but his prestige had suffered an important blow.[71]

The view soon gained currency that the new cabinet was a team which had neither the drive nor the imagination to resolve the problems of regional autonomy, terrorism, unemployment and military subversion. It was dominated by the President's close friend Abril Martorell who became second Vice-President with responsibility for economic affairs. General Gutiérrez Mellado remained as Vice-President for National Security and Defence, although the Ministry of Defence went, for the first time since before the Civil War, to a civilian, Agustín Rodríguez Sahagún. The impression of mediocrity derived from the departure of major figures. Rodolfo Martín Villa had asked to be replaced at the Ministry of the Interior after three years of intense and exhausting labour. Unable to find a suitable substitute, after Martín Villa's Under-Secretary Jesús Sancho Rof (called 'the Sheriff' by Alfonso Guerra) had refused, Suárez turned to General Antonio Ibáñez Freire. Francisco Fernández Ordóñez, the leader of the Social Democrats within UCD, who had been rumoured to have flirted with the PSOE, was replaced by one of his younger followers, Jaime García Añoveros. In fact, in addition to the problems that he met in forming a cabinet, Suárez was suffering pain and discomfort from a dental complication which made it increasingly difficult for him to talk.[72]

It was hardly surprising then that, a mere two months after his general election victory, the press could be found to be complaining of the President's isolation and paralysis. The opinion of the politically aware public was summed up by a daubing on a Madrid wall which read *'Franco estaba loco: se creía Suárez'* ('Franco was mad: he thought he was Suárez').[73] Even leaving aside his health, the problems faced by the Prime Minister were sufficiently daunting to provoke some kind of withdrawal. The achievements of the two years since the elections of 15 June 1977 were considerable – the Pacto de la Moncloa, the Constitution, the beginnings of autonomy legislation – but they were far from spectacular. In contrast, the negative features of terrorism, crime and military subversion captured the headlines virtually every day. ETA-Militar was more committed to violence than it had been two years before and now it actually had the backing of a coalition of political parties, Herri Batasuna, which enjoyed the support of at least 15 per cent of the Basque population. The dominance of the ultras in the army, and especially in the intelligence services and key units such as the DAC at Brunete, was greater than ever. After its recent election defeat, the PSOE was also about to undergo the process which would eventually lead it to power in 1982. It could be argued that Suárez's moment had passed. The historic task of steering democratic reform through the Francoist institutions had been fulfilled. For that, albeit pushed down the road to democratization by pressure from the opposition, Suárez had been the perfect man. Torcuato Fernández Miranda once said, with incomparable arrogance, that the drama of the transition had had an impresario, Juan Carlos, a script-writer, himself, and an actor, Adolfo Suárez.[74] In fact, Suárez was an actor who, in a given situation, was able to make up many of his own best lines. That situation prevailed no more. With the audience becoming ever more restless, Suárez sat in his dressing-room wondering how the play would end.

6
Chronicle of a death foretold: the fall of Suárez 1979–81

From the elections of 1979 until his resignation in January 1981, Suárez's rule was in stark contrast to the apparently unending series of triumphs of the period 1976–7. There was a dramatic decline too in contrast with the period 1977–9 during which, despite the attrition of ETA and ultra hostility, major legislative achievements had been carried through. After 1979, however, the continuing failure to solve the overwhelming economic and social problems that beset Spain, along with terrorism and military subversion, took its toll. The press began to talk more and more of widespread *desencanto* or disenchantment with Suárez and UCD. It was inevitable perhaps that this would be reflected in a generalized disappointment that democracy had not fulfilled all the expectations put on it. However, the bunker mistakenly concluded that the reduction in popular enthusiasm meant an active rejection of the democratic regime. Plotting was thus intensified in the misplaced confidence that the *desencanto* of which the media talked somehow implied that, contrary to the evidence of electoral results and opinion polls, the people longed for a return to authoritarian government.

There were many reasons why the President found the nation's various problems so intractable: their sheer immensity; the limitations of his Francoist background; the well-kept secret of the painful dental troubles from which he was to suffer throughout much of 1979. However, one of the worst obstacles that he faced was his preoccupation with growing evidence that the flimsy unity of his party was crumbling. This dramatically exacerbated the difficulties arising from UCD's lack of an overall majority in the Cortes. The transformation of the 1977 electoral coalition into a party had been achieved with some difficulty in the course of 1978. Nevertheless, there remained considerable tension between those who had been, albeit belatedly, part of the moderate opposition to Franco and those who had been servants of the old regime until the last minute. At the UCD Congress of October 1978, there had surfaced the *bon mot* of the old Christian Democrat leader, José María Gil Robles, to the effect that the ex-Francoist reformists of UCD had not had their conversion falling from a horse on the road to Damascus but while snoozing gently in the back of an official limousine. With hindsight, the attempted unification came to seem to be a major strategic error. As a coalition, the component groups could have come or gone without destroying the whole. They would, in any case, have had to attune their movements to electoral realities. Adjustment and compromise would have been obligatory. Inside a single party, however, the fear of electoral isolation was less great and so they were more reckless and readier to unleash a destructive power struggle to impose their views on others.

Already in early 1979, Christian Democrats within UCD, like Landelino Lavilla and Miguel Herrero Rodríguez de Miñón, had been affronted by the concessions on divorce and education which Abril Martorell had made to the PSOE during his backstairs negotiations on the Constitution. There were also signs that UCD's Social Democrats, led by Francisco Fernández Ordóñez, were negotiating their transfer to the PSOE. The horse-trading over candidacies for the March 1979 general elections and over the conduct of the campaign had left some bitterness within the party.[1] In consequence, Suárez was sufficiently worried about possible defections to demand from every UCD parliamentary deputy an undated letter of resignation and to arrange for their salaries to be paid not directly to them but via the party.[2] It was hardly surprising, given the scale and variety of his problems, that Suárez withdrew into the presidential palace.

His fortunes seemed to have reached their lowest ebb during the weekend of 25–27 May 1979. On the morning of Friday 25 May, an ETA-Militar *comando* gunned down Lieutenant-General Luis Gómez Hortigüela, head of the personnel section of the Army General Staff, Colonels Agustín Laso Corral and Jesús Avalos Gomáriz, and their driver. Two days before the annual military festival, the Día de las Fuerzas Armadas, the attack was a viciously thought-out provocation. Tension in the barracks could hardly have been greater. Rightist gangs roamed the streets of Madrid in search of victims for retaliation. At the funeral service held on 26 May, ultras provoked incidents and yet again there were chants of '¡*Ejército al Poder!*'. Suárez failed to attend the ceremony, did not visit army headquarters and did not even appear in the Cortes until the following Wednesday. A few hours after the service, a bomb exploded in a crowded Madrid cafeteria, the California 47, in the Calle Goya. Goya was near Fuerza Nueva headquarters and right in the heart of the ultra stronghold, the Barrio de Salamanca, nicknamed the *zona nacional* or nationalist zone. At 6.30 p.m. the premises were crowded for the early evening *merienda* and eight people were killed and another fifty injured. Curiously, no ultras were present and the usual Fuerza Nueva souvenir stalls were gone from the street outside.[3] The attack was attributed to GRAPO.

Rumours of a *coup d'état* were deafening. At a meeting between Generals Félix Alvarez Arenas and Luis Cano Portal and Colonel José Ignacio San Martín the need for military intervention was discussed.[4] Even before the tragic events of 25 and 26 May, Suárez was retreating before the military ultras. In the cabinet reshuffle of April, he had appointed the civilian Agustín Rodríguez Sahagún, as Minister of Defence. Suárez had come to the conclusion that the build-up of hostility against General Gutiérrez Mellado made it essential to remove him from the firing line. Accordingly, he was pushed upstairs to be Vice-President of the Government with responsibility for Defence and Security. The authority which he had managed to concentrate in his Ministry was now effectively devolved back to the general staffs of the three services. The new Minister of Defence began to take to extremes the policy of concession to the military hard-liners. His efforts were to little avail. Already in May, their exasperation with the government had reached a new peak. The post of Chief of the General Staff of the Army had fallen vacant. An appointment by strict seniority would have put this crucial post into the hands of the ultras who dominated the upper echelons of the army.

It was inevitable that the bunker press would latch on to the issue of seniority simply because many of the older generals who had fought in the Civil War and then in the Blue Division in Russia were fervent anti-democrats. The government, however, saw the vacancy as an opportunity to further its own ambition of liberalizing the armed forces. The logical candidates, if seniority were the only qualification, were both extreme rightists, Jaime Milans del Bosch, Captain-General of Valencia, and Jesús González del Yerro, Captain-General of the Canary Islands. The normal appointments procedure called for consultation with the Consejo Superior del Ejército, which had duly pronounced in favour of Milans. Accordingly, furious indignation greeted the appointment of General José Gabeiras Montero, an associate of Manuel Gutiérrez Mellado.

Gabeiras had to be promoted from Divisional General to Lieutenant-General and then leap-frog over five other generals. His speech on taking possession of his new post took the theme of the need for the army to respect the Constitution. A further reinforcement of General Gutiérrez Mellado's position took the form of the promotion of another relatively liberal general, Guillermo Quintana Lacaci to be Captain-General of Madrid.[5]

The verdict of the military hierarchy on Gutiérrez Mellado's promotion policy, which had been partly executed by General Gómez Hortigüela, and on the terrorist incidents of 25 and 26 May, was made starkly clear at the trial of General Atarés Peña. The court martial for his attack on Gutiérrez Mellado during the attempted Galaxia coup in November 1978 was held on 28 May 1979. Atarés Peña's offence fell within the sympathetic jurisdiction of the Valencia military region commanded by General Milans del Bosch. The court's decision of not guilty was a judgement on General Gutiérrez Mellado rather than on the defendant. Significantly, both government and opposition were silent about the acquittal of Atarés. Instead, politicians chose to pay heed to frequent declarations by various generals that the army would always respect Article 8 of the Constitution which defined its role as defender of Spain's constitutional order and territorial integrity. However, the sudden enthusiasm of the high command for this article of the Constitution was not unconnected with their erroneous belief that it provided them with a legal justification for intervening in politics. They chose to ignore the fact that any attempt to suffocate democracy would be by its very nature anti-constitutional.[6]

In fact, the increasingly open and confident statements by generals about their readiness to defend the existing order were closely linked to a belief that negotiations to concede Basque and Catalan autonomy would seriously alter that order. Again, the generals seemed oblivious of the fact that under the Constitution, that order could be changed by the popular will. Suárez was in an appalling position, exposed to the hatred of both ultras and *abertzales*. In December 1978, the local councillors from all the municipalities of Euskadi had approved a draft text of an autonomy statute based on the one granted by the Second Republic. Some of its clauses were at odds with the Constitution and negotiations between the Basque parties and the government centred on these incompatibilities. The Partido Nacionalista Vasco was the most open to compromise. EIA and Euskadiko Eskerra were anxious for the 'Statute of Guernica', as the draft was known, to remain unchanged. Herri Batasuna was hostile and regarded the text as falling far short of its goal of the Alternativa KAS. Speed was clearly of the essence, yet Euskadi was baffled by the way in which the government consistently dragged its feet.

The UCD representatives on the Cortes Constitutional Committee encharged with the negotiations were split into hawks or *'Constitu-cionalistas'* who stood by the letter of the Constitution and doves or *'pactistas'* who were prepared to compromise. The most prominent *'Constitucionalista'* was Gabriel Cisneros; the leading *'pactista'* was Miguel Herrero Rodríguez de Miñón. Herrero's Basque wife and his monarchist speculations about the possibility of reviving an ancient formula whereby an independent Euskadi would be united to Spain by agreement with the crown provoked suspicion among the more patriotic sections of UCD. Herrero was removed from the Committee on 23 June because he was considered to be too sympathetic with both Basques and Catalans. Even the closely concerned Minister for Territorial Administration, the *'pactista'* Antonio Fontán Pérez was rumoured to have been marginalized from the negotiations by Suárez. At this point, ETA-Político-Militar intervened in an effort to impel the government to speed up the process. A bombing campaign against Spanish beaches was started and an abortive attempt was made to kidnap Gabriel Cisneros, which left him seriously wounded. It was the clearest illustration imaginable of ETA-PM's policy of using violence as a supplement to more conventional measures. On 18 July 1979, Suárez agreed the autonomy statute with the Basque leader or *Lendakari*, Carlos Garaicoetxea.[7]

A referendum to ratify the statute was scheduled for 25 October. It was to be a watershed in Basque politics. The PNV and Euskadiko Eskerra campaigned for a Yes-vote. ETA-PM accepted the statute while ETA-M declared that the war would go on. Herri Batasuna denounced the text as having been concocted behind the backs of the people. It marked the beginning of the long process whereby ETA-M would eventually be isolated. On 14 July in the prison at Soria, ETA-PM and ETA-M prisoners came to blows over the statute. In the streets of San Sebastián, there were clashes between followers of Euskadiko Eskerra and militants of Herri Batasuna who threw money at them and called them traitors. Throughout the referendum campaign, ETA-M maintained a steady rhythm of murders and even made attempts on the lives of *abertzales* of Euskadiko Eskerra. Mario Onaindía, who had been one of the defendants at the Burgos trial of 1970 and had led EIA into Euskadiko Eskerra, accused Herri Batasuna and ETA-M of using Nazi methods. Both organizations were making increasingly clear a readiness to impose their views on the rest of the Basque population irrespective of its democratically expressed views. When the referendum was held, 60.7 per cent of those entitled to vote exercised their right. 81.14 per cent of those who voted did so affirmatively. It was a triumph for the PNV and Euskadiko Eskerra, and even, to a lesser extent, for Suárez. Abstentions and negative votes were slightly lower in the Basque Country than in the simultaneous Catalan referendum.[8]

At last the road to peace in Euskadi could be discerned. ETA-PM was not to abandon arms for some years to come but its gradual commitment to conventional politics was greater than ever before. The intractable problem remained ETA-Militar. Popular support for its activities was maintained by the continued activities of ultra-rightist terror squads, the so-called *incontrolados*, in which off-duty policemen and Civil Guards were known to take part. However, the insanity of its efforts to provoke a military intervention were condemned by ETA-PM spokesmen.[9] Unfortunately, those efforts were bearing ever more fruit. On 20 September 1979, ETA-M had murdered Colonel Aurelio Pérez Zamora and Major Julián Ezquerro in Bilbao and the consequent army indignation knew no bounds. The extreme rightist press was stepping up its incitements to military intervention. Gangs of rightist youths were back in action attacking trade unionists, Jewish-owned businesses and liberal individuals.[10] While the vast majority of the Spanish population came to terms happily with the new democratic regime, the two extremes of ETA-Militar and the ultras worked in contrapuntal harmony to destroy it.

The fact that something was in the air might have been deduced from the coincidence of provocative declarations by the three most senior ultra generals still on active service, Jaime Milans del Bosch, Jesús González del Yerro and Pedro Merry Gordón, Captain-General of the Seville Military Region. The first two were still seething at the appointment of the liberal General Gabeiras as Chief of General Staff. In an interview, given some time before and now published in *ABC*, Milans denounced, in extremely obscure terms, the terrorism, insecurity, inflation, unemployment, pornography and other ills which he considered to be attributable to democracy. González del Yerro, participating in a tribute to the Spanish Foreign Legion, was less equivocal, condemning the failure of the government to reverse a process in which 'Spain is dying on us'. General Merry Gordón, speaking to the garrison at Ceuta, was even more direct, referring to 'a series of murdering dwarves, sewer rats, who attack us from behind' and threatening in veiled terms that the army would soon turn on its tormentors. Unperturbed, ETA-M replied on

23 September by murdering the military governor of Guipúzcoa, General Lorenzo González-Vallés Sánchez, in San Sebastián.[11]

Just as the incident provoked by General Atarés Peña's outburst against Gutiérrez Mellado in November 1978 was linked to the Galaxia plot, so too these outbursts seemed to be directed at alerting ultra sympathizers to the fact that action was imminent. After the Galaxia fiasco, the conviction had taken root among military ultras that success in such an operation depended on the participation of an important Madrid-based unit. Their thoughts centred on the Brunete Armoured Division, the DAC. The División Acorazada was the key to the capital and, if it led, much of the rest of the army would follow. Since mid-1979 it had been commanded by an ultra, General Luis Torres Rojas. In fact, Torres Rojas was merely the latest stage in a long process whereby the DAC had become an ultra stronghold. Practically from the beginning of the transition to democracy, right-wingers had been requesting and obtaining postings to the DAC. Under the command of Milans del Bosch, who had a remarkable capacity to capture the unquestioning loyalty of his subordinates, the DAC had been brought into the bunker. Its Chief of Staff was Lieutenant-Colonel José Ignacio San Martín, who had been the head of Carrero Blanco's intelligence service, the SIPG, and was devoted to helping Milans turn the DAC into the élite force necessary to 'save Spain'. Curiously, San Martín's appointment in 1979 was partly as a result of a recommendation from General Alfonso Armada.[12]

Within a month of Torres Rojas taking command on 1 June 1979, a series of unauthorized manoeuvres began, with patrols carrying out exercises in the control of the nerve centres of Madrid, armoured vehicles dominating the main access roads and troop carriers patrolling the industrial belt. Officers of the DAC were burning with rage because they were convinced that the forthcoming referendum to approve the Basque autonomy statute meant acquiescence in separatism. It appears that Torres Rojas was at the heart of a planned coup to take place just before the referendum. The plan was for the Brigida Paracaídista (parachute brigade) of Alcalá de Henares, known as the BRIPAC, to seize the Moncloa Palace with helicopter support, while armoured vehicles of the DAC neutralized the capital. Having forced the government to resign, the conspirators aimed to form a military directorate under either General Santiago y Díaz de Mendívil or General Vega Rodríguez. The Cortes would be dissolved, the Communist Party banned and the regional autonomy process reversed. The continuity with the 1977 Játiva meeting and the 1978 Galaxia attempt was obvious. The conversion of normal manoeuvres by the BRIPAC on 21 October into a full-blown coup was, however, still beyond the ultras' reach. In the first place, there was the practical difficulty of obtaining sufficient fuel and munitions which were kept in short supply by a suspicious government. Moreover, the plotters were still in a minority within the armed forces. There were large numbers of officers who would not lightly go along with the enormity of an assault on the democratic regime. The ultra press continued, however, to urge military intervention despite the missed opportunity. Nevertheless, the conspiracy bubbling around Torres Rojas came to an abrupt end on 24 January 1980 when he was removed from command of the DAC and sent to be military governor of La Coruña.

The way in which the government handled the Torres Rojas affair paved the way to the ultimate coup attempt of 1981. It was announced that the transfer had been planned even before Torres Rojas had taken over the DAC. This was patently absurd and did nothing to mitigate the annoyance felt in military circles that he was dismissed while absent from the unit on holiday with his family in Las Palmas. The fact that the Minister of Defence, Agustín Rodríguez Sahagún, hid the real reasons for the dismissal led many politicians to think that the government merely raised the spectre of military threats, '*el ruido de sables*' (the rattle of sabres), in order to distract attention from difficulties in other spheres. Such a policy could only spread complacency in political circles and contempt in military ones. Such was the effect of the disgraceful treatment meted out to Miguel Angel Aguilar. One of Spain's most distinguished journalists and the best-informed expert on military questions, he was then editor of *Diario 16*. He had published the real reasons behind Torres Rojas's transfer and was greeted with government denials as a result of which he was prosecuted for insulting the army and eventually forced from the editorship of the paper.[13]

The government's understandable reflex of massaging the military ego after ETA outrages, combined with sheer relief that Basque terrorism had not had its desired effect of provoking a successful coup, fostered a head-in-the-sand mentality among the political élite. This was illustrated by the contrast between the relatively tough vigilance to which Rodolfo Martín Villa had been subjected by the opposition and the benevolence accorded his successor since April 1979, General Ibáñez Freire. The nervous anxiety not to offend the army was compounded by the trial of the Galaxia conspirators in early May 1980. Tejero and the newly promoted Major Sáenz de Ynestrillas were sentenced to only seven and six months detention respectively. Given the time that they had already served while awaiting trial, this meant their immediate release. A greater encouragement for plotters could hardly have been imagined.

A week later, the Joint Chiefs of Staff rejected a petition for the return to the army of the democratic officers who had led the Unión Militar Democrática. The Captain-General of Madrid, Guillermo Quintana Lacaci, by military standards a moderate, commented ominously that 'the Army should respect democracy, not introduce it into its ranks'.[14] The failure of the government to press for the revindication of the UMD was a further act of weakness which helped to convince the rightists within the armed forces that they could act with impunity. Thus, as soon as he was released from custody, Tejero entered into conspiracy with Milans del Bosch with whom he was brought into contact by Juan García Carrés. Throughout the middle of 1980 the ultra press worked ever more openly to foment military discontent with the democratic regime. Considerable success in this regard was achieved through a spring campaign against the government's plans to bring the Civil Guard under civilian jurisdiction. Together with García Carrés, Tejero played a major role gathering petitions in the course of which he widened his circle of extreme rightist acquaintances.[15] The main focus of this and other rightist efforts was to intensify military pressure for the departure of Suárez.

Discontent with the President was not confined to military circles. Terrorism, street crime, inflation and unemployment were all resented by a population which had expected perhaps more than was reasonable of the new democracy. The growing levels of electoral abstention throughout 1979 and into 1980 could be largely attributed to sheer weariness with an apparently endless round of electoral consultations. However, they also reflected a creeping feeling, born in part of Suárez's silences, that real decisions were taken elsewhere. It became fashionable in 1980 to talk of *desencanto* and to undervalue the very real achievements of Adolfo Suárez. Not only had he steered the country through the immediate formal and legal transition to democracy, but since 1977 his governments had also worked to create the institutional framework of a democratic Spain. Unfortunately, the work of constitutional committees was not the sort of thing to excite intense popular enthusiasm. By 1980, encouraged by the ultra press and scurrilously sensationalist magazines like *Interviú*, some politically unsophisticated sections of the Spanish population began to feel that things had got worse since Franco's time. Numerous commentators pointed out that little had changed, with many Francoists still in power thanks to their conversion to UCD. Suárez's closest collaborators, first Rodolfo Martín Villa and later Fernando Abril

Martorell, despite their great political acumen, seemed to the public to be grey men. Even the Prime Minister's own charm and charisma could be used only selectively, above all on television and in private. That was partly the consequence of his acute dental problems which rendered talking extremely painful. None the less, his undoubted talents and skills seemed to have found adjustment to parliamentary life rather difficult. Moreover, the economic and political difficulties that he was facing were not susceptible to his special brand of behind-the-scenes negotiations.

The pressure on Suárez did not come only from the right. He was increasingly the target of concentrated attacks by the PSOE. After resolving his party's inner crisis, Felipe González set about defeating UCD which effectively meant trying to unsaddle Suárez himself. The PSOE's efforts took two forms. The more public was the unrelenting criticism of Suárez's inactivity and isolation together with attacks on his immediate circle of collaborators. In particular, virulent attacks were directed against Abril Martorell, whose economic policies were described by Felipe González as comparable to the efforts of a gypsy trying to teach a donkey not to eat.[16] More privately, Socialist attempts to undermine Suárez consisted of continuing negotiations with the social democrat wing of UCD. This was facilitated by the fact that UCD was a party held together fundamentally by the enjoyment of power. It had capitalized on the popular hunger for change in Spain while offering guarantees of stability. However, many of its leaders barely tolerated the social democrat reformism of Fernández Ordóñez or even of Suárez himself. If they had restrained their social conservatism until now, it was to ensure their own political survival. They were inhibited at first by fears that, if they jumped overboard, Suárez's ship might still right itself and sail off to greater things leaving them to paddle to oblivion. In 1980 the tide was beginning to turn against Suárez sufficiently to embolden some of his erstwhile supporters to reveal their incipient hostility.

The four main groups within UCD – the Christian Democrats, the ex-Movimiento bureaucrats associated with Rodolfo Martín Villa, the social democrats and the Liberals under Joaquín Garrigues Walker – disagreed on a range of social, economic and religious issues. Nevertheless, it became clear in 1980 that they shared a growing resentment of Suárez's accumulation of power and especially of his control of the party's electoral machine. Signs of a deterioration in his popularity also provoked speculation as to whether they might not survive better without him. There was a feeling that Suárez revealed his Francoist origins by behaving as head of state rather than merely head of government. The President had to take some responsibility for this state of affairs because of his readiness to surround himself with a close inner circle of ex-*Azules* to the exclusion of the other fractions in the party. Moreover, he had certainly failed to hold the party together during the daily vicissitudes of parliamentary life simply by his failure to appear on a daily basis in the Cortes.[17] Garrigues took the lead in pushing for a more collective leadership of UCD. Fernández Ordóñez was reconsidering his future. However, by far the most disturbing rumblings of rebellion came from the Christian Democrats who constituted the most coherent component group within the party. The ambition to turn the UCD into a more openly conservative and confessional party had deep historic roots. Throughout 1980 it was boosted by the growing impact in Spain of the newly elected Pontiff, Carol Woytijla, whose attitudes were reinforcing the more reactionary sectors of the hierarchy. The immediate consequence of that was increasingly vocal criticism by the Christian Democrats of UCD's projected divorce reform.[18]

Internal divisions and the impression of incapacity and inactivity contributed to a series of damaging electoral reverses for UCD in Andalusia, the Basque Country, Catalonia and Galicia. These setbacks went far beyond the poor showing that might have been expected of a centralist party in government in such consultations. In the case of the Andalusian autonomy referendum, held on 28 February, the government could hardly have handled things worse. In mid-January, Suárez had decided to slow down the autonomy process outside Catalonia and the Basque Country. He thereby provoked the resignation of his Minister of Culture, Manuel Clavero Arévalo, the one-time Minister for the Regions. Suárez had then set off waves of outrage and ridicule by appointing as Clavero's successor the ex-head of the Francoist censorship machine and 'official' biographer of the dictator, Ricardo de la Cierva.[19] Since Andalusia was already in the 'fast lane' of the autonomy process, via article 151 of the Constitution, UCD attempted to sabotage its progress by campaigning for abstention in the referendum. This astonishing stance led to Clavero and several other disillusioned UCD deputies from Andalusia resigning from the party to campaign for a Yes-vote. To encourage abstention, the government invented a virtually incomprehensible question: 'Do you give your agreement to the ratification of the initiative contemplated in article 151 of the Constitution with regard to its being carried out according to the procedure established by the said article?'

Despite the bizarre efforts of the government, 54 per cent of the four-and-a-half-million-strong Andalusian electorate voted Yes. They were not so much answering the referendum question itself but generally affirming their support for the autonomy statute. In a sense, the government was victorious because article 151 required that every one of the Andalusian provinces should register a majority of Yes-votes. Since one province, Almeria with only 42 per cent affirmative votes, did not reach the required level, Andalusian autonomy was redirected to the 'slow lane' of article 143 of the Constitution. This meant that an autonomy statute would have to be elaborated by an assembly of all the Andalusian Cortes deputies, senators and representatives of the eight provincial councils (*diputaciones*). The victory for UCD was a thoroughly tainted one. By putting party interest ahead of Andalusian sentiment, Suárez ensured that the party lost massive reserves of local support. The moral victory of the Andalusian left, the PSOE and the Partido Socialista de Andalucía, provoked bitter recrimination within UCD. For the first time, the myth of Suárez's infallibility was broken and he was subject to severe criticism by both Rodolfo Martín Villa and Landelino Lavilla.[20]

While UCD was still reeling from the Andalusian blow, elections to the Basque parliament were held on 9 March 1980. Since the Basque autonomy referendum of 25 October 1979, violence had continued to be the order of the day. ETA-M maintained a steady rhythm of killings which was stepped up prior to the elections. Although ETA-PM accepted the Guernica Statute of Autonomy and committed no assassinations, on 11 November 1979, one of its *comandos* had kidnapped the UCD deputy Javier Rupérez. Eventually released unharmed, Rupérez had been seized as part of a campaign fronted by Euskadiko Eskerra against the continued use of torture against ETA detainees and in favour of the release of prisoners.[21] That episode aside, Euskadiko Eskerra continued to move towards integration into conventional Basque politics. ETA-Militar, backed by Herri Batasuna, still worked for the outright rejection of Spain by Euskadi. The justification for its assassinations was the increasing scale of violence committed by the police and the *incontrolados*. Protests against the use of torture abounded. Murders were being committed in both Spain and the South of France by the ultra-rightist terror squads, now killing under the name Batallón Vasco-Español.[22] In response to violence in the new year, on 1 February 1980, the government named the liberal General José Sáenz de Santamaría as its delegate in Euskadi with full powers to control and co-ordinate the fight against terrorism. With him went the Spanish equivalent of the SAS, the GOE or the Grupos de Operaciones Especiales of the police and the Unidades Antiterroristas Rurales of the Civil Guard. It was all grist to Herri Batasuna's mill and the reinforcement of repression helped overcome an internal crisis within the *abertzale* party.

The elections held in the Basque provinces on 9 March were even more disappointing to Suárez than the Andalusian referendum. The Partido Nacionalista Vasco won with twenty-five of the sixty seats and 38 per cent of the vote. Ominously, Herri Batasuna came second with eleven seats and 16 per cent of the vote. Any satisfaction that Suárez might have derived from seeing the PSOE come third with only nine seats and 14 per cent was swamped by the humiliation of UCD. The Prime Minister's party was beaten into joint fourth place with Euskadiko Eskerra, gaining only six seats and losing 55,000 votes by comparison with the 1979 general elections. Suárez had broken out of his lethargy sufficiently to visit Euskadi and brave the placards and chants of '*Suárez kampora*' ('Go home!'). His intervention had been to no avail and the internal crisis within UCD was worse than ever.[23] Less than two weeks later, on 20 March, a third body blow was delivered in the form of the results of elections to the Catalan parliament. UCD trailed home fourth with only eighteen out of the 135 seats behind the twenty-five of the Communist PSUC, the thirty-three of the Socialist PSC and the forty-three of the victorious Convergència i Unió. It was little consolation that the PSOE/PSC had confidently hoped to win and yet had lost 277,000 votes in comparison with 1979. UCD had lost 286,000 votes. Nor was it great compensation for Suárez to be told by Tarradellas that a victory for Jordi Pujol's conservative Convergència was effectively a triumph for UCD since they were bound to vote together in parliament. No matter how things were viewed, Suárez now faced a gigantic credibility crisis. There were rumours that he would invite the PSOE to join a coalition but the Socialists rejected the idea before it got off the ground. They were, in any case, toying with the idea of subjecting Suárez to a motion of censure in the Cortes.[24]

UCD was in dramatic trouble. One poll showed that slightly more than half of those who had voted for the party in the March 1979 general elections had decided not to do so again. Fewer than 25 per cent of those polled expressed approval of Suárez's record in government. The key to this decline was the popular feeling of *desgobierno*, of not being governed at all. A minor cut in inflation had been achieved by monetarist policies but at the price of substantial increases in unemployment. During the winter of 1979–80, energy restrictions had seen the heating systems dramatically turned down in homes, offices and factories, the consequence of which was a major upsurge of unpopularity for the government. In the meanwhile, the traditional structural weaknesses of the economy were being left untouched. This led to an intensification in friction between the Vice-President with overall responsibility for the economy, Abril Martorell, and the social democrat Ministers of Commerce, Juan Antonio García Díez, and of Industry, Carlos Bustelo. Suárez was impatient with the skirmishes between his ministers, particularly those to do with the economy. It was not an area which engaged his interest.

He was, in any case, overwhelmed by the ongoing and interrelated problems of ETA terrorism, the military attitude to politics and the increasingly chaotic progress of the autonomy process. In part, Suárez seemed to be trying to defuse the situation by treating ETA as if it were no more than a minor irritant and by ignoring the fact that the extreme right was virtually on a military footing. To most observers, however, it appeared as if he were simply doing nothing. There was a widespread feeling that the reins of government really were in the hands of Suárez's Vice-President and long-standing friend, Fernando Abril Martorell. It was frequently remarked that Suárez was behaving as if he were Head of State and Abril Martorell the President of the Council of Ministers. This was an understandable criticism since months passed between the Prime Minister's parliamentary appearances and press conferences. His absences even from cabinet meetings were increasingly frequent. Suárez was becoming the hermit of the Moncloa Palace, reluctant to face parliament and isolated even from his own party. Emilio Romero, the scabrous right-wing journalist, commented that Suárez's style of politics was more befitting to the head of a secret parallel state unanswerable to the institutions of democracy.[25]

To some extent, the Prime Minister was cut off from the bulk of the political élite by a lack of confidence deriving from his own exiguous educational achievements. Many of them were ex-university professors, legal experts or men who had come top in their *oposiciones*, the competitive entry examinations for the Spanish civil service. Accordingly, he was said to feel panic at the prospect of facing parliament or the cabinet, in contrast to his consummately assured appearances in the controlled environment of television.[26] He thus remained in his office, cocooned by muzak and screened from the real political world by an inner circle of advisers known as the 'plumbers' (*fontaneros*). The Watergate-inspired nickname derived from a belief that they constituted a small espionage service working for Suárez. They included his brother-in-law and personal private secretary, Aurelio Delgado; his chief Cabinet Secretary, Alberto Aza; the economist, Alberto Recarte, who was alleged to keep files on the UCD leadership; and the one-time Secretary of State for Information and later Governor-General of Catalonia, Josep Melià. The *fontaneros* almost certainly caused Suárez more problems than they solved. Their biased and sycophantic advice intensified his feelings of besieged solitude. They formed a barrier around him which cut him off from the rest of the party élite. Suárez's long-standing friend, Fernando Abril Martorell, was particularly alienated by their existence.[27]

More crucially, the *fontaneros* were the target of venomous resentment within the higher reaches of the UCD where conspiracy against the Prime Minister was coming out into the open. Representatives of the various factions happily recounted to the media their grudges and their versions of inner-party conflict without worrying about the impact on public opinion of such indiscretions. UCD deputies were beginning not to turn up for Cortes debates and some even began to vote against the government.[28] The scale of dissent became apparent during the six painful weeks in the spring of 1980 during which Suárez cobbled together a new cabinet. Laborious, and back-stabbing, negotiations, described by *Cambio 16* as a 'macabre dance of the vampires', were a rehearsal for the power struggle to come at the second UCD Congress scheduled for October. Announced on 2 May, the reshuffled cabinet was marked by the absence of Joaquín Garrigues's liberals and of the more senior of Francisco Fernández Ordóñez's social democrats. The Christian Democrats saw their position consolidated by the addition of José Luis Alvarez (Transport), José Antonio Ortega y Díaz Ambrona (Legislative Co-ordination) and Ignacio Bayon Marine (Industry). General Ibáñez Freire was replaced as Minister of the Interior by a close crony of Rodolfo Martín Villa, Juan José Rosón.[29]

The dissatisfaction of Garrigues and Fernández Ordóñez was ample proof of the inadequacy of the cabinet changes to deal with the crisis which had arisen out of the electoral defeats and the continuing problems of ETA and ultra-rightist violence. On 21 May, in an effort to capitalize on the general disillusion with Suárez, the PSOE tabled its motion of censure. Felipe González delivered a blistering but dignified attack on the failings of the UCD in government. The cabinet survived the motion in the subsequent debate held between 28 and 30 May only because of the abstentions of Alianza Popular and Convergència i Unió. In dramatic contrast to Suárez's inability to repair his tarnished image, Felipe González was able, in the first parliamentary debate televised in its entirety in Spain, to enhance his prestige with a performance of presidential quality. The Prime Minister did not choose to reply to the censure motion, but instead threw his Vice-President to the lions. In the course of the debate, Suárez was deeply wounded by Alfonso Guerra's statement that 'Suárez does not tolerate democracy and the democratic regime can no longer tolerate Suárez' ('*Ni Suárez soporta la democracia, ni la democracia soporta por más tiempo a Suárez*').[30] Demoralization was rife in the UCD ranks and criticism of Suárez spreading fast. One of the most prominent of his Christian Democrat critics, Landelino Lavilla, was President of the Cortes. The *fontaneros* were soon to be whispering that he had exercised his functions during the censure debate in such a way, that is to say with such impartiality, as to let the Socialists shine. Public statements by Lavilla in the early summer made it clear that he regarded himself as a viable substitute for Suárez.[31]

Suárez and his immediate circle believed that it would only be possible to mount an adequate counter-attack by getting rid of Abril Martorell and thereby renovating the image of the government. After Abril's rambling and inconsequential performance in the censure debate, it was easier for the *fontaneros* to insinuate to Suárez that his own survival depended on the departure of his friend. Moreover, with Abril constantly in the public eye, it was easy for them to blame him for everything that seemed to be going wrong. Equally, the fact that dealings between the government and the opposition were carried out by negotiation between Felipe González or Alfonso Guerra and Abril made it easy to generate Suárez's jealousy. However, given the level to which anti-Suárez intrigue was rising, the hope of saddling Abril with the responsibility for the government's failures was a vain one. The extent of dissent was revealed at a meeting of the UCD's permanent committee held at the Casa de la Pradera on the banks of the reservoir of Manzanares el Real, forty kilometres outside Madrid, from 7 to 9 July 1980. The 'barons', or leaders, of the various party factions demanded a greater share in the running of both UCD and the government. There followed a lengthy and acrimonious discussion of possible methods of replacing Suárez.

Apparently, Joaquín Garrigues, Francisco Fernández Ordóñez, Rodolfo Martín Villa and Fernando Alvarez de Miranda of the Christian Democrat wing had made a prior agreement to push the candidacy of Lavilla. In the event, when challenged directly by Abril and by Suárez's new right-hand man, the Minister of the Presidency, Rafael Arias Salgado, none of them had the courage to play Brutus. In part, the dissidents' failure of will derived from the fact that Lavilla was at best a compromise candidate. They were also swayed by arguments to the effect that the removal of Suárez could only favour the PSOE. Finally, they were given pause by the enormity of overthrowing the popularly elected President by exactly the same kind of back-room manoeuvre which was cited as his greatest fault.[32] None the less, the writing was on the wall and Suárez was obliged to make concessions to the demands for a more collective leadership or *dirección colegiada* as they termed it.

It was leaked to the press that Francisco Fernández Ordóñez's Partido Social Demócrata, which had been dissolved into UCD, would soon be reformed as an independent party. This in turn fuelled press speculation that such a group would be a *partido bisagra* or 'hinge' party between UCD and the PSOE, and might promote demands for a coalition.[33] That kind of threat could only hasten the process whereby 'barons' would soon be incorporated into the cabinet, although it also intensified the collapse of morale. The prevailing atmosphere was revealed by an incident in the corridors of the Cortes on 12 June 1980. Francisco Fernández Ordóñez complained to Suárez that he was being spied on and his financial affairs being investigated by the *fontanero* Alberto Recarte.[34]

In the meanwhile, another of Suárez's closest collaborators, the sleek Minister for Territorial Administration, José Pedro Pérez Llorca, was working hard to strengthen the government by trying to negotiate parliamentary agreements with the principal Catalan and Andalusian groups and even with the Partido Nacionalista Vasco. The idea was that, with their support previously agreed, the government could ask for a parliamentary vote of confidence in the autumn. In return, there would have to be representatives of Convergència i Unió brought into the cabinet. Such deals would not only bolster the UCD in the Cortes, but they would also smooth the path to a resolution of the increasingly tangled autonomy process. They appealed to Suárez because they would help diminish the growing parliamentary strength of the PSOE. However, if they provided a parliamentary respite, they did nothing to heal the gaping self-inflicted wounds within the party itself. Abril Martorell and the UCD's Secretary-General, Rafael Calvo Ortega, disagreed strongly with a policy of appeasing, and even becoming dependent on, the regional parties. They considered that it made more sense to try to maintain the democratic pact or consensus which had served the country so well during the constituent period. Abril Martorell in particular preferred to maintain his solid working relationship with the PSOE both for personal reasons and also because of a belief that major problems like terrorism, military subversion and regional devolution required the co-operation of the two great national parties. Above all, he feared that the growing bellicosity between UCD and the PSOE suited the purposes of military plotters.[35]

The situation was worsening inexorably for the Prime Minister. On 21 July, Abril Martorell had resigned, largely in the hope that Suárez would be obliged to reinforce his position. Abril was a parliamentary deputy for Valencia. He had been outraged by reports in *El País* that the Minister of Transport, Salvador Sánchez Terán, had made a secret deal with Morocco whereby, in return for an agreement on fishing limits, North African oranges would be permitted free transit through Spain to their markets in the EEC. Since such a deal would seriously damage the interests of Abril's most powerful Valencian constituents, rumours circulated that the entire operation had been set up to provoke Abril's resignation. After fierce cabinet clashes between Abril and Sánchez Terán, Suárez intervened with King Hassan of Morocco to find a solution. However, the relations between the President and his deputy were now irreparably soured. Suárez was resentful that Abril showed little gratitude for his intervention; while Abril was embittered that the affair had been allowed to blow up in the first place. After some weeks' vacillation, Abril's resignation was accepted.[36] The *fontaneros* were confident that the sacrifice of Abril Martorell would benefit Suárez. However, while it was true that his stint as economic affairs supremo had done little to halt the steady rise in unemployment, Abril had been the artificer of a degree of parliamentary co-operation with the PSOE. Without his loyal support, Suárez was ever more exposed to the intrigues of his enemies.

The critics of the President were briefly thrown into total disarray on 29 July 1980 by the sad death from leukaemia of the Liberal leader, Joaquín Garrigues Walker. A genuine liberal of political talent and personal charm, Garrigues was considered in some circles to be the John F. Kennedy of Spanish politics and the most plausible rival to replace Suárez. He had enjoyed the unreserved support of the powerful and influential Grupo 16 press network and, in his last interview in *Cambio 16*, he had expressed his conviction that Suárez was finished and knew it.[37] In late August, it was rumoured that José María de Areilza was trying to gain the support of Socialists, Communists and certain elements of UCD to put together a coalition government to replace Suárez. The notion was far-fetched since Felipe González had no more desire than had Suárez three years before to fall into the clutches of the Conde de Motrico. Nevertheless, the fact that it could be bruited about at all was an unmistakable indication of the collapse of confidence in the President and of the growing hostility of the press. More disturbing rumours suggested that the PSOE was prepared to enter a *'gobierno de gestión'* (caretaker coalition) under the presidency of a general, possibly Alvaro Lacalle Leloup. Suárez, who was in Lima at the time, told the Spanish journalists who had accompanied him to Peru, 'I know all about the PSOE's plans to make a soldier president. It is absolutely absurd' (*descabellado*).[38]

By the autumn of 1980, Suárez found himself isolated from his cabinet, his party and the press. The working agreement with the PSOE was in tatters. Felipe González declared that the Prime Minister no longer had a meaningful contribution to make (*su papel ha terminado*). Unemployment had risen to one and a half million. The government's policy on regional autonomies was at a stalemate. Ill-feeling in Andalusia remained intense after the referendum fiasco. The slowness of the transfer of powers to the newly elected Basque and Catalan regional governments was both an embarrassment and a provocation. In the Basque Country, the government's delegate, General Sáenz de Santamaría, complained that Madrid's dilatoriness was generating support for ETA. Indeed, at a time when public opinion in Euskadi was rallying around the Statute of Guernica and moving away from commitment to the Alternativa KAS, the government's apathy with regard to Euskadi bordered on criminal neglect.

The consequent resurgence in mid-1980 of both wings of ETA could hardly have been more alarming. As in the previous year, ETA-Político-Militar carried out an unsuccessful bombing campaign against tourist resorts to back its demands for the release of prisoners and for the acceleration of an autonomy referendum for Navarre. Despite its failure, the inconvenience, fear and resentment generated by this disruption of the holiday season contributed to the widespread feeling that the government was incompetent. However, ETA-PM's activities paled into insignificance by comparison with those of ETA-Militar. The organization's callous field commander, Miguel Angel Apalátegui ('Apala'), who had disppeared from France in October 1977 while awaiting extradition proceedings, had reappeared in Spain. He had formed a *comando* with Juan Lorenzo Santiago Lasa Michelena ('Txikierdi'), the alleged assassin of Generals Sánchez Ramos, Ortín Gil and Gómez Hortigüela. On 25 July, disguised as civil guards, 'Apala' and 'Txikierdi' had stolen 7000 kilos of plastic explosive (*goma 2*) from a poorly guarded storage dump at Soto de la Marina in the province of Santander.

A chill ran through Spain's political class since possession of such enormous quantities of explosive substantiated ETA-M's announced readiness to unleash total war against the Spanish State to secure the inclusion into Euskadi of the province of Navarre. ETA-M and Herri Batasuna shared an almost imperialist attitude to Navarre. HB meetings were often punctuated with the shout *Nafarroa Euskadi da* (Navarre is Euskadi). The results of the 1979 elections in Navarre showed that the vast majority of the province's population had no desire to be part of Euskadi. It was evidence of ETA-M's increasing contempt for democracy that the annexationist ambition quickly led to grenade attacks on Civil Guard posts in Navarre. On 22 August, an ETA-M *comando* attempted to murder José Javier Uranga, editor of the *Diario de Navarra*. Uranga's newspaper was committed to defending the view of the majority of Navarrese who were determined that Navarre should remain part of Spain and thus be independent of Euskadi.[39]

The ETA aspiration of annexing Navarre provoked apoplexy among senior army officers who regarded Navarre as an inalienable part of Spain as well as a cradle of right-wing patriotic values. Navarre had provided Franco with the *Requetés*, the ferocious Carlist militia which had accompanied his armies during the Civil War, and had enjoyed an especially privileged position under his regime. Military discontent was, in any case, boiling up again during the summer of 1980. The cause of their anger was a draft military amnesty law put before the Cortes in June. The project aimed at facilitating the reintegration into the ranks of those officers who had fought with the Republic during the Civil War and of the members of the Unión Militar Democrática. Anger in army quarters was reported to be even more intense than it had been after the legalization of the PCE. To make matters worse, military dissidence had been kept at flash point throughout the spring and summer of 1980 by a series of assassination attempts on senior generals carried out by both ETA-Militar and GRAPO.[40]

Suárez had his back to the wall but he rallied one last time. On 9 September he reshuffled his cabinet to create the so-called 'government of the barons'. He created a new category of super-ministers, with the title of Minister of State. The distribution of the new titles clinched the temporary loyalty of some of the more important 'barons'. However, this purchase of breathing space inadvertently complicated the situation within the UCD. In particular, the appointment of Francisco Fernández Ordóñez as Minister of Justice was taken as a challenge by the Christian Democrats. Formally in charge of Church–State relations, the social democrat leader was committed to divorce reform and was thus fated to clash with the confessional right. In fact, Suárez had little choice but to promote Fernández Ordóñez if he was to neutralize the overtures being made to him by the PSOE. Given his record of commitment to fiscal reform, Fernández Ordóñez was so deeply resented in some powerful circles that Suárez was unable to give him the Ministry of the Economy, which went to another social democrat, Juan Antonio García Díez. Landelino Lavilla suffered the President's revenge for his role as possible substitute at the Manzanares el Real meeting. He was excluded from the division of the ministerial spoils. However, he remained as President of the Cortes, a position from which he was able to organize the 'críticos' as the internal UCD opponents of Suárez were known.[41]

The 'government of the barons' was well received by the press. To remedy the government's most glaring weakness, Rodolfo Martín Villa was made Minister for Territorial Administration. He was to put new energy into the autonomy process, although his previous stint as Minister of the Interior and his leadership of the UCD's ex-Francoist machine-men, the *Azules*, did not immediately endear him to the Basques. In general, the cabinet of barons was almost certainly the most talented that Suárez had ever assembled. However, it merely prolonged rather than resolved the crisis. A central problem derived from the absence of Abril Martorell, the President's erstwhile parliamentary shield. Suárez tried to replace him as his right-hand man by appointing Pío Cabanillas to be Attaché to the President (*Ministro de Estado Adjunto al Presidente*). Unfortunately, the possible benefit of Cabanillas's devious negotiating skills was minimized because he clashed with Suárez's other main supporter in the cabinet, Rafael Arias Salgado, the Minister of the Presidency. As one of Spain's shrewdest political commentators, José Oneto, put it, 'without Abril as fireman, the fire soon reached the palace'.[42]

By dint of prior agreements with both Catalans and Andalusians, Suárez managed to survive a parliamentary vote of confidence on 18 September, although he was given a rough ride in the Cortes. Blas Piñar remarked that the new cabinet was a fashion parade in which the same old models wore the same old clothes. In similar vein, Fraga said that the President's speech was 'like a John Travolta movie: always the same plot, always the same actor and always made for children' (*'el discurso del presidente es como una película de Travolta: siempre la misma comedia; siempre el mismo personaje y siempre para chicos'*). Much more significantly, the Socialists enhanced their standing with a reasoned critique of the government's inability to resolve economic and social problems.[43] However, the contrast with Suárez's recent performances was noticeable.

The President seemed to have recovered his old verve, meeting the UCD *críticos*, giving press conferences and even speaking at meetings in the provinces. A series of meetings with Felipe González, on 1 October, with Santiago Carrillo, on 6 October, and with the Basque *Lendakari* Carlos Garaicoetxea, on 12 October, stimulated speculation that a new Moncloa Pact was in the offing. The meeting with Garaicoetxea was especially promising and reflected the injection of energy that Martín Villa had brought to the autonomy process. ETA-M, alarmed by the possibility that the talks with the *Lendakari* might foster better relations between Euskadi and Madrid, murdered eight people in the course of Garaicoetxea's visit. However, the overall balance of the talks was positive. Although the Basque demand for an acceleration in the creation of an autonomous Basque police force remained unsatisfied, agreements were reached over state funding for Euskera-speaking schools, or *Ikastolas*, for aid to the Basque steel industry and for the inauguration of a Basque television channel.[44] Unfortunately, Suárez was unable to capitalize on this promising beginning. His apparent recovery had come too late.

The situation soon began to worsen inexorably. Conspiracy was rife in the army at various levels. A number of colonels were discussing the possibility of emulating the recent coup in Turkey and establishing a junta to smash ETA. Senior generals were examining ways of putting an end to what they saw as an intolerable political situation. Even before the Turkish events, the ultra magazine *Heraldo Español* had published on its cover a picture of a white horse under the title *Se busca un general* (general wanted). On the inside pages, there was open speculation about the most suitable military candidates to take over the government. On 17 October, twenty-six of the most prominent ultras in Spain met in Madrid to discuss finance and civilian support for a projected coup. The ultra press was muttering darkly about a so-called '*Operación De Gaulle*'. This was almost certainly an obscure reference to the activities of General Alfonso Armada. Since the beginning of 1980, Armada had been Military Governor of Lérida. He was trying to drum up support for a non-violent substitution of UCD by a government of national salvation under his own presidency. On 22 October, at a lunch in the home of the Socialist *Alcalde* of Lérida, Antonio Ciurana, Armada went so far as to approach Enrique Múgica of the PSOE and Joan Raventós of the PSC. Felipe González was immediately informed and passed on the information to Suárez. On 17 November, Armada visited the Captain-General of the Valencia Military Region, Jaime Milans del Bosch, and spoke to him in similar terms, insinuating that he was acting under the discreet orders of the King. Milans's existing dissatisfaction with the political situation could only be fired by these hints of royal approbation. The scene was repeated during a subsequent visit to Valencia on 10 January 1981. In his memoirs, however, Armada attempted to diminish the importance of these meetings. He even went so far as to claim that the main topic of conversation at the lunch in Lérida had been the need to encourage mule-breeding for army mountain units.[45]

In addition to rumblings of military conspiracy, Suárez also had to cope with the fact that the PSOE remained hostile despite the cabinet reshuffle. As Abril had foreseen, the deal with the regionalist groups had embittered the opposition. Alfonso Guerra was especially enraged by the UCD's arrangement with Alejandro Rojas Marcos's Partido Socialista de Andalucía to speed up autonomy for the south. It was interpreted as a manoeuvre against the PSOE in its own stronghold. Unconvinced that the new cabinet would be able to produce fresh measures against terrorism or carry out its austerity programme, Felipe González was talking about the possibility of another motion of censure. Furthermore, the cabinet's fragile image of unity was belied by the stream of criticism of Suárez emanating from the ranks of the excluded Christian Democrats.[46] Despite Suárez's apparent readiness to turn over a new leaf, his position deteriorated inexorably. He had even broken up the *fontaneros* by giving them jobs elsewhere, but he soon drifted back into apparent apathy and silent isolation.

Suárez's bankruptcy was graphically exposed on 23 October 1980. On that day, forty-eight children and three adults were killed in an accidental propane gas explosion at the village school of Ortuella in Vizcaya. At the same time, the ETA-M wave of killings culminated in the assassination of three Basque UCD members. The murders were carried out by an ETA-M offshoot known as the *comandos autónomos*. In the midst of these horrors, Suárez displayed an icy indifference. He remained coldly in the Moncloa Palace and refrained from making any parliamentary statement about either the disaster or the terrorist attacks. He neither visited the stricken village nor attended the funerals of his party colleagues. He was reported to have said that, if he went to one funeral, he would have to go to them all. In stark contrast, Queen Sofía flew immediately to Bilbao to be with the families of the victims of Ortuella. Suárez's seeming callousness was loudly condemned by the press and the three principal opposition parties.[47]

At a time when opinion in the Basque Country was finally moving against ETA, Suárez seemed to be displaying public contempt for the Basques. It was not without significance that one of the murdered UCD members was Jaime Arrese Arizmendiarreta, who had narrowly failed to gain a parliamentary seat for Guipúzcoa in the 1979 general elections. Arrese was about to be called upon to be the replacement member of parliament for Marcelino Oreja Aguirre, the ex-Minister of Foreign Affairs. Oreja was obliged to resign his Cortes seat because he had just been appointed 'Governor-General' for the Basque Country. Since both article 154 of the Spanish Constitution and article 23 of the Statute of Guernica provided for the government's representative in the Euskadi to be called a 'Delegate', Oreja's title seemed to reflect either calculated insult or else culpable negligence.[48] In fact, Oreja was to work hard, with Martín Villa, to restore Basque faith in Madrid.

However, within a week of Arrese's murder the media's talk of 'paralysis' and 'putrefaction' seemed to be justified by ten days of mindless violence in the Basque Country. The year to the end of October 1980 had seen 114 deaths as a result of terrorism, an average of one victim every three days, including fifty-seven civilians and twenty-seven civil guards, eleven army officers and nine policemen. Now, on 31 October, ETA-PM murdered Juan de Dios Doval Mateos, a San Sebastián law professor who was next on the UCD candidate list for Guipúzcoa and thus the replacement for Arrese Arizmendiarreta. Then, on 3 November, an ETA-M *comando* machine-gunned a bar in Zarauz, killing four civil guards and a PNV member and wounding six other customers. To the outrage of the Basque UCD, Suárez chose not to attend the funeral of Professor Doval. The demoralization of the centre party there had reached its lowest ebb. Under the weight of ETA threats to themselves and their families, several of its senior figures were leaving the area and going to live elsewhere in Spain. The sense that the government was not governing had reached its highest point.

Yet, paradoxically, the violence of the autumn of 1980 was finally to provoke a reaction in the Basque Country itself. On 9 November, a silent all-party demonstration of 30,000 marched through San Sebastián, local PSOE, UCD and PNV leaders linking arms. Herri Batasuna supporters erected a road block, chanted '*PNV traidor*' ('PNV traitor') and '*Gora ETA-Militarra*' ('Long live ETA-Militar') and stoned the procession. The marchers, however, turned upon them and finished the demonstration successfully. It was an important turning point. Increasing numbers of businessmen were also beginning to refuse to pay the 'revolutionary tax' demanded by ETA.[49] If once upon a time, in the belief that Madrid could not supply justice, the Basque population had looked to ETA to do so, that time had gone. Within a week, while ETA-M continued to kill policemen, a Basque Peace Front (*Frente por la Paz*) was set up by the PSOE, the PNV, Euskadiko Eskerra, the PCE-EPK or Basque Communist Party, UCD and the Carlists. They were brought together by an awareness that ETA's assault on Spain's democratic regime had to be countered before it was too late. However, it was only a tentative beginning. Euskadiko Eskerra could not fully reconcile itself to collaboration with 'Spanish' parties like the PSOE and UCD for fear of losing support to Herri Batasuna. The PNV was also to encounter some difficulties in selling the idea to its militants and, in mysterious circumstances, eventually pulled out of the *Frente.* In any case, as Mario Onaindía, the Euskadiko Eskerra leader, suggested, it was difficult to avoid the suspicion that the PNV was less than totally hostile to ETA terrorism. Indeed, the PNV always side-stepped a full condemnation of the violence which ultimately facilitated the negotiation of more concessions from Madrid.[50]

The sense of urgency was provided by fears within the political élite that the army was about to lose its patience. On 5 November, at a private party in a military housing complex, fifty officers had apparently discussed a report on the Turkish military coup of two months earlier. The report had been composed by the Spanish military attaché in Ankara, Colonel Federico Quintero Morente, the US-trained counter-insurgency and intelligence expert who, it will be recalled, had exposed the Galaxia plot. His report, which discussed the effects of terrorism and economic stagnation on unstable Mediterranean democracies, was leaked to the press on 6 November. The elaboration of such a report would have been a routine duty for a military attaché although it was later alleged that the CIA station in Turkey had had a hand in it. The press and many politicians began to talk of the 'Turkish temptation' and the 'Ankara syndrome'. Coming in the wake of the rumours about General Armada's *Operación De Gaulle*, both Manuel Fraga and Felipe González were sufficiently worried to speak of their readiness to join in a caretaker coalition government (*gobierno de gestión*) in circumstances of extreme gravity. It is likely that they saw such an initiative as a lesser evil, a sacrifice that might have to be made to forestall a full scale *golpe a la turca.*[51]

In the light of the Basque situation, it was hardly surprising that political nerves should be on edge. The idea of a strong all-party *gobierno de gestión* to replace Suárez had been in the air since the summer of 1980.

In mid-December, the Prime Minister told Fernando Alvarez de Miranda of his distress at the talk of coalitions under the leadership of General Armada. Rumours about the plans of Armada were matched by open speculation about a broad coalition under Alfonso Osorio, who had been hostile to Suárez since the legalization of the Communist Party and his own subsequent exclusion from the cabinet after the June 1977 elections. Osorio was incidentally a friend of Armada. Osorio had apparently discussed the idea of a strong all-party government with important members of the PSOE including Enrique Múgica and Javier Solana, with his own Christian Democrat following within UCD and even with Jaime Ballesteros of the PCE. These exploratory talks had countenanced the possibility that the coalition might be better led by a general than by Osorio. In the light of alarming rumours about a violent coup of the colonels, and faced with the patent incapacity of the UCD government to resolve the problems of ETA and unemployment, such a middle way began to seem almost an attractive option.[52]

Against the background of army sedition and turmoil in Euskadi, the apparent unconcern of the government was scandalous. Suárez was in fact dramatically preoccupied by the situation inside UCD. The party was a cauldron of conspiracy. Infuriated by Fernández Ordóñez's divorce reform plans, the Christian Democrat wing went on to the attack. The post of UCD *portavoz parlamentario* (parliamentary spokesman and effectively president of the parliamentary party and government chief whip) needed filling after the resignation of the previous incumbent, Antonio Jiménez Blanco. Suárez's party apparatus had a candidate, Santiago Rodríguez Miranda, ready. The *críticos* went into action and, to assert their power and teach the party leadership a lesson, they mobilized to elect instead the brilliantly vituperative Christian Democrat and one-time follower of Gil Robles, Miguel Herrero Rodríguez de Miñón. He campaigned on the need for the democratization of the party. Herrero compared Suárez's mode of leadership of both the country and the UCD as *Movimientista*, that is to say redolent of Franco and the Falange. He gained the post by 103 votes to 45 in a vote which had curiously seen Martín Villa allow his followers a free choice. This was interpreted as clear evidence that he had abandoned the Suárez cause.[53]

A manifesto signed by 200 UCD *críticos* made public the extent of the Christian Democrat assault on Suárez. However, increasingly frequent contacts between the *críticos* and Fraga's Alianza Popular and reports of substantial bank support suggested that democratization of UCD was not precisely the main object of the operation. The idea behind the so-called *Operación Quirinale* was to push UCD towards emulation of the Italian Democrazia Cristiana, a rightwards swing opposed by Suárez. That the President himself was the target could no longer be hidden after the cudgels were taken up by Landelino Lavilla. On 12 January 1981, he made a devastating and widely publicized declaration to a Madrid newspaper. He not only accused Suárez of accumulating arbitrary power, but, what was worse, not using it and thereby making UCD into 'the pillar of salt' of Spanish politics. It was starkly obvious that the forthcoming Second Congress of UCD, scheduled to be held in Mallorca on 29 January, would see the culmination of the intrigue against the President begun at Manzanares el Real six months earlier.[54]

Under the circumstances, it was hardly surprising that Suárez began to consider resignation. Physically and psychologically exhausted after leading Spain through the transition, he had little stomach for a fight with his erstwhile colleagues. His immediate entourage, the remaining *fontaneros* and the ever-faithful Abril Martorell, had worked hard and were confident that Suárez would be able to carry the Congress with him. Nevertheless, over the weekend of 24–25 January 1981, Suárez was reaching the momentous decision to resign. It appears that seventeen senior generals had met on 23 January to discuss the need for a military intervention in politics. The King, who was away from Madrid on a hunting trip, made a rapid return to the capital.[55] In an atmosphere of immense tension, Suárez had come to the conclusion that victory in the Congress would at best gain him five or six months' respite. Conflict would soon break out again over divorce reform and the question of incorporating Catholic universities into the state system. By then, one of the main instruments of party discipline – the letters of resignation signed by all UCD parliamentary deputies – would be useless since the Cortes would have gone beyond the point after which deputies could still be substituted. Thereafter, with the party crumbling, there would be the prospect of coalition government, an outcome that Suárez could not countenance. In any case, opinion polls suggested that only 26 per cent of the population supported him as against 43 per cent for Felipe González. Having decided that there could be no real unity in UCD under his leadership, he felt that there was no alternative to resignation and planned to make an announcement at the Party Congress. As he told his closest collaborators in the UCD leadership, he had no more rabbits to pull out of his top-hat.[56]

In the event, this plan was thwarted by an air controllers' strike which forced the postponement of the Congress. Accordingly, after informing the cabinet, the party leadership and the King, Suárez announced his departure in a television broadcast on 29 January. The ultra-right was jubilant, its haunts buzzing with rumours that Suárez had been forced to resign by the King and the generals together. The headline in *El Alcázar* on the day following the announcement was 'Suárez is right: "My departure is more beneficial for Spain than my continued presence in the Government". Pity he didn't realize earlier!' There is little published evidence to prove that the King's reaction was other than one of surprise although some commentators persisted in the belief that there had been a *guiño real* or 'royal wink'. That the King was aware of the anti-democratic sentiment in the army cannot be doubted. He was always immensely sensitive to military feelings and General Armada, among others, made a point of keeping him informed on the atmosphere in the officers' messes.

The King's new year message to the armed forces, delivered on 5 January, had indicated his preoccupation. He warned the officer corps not to get involved 'in political activities distinct from that elevated endeavour which interests us all, the grand endeavour of the greatness of Spain and the permanent vigilance of its security'. Suárez visited the royal family during their Christmas holiday in the ski resort of Baqueira Beret in the province of Lérida. There was inevitable speculation that Juan Carlos and the Prime Minister discussed the possibility of a military coup and ways of diverting it. It was also remarked later that, on his return from Baqueira Beret, Suárez seemed to have lost his will to fight. Moreover, rumours were fed by a line in the resignation speech where Suárez said 'I do not want the democratic regime of co-existence to be once more a parenthesis on the history of Spain.' Although Suárez was later to deny that there had been military pressure, the remark was an unmistakable reference to the army's rising against the Second Republic in 1936.[57]

In the light of what was to happen less than a month after his resignation, it is difficult not to see Suárez's departure as, in some way, a response to military pressure. However, his courageous behaviour during the military seizure of the Cortes on 23 February 1981 when he confronted the armed civil guards who had burst into the chamber eliminates any suggestion that he had thrown in the towel out of cowardice. He was profoundly exhausted and had done all that he could. The attrition of ETA terrorism, army subversion, the constant intrigue of his rivals in UCD, the inability of his governments to come up with solutions to the economic problems of Spain had all contributed to rubbing the shine off Suárez's once glossy image. That was one of the prices to be paid for power in the democratic system. He had enjoyed massive popular support in 1977 and 1979 when his contribution to the nation was perceived as positive. After months of isolation in the Moncloa and political failures on several fronts, he had lost it. The deterioration of Suárez's image, his secretiveness, his unease in the Cortes and his retreat behind a wall of *fontaneros* should not, however, obscure the enormous contribution that he had made to Spanish politics.

He had come to the Moncloa Palace at a time when Spain was in a ferment of strikes and demonstrations. Fatal conflict between the regime and the opposition seemed to many to be inevitable. Suárez had no democratic legitimacy and was no more than the nominee of the King. There had been prophets of doom ready then to predict that he would be lucky to last more than a few weeks. Four and a half years later, he left the presidential palace with terrorism, subversion and popular disenchantment the order of the day. None the less, his very departure in response to the wishes of his own party and to hostile opinion polls was a reflection of the enormous changes that Spain had undergone during his period in office. In 1976 and 1977, he had exchanged the sterile obstructionism of the Francoist élite for an open and positive flexibility. Between 1977 and 1980, even despite his tendency to prefer secret negotiations to parliamentary business, and at the cost of many regrettable delays, remarkable progress was made towards the creation of a constitutional democracy, the nurturing of parliamentary co-existence and the concession of regional autonomy. Whatever Suárez's shortcomings, neither the lunacy of Tejero nor that of ETA should be allowed to deprive him of his place in the history of Spanish democracy.

7
Out of the ashes: the consolidation of democracy 1981–2

The immediate reaction of the press and the political élite to the departure of Suárez was one of surprise. After long months of growing hostility to the President, it was difficult to believe that he had actually gone. There were a few complacent comments that for him to be replaced at all was evidence of the strength of Spanish democracy. Neither politicians nor journalists realized how severely that strength was soon to be tested. It was widely whispered in Madrid that Suárez had had advance notice of a forthcoming military action against him. At the very least, he was aware that General Armada was meeting politicians with a view to launching what came to be known as his *golpe blando* (soft coup). Only two days after Suárez's resignation, the right-wing columnist Emilio Romero, a close friend of García Carrés, published an article in *ABC* which discussed the *'solución Armada'* (a pun on armed solution and Armada solution). Suárez cannot have been ignorant of the fact that some colonels were said to be preparing a more brutal Turkish-style coup. The long-smouldering army hostility reached new intensity, especially in units of the DAC, after news that Suárez had been trying to calm the Basque Country with pardons for some ETA prisoners. On 24 January, *El Alcázar* had published sinister ruminations to the effect that another Galaxia-style plot was on the horizon.[1] Whatever the case, Suárez had every reason to fear something of the sort. If he hoped to forestall it by disappearing from the scene, he was to be disappointed. Indeed, his resignation was to set off a train of political disintegration which merely consolidated the views of many officers that their intervention was a patriotic duty.

The internal divisions of UCD had gone too far to be resolved by

Suárez's departure. Resentment of the President had become one of the few issues which united many groups in the party. His replacement by Leopoldo Calvo Sotelo, the Vice-President of the Cabinet, could hardly be seen as a new dawn. Calvo Sotelo owed his selection to the fact that, although not actively supported by any particular faction, he was the most widely tolerated candidate. The main barons had effectively neutralized one another. The conservative Landelino Lavilla was considered by Francisco Fernández Ordóñez and the social democrats to be unacceptably close to the Church and to the banks. In turn, Fernández Ordóñez was seen as too dangerously committed to divorce and tax reform to be admitted as party leader by the Christian Democrats. Rodolfo Martín Villa's past as a Falangist and as a tough Minister of the Interior was thought to render him unacceptable to public opinion. The taciturn Calvo Sotelo, however, had both good banking contacts and membership of the ACNP to endear him to the Church. Moreover, having masterminded the selection of candidates for the 1977 elections, he was well-known within UCD and seemed to have no active enemies. He was thus the best compromise candidate. The *críticos*, however, still flying the flag of inner-party democracy, were enraged by the manner of Calvo Sotelo's selection. He was chosen not by the entire parliamentary group but by a caucus of senior UCD leaders.[2] This ensured that he began his rule with a handicap. However, no matter what the circumstances of his elevation he would have been unlikely to find a united party. The departure of Suárez had not diminished the conflicts within UCD.

The new Prime Minister was to find his parliamentary position dramatically undermined by an awareness of the continual plotting of the *críticos*. Moreover, even before he could formally take over, the military situation he faced was extraordinarily hostile. Army readiness for a political intervention could hardly have been higher. Much to the chagrin of many senior officers, Juan Carlos and Queen Sofía made an official visit to the Basque Country from 3 to 5 February 1981. Some nationalists welcomed the notion of a direct dialogue between the crown and the Basque institutions. It recalled for them the historic situation before Basque privileges were lost. That point was implicit in the ostentatious marginalization from the ceremonies of the government's official representative in the Basque Country, Marcelino Oreja. The King and Queen were greeted warmly in some areas but the first royal visit to the area since 1929 was seriously marred by desultory anti-Spanish demonstrations at Vitoria airport and by an incident at the Basque parliament, the Casa de Juntas in Guernica.

Before he could begin his speech, the King was interrupted by the deputies of Herri Batasuna who gave an impromptu rendition of the Basque national anthem, the *Eusko Gudari*. When the stewards tried to evict them, noisy scuffles broke out. When order was restored, Juan Carlos declared 'Against those who make a practice of intolerance, who are contemptuous of co-existence and who have no respect for our institutions, I proclaim my faith in democracy and my confidence in the Basque people.' The King handled the insulting outbreak with great dignity and aplomb, gaining a standing ovation from the PNV and other members of the Basque parliament. Despite the gratuitous discourtesy of Herri Batasuna, the royal trip, coming after Queen Sofía's visit to the site of the Ortuella disaster, could not have had a more positive impact on Basque public opinion. However, the military was appalled.[3] To make matters worse, massive publicity was being given to two kidnappings by ETA. The first, of the Valencian industrialist Luis Suñer, the biggest taxpayer in Spain, could hardly be presented as anything less than a crime of extortion. He was not released until 14 April 1981 after large sums of money had changed hands.[4]

The second kidnapping, of José María Ryan, the chief engineer at the Lemoniz nuclear power station, had taken place on 29 January. ETA had once favoured nuclear energy as a means towards the self-sufficiency of Euskadi, but had been quick to see the potential of popular anti-nuclear sentiment. With the same ideological confusion that permitted the co-existence of rhetorical pacifism and daily violence, progress towards the completion of the Lemoniz plant was now interpreted as further Spanish exploitation. Iberduero, the company building Lemoniz, was given seven days to destroy installations in which over 130,000,000,000 pesetas had been invested, if Ryan was not to die. There was a wave of outrage throughout Spain and the Basque Country. The workers of Lemoniz, backed by the UGT, the Comisiones Obreras and the union linked to the PNV, ELA-STV, formed a Ryan Liberation Committee. Urgent appeals for Ryan's life came from European anti-nuclear organizations, from Amnesty International which had so often defended ETA prisoners, from the Church and, most movingly, from the Ryan family. A huge demonstration calling for his release took place in Bilbao on 5 February. It was to no avail. An absurd and truculent note from ETA-M declared that this massive expression of popular feeling was an expression of 'contempt for the majority will of the people'. It went on to state that Ryan had been tried and found guilty of putting into practice the plans of Iberduero. ETA-M announced that the death sentence would be shortly put into effect. Unlike ETA, the democratic state had abolished the death penalty and yet was denounced by the killers of Ryan as a fascist dictatorship.[5]

The news of the vicious murder of this non-political family man on 6 February 1981 aroused mass indignation. There was a general strike across the entire Basque Country. 300,000 people took part in protest demonstrations in San Sebastián, Bilbao and Vitoria. Only Herri Batasuna stood aside and some of its militants stoned the demonstrators. The cynicism of Herri Batasuna surpassed even its previously remarkable record. The strikes and demonstrations were dismissed as the consequence of *maniobra patronal* (employers' tricks) and *intoxicación de la prensa* (press distortion). As far as Herri Batasuna was concerned, the main significance of Ryan's murder was that it allowed the press to turn the people against ETA-M and HB. The fact that he had been cold-bloodedly shot in the back of the neck was referred to in its communiqué merely as his *fatal desenlace* (fatal end) as if ETA-M had somehow had nothing to do with it. Indeed, as far as Herri Batasuna was concerned, Ryan had been killed by Iberduero.[6]

As ETA-M seems to have hoped, Ryan's murder sparked off ultra-rightist fury in the army. The focus for this was an inflammatory article by the retired General Fernando de Santiago y Díaz de Mendívil. Under the headline *Situación Limite* (roughly, This Cannot Go On), he wrote that the incident in Guernica, in which the Supreme Commander of the Armed Forces (the King) had been insulted, was typical of the state of decomposition into which Spain had fallen. Of the Ryan murder, he wrote ominously that 'We can no longer remain impassive before such chaos'; of the long list of ETA kidnappings and assassinations, that they were 'the most obvious proof that here there is no authority and authority must be re-established'. Recent evidence of growing electoral abstention was taken by General Santiago as meaning that the population had rejected the 'contubernio político' (the politics of intrigue) and was looking to the army to save Spain.[7]

Since mid-December 1980, *El Alcázar* had published three more or less open appeals for a military coup under the by-line of '*Almendros*' (almond trees). Acute analysts assumed that the collective signature of the *Colectivo Almendros* was a coded message that something was being plotted for the second half of February which is when the almond normally blossoms. The idea for the collective signature had been elaborated at the *El Alcázar* offices on 19 November in order to help create the necessary expectation for the forthcoming *golpe*. Among the members of the collective were Antonio Izquierdo, the paper's editor, one of its leading writers, Joaquín Aguirre Bellver, and two other of its journalists, Angel Palomino and Ismael Medina. A number of well-known ultra officers were also involved in the foundation of *Almendros*, including General Santiago, Colonel José Ignacio San Martín, the Chief of Staff at the DAC, and Captain Camilo Menéndez Vives, the naval officer who had attacked Gutiérrez Mellado in 1977. The collective felt secure in publishing its three seditious articles because five hundred officers had agreed that, in the event of the newspaper being prosecuted, they would all claim to have written them. The group also had wide ramifications among a whole range of civilian ultras, including José Antonio Girón de Velasco and Juan García Carrés. They hoped for a coup more openly Francoist than either the soft option of Armada or the 'Turkish' plans of the colonels.[8] These hopes were pinned on General Jaime Milans del Bosch.

Military complaints about the lack of authority shown by the government were given some substance by the second Congress of UCD which eventually got under way on 6 February 1981 in Palma de Mallorca. Out of government, Suárez no longer had the resources of patronage, nor perhaps the will, to keep his loose coalition together. Accordingly, centrifugal tension re-emerged with a vengeance at the Congress. The crucial division was between the Christian Democrat *críticos* and an alliance of so-called *oficialistas*. This consisted of party *apparatchiks* led by Fernando Abril Martorell, Agustín Rodríguez Sahagún, Rafael Arias Salgado and Rafael Calvo Ortega, together with the followers of Martín Villa and the social democrats of Fernández Ordóñez. It was a group united by a suspicion that Landelino Lavilla and the *críticos* wished to turn UCD into a confessional and reactionary party like the CEDA of the 1930s. The delegates or *compromisarios* were divided into approximately 1400 *oficialistas* and 600 *críticos*. However, the party apparatus ensured that the new executive committee would not embody proportional representation but rather be dictated by their majority. Calvo Ortega became Secretary-General of UCD and Rodríguez Sahagún President. Lavilla's *críticos* obtained only seven of the thirty-nine seats on the executive.[9] However, the apparent unity imposed by the *oficialistas*, in part facilitated by a general desire not to squabble in the wake of Suárez's departure, would be short-lived. The Congress did little for the credibility of Leopoldo Calvo Sotelo since its proceedings failed dramatically to project the much-needed impression that his leadership would have a strong basis of parliamentary support.

To make matters worse, the tide of opinion against ETA unleashed by the murder of Ryan was reversed on 13 February by the death of the *Etarra*, Joseba Iñaki Arregui Izaguirre, who had been captured on 4 February after a spectacular shoot-out in Madrid. His death reflected at best stupidity on the part of his jailers; at worst a deliberate provocation just when the tide was turning against ETA. He had been beaten and it was clear that he had died as a result of police torture. The authorities claimed that Arregui was also suffering from serious bronchial pneumonia as a result of crossing the Pyrenees on foot in mid-winter. There were anti-Spanish demonstrations in the Basque Country against the police, smaller but much more vehement than those against ETA the previous week. Eleven policemen, of whom at least one was a self-confessed ultra, were put at the disposal of an investigating judge. There was a wave of resignations within the forces of order. They included that of the Director-General of the Police, José Manuel Blanco, and the Comisario General de Información, Manuel Ballesteros García, who both believed that the interrogation carried out by their men had been positive because it had led to revelations that the *comando* of which Arregui had formed part was in Madrid to prepare an attack on a senior military figure and to kidnap a prominent banker. The death of Arregui was too convenient for the plans being hatched by the ultras not to provoke speculation that it was a deliberate attempt to maintain the ferment in the Basque Country and to make the government appear to have lost control of events.[10]

Accordingly, when Calvo Sotelo finally addressed the Cortes on 21 February 1981, it was in an atmosphere charged with wild rumours about an imminent military coup. The death of Arregui had ruined hopes for a smooth transfer of power to the new Prime Minister. José Pedro Pérez Llorca had been negotiating with numerous small groups in the Cortes to ensure their support in the investiture votation. He had secured promises of votes from the Catalans of Convergència i Unió, from small Aragonese and Navarrese regionalist groups and even from a section of Coalición Democrática, including Alfonso Osorio and José María de Areilza. He was on the verge of a similar agreement with the PNV when news of Arregui's death was released. Under such circumstances, the Basques felt unable to vote for the government.[11] In consequence, Calvo Sotelo faced an uphill struggle. He declared that the transition from dictatorship to democracy was complete and he effectively offered a government programme of retrenchment. Although he received a simple majority of 169 votes to 158 against and 17 abstentions, his performance did not gain him the overall majority of 176 votes necessary to confirm him as President.

Santiago Carrillo commented that Calvo Sotelo's government was born dead.[12]

Certainly, the failure to win the investiture vote implied a fatal weakness. That was clear from the back-stage negotiations which had accompanied his efforts to form a new cabinet. The split between the Christian Democrat *críticos* and other UCD factions constituted a major difficulty. Francisco Fernández Ordóñez had made it clear that social democrat co-operation in the new cabinet was dependent on a commitment to divorce reform which could only infuriate the Christian Democrats. Moreover, just as UCD was beginning to crumble in earnest, there were signs of a substantial revival of Alianza Popular. Opinion polls suggested that Alianza Popular could double its vote at the expense of UCD. To take advantage of the flood of refugees alarmed by the UCD leadership crisis, Manuel Fraga saw the need for a move to the centre. At the IV Alianza Popular Congress held in Madrid from 13 to 15 February, the more trogloditic Francoists were marginalized and prominence was given to somewhat more liberal figures like the Madrid lawyer Félix Pastor Ridruejo and the writer Carmen Llorca.[13]

After the failure on 21 February, the would-be President was obliged to wait two days for a second vote of investiture for which only a simple majority was necessary. The voting had just begun on 23 February when at 6.20 p.m. a group of civil guards under Colonel Tejero arrived at the Cortes in private buses specially bought by Tejero's wife. They burst into the chamber and held the entire political class hostage. Great personal courage was shown by General Gutiérrez Mellado, who ordered them to leave and was violently jostled, and by Adolfo Suárez who went to his assistance. Felipe González, Alfonso Guerra, Santiago Carrillo, Gutiérrez Mellado, Suárez and Agustín Rodríguez Sahagún were locked in separate rooms as super-hostages. Tejero telephoned the headquarters of the Captain-General of the Valencia Military Region, Jaime Milans del Bosch. His message was brief and incriminating: '*Pavia* here. Everything in order. Objective achieved. All quiet.' The code-name *Pavia* referred to the nineteenth-century general who put an end to the First Republic when he threatened the Cortes with artillery. Tejero then returned to the chamber and announced that a senior military personage would shortly arrive to take control.

A few minutes after Tejero's arrival in the Cortes, Milans del Bosch declared a state of emergency in the Valencian region. Every fifteen minutes, the local radio broadcast a proclamation or *bando* by Milans which began with the preamble 'in the light of events in the capital and the consequent vacuum of power, it is my duty to guarantee order in the military region under my command until I receive instructions from His Majesty the King'. The unauthorized use of his name especially offended Juan Carlos. The *bando* ordered the militarization of all public service personnel, imposed a nine o'clock curfew and banned all political activities. Tanks took up positions alongside important public buildings. In the offices of trade unions and political parties, frantic efforts were made to destroy membership files and documents which might have facilitated a purge by the ultra-right. From the Basque Country, cars flooded across the border into France. In Asturias, however, the local PSOE and UGT issued a denunciation of the coup and the mineworkers' union SOMA-UGT declared a general strike.[14]

Mysterious troop movements took place in different parts of Spain and in Madrid, where the streets were deserted, the radio and television broadcasting studios at Prado del Rey were taken over by a unit from the División Acorazada de Brunete at 7.48 p.m. They insisted that the radio broadcast only military marches. At 9.20 p.m. they received orders to withdraw and did so. It later emerged that these orders had emanated from General Alfonso Armada Comyn who, as second-in-command of the General Staff, was ostensibly working to make Tejero release the Cortes deputies. In fact, Armada was playing a dangerous and ambiguous game throughout the events known as the *Tejerazo*. Cunningly exploiting the blindly fanatical Tejero, the aristocratic Armada was actually seeking the moment to implement his solution of a De Gaulle-style government of national salvation. As a 'patriotic sacrifice' and in order to end the dangerous situation in the Cortes, he would offer to form a government without ever seeming to have played any part in initiating the coup. Presumably, the more plebeian Tejero would then have been sacrificed.

Ultimately, the coup was to fail because the decisive action of the King and his close collaborators exposed the ambiguities and inadequate preparations of the plotters. The principal conspiracies simmering throughout 1980 had come together in a rashly precipitate manner. Milans and the DAC colonels planned a Turkish or Chilean-style coup to be followed by a draconian purge of the left, a 'dirty war' against ETA and a return to rigid centralism. Hopes that this would have the support of the King led to the link-up with Armada who fraudulently presented himself as the royal agent. Dreaming of the milder *Operación De Gaulle*, with himself cast in the role of the great man, Armada hoped to use the threat of the colonels to blackmail the political class into supporting his *gobierno de gestión*. Both sets of plans were thrown out of joint by

Suárez's early resignation. The ultimately fatal decisions were made to bring forward the date for the coup and to let the volatile and uncontrollable Tejero be its battering ram.

Behind Armada's behaviour was a strange mixture of arrogance and paternalism which led him to believe that he could both interpret the unspoken wishes of Juan Carlos and then present himself to his brother officers as the King's spokesman. He had already approached politicians of the PSOE, the PCE and Coalición Democrática with the idea of a strong coalition government of national salvation under his leadership. Armada had been for many years one of Juan Carlos's tutors and Secretary-General of the Royal Household until he was dismissed in July 1977 allegedly for political meddling. After various postings, he had been brought back to Madrid on 12 February 1981, against the advice of Adolfo Suárez, to the post of second-in-command of the General Staff. Armada's much-vaunted proximity to the King permitted him to convince Milans and a number of other key officers that he had royal authority for a coup and for a cabinet under his own presidency. His friendship with Milans went back to their days together in Russia with the *División Azul*. He was also a close friend of General Torres Rojas.

At his lunch with Milans on 10 January, Armada had stressed that the King was worried about the drift of the political situation and was anxious to remove Suárez. The erroneous implication picked up by Milans was that Armada was actually the King's emissary. Thereafter, Armada was kept informed by Colonel Diego Ibáñez Inglés, one of Milans's aides, of the progress of the conspiracy. Milans, Torres Rojas, Tejero and the civilian ultra Juan García Carrés met in Madrid on 18 January. In fact, all three of the principal protagonists of the coup, Tejero, Milans and Armada, had differing ambitions and this was to be a significant handicap for them. Nevertheless, it is clear that throughout the entire operation both Milans and Tejero were convinced that what they were doing would meet with the King's approval. That conviction can only have come from Armada who seems to have hoped that the Tejero–Milans del Bosch *fait accompli* would oblige Juan Carlos to acquiesce in his plan for an all-party government of national salvation. That he was playing a double game might have been deduced from the fact that he was always careful never to meet more than one of the conspirators at a time. The lack of witnesses would always enable him to claim to have had nothing to do with the plot and to present his 'solution' as a disinterested gesture.

Doubt still hovers about what he was telling the politicians that he wanted in his coalition. He was known to be friendly with Alfonso Osorio. He had already contacted the PSOE through Múgica. It would seem that he was sounding them out in terms so general as not to alert them to what he planned. If anything went wrong, he would not be committed. At the same time, he was using his contact with the politicians to convince himself and his fellow conspirators of his suitability as the head of a government of national salvation. This is the most plausible conclusion to be drawn from a dinner held at his home on 16 February. The guests included the Captain-General of Catalonia, Antonio Pascual Galmés, the Chief of the General Staff, José Gabeiras Montero, the head of the Royal Household, the Marqués de Mondéjar, Nicolás Cotoner y Cotoner, and the Catalan Communist deputy, Jordi Solé-Tura. The reason for the dinner was to discuss preparations for the forthcoming royal visit to Barcelona. The King was to preside at a parade on the Armed Forces Day which was being held outside Madrid for the first time. It was obviously a subject of concern to all the guests and almost certainly the *raison d'être* of the dinner. In the eyes of Armada's fellow plotters, such a gathering could only mean that he was getting support for his plans from the King, from the highest echelons of the army and from politicians. Whatever the conspirators may have thought about his projected cabinet – and for Tejero, it was to be unacceptably liberal – such meetings permitted them to go into 23 February confident that Armada had surrounded the coup with an aura of legitimacy.[15]

The job of dismantling the coup was undertaken by a triumvirate of the King himself, the Secretary-General of the Royal Household, General Sabino Fernández Campos, and the new Director-General of Security, Francisco Laína García. They were backed by the Chief of the Army General Staff, General José Gabeiras Montero, and the Captain-General of Madrid, Guillermo Quintana Lacaci. A provisional government consisting of the under-secretaries of each ministry was established under the direction of Laína in the Ministry of the Interior. In the Hotel Palace opposite the Cortes, the Inspector-General of the Police, General José Sáenz de Santamaría and the Director-General of the Civil Guard, General José Aramburu Topete, directed local operations. At one point, Aramburu entered the Cortes and tried single-handedly to make Tejero desist. Tejero's response was to threaten to kill both General Aramburu and himself. Sáenz de Santamaría surrounded the Cortes with police units to prevent further subversives joining those inside. It is significant that the police, despite well-founded doubts about their loyalty over the previous four years, made an important contribution to blocking the coup. Although in the event it was not to be necessary, General Sáenz de Santamaría was also preparing for the ultimate contingency of an assault by the GOE (*Grupos de Operaciones Especiales*), Spain's special services.

Aided by General Gabeiras Montero, the King and his aides engaged in a battle by telephone to secure the loyalty of the Captains-General of the other military regions. It was feared that Milans might have already gained crucial support by convincing them that there was royal backing for the Armada solution. There was much dithering and some of the Captains-General kept in frequent contact throughout the night with Milans as well as with the Zarzuela Palace. If the King had been prepared to abandon the Constitution, there is little doubt that the Captains-General would happily have brought their troops out into the streets. In that sense, only he stood between Spanish democracy and its destruction. The task of his emergency committee was rendered somewhat easier by the rapid declarations of loyalty and support from Antonio Pascual Galmés, the Captain-General of the Fourth Region, Catalonia, and of Jesús González del Yerro, Captain-General of the Canary Islands. That González del Yerro, reputed to be a hard-line reactionary, stood by his oath of loyalty to the King and the Constitution was a tribute to the role played by Juan Carlos both on the night of 23 February and throughout the entire transition period.

The Captain-General of Zaragoza, Antonio Elícegui Prieto, after some hesitation, also declared for the Crown. However, one known ultra, Pedro Merry Gordón, Captain-General of the Second Region, Seville, was thought to be on the verge of taking tanks into the streets of the Andalusian capital. He spent much of the night on the telephone both to the Zarzuela and to the headquarters of Milans del Bosch. His loyalty was not confirmed until the early hours of the morning. The attitude of another, Angel Campano López, Captain-General of Valladolid, did not inspire confidence. In both cases, the determined intervention of the military and civil governors of each city, General Manuel María Mejías and Román Ledesma in Valladolid and General Manuel Esquivias Franco and José María Sanz Pastor in Seville, imposed caution on the two Captains-General.

The coup's greatest strength and its fatal weakness were the ambiguity of General Armada. This was made clear by the role played by the Brunete Armoured Division or DAC, which was to have been one of the crucial elements of the coup. Dominating Madrid, the DAC came within an inch of intervening decisively. When the coup started, the DAC's

commanding officer, General José Juste Fernández, was en route to
Zaragoza to inspect some DAC units which were on manoeuvres there.
The previous commander and an important member of the conspiracy,
General Torres Rojas, was present at DAC headquarters ready to take
over in the absence of Juste. Military governor of La Coruña since his
dismissal from the DAC in January 1980, Torres Rojas had used a pretext
to gain permission to be in Madrid from the Captain-General of La
Coruña, General Manuel Fernández Posse. The DAC's Chief of Staff,
Lieutenant-Colonel San Martín, one-time head of Carrero Blanco's
intelligence service, was also one of the main conspirators behind the
coup. Accompanying Juste, he telephoned the DAC and then informed
Juste that they must return to Brunete.

On arrival at his headquarters, General Juste was informed, if he did
not already know, of the intentions of Milans del Bosch. He rang up the
Zarzuela Palace expecting to find Armada directing operations under the
King's aegis. On being told that Armada was neither there nor expected
(*ni está, ni se le espera*), he apparently said 'that changes everything' ('*eso
cambia todo*'). He then telephoned the headquarters of the Captain-
General. Under the close vigilance of General Quintana Lacaci, Juste
imposed his command on the bulk of the Division and Torres Rojas was
obliged to return to La Coruña. It was thus possible to prevent the
mobilization of most of the units which were to have occupied Madrid,
except for some military policemen under Major Ricardo Pardo Zancada
who had already joined Tejero. Juste's phone call raised serious doubts
about his own position. Tejero was to claim later that Juste knew before
leaving for Zaragoza about the coup and about Torres Rojas but was not
prepared to be involved directly. On the other hand, Juste's stance later in
the course of the night of 23 February helped to save the situation. More
importantly, his phone call to the Zarzuela alerted the King and his staff
to the fact that Armada was somehow involved and therefore not to be
trusted.

The task of Laína, Gabeiras and Quintana Lacaci was made more
difficult because they only gradually realized the complex game that
Armada was playing. His hints that the King was involved were the
strongest card in the hands of the *golpistas*. It finally emerged that
Armada was in fact the 'senior military personality' that Tejero had been
waiting for. Suspicions raised by General Juste's telephone call to the
Zarzuela were confirmed when Tejero refused any other mediator but
Armada or the King himself. Armada entered the Cortes at 12.30 a.m. on
the morning of the 24th and spoke to Tejero for about three quarters of an

hour. He proposed offering to the hijacked deputies the idea of a government of national salvation under his own presidency. Within this 'constitutional solution', the Cortes would then put the proposal to the King. It was an idea which, if successful, would have left Armada both clear of suspicion and head of government. Unfortunately for him, Tejero rejected out of hand the idea of a government containing Socialists and possibly even a token Communist. He wanted a Pinochet-style junta to crush the left and revoke regional autonomies not a bland compromise acceptable to the majority in parliament. In any case, Armada's duplicity was already suspected both at the Zarzuela and at the Ministry of the Interior.

Eighteen hours in all were necessary to secure the surrender of Tejero. However, the coup had been seen to falter when Juan Carlos appeared on television at 1.15 a.m. on 24 February. It had been delayed by the presence of the troops at Prado del Rey and the difficulties of getting a camera crew to the Zarzuela Palace until after 9.30 p.m. The decisive broadcast announced that the Crown would not tolerate actions which aimed to interrupt by force the democratic process determined by the popularly ratified Constitution. Milans was telephoned by the King who made it clear that he opposed the coup, that he would not abdicate nor leave Spain and that in order to prevail the rebels would have to shoot him. A telex sent an hour later confirmed the message of the phone call and warned Milans that he and his fellow conspirators were risking civil war. Realizing that the pretence of enjoying royal support could no longer be sustained, and that the other Captains-General had not backed him, Milans withdrew his troops from the streets at 4 a.m. Tired and abandoned, Tejero finally negotiated his surrender with the ubiquitous General Armada. Armada was himself arrested on the following day.

The Cortes deputies left the chamber at midday on 24 February. Several hours later, after a prolonged and heartfelt ovation for the King, they gave their approbation to Calvo Sotelo's investiture by 186 votes to 158. Felipe González offered to take part in a coalition government. The extent to which the King had interpreted the wishes of his people was graphically shown on 27 February when three million people demonstrated in favour of democracy in Madrid and other cities. However, because of disagreements provoked by Herri Batasuna, such unity was not possible in the Basque Country. Indeed, the defeat of the coup did not resolve the democratic regime's outstanding difficulties. This point was made by Juan Carlos to Adolfo Suárez, Felipe González, Agustín Rodríguez Sahagún, Santiago Carrillo and Manuel Fraga when he received them on the evening of 24 February. The very fact that the King had been obliged to place his personal prestige and safety at risk suggested that Spain's political class in general and the leadership of UCD in particular had severely miscalculated the mood of the army during the transition period. It was true that the plotters had miscalculated their potential support. However, both their original hopes and their ultimate disappointment hinged on the stance taken by Juan Carlos.

23-F, as the coup came to be known, brutally exposed the UCD's conciliatory tactics with regard to the armed forces. Somehow Spain had lost its way after 1979. The great achievements of the period 1976–9, the democratic pact, the consensus which had helped create a democratic state with a high level of regional autonomy, had been obscured by the incapacity of Suárez and his various governments. To a certain extent, Suárez had governed according to the pragmatic principle of leaving things alone unless forced to do otherwise by popular protest or terrorism. Substantial achievements there were, but there was also a growth in the politics of blackmail and of terror. It showed that the team which, with the opposition baying at its heels, had been ideal to steer democratic change through the Francoist institutions was not similarly suited to deal with the problems of inflation, unemployment, terrorism and military subversion. The defeat of Tejero, however, gave the country a second chance. If the formal legal transition could somehow be converted into real substantial change, the *desencanto* would soon be dissipated.

The national spirit of post 23-F co-operation was reflected in the new cabinet of the taciturn Leopoldo Calvo Sotelo. To ensure immediate administrative continuity and to eliminate any suggestion of what the *golpistas* had eagerly called a power vacuum, the Prime Minister made few changes. His team was also, like Suárez's cabinet of 'barons' which it resembled closely, an attempt to distribute power evenly within UCD. Martín Villa continued to oversee the autonomy process from the Ministry of Territorial Administration. There were two other Martín Villistas. His close friend and collaborator, Juan José Rosón Pérez, stayed on as Minister of the Interior and Jesús Sancho Rof took over the combined Ministry of Labour, Health and Social Security. The Christian Democrats were also well represented through Juan Antonio Ortega y Díaz Ambrona at Education, Iñigo Cavero Lataillade at Culture, José Luis Alvarez Alvarez, once UCD's *Alcalde* of Madrid, at Transport and Luis Ortiz González at Public Works. Curiously, given Calvo Sotelo's own very conservative instincts, there was also a strong social democrat tendency.

The powerful Ministry of the Economy and Commerce remained in the hands of Juan Antonio García Díez, who combined a high level of competence with a close personal friendship with the new President. Also within the social democrat orbit of economics was the Ministry of Finance (*Hacienda*) under Jaime Añoveros García.

The remaining 'baron', Francisco Fernández Ordóñez continued as Minister of Justice. Given his commitment to legalizing divorce, his appointment was the rock on which the cabinet would eventually split. It was the glaring exception in a government in which the President had generally managed to distribute satisfactorily the parcels of power which the various UCD factions considered to be their own. The ex-*Azules* led by Martín Villa held ministries which closely corresponded to the areas once controlled by the Movimiento, labour, social security and local administration. As the UCD faction that could most convincingly present itself as reformist, the social democrats had sought and achieved a high degree of control in the area where reform was most urgent, the economy. The Christian Democrats held ministries of traditional Catholic interest, Education and Culture. However, the Ministry of Justice, under Franco at least, normally held by a figure close to the Church, had escaped their grasp. Eventually, their opposition to the reform projects of Fernández Ordóñez would accelerate the collapse of UCD. In the short term, however, all attention was concentrated on the Ministry of Defence. The job of rooting out *golpismo* and rebuilding civil–military relations was entrusted to Alberto Oliart Saussol. Not a baron, little known in the country at large, Oliart was a lawyer who had had a brilliant career in various state departments in the Francoist period and had powerful banking connections. He was considered to be a liberal and he quickly declared that his aim was to adjust military legislation to the Constitution.[16] It was to be a difficult and delicate task. More than once in the next eighteen months, Oliart's apparent ductility *vis-à-vis* the army led to suggestions that on the contrary the military was adjusting the Constitution to its desires.

Indeed, as 1981 progressed, there was to be a growing conviction that in a sense Armada's *golpe blando* had succeeded, that policies were being radio-controlled by the military authorities who became a kind of government in the shadows. This feeling was based in the first instance on the King's statement to the leaders of the parliamentary groups when he had received them on 24 February. In it he had said that 'an open and tough reaction by the political parties against those who committed acts of subversion in the last few hours would be most unadvisable and it would be even more counter-productive to extend such a reaction to the entire Armed Forces'. He had called on them to reconsider their positions in order to foster the highest possible level of unity and concord in Spain and pointed out that he could not do again what he had just done.[17]

None the less, out of the ashes of the 23-F, the phoenix of Spanish democracy was to rise again. The demonstrations of 27 February marked the end of the *desencanto*. Tejero had the inadvertent effect of making the population as a whole revalue their democratic institutions. Calvo Sotelo quickly showed a readiness to break with the more negative aspects of Suárez's rule. He expressed a wish – quickly blocked by his security team – to leave the Moncloa Palace and move the President's office back into central Madrid in order to be less isolated. It was made clear that he would appear more frequently in parliament and before the press. He quickly showed that he meant what he said. Regular consultations were started with the leaders of the other parties and with senior generals. In general, there was a new sense of gravity at the Moncloa Palace. Within three months, Calvo Sotelo's personal opinion poll ratings began to reflect public satisfaction with the new approach.[18]

The change of mood was evident too in the offers made by Felipe González, Manuel Fraga and Santiago Carrillo to support the government in the Cortes. Even ETA-PM made a contribution. On 21 February, the organization had kidnapped three foreign consuls in a bizarre protest against the death of Arregui. The three were now released and an indefinite ceasefire announced. Coming in the wake of a Basque peace initiative launched by Mario Onaindía of Euskadiko Eskerra on 22 February, it marked the beginning of the gradual, albeit troubled, disappearance of ETA-PM. It was interpreted by the bunker press as proof that the *Tejerazo* had been a positive and patriotic initiative.[19] Fear of the blood-bath likely to be unleashed by Tejero and reflection on the absurdity of the military attempting to resolve Spain's massive economic problems contributed in equal measure to Spanish democracy having a second chance. Stripped now of the elements of euphoria which accompanied the change of regime in 1977, democracy was now seen as a deadly serious business, a matter of life and death for the entire nation. Had it not been for the divisions in his own party, it is possible that Calvo Sotelo might have been able to make more of the new spirit of national co-operation.

Calvo Sotelo's programme, already announced before the events of 23 February, was moderate in the extreme: entry into NATO, commitment to the market economy, reduction in the level of public expenditure, stimulation of private investment and wage restraint. On 7 March, the new President gave his first press conference and somewhat unconvincingly dismissed the coup as an isolated incident within a general context of military loyalty to democracy. This delicate regard for army sensibilities was reflected at the secret Cortes session held on 17 March to discuss the coup. Both the government and the opposition agreed that the anti-terrorist campaign should be intensified. There was also a consensus that the relatively rapid progress towards regional autonomy, which had so incensed the military, should be slowed down. Declarations that the regions must not make exaggerated demands eventually led to the elaboration of the notorious Ley Orgánica de Armonización del Proceso Autonómico (LOAPA). The LOAPA, born of an agreement between UCD and the PSOE, was presented to the Cortes on 29 September 1981, and was an attempt to emasculate concessions to the regions. It was not surprising then that journalists commented that it was as if the military, far from suffering the consequences of the coup's defeat, were enjoying the successful achievement of some of its ends. In fact, appeals made to the supreme court by the Basque and Catalan regional governments in 1982 managed in their turn to emasculate or at least freeze the LOAPA. None the less, at the time the LOAPA was the most visible symbol that during 1981 Spain was a democracy under hostile surveillance.

This impression was confirmed when many of the minor participants in the 23-F were released throughout March and April. The publication of an article by Tejero defending the coup brought home to public opinion the extent of the privileges being enjoyed by the imprisoned conspirators. The *golpistas* were awaiting trial in conditions of considerable physical comfort and received virtually unlimited visits from their sympathizers.[20] The apparent military tutelage of the government seemed to be confirmed in April when liberal officers of the UMD were yet again refused re-admission to the ranks. In the light of UCD's eagerness to appease the armed forces at every turn, the indecent haste with which the government pressed for entry into NATO was seen as another attempt to curry military favour. It is almost certainly the case that the cabinet believed that the integration of the Spanish armed forces into the Western defence system would divert them from their unhealthy readiness to interfere in domestic politics. When the PSOE opposed entry, it was accused of rocking the boat. Paradoxically, the PSOE's position did it little but good in army eyes. Even officers who relished the access to modern weaponry implicit in NATO entry agreed with the Socialist stance because they regarded UCD's failure to negotiate more concessions in return for integration as tantamount to a national humiliation. It was felt in military circles that more should be made of the fact that Spain was offering NATO more than she was receiving in return.[21]

In general, however, the prevailing atmosphere in 1981 was one of trepidation. Regular articles in *El Alcázar* in defence of Tejero suggested that there was little repentance in ultra circles.[22] Fear of what the army might do was fuelled by the continuing terrorist activities of both ETA-M and GRAPO. The ceasefire offered by ETA-PM was not emulated by the 'Milis'. On 1 March, an attempt to blow up two police cars on the road between Sestao and Portugalete near Bilbao having failed, a machine-gun attack was launched in which an innocent woman passer-by was wounded. On 5 March, a senior police inspector, José Luis de Raymundo Moya, was assassinated in Bilbao. True to the new presidential style, Calvo Sotelo attended the funeral. The Basque PSOE leader, Txiki Benegas, declared that ETA-M was objectively lined up with the *golpistas*. Indeed, the continuing terrorism of ETA-M – with one army colonel murdered in Bilbao on 19 March and another in Pamplona on the 21st – proved the point beyond any doubt.[23] ETA-M refused to acknowledge either the existence of democracy or the popular support that it enjoyed. To justify itself, ETA-M needed the establishment of a cruel military dictatorship and was prepared to go on killing in order to pursue its own lunatic logic. Benegas's point was to be tragically proved in 1984 when ETA-M murdered General Guillermo Quintana Lacaci, the Captain-General of Madrid who had done so much to block the *Tejerazo*.

The determination of Calvo Sotelo to deal energetically with threats to democracy was quickly revealed by the presentation in the Cortes of a law for the defence of the Constitution which permitted action to be taken against the press networks of both the bunker and ETA-M. This was followed by the announcement on 23 March of new measures to combat ETA. The army was to be brought in to seal the Franco-Spanish frontier. A single anti-terrorist command (Mando Unico Antiterrorista) was established in the Ministry of the Interior to co-ordinate police, civil guards and the army. The tough Manuel Ballesteros, once chief of police in Bilbao, was put in command. Frontier posts were to be more tightly controlled and the forces of order in Euskadi and Navarre were to be better equipped. There were some fears that this might be playing into the hands of ETA-M. However, the weight of popular hostility against the terrorists gave Calvo Sotelo and his Minister of the Interior, Juan José

Rosón, the confidence to take energetic steps without fear of being accused of heavy-handed authoritarianism.[24]

Three months after assuming power, Calvo Sotelo could note with satisfaction that public opinion approved of his style of government and that the post-*Tejerazo* spirit of co-operation still prevailed among the political parties. However, there were dark clouds on the horizon and they began to gather in earnest in early May. Having had its offers of coalition government rejected, the PSOE became increasingly resentful of the speed and secretiveness of the government's dealings with NATO. There was talk of breaking the consensus and a return to the outright hostility that had marked Suárez's last days.[25] In the event, the politics of co-operation (*concertación*) prevailed for the moment. Nevertheless, Calvo Sotelo was soon to find himself, like Suárez before him, caught in a cross-fire between terrorism and subversion at the same time as his party dedicated its efforts to internal squabbling.

Difficulties began on 4 May when a suspiciously resuscitated GRAPO burst on to the scene. In Madrid, one gang murdered the liberal artillery General, Andrés González de Suso. Almost simultaneously, more GRAPO killers shot dead two civil guards in Barcelona. Throughout its history, GRAPO's leftist veneer had been belied by the fact that its actions consistently favoured the objectives of the extreme right. The strange coincidence of interest between terrorism and *golpismo* was shockingly illustrated a mere seventy-two hours later. An ETA-M *comando* bombed the car of General Joaquín María de Valenzuela, the new head of the King's Household, killing outright his chauffeur, an aide and a sergeant and leaving him on the brink of death. Ultra-rightists were quickly out on the streets calling for military intervention. More crucial, however, was a remarkable action of mass solidarity in favour of democracy, recalling the demonstrations of 27 February. Two minutes' silence reigned in the streets, homes and factories of Spain at midday on 8 May. On the following day, the police managed to capture the group that had murdered General González de Suso.[26]

However, these positive features were more than neutralized by two extraordinarily sinister incidents which kept popular uncertainty at the highest pitch. On 9 May, three innocent young men were killed in Almería by civil guards in the most bizarre circumstances. Detained on the grounds that they might possibly be ETA suspects, they died on the way to interrogation when their car was mysteriously destroyed. Tension was screwed even tighter over the weekend of 23–24 May when a group of armed men, rumoured to be civil guards, seized the Banco Central in

Barcelona and held everyone in it hostage. They demanded the release from custody of Colonel Tejero, Colonel San Martín, General Torres Rojas and Milans's ADC, Colonel Pedro Mas Oliver. The bank was finally liberated after the intervention of the special forces of the GOE.[27] A frequent series of ultra gatherings kept up the pressure. The fact that only thirty of the nearly three hundred officers involved in the 23-F coup were to be tried contributed to the general impression that the democratic regime was again failing to show the strength and determination necessary to defend itself. Efforts were also being made to undermine faith in the King and the political class by ultra leaks of statements by Tejero and other *golpistas* insinuating that there had been complicity in their actions and those of General Armada.

Anxieties were somewhat calmed by the skill with which the Socialist *Alcalde* of Barcelona, Narcis Serra, organized the Armed Forces Day on Sunday 31 May. Since the event had replaced Franco's major military festival, the Day of Victory, it was indeed remarkable that the military should accept Barcelona as the venue for a parade which had previously always taken place in Madrid. The symbolism of the change was seized upon by the media as proof of the army's integration into the democratic polity. Whatever the behind-the-scenes negotiations to make it possible, the holding of the ceremony in Catalonia, with the regional and national flags flying side by side, was a significant military concession to the autonomy process. Narcis Serra pleased the senior officers present by his courtesy, good sense and efficiency. Serra was one of the most talented members of the PSOE. Widely credited with having made the event a symbol of reconciliation and national unity, he established himself as a man with a certain authority where the armed forces were concerned.[28] Eighteen months later, he was to be Minister of Defence.

The image of efficacy projected by Narcis Serra was in sharp contrast to that presented by Calvo Sotelo's government. On 21 June a series of arrests revealed that several rightist colonels had tried to organize another coup.[29] Curiously, evidence of continued *golpismo* did the government less harm than a growing scandal concerning public health. Since early May, forty-eight people, including several children, had died from a mysterious illness diagnosed as 'atypical pneumonia'. Over 8000 more were in hospital suffering from appallingly painful symptoms. By mid-June, it was concluded that the cause of the epidemic was rape-seed oil (*aceite de colza*). The oil in question had been adulterated with industrial oil and various chemicals to make it smell like olive oil. It had then been sold illegally from street stalls for domestic consumption. The main association of olive oil producers, the Unión del Olivar Español, had repeatedly warned the Ministry of Agriculture about the traffic in illegal cooking oil. The exiguous nature of Spain's limited consumer protection laws and the apparent unconcern of the Ministry of Health led to a wave of public hostility against the government.[30]

The increasingly bad press suffered by Jesús Sancho Rof was not the only problem suffered by Calvo Sotelo's government in the spring and summer of 1981. Rumours of military conspiracies were apparently endless. However, Calvo Sotelo was to find, like Suárez before him, that the internal squabblings of his party were to be one of his greatest handicaps. There were two major areas of conflict. On the one hand, there was the hostility between the anti-divorce Christian Democrats and the Minister of Justice, Francisco Fernández Ordóñez. Then, on the other, there was a power struggle against the caretaker party leadership left behind by Suárez. The Christian Democrats of UCD were moving ever closer to Alfonso Osorio and Coalición Democrática. Both Miguel Herrero and Oscar Alzaga were talking of the need to establish a great right-wing coalition (*la gran derecha*) including Alianza Popular. Such a development was likely to push Francisco Fernández Ordóñez out of the UCD. Indeed, when a liberal section of the party voted with the PSOE on 22 June in a vote on divorce, the Christian Democrat *críticos* were loud in their accusations that Fernández Ordóñez was likely to leave the party and join the Socialists. At the same time, what seemed like an attempt by Suárez to run the party by radio control through Rodríguez Sahagún and Calvo Ortega was provoking discontent. There were now attempts to persuade Rodolfo Martín Villa to take over the leadership.[31] In a sense, what was happening was a long overdue clarification of the ideological ambiguities of UCD. However, with elections due in two years, there was an element of panic about the process.

The impression given by UCD's permanent internal crisis was that the party of government was fiddling while Rome burnt. This sensation was particularly acute after the arrests of 21 June. Military intelligence and a new police department called the *Brigada anti-golpe* (anti-coup brigade) had uncovered an ambitious ultra plot. Its ramifications emerged in the weeks following the arrest of two colonels, Ricardo Garchitorena Zalba and Antonio Sicre Canut, and Tejero's crony, Major Ricardo Sáenz de Ynestrillas. The idea behind the conspiracy was that a strategy of tension would be created by an escalating bombing campaign to be carried out by groups of well-armed ultra-rightist militants. Its culmination would have come in Barcelona on 23 June at the Nou Camp football stadium where a huge Catalanist rally was scheduled. Simultaneously, the King would be seized and forced to abdicate. A military junta would be established. Blacklists of democrats to be liquidated had been drawn up.[32] Confined to extreme ultra circles and with only limited impact within the army itself, the projected coup nevertheless provoked considerable apprehension in the country at large.

Calvo Sotelo's attempts to combat the consequent uncertainty were dramatically undermined by the rumblings within his party. On 24 July 1981, a group of thirty-nine UCD parliamentary deputies, led by Oscar Alzaga and Miguel Herrero Rodríguez de Miñón, announced the creation of a so-called Plataforma Moderada (moderate platform). Their aim was to expose what they saw as the false unity and hybrid nature of UCD imposed by Adolfo Suárez. They wanted to eliminate its social democrat pretensions and make it an unequivocally conservative party. For this reason, they were anxious to turn the clock back to the time before Suárez's 1977 landing in Centro Democrático. They hoped to incorporate Alfonso Osorio and José María de Areilza. Manuel Fraga was quick to see the potential of this division and began to talk of the need for UCD and Alianza Popular to make an alliance in search of what he called the 'natural majority'. The liberal tendency within UCD, mute since the death of Joaquín Garrigues Walker, was also reviving under his brother Antonio but in a rather more conservative guise.

The various schemes of the Christian Democrat *críticos* who had joined in the Plataforma Moderada could only provoke the hostility of Adolfo Suárez. Together with Abril Martorell, Rodríguez Sahagún, Arias Salgado and Calvo Ortega, the ex-President still had considerable power within the party. Suárez gave interviews during the summer which suggested that he was considering leaving UCD, in electoral terms a not inconsiderable threat. The potential division in UCD was thus increasingly likely to be fatal. The beginning of the end came in late August. The obvious signs of a swing to the right made it clear to Francisco Fernández Ordóñez and his social democrat followers that their days within the party were numbered. Anticipating events, he resigned as Minister of Justice on 31 August. He was replaced by Pío Cabanillas. Two months later, together with seventeen social democrat senators and Cortes deputies, the eternally restless Fernández Ordóñez left UCD and founded a new party called Acción Democrática.[33]

The UCD's parliamentary strength was now within thirty seats of that of the PSOE. The extent to which the internal crisis of UCD was having an external effect was made brutally clear on 20 October in the elections for the regional parliament in Galicia. In a crushing victory for Alianza Popular, UCD lost nearly three quarters of the votes which had been cast for it in the general elections of 1979. The usual excuses that regional elections see votes for regional parties would not do since Alianza Popular with twenty-six seats, UCD with twenty-four and the PSOE with seventeen won the first three places. The Socialists came second in all big towns, except Pontevedra, being knocked into third place overall by the rural vote. It was a major humiliation for the government.[34] Increasing numbers of desertions from UCD would not be long in becoming the norm.

The crumbling unity of UCD was in dramatic contrast to the seemingly inexorable surge of strength being enjoyed by the PSOE. The disintegration of the PCE, which was breaking apart in rebellion against Carrillo's rigidly authoritarian leadership, had also helped the PSOE by leaving it as the only plausible party on the left. Circumstances were spotlighting the PSOE as the inevitable alternative party of government. Felipe González consistently topped opinion polls as the nation's most popular leader. His image neatly combined freshness and common sense. It was quite unlike the lugubrious note consistently struck by Calvo Sotelo. The Socialists' appearance of unity and efficacy was greatly enhanced by the unveiling in June 1981 of a plan of action for the consolidation of democracy. Its objective of the 'effective but democratic fight against terrorism', the thoroughgoing investigation of 23-F and a moderate economic programme eschewing nationalizations suggested that the PSOE had a clearer vision of how to confront the nation's problems than did a UCD obsessed with its own internal haemorrhaging. In the autumn, both Alfonso Guerra and Felipe González launched attacks on the UCD's *desgobierno* or failure to govern.[35]

The capacity of the PSOE to project an image of reliability was greatly enhanced by its XXIX Party Congress held in the third week of October 1981. The main danger of internal dissent arose from the fact that, with the PCE in disarray, many unattached leftists had made the PSOE their home. They had united to form the Izquierda Socialista (socialist left). However, neither they, nor the more veteran *sector crítico* led by Luis Gómez Llorente and Pablo Castellano which had been defeated in 1979, were able to make any impact at the Congress. This was because the winner-take-all system of election of provincial delegates virtually wiped them out beforehand. At the Congress itself, the left's few surviving representatives were swamped in the procedure whereby delegations voted as a block, according either to the majority view or the judgement of the delegation chief. Thus, the outgoing Executive Committee's report was approved by 96.6 per cent of the delegates, thereby justifying its pre-Congress decision not to admit proportional representation or individual votes for delegates. Felipe González was unanimously re-elected Secretary-General. After his victory, he was able to re-affirm more strongly than ever that the PSOE, with its moderate programme, could undertake the democratic transformation of Spain in a way that the UCD, with its Francoist origins, never could.[36]

With the UCD on the ropes, the Socialists pressed their advantage throughout the autumn of 1981. The government was badly shaken by its inept handling of the rape-seed oil (aceite de colza) scandal in which the death toll had reached over 130. Led by its health spokesman, Ciriaco de Vicente, the PSOE acted as a firm and responsible opposition, pressing for the resignation of those ministers whose dereliction of duty had put thousands of lives at risk. The clear impression was given that only the Socialists truly represented the interests of ordinary Spaniards. This was also the effect of the PSOE's anti-NATO campaign. Not only was the party able to capitalize on the emergent peace movement in Spain, but it also drew strength from the fact that, having had no experience of Nazi occupation, Spaniards were less prone to scaremongering about the dangers of take-over by a totalitarian superpower.

UCD's internal collapse, the colza outcry and the NATO debate were pushing hundreds of thousands of one-time centre–left UCD voters into the orbit of the PSOE. At the same time, the collapse of the Communist Party was of considerable electoral benefit to the PSOE in that its voters were likely to cast a vote for the only feasible left-wing option. In addition, the PCE's obsession with its own collapse removed a source of potentially damaging criticism of the PSOE's ever more moderate line. The PCE had long been smouldering at the imposition of the aged exiled leadership team brought by Santiago Carrillo from Paris in 1977. His heavy bureaucratic style had led to considerable internecine dispute, the consequences of which had been a steady loss of militants throughout the late 1970s. Part of the conflict arose from the party's participation in the Pacto de la Moncloa in October 1977 risking the slur of helping to make the working class pay the costs of the economic crisis. Debate over whether to adopt more revolutionary or more moderate policies had surfaced at the IX Congress in April 1978 when Carrillo forced through the abandonment of Leninism against substantial opposition.[37]

Thereafter, Carrillo's leadership had been challenged on two fronts.

On the one hand, a Soviet-sponsored opposition, which was especially successful in Catalonia, pushed for a more revolutionary, harder line. Because of their support of the Soviet invasion of Afghanistan, they came to be known as *Afganos*. On the other hand, an 'ultra-Eurocommunist' group, known as the *renovadores* (renovators), demanded that the party be opened up to currents in society at large. Reverting to the Stalinist instincts of his youth, Carrillo reacted violently against the *renovadores*, expelling many of the PCE's most talented elements and several of his own closest collaborators. In November 1981, the application of 'administrative sanctions' to well-known figures like the PCE's foreign affairs expert, Manuel Azcárate, and the Communist members of the Madrid city council (*ayuntamiento*) brought home Carrillo's residual Stalinism to the general public. There were constant crises in the Catalan, Basque and Asturian parties. In the autumn of 1981, the bulk of the Partido Comunista de Euskadi-EPK broke away under Roberto Lertxundi and joined up with Mario Onaindía in Euskadiko Eskerra.[38] This, together with the endless drifting away of party intellectuals, led to widespread conviction that the PCE was moribund and likely to be annihilated in the next elections.

A not entirely dissimilar feeling about UCD was becoming equally common. A meeting of the party's executive committee was held on 2 November 1981 to discuss the electoral disaster in Galicia. At the meeting, at which Fernández Ordóñez's departure was announced, Calvo Sotelo spoke openly about the impact of the internal crisis. 'While the party appears every day in the crime pages', he commented mordantly, 'it is impossible to govern seriously.' ('*No se puede gobernar con seriedad mientras estamos saliendo en las páginas de sucesos.*') Coming so shortly after the PSOE's shining display of unity, the conflicts appearing at the UCD meeting created a lamentable spectacle. Adolfo Suárez commented that 'the scale of our deterioration is such that if we weren't all in UCD we wouldn't even vote for ourselves' ('*Es tal el deterioro que nos hemos infringido que si no fueramos nosotros de UCD, no nos votaríamos a nosotros mismos*'). The division of the two posts of Prime Minister and party President which had taken place at the II UCD Congress in Palma de Mallorca was now seen to be destructive. It had permitted Suárez to maintain control over the party through the President, Agustín Rodríguez Sahagún, and the Secretary-General, Rafael Calvo Ortega. This had inevitably weakened the position of Calvo Sotelo. At a time when he needed the party united behind him, it had been wracked by the power struggle between the Christian Democrat *críticos* and the alliance of social democrats and Suárez supporters. Now with Fernández Ordóñez out of the party, Suárez was more isolated.[39] Calvo Sotelo thought that he at last had some chance to stamp his own authority on the party. He reckoned without the destructive capacity of the conservative Christian Democrats led by Miguel Herrero and Oscar Alzaga.

The meeting of 2 November generated a conviction within the party that Calvo Sotelo should assume the UCD presidency. In particular, the ever-efficient Martín Villa had come to the conclusion that the hostility between Calvo Sotelo and Rodríguez Sahagún was damaging for the party. Accordingly, he swung his not inconsiderable weight behind Calvo Sotelo. Rodríguez Sahagún's sorrowful resignation was provoked at a further executive committee meeting on 13 November. Suárez was not present at the meeting but at a Madrid hospital where his son had been taken after an accident. After rumours that he had been talking of leaving UCD altogether, he announced his resignation from the executive committee. A week later, the UCD's political council met to choose a new leader. Calvo Sotelo was elected and in his acceptance speech described himself somewhat optimistically as *el clavillo del abanico, que mantiene unidas las varillas de UCD* (the pin which holds together the ribs of the UCD fan). It was a nice metaphor but it bore little relation to the reality of a party now in its death agony.[40]

Against the advice of Rodolfo Martín Villa, Juan Antonio García Díez and Pío Cabanillas, Calvo Sotelo immediately proceeded to the creation of a new cabinet. They believed that he should call early elections before the galloping weakness of UCD was exposed further in the Cortes. For a variety of reasons, Calvo Sotelo chose not to heed their warnings. Above all, he had hopes of a revival of the party and he also believed that his government should be in power to oversee the trial of the 23-F plotters. His new team, announced on 1 December, did little to suggest that he made the right decision. It was the same old story, a compromise team with little new talent. The Christian Democrats, Oscar Alzaga and Miguel Herrero Rodríguez de Miñón, already drawing nearer to Alianza Popular, refused portfolios and thereby left the government significantly weaker. Rodolfo Martín Villa assumed the first vice-presidency and relinquished his responsibilities in the autonomy process. Calvo Sotelo's idea was that Martín Villa would undertake to reorganize the UCD and prepare it for the next elections. As it was, he fell between two stools, being able to devote adequate time neither to the party nor to the government. He commented in his memoirs that to accept the vice-presidency had been a 'grave error'.[41]

Rosón remained at the Ministry of the Interior. As the second vice-president, with overall responsibility for the economy, Juan Antonio García Díez headed the social democrats who were thus rewarded for not joining Fernández Ordóñez's break-away group, Luis Gamir at Transport and Santiago Rodríguez Miranda at Labour and Social Security. Suárez's supporter, Rafael Arias Salgado became Minister for Territorial Administration. The liberal, Soledad Becerril Bustamante, became the Minister for Culture and the first woman to hold ministerial office in Spain since Federica Montseny during the Civil War. In theory at least, all the main UCD families had been represented. However, this division of the spoils appeared to be the cabinet's main positive feature. There was little to suggest a creative or dynamic response to problems like unemployment, the rape-seed scandal or the continuing rumblings of military discontent.

Indeed, the most disappointing feature of the cabinet was the continued presence at the Ministry of Defence of Alberto Oliart. A number of incidents had led to accusations that Oliart was behaving like the tail of the military dog. On 25 July the Captain-General of La Coruña, Manuel Fernández Posse, had made a speech attacking the liberalism of Spanish politics and society in terms which suggested outright nostalgia for Franco. Then on 20 August, General Luis Caruana y Gómez de Barreda, who had been military governor in Valencia on the night of 23 February and acted then in a rather ambiguous manner, was made Captain-General of Zaragoza. Further astonishment had been generated by the award of a medal for 'sufferings for the Fatherland' to General Milans del Bosch. Outrage greeted the imposition of a period of only one month's detention for his son, Captain Milans del Bosch, for offensively insulting remarks made about his Commander-in-Chief, the King, to whom he referred as a 'pig'. Comparisons were made a few weeks later with the identical sentence imposed upon Major Alvaro Graiño whose offence was to publish a newspaper article warning of *golpismo* in the armed forces. On 29 November there was an incident which recalled Tejero's suppression of a legally authorized demonstration in Malaga in 1977. The extreme rightist Captain Lorenzo Fernández Navarro ordered his men to charge against a legal and pacific anti-NATO demonstration in La Coruña. In all of these cases, Oliart had been seen to be lacking in the necessary authority.[42]

Moreover, in the weeks following his confirmation in his post, there were more worrying occurrences of military indiscipline. The most disturbing were the reappearance of an ultra organization called the Unión Militar Española and the publication of an anti-Constitutional manifesto signed by one hundred army offers, the bulk of them from the DAC. It was part of an ultra scheme to stimulate support for the 23-F plotters prior to their trial but it was also linked to the endlessly bubbling colonels' coup. The authors of the *manifiesto de los cien* hoped that it would be signed by 90 per cent of the officer corps. Only the determined reaction of the Joint Chiefs of Staff (Junta de Jefes de Estado Mayor or JUJEM) under General Ignacio Alfaro Arregui prevented the spread of revolt throughout the ranks. The signatories were put under detention and all units were warned of the total prohibition on political statements by officers. *El Alcázar* was the first newspaper able to publish the complete text. Accordingly, it was rumoured that the manifesto had been drawn up by the same group of ultras that had made up the *Colectivo Almendros* which had helped to prepare the way for the 23-F. Two days before its publication, José Antonio Girón de Velasco apparently lunched with some of the more prominent signatories including Colonel Jesús Crespo Cuspineda of the DAC. In fact one of the principal authors, Crespo would later be arrested as the key man behind the revival of the colonels' coup planned to destroy the elections of October 1982. Oliart's declarations about the manifesto to the effect that there was nothing to worry about provoked Manuel Fraga into remarking that the Ministry of Defence existed only on paper.[43]

The Minister's relaxed attitude contrasted to the determined display of authority by the King. Juan Carlos called a meeting of the Joint Chiefs of Staff and issued a call for discipline in the armed forces. Out of this meeting came a decision to replace the JUJEM in its entirety. The official explanation given was that, with many of its members coming up for retirement, total renewal was the only way to guarantee a coherent team to work together to oversee entry into NATO. Another view was that the JUJEM's authority was somewhat flawed after 23-F and that a fresh team would be needed to restore discipline especially with the trial of the conspirators on the horizon. Since General Gabeiras, Chief of the Army General Staff, was due to appear at the trial as a witness, it was feared that the authority of the JUJEM might be challenged in some way. The new president of the JUJEM announced in mid-January was General Alvaro Lacalle Leloup, a tough *Constitucionalista*.[44]

The atmosphere of uncertainty generated by the renewed talk of *golpismo* underlined the fact that, within weeks of its formation, Calvo Sotelo's cabinet seemed to lack determination and direction. The psychosis of the 'Armada solution' was being repeated. Rumours abounded that a government of concentration was going to be formed under the presidency of General González del Yerro. The PSOE made frequent declarations of its readiness to join in a coalition to deal with the crisis. Calvo Sotelo, however, preferred to go on alone despite the self-evident weakness of UCD. Alfonso Guerra commented that 'this is like Venice; every day we sink another centimetre'. He accused Calvo Sotelo of the arrogance of not bothering to look out of the window. It was hardly surprising, since the Prime Minister had enough to occupy him in trying to keep his own house in order. In the first week of February, three UCD deputies abandoned the sinking ship. Miguel Herrero Rodríguez de Miñón, a social democrat, Francisco Soler Valero, and the voluble Francoist historian Ricardo de la Cierva all joined Coalición Democrática.

After the major destabilizing operation that Herrero had organized within UCD, forming the Plataforma Moderada, forcing out Fernández Ordóñez and then breaking the power of Adolfo Suárez, his was an astonishing and opportunistic desertion. Having pushed hard for the UCD to make an electoral alliance with Coalición Democrática/Alianza Popular and failed, Herrero had been sacrificed as the UCD parliamentary spokesman and seems to have feared that his career in the party was finished. His transfer to Fraga's team was made the more attractive by the damage that he left behind him. The presence of the rightist La Cierva in UCD had long puzzled observers. UCD's difficulties were making many of its Cortes deputies wonder seriously if they would get a seat at the next elections. La Cierva was no exception. Inevitably, rumours abounded that these early departures were merely the first trickle before the dam burst. The position of Calvo Sotelo was weakening by the day.[45]

The situation in UCD and the consequent crisis of authority was exacerbated by a revival of ETA activity in the new year. A massive extortion campaign had been mounted by ETA-M with thousands of Basque businessmen and professionals receiving death threats and demands for payment of the 'revolutionary tax'. Many of those threatened were of modest means, many were PNV members and some of them had even fought with the Basque forces during the Civil War. The threats were backed up by the kidnapping on 5 January of the industrial magnate José Lipperhiede. The consequent wave of outrage recalled the demonstrations after the murder of José María Ryan. The Basque autonomous government and the PNV through its leader, Javier Arzallus, declared war on ETA. There were spontaneous demonstrations throughout the Basque Country and in rural areas for the first time villagers began to stand up to the covert threats of Herri Batasuna. This was a hopeful sign but hardly one for which Calvo Sotelo's government could take credit. Moreover,

Lipperhiede was released only after his family and friends had raised a ransom of 100 million pesetas (approximately £500,000).

At the same time as the renewed ETA-M activities, a crisis broke out within ETA-PM. Since the post 23-F ceasefire, many within the organization had been attracted by the efforts of Mario Onaindía and Juan María Bandrés of Euskadiko Eskerra to secure their reintegration into civil society. The Onaindía/Bandrés plans were a major contribution to the pacification of Euskadi. However, just as six years earlier the political initiatives of 'Pertur' had led to the breakaway of the *Comandos Bereziak*, now a militant section of ETA-PM rejected the peace initiative and moved closer to ETA-M. As a demonstration of their methods, at the beginning of January 1982 they kidnapped the father of the singer Julio Iglesias. He was released by an intervention of the special services of the GOE. At the same time, the Mando Unico Antiterrorista under Manuel Ballesteros scored a substantial triumph when it captured ETA-PM's entire arsenal.[46] However, the threat of ETA-M remained and public opinion began to wonder if perhaps the Socialists deserved a chance to try where UCD had failed.

Curiously, despite and perhaps even because of the constant rumours and realities of military subversion and ETA terrorism, the popular mood was changing. Confidence in the King and in the country's democratic institutions was paradoxically boosted by the *golpistas* themselves during the course of their trial. The proceedings began on 19 February and dominated Spanish politics until well into the spring.[47] They took place in a febrile atmosphere in which the ultra press was permitted to express open support for the defendants. Walls were not daubed but professionally stencilled with the slogan *Libertad Militares Patriotas Detenidos* (freedom for the jailed patriotic officers). In court, the defendants revealed themselves to be ill-mannered bullies. The extent of their arrogance, disloyalty – even to one another – petty-mindedness and moral bankruptcy was to have an enormous and unexpected impact on civil-military relations. There was public dismay at the behaviour of the self-regarding defendants. The *golpistas* talked of nothing but patriotism and their self-appointed role as guardians of the nation's values, yet they were blind to the extent to which their actions had done nothing but bring international ridicule and shame on Spain. Despite the efforts of *El Alcázar* to present the proceedings as a trial of the entire army, many officers were shocked and repudiated the defendants. Their disquiet was summed up by José Sáenz de Santamaría, now Captain-General of Valladolid, who declared that 'the Army has begun to be feared by its own people, ceases to be respected by its enemies and has begun its own self-destruction' ('*el Ejército empieza a ser temido por su propio pueblo, deja de ser respetado por sus enemigos y a comenzado su autodestrucción*').[48]

The trial had provided the stimulus for debate in officers' messes about the rights and wrongs of *golpismo*. Previously, the Francoist values of the old guard had been taken for granted. Now, there could be seen the appalling spectacle of officers who had always projected themselves as the embodiment of honour and discipline behaving in a boastful and undignified fashion. Their loutish attitudes in the courtroom and evidence of their disobedience of orders from superior officers undermined the certainties of the more thoughtful officers. The fact that the accused were tried by court martial rather than by a civilian court was originally a concession to military sensibilities. Yet, in a civilian court, the *golpistas* would have been able to claim that the entire military estate was being tried by civil society. As it was, the armed forces were forced to purge themselves. After the trial, defence of the Constitution, if not exactly fashionable, was less frowned upon within the ranks of the armed forces. Anti-democratic declarations which previously had enjoyed silent approbation if not open admiration were now more likely to draw severe rebukes from the military authorities.

Constitutionalist officers even began to appear on television and write articles in the press. The *pro-Constitucionalistas* began to come out of their shells and the *golpistas* to withdraw into the shadows, where needless to say they continued to plot the resuscitation of their never fully implemented 'coup of the colonels'. The bulk of the officer corps had become what was known as the *sector prudente*, concerned above all to safeguard their careers. *El Alcázar* began gradually to be replaced by moderate conservative newspapers like *ABC* and *Ya*. The beginning of a change of attitudes was also a response to the continuation in a slightly watered-down form of the promotions policy originally initiated by General Gutiérrez Mellado. Helped by the passage of time, the strategy of hastening the transfer to the reserve list of Francoist generals, putting key units in the hands of loyal *Constitucionalistas* and using criteria other than mere seniority when it came to appointments and promotions was gradually bearing fruit. The application of that policy owed less to the hesitations of the Minister of Defence than to the stern authority imposed on the Junta de Jefes de Estado Mayor by its new president, Alvaro Lacalle Leloup.

Even after the trial, however, Calvo Sotelo's position continued to deteriorate. ETA-M continued its endless round of kidnappings and bombings in support of its extortion campaign against businessmen. It struck a major blow against the government's popularity in mid-April by destroying the Madrid telephone exchange and causing massive inconvenience in both the capital and the surrounding provinces. The Mando Unico Antiterrorista was scoring some successes but not enough to convince public opinion that the war against ETA would soon be over. The most positive advance against ETA was coming as a result of the co-operation between the Minister of the Interior Juan José Rosón and the Euskadiko Eskerra leadership to help repentant members of ETA-PM lay down their arms. This was a sufficiently important initiative to infuriate the dwindling group within ETA-PM committed to continued terrorist activities. Reprisals were threatened against ex-*Etarras* who accepted what were called government 'bribes'. Nevertheless, the successes of the Onaindía/Bandrés plan for the pacification of Euskadi were not sufficient to calm the storm into which UCD was heading.

Daily reminders about the 23-F through the media's blanket coverage of the trial and the apparently endless violence of ETA-M had done little for the government's image. Opinion polls showed unmistakably that the PSOE would win the next general election. The most devastating proof came in the elections to the Andalusian parliament on 23 May. The bitterly fought campaign was seen on all sides as a rehearsal for a national contest. Andalusia represented one sixth of the total Spanish electorate. In addition to carrying the burden of its errors over Andalusian autonomy in 1980, UCD had to go into the campaign under the shadow of rumours that Adolfo Suárez was about to depart definitively from the party. He refused to participate in the election campaign. The PSOE, led by the charismatic Rafael Escuredo and with a dynamic message of change, received 52 per cent of the vote and sixty-six seats. Alianza Popular came second with seventeen seats and UCD trailed in third with only fifteen. In one village in the province of Granada, UCD received fewer votes than the number of UCD representatives on the municipal council.[49]

After the Andalusian results, the higher echelons of UCD became a cauldron of recriminations. Inevitably, dissatisfaction focused on Calvo Sotelo. There was talk of him being replaced by Landelino Lavilla and rumours that Martín Villa was trying to persuade Suárez to return. The most conservative Christian Democrat elements, like Oscar Alzaga, Marcelino Oreja and José Luis Alvarez, were giving more serious consideration than ever to following the example of Miguel Herrero and joining Coalición Democrática. They cannot have been unaware that the banks were beginning to pump money into Alianza Popular and to treat UCD with a growing coolness. Fraga was looking an ever more attractive ally since his triumphs in the Gallego and Andalusian elections. Reports appeared to the effect that Alianza Popular was experiencing a recruiting boom of 1000 new members per week. Calvo Sotelo realized that he would have to face a general election in the short to medium term. Immediately after the Andalusian results were digested, he began to prepare. However, his position was not helped by the publication on 3 June of the sentences of the trial of the 23-F conspirators. Although Tejero and Milans del Bosch received the maximum possible thirty years, Armada was sentenced to only six. Twenty-two of the thirty-two defendants were given less than three years which permitted them to return to the ranks after they had served their sentences. The government would eventually appeal to the Supreme Court (*Tribunal Supremo*) and the sentences would be substantially increased, most notably in the case of Armada. However, in the meanwhile, the sentences were received by a stunned political class. It seemed, briefly at least, as if nothing had changed.[50]

Leopoldo Calvo Sotelo, whose self-confessed difficulty in smiling did little for his image, seemed as lonely a figure as Suárez had in January 1981. He was an efficient administrator rather than a political communicator, let alone a great statesman. During the summer of 1982, his standing crumbled as that of both Manuel Fraga and Felipe González rocketed. Opinion polls left little doubt that the PSOE would be in a position to form a government after the next elections. Felipe González refrained from efforts to bring down the government or to force early elections, pointing out that the PSOE's primordial objective was to ensure the survival of the democratic regime. He was biding his time, creating an image of moderation and strength, gaining in democratic credibility and confident of his ultimate victory. Felipe González and Adolfo Suárez were in contact, discussing the possibility of a centre–left coalition. In recognition of the hopelessness of his situation, Calvo Sotelo resigned as President of UCD. He had never really wanted the Presidency and had done nothing with it. At a meeting of the party's political council on 6 July, Landelino Lavilla assumed the Presidency and the job of seeing the party through the next elections. Three members of the cabinet, Martín Villa, Arias Salgado and Lamo de Espinosa, resigned their posts in order to devote themselves to helping Lavilla rebuild the party. On 30 July, Calvo Sotelo announced that he would not be the UCD's presidential candidate in the next elections.[51]

By comparison with UCD, on which could be discerned the whiff of death, the PSOE could hardly have been in better health. Felipe González had announced that he had a programme of government and declared that his cabinet was already chosen. The liberal press was behind him. Francisco Fernández Ordóñez's Partido de Acción Democrática had negotiated an electoral coalition with the PSOE. The Socialists' growing strength permitted Felipe González to give the confident impression of being the future Prime Minister quietly biding his time. He had every reason to be confident since the self-destruction of the UCD was only matched by that of the PCE. Internal feuding among the Communists had reached such a peak that Carrillo was able to hold on to power only by the dangerous gesture of a short-lived resignation on 7 June. It presaged his ultimate loss of control of the party apparatus. UCD's disarray reached its most dramatic point at the end of July when it began to break up into its component parts.

Like a film running backwards, UCD returned to its fragmented origins. The more conservative Christian Democrats had only ever reconciled themselves to existence under Suárez because they were beguiled by the prospect of power. Now, under Oscar Alzaga, they followed the trail blazed by Miguel Herrero and formed the Partido Demócrata Popular and announced their electoral coalition with Fraga. The liberals, restless since the death of their leader, Joaquín Garrigues, were now reformed under his brother Antonio as the Partido Demócrata Liberal. The social democrats had already gone. Now Suárez, angry at being offered only the third place on the party's electoral list for Madrid, decided to leave and form a new party, to be called Centro Democrático y Social.[52] The electoral boost that this implied for the PSOE was magnified when Suárez refused categorically to co-operate with UCD and declared that, after the poll, his party would support a Socialist government. The departure of its first leader signified the granting of UCD's death certificate. Calvo Sotelo and Landelino Lavilla recognized the fact. On 27 August, the President called general elections to be held within the legal minimum period of two months. It was a final act of defiance aimed at preventing Suárez and the other defectors consolidating their new parties and thus even more taking votes away from UCD.[53]

A frantic effort now began to form coalitions before the deadline of 14 September. In a sea of opportunism, Landelino Lavilla showed himself briefly to be the determined and authoritative leader that UCD had been lacking. He refused to link UCD to the great rightist alliance being formed around Fraga with the sponsorship of the employers' federation, the CEOE, on the grounds that to do so would destroy the centre ground in Spanish politics. His attempt to form a coalition with the Centro Democrático y Social failed because Suárez was committed to a future co-operation with the PSOE. Lavilla's main success was to ensure that both Antonio Garrigues and his liberals and Juan Antonio García Díez and the remaining UCD social democrats would go into the elections as part of the centre coalition. It was all in vain and Lavilla must have known it. The electoral law which he himself had helped elaborate would implacably penalize a divided centre. Curiously, much of the effort put into the quest for coalitions was expended in the fond belief that groups like Suárez's CDS would gain about thirty seats. Opinion polls pointed more accurately to a sweeping Socialist victory and a strong showing for Alianza Popular.[54]

The CEOE tried to put a brake on the accelerating popularity of the Socialists by launching accusations that the PSOE aimed to impose a Soviet economic model on Spain. In fact, the PSOE's programme could not have been more moderate. Long-term ambitions for the creation of a just and egalitarian society were subordinated to immediate practical tasks like the restructuring of Spanish industry, the stimulation of employment, the reform of Spain's cumbersome civil service and the elaboration of a more positive and independent foreign policy. Most public attention focused on a promise to create 800,000 new jobs. Public investment was to be the key, backed by agreement with private enterprise. Immediate measures would include the reduction of the working day and the lowering of the retirement age. The quest for social justice was to be satisfied by increased spending on the social security system, the health service, education and housing. In foreign policy, an idealistic programme was elaborated which envisaged Spain remaining non-nuclear, adopting a more decisive role in Latin America, seeking an independent position between the two major alliance systems, freezing NATO integration and calling a referendum on membership, successfully concluding negotiations for entry into the EEC and advancing claims to sovereignty of Gibraltar.[55]

After the self-destruction of the centre, the substantial challenge to the PSOE came from Alianza Popular. Fraga's programme was unequivocally conservative, its catchwords efficiency and solutions. Law and order, freedom of education, the reduction of public spending, the maintenance of the free market economy, the defence of the family and national unity were the key points which managed to combine modern monetarism with traditional Spanish nationalist values. The creation of jobs was given less priority in the programme than the provision of what was called 'labour flexibility and mobility' which effectively meant an end to restrictions on lay-offs and redundancies. The Alianza Popular campaign was aimed at the middle classes and was rather less brash than had been expected from the energetic Fraga.

The election campaign was carried out with a high degree of civic spirit. This was not unconnected with the fact that on 3 October news broke of a projected coup. Scheduled for 27 October, the day before the polling was to take place, it was a more thoroughgoing version of the long simmering 'coup of the colonels'. Military intelligence services and the *Brigada Anti-golpe* had discovered that three ultra-rightist colonels, closely connected with Fuerza Nueva, were involved in a conspiracy whose ramifications led back to Milans del Bosch. Arrests in the early hours of the morning of 2 October had been followed by the interrogation and imprisonment of Colonel Luis Muñoz Gutiérrez, whose wife was a Fuerza Nueva candidate for the Senate, Colonel Jesús Crespo Cuspineda of the DAC, one of the plotters behind the manifesto of one hundred published in December 1981, and his brother, Colonel José Crespo Cuspineda. At the home of Muñoz Gutiérrez were found immensely detailed plans for the coup. The Zarzuela and Moncloa Palaces, the headquarters of the JUJEM, various ministries and key public buildings were to be taken over by commandos in helicopters. Railway stations, airports, radio and television transmitters and newspaper offices were to be seized. The political élite was to be 'neutralized' in their homes. The King was to be deposed for having betrayed his oath of loyalty to the Movimiento.[56]

The plotters had clearly learned the lessons of 23-F. *El Alcázar* tried to dismiss the coup as a government invention, referring to it as a *golpe de risa* (a pun on 'laughable coup' and 'fit of laughing'). The nation's politicians and the majority of the public were appalled. Fraga curiously stated during the Cortes debate on the coup that he understood the conspirators. Alfonso Guerra commented mordantly that 'Fraga has turned himself into the psychiatrist of the *golpistas*, which is dangerous because some psychiatrists end up getting their patients' illnesses.'[57] There were, however, some grounds for cautious optimism. The Centro Superior de la Información de la Defensa (CESID), the central military intelligence co-ordinating authority, had acted swiftly and efficiently, in dramatic contrast to February 1981. Moreover, the indignation produced by the plans for the physical elimination of the Chiefs of Staff contributed to the isolation of the *golpistas*. On the other hand, only the three main protagonists were arrested despite the discovery of documents implicating at least 200 more. Nine more officers thought to be involved were posted away from Madrid, including Major Ricardo Sáenz de Ynestrillas and Colonel Antonio Sicre Canut, who apparently remained as committed as ever to holding back the tide of democracy.[58]

However, the era of UCD appeasement of the military was about to give way to a more equal relationship between the Socialists and the armed forces. The elections of 28 October 1982 took place under the shadow of military intervention but fear did not deter the population from giving the PSOE a substantial mandate. Indeed, the election results were a gigantic popular rejection of the *golpistas* and their bizarre claim to be doing what was best for the people of Spain. The Socialists received 10,127,092 votes, 47.26 per cent of those cast, which gave them 202 seats. This was the biggest majority enjoyed by any party during the post-1977 period or even during the Second Republic. Alianza Popular came second with 5,548,335 votes, 25.89 per cent, and 107 deputies, thereby substantiating Fraga's predictions about a two-party system. UCD limped home behind the Catalan regional party Convergència i Unió with 1,323,339 votes, 6.17 per cent and 11 deputies. Calvo Sotelo failed to gain a seat. Santiago Carrillo did get a seat but the PCE dropped from nearly 11 per cent to 3.6 per cent and lost three quarters of its deputies.[59] The annihilation of UCD was the greatest electoral defeat suffered by a governing party in Europe since the Second World War. It recalled the disappearance of the Radical Party in Spain in 1936. That too had been a party short of ideals and ideas. It was ironic that Adolfo Suárez, having played the historic role of helping to dismantle Francoism and opening the way to the establishment of democracy under UCD, should go on to play the equally historic role of helping to dismantle UCD and opening the way to substantial change under the PSOE.

The PSOE's gains were well-distributed throughout the country, substantiating Socialist claims that it was a more truly national party than UCD had ever been. That alone would have guaranteed Felipe González a degree of military benevolence. The decisiveness of the popular vote in favour of the slogan 'Vote PSOE for change' had considerable impact in military circles. The scale of the popular commitment to the democratic regime definitively put an end to the claim that the army could interpret the national will better than could elected politicians. The moderation of the PSOE guaranteed considerable good will. The tasks awaiting Felipe González were enormous. The linked problems of ETA terrorism and military subversion required skill and authority. With good relations with both the PNV and Euskadiko Eskerra, the PSOE had perhaps a better chance of success against ETA than UCD ever did. Under the immensely tactful and authoritative figure of the new Minister of Defence, Narcis Serra, the PSOE would inaugurate a programme of military modernization, redeployment, professionalization and depoliticization which would finally undermine the Third World *golpista* mentality in the armed forces. The restructuring of Spanish industry, with its obsolete sectors, its high energy dependence, its regional imbalances and its technological subservience, would require vision and sacrifice. The same was true of agrarian reform. No one expected short-term triumphs. However, the fact that the PSOE was prepared to confront tasks shirked by UCD ensured remarkable public tolerance for immediate measures like devaluation of the peseta, tax increases and fuel price rises. The Socialists had been elected by a serious electorate which had undergone the agonies of terrorism and military conspiracy. They were expected to provide serious government.

Spain had come a long way since 1969. The Spanish people had walked the tightrope of terrorism and subversion. If they had been humiliated by Tejero and ETA, they also had much of which they could be proud. A major protagonist of the period had been a courageous and democratic press, some of whose most important figures like Juan Tomás de Salas, the director of *Cambio 16*, had faced death threats, and others like José María Portell had actually been murdered. Politicians from the old regime like Adolfo Suárez and from the opposition like Felipe González had belied Franco's doom-laden conviction that Spaniards were unfit for democracy. In the course of the transition, they and many others, Areilza, Martín Villa, Carrillo, Fraga and many more, had worked, above and beyond their mistakes or their party interest, in a spirit of compromise and sacrifice to establish democracy. Spaniards too had much to be proud of in the person of Juan Carlos, a democratic King who had risked his life in the service of the Constitution.

The road from 1969 had not been an easy one and there had been painful moments along the way. The Carrero Blanco period had seen the reluctant break-up of the Francoist clans. The moderate opposition had been strengthened but in response the regime had lashed out with ultra-rightist terror. Under Arias Navarro, the impossibility of Francoist *continuismo* had been agonizingly exposed. Then, against the expectations of all but a tiny few, Adolfo Suárez had done the impossible in overseeing the legal transition from Francoist 'legality' to democracy. Thereafter, all the democratic parties had worked together to create the framework of the Constitution and the structures of regional autonomy. The daunting obstacles of recalcitrant military nostalgia and the bloody schemes of ultra-nationalist adolescents stood in the way of the consolidation of democracy. Yet in the elections of 28 October 1982, the popular will prevailed. The transition was over. Real change could now begin.

Dramatis personae

Fernando Abril Martorell – close friend and collaborator of Adolfo Suárez, part of the 'Segovia mafia', held various ministries until dropped in 1980.

Fernando Alvarez de Miranda – liberal Christian Democrat, joined UCD, President of the Cortes from 1977 to 1979, thought to be the 'conscience' of UCD.

Miguel Angel Apalátegui 'Apala' – hard-line activist leader of ETA-PM's violent *Comandos Bereziak*, took them into ETA-M.

José María de Areilza, Conde de Motrico – ambitious and cosmopolitan ex-Francoist, a prominent leader of the liberal monarchist opposition and key figure in efforts to create a centre-right party until ousted by Suárez.

Carlos Arias Navarro – staunch Francoist, successively Director-General of Security, Mayor of Madrid, Minister of the Interior, then Franco's last Prime Minister, attempted half-heartedly to introduce limited cosmetic reform.

Alfonso Armada Comyn – ambitious general, conservative monarchist once close to Juan Carlos, tried to exploit the 1981 coup attempt for his own benefit.

Emilio Attard Alonso – amiable and ambitious Christian Democrat from Valencia, joined UCD, presided over Constitutional Committee of Cortes.

José María 'Txiki' Benegas – leader of the Basque branch of PSOE, campaigner for peace in Euskadi.

Pío Cabanillas Gallas – wily Gallego follower of Fraga, progressive Minister of Information under Arias Navarro, dismissed in 1974 then helped found UCD.

Rafael Calvo Serer – Opus Dei theorist, director of liberal newspaper

Madrid, joined opposition when it was closed down, member of Junta Democrática.

Leopoldo Calvo Sotelo – lugubrious UCD leader, succeeded Adolfo Suárez as Prime Minister in February 1981.

Angel Campano López – prominent ultra general, played ambiguous role on night of 23 February 1981 coup.

Luis Carrero Blanco – Franco's loyal Cabinet Secretary, hard-liner linked to Opus Dei, assassinated by ETA in 1973.

Santiago Carrillo Solares – veteran leader of the PCE, helped push Suárez to more thoroughgoing democratic reform.

Vicente Enrique y Tarancón – liberal leader of the Catholic Church.

Torcuato Fernández Miranda – Vice-President under Carrero Blanco, Falangist constitutional lawyer, once tutor to Juan Carlos, gave Suárez crucial advice and assistance in steering through the reform project.

Francisco Fernández Ordóñez – gregarious and restless social democrat 'baron' of UCD who passed over to the PSOE in 1982.

Manuel Fraga Iribarne – energetic and irascible Francoist, emerged in 1975 as a liberal, than swung to the right and founded Alianza Popular.

José Gabeiras Montero – loyal *constitucionalista* general, as Chief of the General Staff opposed the Tejero coup attempt of 1981.

Carlos Garaicoetxea – Basque *Lendakari*.

Juan García Carrés – prominent ultra.

Joaquín Garrigues Walker – liberal 'baron' of UCD.

Dr Vicente Gil – Franco's excitable but totally loyal personal physician.

José María Gil Robles – veteran Christian Democrat leader.

José Antonio Girón de Velasco – close to Franco, hard-line ultra-rightist.

Felipe González Márquez – leader of PSOE and Prime Minister from 1982.

Jesús González del Yerro – conservative general who as Captain-General of the Canary Islands remained loyal on the night of the 1981 military plot.

Alfonso Guerra – organizational brains of the PSOE and intimate friend of Felipe González, known for his organizational skills and mordant wit.

Manuel Gutiérrez Mellado – liberal general, as Minister of Defence assumed the difficult task of dealing with the army during the transition.

Miguel Herrero Rodríguez de Miñón – brilliant Christian Democrat lawyer, began his career close to José María Gil Robles, joined UCD then helped break it up.

Fernando Herrero Tejedor – Opus Dei member and prominent Movimiento figure who sponsored Adolfo Suárez's early career.

Carlos Iniesta Cano – prominent ultra general, close to Girón.

Landelino Lavilla Alsina – one-time *Tácito*, then Christian Democrat 'baron' within UCD, President of the Cortes from 1979 to 1982.

Gregorio López Bravo – a leading Opus Dei technocrat, survived Matesa scandal, disappeared after death of Carrero, re-emerged in Alianza Popular in 1977.

Laureano López Rodó – monarchist, the most prominent Opus Dei technocrat, disappeared after death of Carrero, reappeared in Alianza Popular in 1976.

Rodolfo Martín Villa – shrewd and hard-working Movimiento bureaucrat, became Suárez's Minister of the Interior and 'baron' of the *azules* within UCD.

Cristóbal Martínez-Bordiu, Marqués de Villaverde – ultra-rightist surgeon and Franco's son-in-law.

Pedro Merry Gordón – conservative general, as Captain-General of Seville wavered on night of 1981 military coup.

Jaime Milans del Bosch – ultra general, member of prominent military dynasty, Captain-General of Valencia and one of the leaders of the 1981 military coup.

Eduardo Moreno Bergareche 'Pertur' – ETA-PM political theorist, advocate of the return to conventional politics, murdered in 1976, allegedly by 'Apala'.

Alberto Oliart Saussol – UCD Minister of Defence under Calvo Sotelo.

Mario Onaindía Nachiondo – ETA militant, tried at Burgos, later leader of EIA, then Euskadiko Eskerra, leading figure in movement for peace in Euskadi.

Alfonso Osorio García – one-time *Tácito*, Catholic monarchist, Vice-President in Suárez's first government then broke with UCD to form Coalición Democrática.

Guillermo Quintana Lacaci – loyal *constitucionalista* general, who as Captain-General of Madrid opposed the 1981 military coup, murdered by ETA-M in 1984.

Federico Quintero Morente – colonel specializing in counter-insurgency questions, author of influential report on 1980 Turkish military coup.

Blas Piñar López – leading ultra-rightist, editor of *Fuerza Nueva*.

José María Portell – Basque journalist, expert on ETA, occasionally used as mediator between ETA and the government, murdered by ETA-M in 1978.

Nicolás Redondo – UGT leader from Bilbao, helped revive PSOE in late 1960s.

Dionisio Ridruejo – liberal and socially aware ex-Falangist who gave respectability to the opposition.

Joaquín Ruiz Giménez – ex-Minister under Franco, sincere social Catholic, crucial interlocutor between the opposition and regime moderates.

José María Ryan – Basque electrical engineer murdered by ETA-M in February 1981.

Ricardo Sáenz de Ynestrillas – inveterate *golpista*, associated with Tejero.

José Ignacio San Martín López – colonel who worked in Carrero Blanco's intelligence service and then became involved in *golpista* activities in 1980.

Fernando de Santiago y Díaz de Mendívil – reactionary Minister of Defence, resigned over Suárez's reform project, the most influential ultra general.

Joaquín Satrústegui – liberal monarchist opponent of Francoism.

Federico Silva Muñoz – conservative Christian Democrat Francoist, later in Alianza Popular.

José Solís Ruiz – Falangist proponent of various attempts at cosmetic reform in the last years of Francoism.

Adolfo Suárez González – ambitious Movimiento *apparatchik* who became a democrat and fulfilled the historic task of presiding over the transition.

Josep Tarradellas – historic President of the Generalitat.

Antonio Tejero Molina – fanatical ultra, Civil Guard colonel, inveterate plotter, behind coup attempts of 1978 and 1981.

Luis Torres Rojas – ultra general who attempted to involve the DAC in coup attempts in 1979 and 1981.

Glossary of frequently used Spanish words

abertzale. Left Basque patriot.

aceite de colza. Rape-seed oil, adulterated supplies of which were thought to be the cause of many deaths in 1981.

Alcalde. Mayor.

Almendros. Almond trees – pseudonym of *golpista* editorial collective in *El Alcázar* prior to *Tejerazo*.

Alternativa KAS. Basque ultra-nationalist minimum demands.

aperturista. Francoist who saw that the regime would have to be opened up to reform, hence *aperturismo* and *apertura* (opening).

Ayuntamiento. Town council/town hall.

Azules. Literally 'blues', but one-time Falangists in UCD.

Bereziak. Violent breakaway group from ETA-PM which joined ETA-M.

bunker. Generic term used to cover the extreme right committed to fighting democracy from the rubble of Francoism.

comando. Terrorist unit, usually of ETA but sometimes of GRAPO.

continuista. Francoist who wanted to keep the regime in being with the minimum change possible, hence *continuismo*.

convenio colectivo. Bi-annual wage agreement.

críticos. Critical anti-leadership faction in both PSOE and UCD.

desencanto. Disenchantment, a term popularized by the press in 1980.

desgobierno. Lack of government, a term popularized by the press during 1980 and 1981.

Ejército al Poder. Ultra slogan – power to the army.

Etarra. ETA activist.

Euskadi. The Basque Country.

Euskera. The Basque language.

fondo de reptiles. Slush fund.

fontaneros. 'Plumbers', term used to denote Suárez's inner circle of advisers.

garrote vil. Barbaric method of execution by strangulation used under Franco.

gobierno de gestión. All-party emergency coalition government.

golpe. Military coup.

golpe blando. Bloodless coup.

golpista. Soldier or civilian committed to overthrowing the democratic regime by means of a military coup.

Ikastola. Euskera-speaking school.

Ikurriña. The Basque flag.

incontrolados. Ultra-rightist terror squads which have got out of control, usually in the Basque Country.

inmovilista. Francoist who was not prepared to make any concessions to the democratic opposition, hence *inmovilismo*.

Lendakari. The Basque leader.

merienda. Late afternoon to early evening snack.

Movimiento. The institutional framework of Francoism.

oposiciones. Competitive state examinations.

pasota. Nihilistic form of punk, who *pasa de todo* or couldn't give a hoot about anything, considered to be one of the first symptoms of the *desencanto* of the late 1970s.

patrimonio sindical. Trade unions' buildings, newspapers and funds confiscated by the Francoists after the Civil War.

poderes fácticos. *De facto* powers, the army, the banks, the Church etc., an expression which became common after 1977.

ponencia. A report or the committee which draws it up.

portero. Concierge or doorman, sometimes used as informers by the Falange.

procurador. A member of the Francoist Cortes.

ruptura democrática. The total break with the structures and personnel of the old regime to which the opposition aspired until the acceptance in 1976 that there would have to be a negotiated break.

ruptura pactada. The negotiated break which was eventually the basis of the transition.

sereno. Night-watchman.

Sindicatos. The state-run vertical or corporate trade unions.

Tácito. Group of Catholic functionaries, associated with the ACNP, and later an important component of UCD.

terna. Three-man short-list, a constitutional device much favoured within the Francoist system to maintain a semblance of consultation while leaving ultimate choice in the dictator's hands.

voto de miedo. Fear vote.

zona nacional. The ultra-rightist-dominated Barrio de Salamanca in Madrid, a pun on the Civil War-time Nationalist zone.

Appendix 1   Spain's eleven military regions and their commanders on 23 February 1981

I Military Region, H.Q. Madrid: Lieutenant-General Guillermo Quintana Lacaci

II Military Region, H.Q. Seville: Lieutenant-General Pedro Merry Gordón

III Military Region, H.Q. Valencia: Lieutenant-General Jaime Milans del Bosch

IV Military Region, H.Q. Barcelona: Lieutenant-General Antonio Pascual Galmés

V Military Region, H.Q. Zaragoza: Lieutenant-General Antonio Elícegui Prieto

VI Military Region, H.Q. Burgos: Lieutenant-General Luis Polanco Mejorada

VII Military Region, H.Q. Valladolid: Lieutenant-General Angel Campano López

VIII Military Region, H.Q. La Coruña: Lieutenant-General Manuel Fernández Posse

IX Military Region, H.Q. Granada: Lieutenant-General Antonio Delgado Alvarez

Military Region of the Canary Islands: Lieutenant-General Jesús González del Yerro

Military Region of the Balearic Islands: Lieutenant-General Manuel de la Torre Pascual

Appendix 2   The evolution of ETA's principal factions

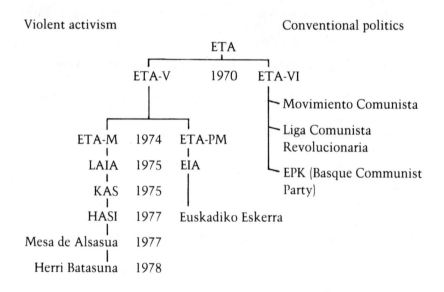

Violent activism

Conventional politics

ETA

ETA-V   1970   ETA-VI

— Movimiento Comunista

— Liga Comunista Revolucionaria

ETA-M   1974   ETA-PM

LAIA   1975   EIA

KAS   1975

— EPK (Basque Communist Party)

HASI   1977   Euskadiko Eskerra

Mesa de Alsasua 1977

Herri Batasuna   1978

Notes

Chapter 1 The internal contradictions of Francoism 1939–69

1 On the origins and nature of the Civil War, see Raymond Carr, *The Spanish Tragedy: The Civil War in Perspective* (London, 1977) and Paul Preston, *The Coming of the Spanish Civil War* (London, 1978) and, as editor, *Revolution and War in Spain 1931–1939* (London, 1984).

2 For the composition of Franco's support, see Amando de Miguel, *Sociología del franquismo* (Barcelona, 1975); Eduardo Sevilla-Guzmán and Salvador Giner, 'Absolutismo despótico y dominación de clase: el caso de España' in *Cuadernos de Ruedo Ibérico*, nos 43–5, January–June 1975; C. Viver Pi-Sunyer, *El personal político de Franco 1936–1945* (Barcelona, 1978) and Miguel Jerez Mir, *Elites políticas y centros de extracción en España 1938–1957* (Madrid, 1982).

3 Raymond Carr and Juan Pablo Fusi, *Spain: Dictatorship to Democracy* (London, 1979) p. 19.

4 Hartmut Heine, *La oposición política al franquismo* (Barcelona, 1983) pp. 41–8; Malcolm Muggeridge, editor, *Ciano's Diplomatic Papers* (London, 1948) pp. 293–4; Charles Foltz Jr., *The Masquerade in Spain* (Boston, 1948) pp. 96–8.

5 The narrow competition between the Francoist families has been denominated 'limited pluralism'. See Juan J. Linz, 'An authoritarian regime: Spain' in E. Allardt and Y. Littunen, editors, *Cleavages, Ideologies and Party Systems* (Helsinki, 1964); Miguel, *Sociología*, passim and Sheelagh Ellwood, *Prietas las filas: historia de Falange Española 1933–1983* (Barcelona, 1984) chapters 3 and 4.

6 Ellwood, *Prietas las filas*, pp. 146–7; Ramon Serrano Suñer, *Entre el silencio y la propaganda, la Historia como fue: Memorias* (Barcelona, 1977) pp. 364–71.

7 This shift in the internal balance of forces is the subject of Paul Preston, editor, *Spain in Crisis: Evolution and Decline of the Franco Regime* (Hassocks, 1976).

8 The more bizarre contradictions are discussed in Agustín Roa Ventura, *Agonía y muerte del franquismo (una memoria)* (Barcelona, 1978).

9 Sima Lieberman, *The Contemporary Spanish Economy: A Historical Perspective* (London, 1982) pp. 73–96; José Manuel Naredo, *La evolución de la agricultura en España* 2nd edition (Barcelona, 1974) pp. 146–71

10 Angel Viñas, *Los pactos secretos de Franco con Estados unidos* (Barcelona, 1981) pp. 26–51, 134–48.

11 Pablo Lizcano, *La generación del 56: la universidad contra Franco* (Barcelona, 1981) pp. 77 ff.; Sergio Vilar, *La oposición a la dictadura: protagonistas de la España democrática* 2nd edition (Barcelona, 1976) pp. 405–7; Javier Tusell, *La oposición democrática al franquismo* (Barcelona, 1977) pp. 282–97.

12   This process was analysed as early as 1964 by Fernando Claudín, *Las divergencias en el Partido* (n.p., 1964) chapters 3, 5 and 6. Less prophetic accounts may be found in F. Javier Paniagua, *La ordenación del capitalismo avanzado en España: 1957–1963* (Barcelona, 1977) *passim*; Carlos Moya, *El Poder económico en España* (Madrid, 1975) pp. 119–42 and Lieberman, *Spanish Economy*, pp. 199–246.

13   Lieberman, *Spanish Economy*, pp. 250–6. On the strikes of 1962 and their implications, see Ignacio Fernández de Castro and José Martínez, editors, *España hoy* (Paris, 1963) and Parti Communiste Français, *2 meses de huelgas* (Paris, 1962).

14   Ellwood, *Prietas las filas*, pp. 183–7; Carr and Fusi, *Spain*, pp. 174–6.

15   Ramon Soriano, *La mano izquierda de Franco* (Barcelona, 1981) *passim*; Laureano López Rodó, *La larga marcha hacia la Monarquía* (Barcelona, 1977), pp. 195–7.

16   López Rodó, *La larga marcha*, pp. 286–9.

17   Amandino Rodríguez Armada and José Antonio Novais, *¿Quién mató a Julián Grimau?* (Madrid, 1976) pp. 109–58; Stuart Christie, *The Christie File* (Seattle, 1980) p. 51; *¿Crimen o castigo? Documentos inéditos sobre Julián Grimau* (Madrid, 1963) *passim*.

18   Octavio Alberola and Ariane Gransac, *El anarquismo español y la acción revolucionaria 1961–1974* (Paris, 1975) pp. 107–12.

19   *Cuadernos de Ruedo Ibérico*, no. 10, December 1966 to January 1967, pp. 28–63.

20   Edouard de Blaye, *Franco and the Politics of Spain* (Harmondsworth, 1976) pp. 186–214; Lorenzo Torres, 'The Spanish left: illusion and reality' in *The Socialist Register 1966* pp. 68 ff.

21   For an account of this crisis in the Communist Party, see Paul Preston, 'The PCE's long road to democracy 1954–1977' in Richard Kindersley, editor, *In Search of Euro-communism* (London, 1981); Claudín, *Las divergencias*, *passim*; Jorge Semprún, *Autobiografía de Federico Sánchez*, *passim* (Barcelona, 1977).

22   Vilar, *La oposición* pp. 397–451, 507–11. For an excellent account of the thinking of the liberal and moderate opposition, see Elías Díaz, *Pensamiento español 1939–1973* (Madrid, 1974) *passim*.

23   Gregorio Morán, *Los españoles que dejaron de serlo: Euskadi, 1937–1981* (Barcelona, 1982) pp. 17–27.

24   Lizcano, *La generación del 56*, *passim*; Salvador Giner, 'Power, freedom and social change in the Spanish university, 1939–1975' in Paul Preston, editor, *Spain in Crisis: Evolution and Decline of the Franco Regime* (Hassocks, 1976).

25   De Blaye, *Franco*, pp. 246–8; Rafael Calvo Serer, *La dictadura de los franquistas: El 'affaire' del MADRID y el futuro político* (Paris, 1973), pp. 64–5, 80–1.

26   Jesus Ynfante, *La prodigiosa aventura del Opus Dei: génesis y desarrollo de la Santa Mafia* (Paris, 1970) pp. 173–7; López Rodó, *La larga marcha*, pp. 263–5.

27   José María Maravall, *Dictatorship and Political Dissent: Workers and Students in Franco's Spain* (London, 1978), pp. 33–8.

28   José Chao, *La Iglesia en el franquismo* (Madrid, 1976) pp. 152–3. I am indebted to Dr Frances Lannon for her comments on the radicalization of the Church.

29   Francisco Franco Salgado-Araujo, *Mis conversaciones privadas con Franco* (Barcelona, 1976), diary entries for 16 January, 8, 22 March, 3 May 1969, pp. 538–9, 544–5, 548.

Chapter 2 Holding back the tide: the Carrero Blanco years 1969–73

1   *Le Monde*, 9–10, 11, 14, 15 March 1969; Chao, *Iglesia*, pp. 154–204; Norman Cooper, 'The Church: from crusade to Christianity' in Preston, editor, *Spain in Crisis*, pp. 66–9.

2   Alfonso Osorio, *Trayectoria política de un ministro de la Corona* (Barcelona, 1980) pp. 16–19; A. Sáez Alba, *La otra cosa nostra: la Asociación Católica Nacional de Propagandistas y el caso de EL CORREO de Andalucía* (Paris, 1974) pp. LXXXII–CII. Manuel Cantarero del Castillo, *Falange y socialismo* (Barcelona, 1973) is an extreme

example of this tendency within the Falange. Cf. Luis Ramírez, 'Morir en el bunker' in *Horizonte español 1972*, 3 vols (Paris, 1972) I, pp. 3–4; Calvo Serer, *La dictadura*, p. 46.

3　Franco Salgado, diary entry for 22 March 1969, *Conversaciones*, pp. 544–5; De Blaye, *Franco*, pp. 255–6.

4　Lieberman, *Spanish Economy*, pp. 199–263; Manuel Jesús González, *La economía política del franquismo 1940–1970: dirigismo, mercado y planificación* (Madrid, 1979) pp. 300–46.

5　López Rodó, *La larga marcha*, pp. 316–78, 650–2.

6　*Arriba*, 29 November 1966, quoted by Sheelagh Ellwood, *Franco's Single Party: Falange Española de la JONS 1933–1983*, unpublished doctoral thesis, University of London, 1983, p. 233.

7　*Le Monde*, 3 September; *Mundo Obrero*, 2 September 1969.

8　Carr and Fusi, *Spain*, pp. 179–88.

9　*Le Monde*, 8, 9, 11, 12, 29 July; 7, 8, 19, 20, 22, 26 August; *International Herald Tribune*, 10, 17 July 1969.

10　*Le Monde*, 31 August to 1 September 1969; López Rodó, *La larga marcha*, pp. 391–5, 653–9; Rafael Calvo Serer, *Franco frente al rey* (Paris, 1972) pp. 188–95; Franco Salgado, diary entry for 11 October 1969, *Conversaciones*, p. 549; De Blaye, *Franco*, pp. 259–64.

11　Ricardo de la Cierva, *Historia del franquismo*, 2 vols (Barcelona, 1975–8) II, pp. 99–100.

12　*Le Monde*, 27 December 1969; 27 April 1970; *Mundo Obrero*, 23 January, 25 May; *ABC*, 25, 26 April, 1970; Franco Salgado, diary entry for 25 April 1970, *Conversaciones*, pp. 556–7; Enrique Tierno Galván, *Cabos sueltos* (Barcelona, 1981) pp. 420–3.

13　*Mundo Obrero*, 8, 23 January, 6 February 1970.

14　Fernando Claudín, 'Las relaciones soviético-franquistas (Crónica de una normalización inconclusa)' in *Horizonte español 1972*, II, pp. 250–262; *Mundo Obrero*, 7 March 1970.

15　*Mundo Obrero*, 9 September; *ABC*, 22 July 1970; *Horizonte español 1972*, I, pp. 203–12.

16　*Ya*, 29 July 1970.

17　*Le Monde*, 16, 31 December 1969; *Horizonte español 1972*, I, p. 191; Cooper, 'The Church', pp. 70–1.

18　*Le Monde*, 1, 5, 9, 12, September; *Mundo Obrero*, 9, 30 September 1970.

19　*Le Monde*, 3, 5, 6 November; *Mundo Obrero*, 14 November 1970.

20　*Le Monde*, 20–21 September 1970; Joseba Elósegi, *Quiero morir por algo* (n.p., n.d., but St Jean de Luz, 1971); Herbert R. Southworth, *Guernica! Guernica! A Study of Journalism, Diplomacy, Propaganda and History* (Berkeley, 1977) pp. 308–9.

21　*Mundo Obrero*, 30 October, 22 December 1970

22　Calvo Serer, *La dictadura*, p. 173; Ramírez, 'Morir en el bunker'; Paul Preston, 'General Franco's rearguard' in *New Society*, 29 November 1973.

23　*Ya*, 1 April 1970; Ginés de Buitrago, 'Un poco de formalidad!' in *ABC*, 2 April; *Mundo Obrero* 29 April 1970.

24　*International Herald Tribune*, 27 May 1970.

25　*Horizonte español 1972*, I, pp. 192, 195, 225.

26　*Madrid*, 30 May 1968, 25 November 1971; Calvo Serer, *La dictadura*, pp. xvii–xxvii, 2–10, 179–209.

27　Kepa Salaberri, *El proceso de Euskadi en Burgos. El sumarísimo 31.69* (Paris, 1971) pp. 102–10; *ABC*, 22, 26 November 1970.

28　Salaberri, *Proceso*, p. 107; La Cierva, *Franquismo*, II, pp. 329–36.

29　*Le Monde*, 2 December 1970; *Horizonte español 1972*, I, p. 235.

30　Gurutz Jáuregui Bereciartu, *Ideología y estrategia política de ETA* (Madrid, 1981) pp. 469–70. For the impact of the kidnapping in Germany, see *IG-Metall Pressespiegel für spanische Kollegen, Servicio de Prensa*, no. 342, 18 January 1971.

31　Angel Amigo, *Pertur: ETA 71–76* (San Sebastián, 1978) p. 26.

32　*Le Monde*, 5, 8 December 1970; Salaberri, *Proceso*, pp. 165–7.

33 *Le Monde,* 11 December; *Nouvel Observateur,* 14 December 1970. The best account of the trial is Salaberri, *Proceso,* pp. 153-238. See also Lurra, *Burgos, Juicio a un pueblo* (San Sebastián, 1978). The regime's point of view can be found in Angel Ruiz de Ayúcar, *Crónica agitada de ocho años tranquilos 1963-1970* (Madrid, 1974) pp. 219-368, and Federico de Arteaga, *ETA y el proceso de Burgos* (Madrid, 1971) pp. 305-34

34 *Mundo Obrero,* 22 December; *Le Monde,* 15, 23 December 1970

35 *Le Monde,* 15, 16, 17 December 1970

36 *Le Monde,* 18, 19, 21 December 1970; Vicente Gil, *Cuarenta años junto a Franco* (Barcelona, 1981) pp. 98-103; Salaberri, *Proceso,* pp. 263-72; *Horizonte español 1972,* I, pp. 266-71.

37 *Le Monde,* 23, 29 December 1970; Salaberri, *Proceso,* pp. 275-81.

38 *Le Monde,* 29, 30, 31 December 1970; Salaberri, *Proceso,* pp. 293-318; Angel Bayod, editor, *Franco visto por sus ministros* (Barcelona, 1981) p. 239.

39 *Le Monde,* 4 February 1971.

40 *Mundo Obrero,* 22 January; *Le Monde Diplomatique,* January 1971; Calvo Serer, *Franco,* pp. 198-9; De Blaye, *Franco,* pp. 324-5

41 *Mundo Obrero,* 6, 19 February 1971; *Horizonte español 1972,* I, pp. 279, 288.

42 *Le Monde,* 31 January; *Mundo Obrero,* 3 April; *Madrid,* 24 November 1971; Ramírez, 'Morir en el bunker', p. 3.

43 *Le Monde,* 11 November 1971; *Horizonte español 1972,* I, p. 289; Calvo Serer, *Franco,* pp. 205-18.

44 *Cuadernos de Ruedo Ibérico,* nos 33-5, October 1971 to March 1972, pp. 3-19; *Horizonte español 1972,* I, pp. 326-35; *Mundo Obrero,* 15 October; *ABC,* 2 October 1971; Calvo Serer, *La dictadura,* pp. 190-3.

45 Cooper, 'The Church', pp. 72-4.

46 *Le Monde,* 12, 22 October, 2, 17, 24 November; *Mundo Obrero,* 15 July, 17 September, 2, 27 October, 12 November, 10 December 1971.

47 *Mundo Obrero,* 10 December 1971; *Horizonte español 1972,* I, pp. 315-16.

48 *Le Monde,* 1-2 February 1970; *Informaciones,* 6 November 1971, 17 April 1972, 26, 30 April 1973; *ABC,* 7 November 1971; *Mundo,* 15 April 1972, 9 June 1973; *Horizonte español 1972,* I, pp. 311-14.

49 De Blaye, *Franco,* pp. 332-3.

50 Amigo, *Pertur,* pp. 44-8; José María Garmendía, *Historia de ETA,* 2 vols (San Sebastián, 1980) II, pp. 164-73; Ortzi (pseudonym of Francisco Letamendía), *Historia de Euskadi: el nacionalismo vasco y ETA* (Paris, 1975) pp. 397-401.

51 Garmendía, *ETA,* II, pp. 173-8.

52 *Observer,* 19 March; *Mundo Obrero,* 14, 30 March, 15 April 1972.

53 *Mundo Obrero,* 5 February, 10, 22 June 1972; *Horizonte español 1972,* I, p. 370.

54 *ABC,* 1 January; *Ya,* 6 January 1972; *Horizonte español 1972,* I, p. 336.

55 *Mundo Obrero,* 3 March, 8 July 1972; 26 April 1973.

56 *Le Monde,* 15 August; *Le Socialiste,* 21 September 1972; PSOE, *Congresos del PSOE en el exilio,* 2 vols (Madrid, 1981) II, pp. 179-204.

57 Dionisio Ridruejo, *Casi unas memorias* (Barcelona, 1976) pp. 427-34; Rafael Calvo Serer, *La solución presidencialista* (Barcelona, 1979) pp. 48-53; Miguel Herrero, *El principio monárquico* (Madrid, 1972); Jorge de Esteban *et al., Desarrollo político y constitución española* (Barcelona, 1973).

58 Carr and Fusi, *Spain,* pp. 194-5; *Mundo Obrero,* 28 April, 23 May 1973.

59 *Le Monde,* 4, 5-6, 7 August; *Informaciones,* 11 June 1973; Calvo Serer, *La solución,* pp. 127-36; Miguel, *Sociología,* p. 81.

60 *Mundo Obrero,* 1, 28 November, 12 December 1973.

61 *Observer,* 23 December; *Le Monde,* 23-24 December 1973; *Mundo Obrero,* 15 January 1974; conversations of the author with Nicolás Sartorius in London, October 1983.

62 The fullest accounts of the assassination are Julen Agirre (pseudonym of Eva Forest), *Operación Ogro: cómo y porqué ejecutamos a Carrero Blanco* (Paris/Hendaye, 1974); Joaquín Bardavío, *La crisis: historia de quince días* (Madrid, 1974); Rafael Borrás Bertriu et al., *El día en que mataron a Carrero Blanco* (Barcelona, 1974); Ismael Fuente, Javier García and Joaquín Prieto, *Golpe mortal: asesinato de Carrero y agonía del franquismo* (Madrid, 1983).

63 ETA communiqué no. 1, 20 December 1973, reprinted in Agirre, *Ogro*, p. 139.

64 *Le Monde*, 3 December 1974.

65 *Le Monde*, 25, 30-31 December 1973.

66 *Sunday Times*, 23 December; *Pueblo*, 22 December; *Guardian*, 27 December 1973. The text as published, and perhaps expurgated, shows an excess of zeal rather than a deliberate plan to make a *coup d'état*. See Bardavío, *La crisis*, pp. 111-16; Borrás, *El día*, pp. 34-6; Carlos Iniesta Cano, *Memorias y recuerdos* (Barcelona, 1984) pp. 218-22; José Ignacio San Martín, *Servicio especial* (Barcelona, 1983) pp. 90-114. See also *El Socialista*, 2ª quincena de enero 1974, and Marcel Niedergang, 'Le franquisme et ses ultras' in *Le Monde*, 5-8 January 1974.

67 *Guardian*, 28 December; *Times*, 29 December; *Le Monde*, 30-31 December 1973; *ABC*, 4 January 1974; Bardavío, *La crisis*, pp. 139-61; Gil, *Cuarenta años*, pp. 139-61; Bardavío, 'Las intrigas franquistas de palacio' in *Diario 16*, 9 October 1983; Antonio Izquierdo, *Yo, testigo de cargo* (Barcelona, 1981) p. 37.

68 Borrás, *El día*, pp. 252-6; *Mundo*, 5 January 1974.

69 *Le Monde*, 26 December; *Informaciones*, 21 December 1973; Anatoly Krasikov, *From Dictatorship to Democracy: Spanish Reportage* (Oxford, 1984) pp. 62-9; Fuente et al., *Golpe mortal*, pp. 50-1.

70 *Daily Telegraph*, 31 December; *Guardian*, 31 December 1973, 4 January; *Financial Times*, 4 January; *Le Monde*, 4 January 1974.

Chapter 3 A necessary evil: the Arias Navarro experience 1974-6

1 Wilebaldo Solano, 'Le développement des conflits sociaux' in *Le Monde Diplomatique*, February 1974; *Mundo Obrero*, 28 November, 31 December; *Frente Libertario*, December 1973.

2 Charles F. Gallagher, *Spain, Development and the Energy Crisis* (New York, 1973) p. 3.

3 Ramón Tamames, 'Expansion économique et démocratie' in *Le Monde Diplomatique*, February 1974; *Financial Times*, 13 February 1974; *Cambio 16*, 18 March; *Treball*, 12 March 1974.

4 Gil, *Cuarenta años*, pp. 145-6.

5 Bardavío, 'Las intrigas franquistas de palacio' in *Diario 16*, 9 October 1983 and *La crisis*, p. 224.

6 Javier Figuero, *UCD: la 'empresa' que creó Adolfo Suárez* (Barcelona, 1981) p. 17; San Martín, *Servicio especial*, p. 101.

7 Sáez Alba, *ACNP*, pp. 293-323; Fernando Jáuregui and Manuel Soriano, *La otra historia de UCD* (Madrid, 1980) pp. 41-2.

8 *ABC*, 3 March 1974; *Declaración programática del nuevo Gobierno* (Madrid, 1974); Osorio, *Trayectoria*, pp. 26-7; Sáez Alba, *ACNP*, pp. CX-CXII.

9. *Guardian*, 13 February; *Times*, 13 February; *Le Monde*, 14 February; *Mundo Obrero*, 27 February 1974. Arias's speech was apparently written by Gabriel Cisneros and Luis Jaúdenes. For the full text, see *Discurso del Presidente del Gobierno a las Cortes Españolas, 12.II.1974* (Madrid, 1974).

10 Bardavío, *La crisis*, pp. 131, 161-4.

11 *ABC*, 18 January 1974; *El Alcázar*, 17 November 1973.

12 Francesc Amover, *Il carcere vaticano: Chiesa e fascismo in Spagna* (Milan, 1975)

pp. 87–99; Fernando Gutiérrez, *Curas represaliados en el franquismo* (Madrid, 1977) pp. 152–81.

13 José María de Areilza, *Diario de un ministro de la monarquía* (Barcelona, 1977) p. 71.

14 *Le Monde*, 26 February, 5, 9 March; *El Alcázar*, 7, 8 March; *Observer*, 10 March; *Guardian*, 11 March 1974; Ortzi, *Euskadi*, pp. 404–7; 'Il bastone e la garrota' in *Panorama* (Rome) 14 March 1974.

15 *La Voz Comunista*, no. 6, May 1974; *Mundo Obrero*, 31 December 1973, 25 April 1974; *Frente Libertario*, April, May 1974.

16 *Agenor*, no. 42, April 1974.

17 *Arriba*, 28 April, 12 May; *Ya*, 30 April; *Cambio 16*, 13 May; *ABC*, 30 April; *Le Monde*, 23 May 1974.

18 *Le Monde*, 15 May; *Financial Times*, 29 May; *Guardian*, 31 May 1974.

19 *Guardian*, 12, 15 June; *Le Monde*, 13, 15, 16–17 June; *Mundo Obrero*, 4 June 1974; remarks made by Santiago Carrillo at a private seminar organized in Toledo in May 1984 by the Fundación Ortega y Gasset (henceforth FOG/Toledo).

20 *ABC*, 29 May, 16 June; *Ya*, 16 June; *El Alcázar*, 16 June 1974.

21 *Le Monde*, 23–24, 25 June; *Mundo Obrero*, 3 July 1974; Fernando Alvarez de Miranda, *Del 'contubernio' al consenso* (Barcelona, 1985) p. 81.

22 *Le Monde*, 11 June, 21–22, 25 July, 4 September; *Observer*, 14 July; *Times*, 20 July; *Guardian*, 20 July; *Ya*, 20 July 1974; Gil, *Cuarenta años*, pp. 167–202; Luis Ramírez, *Franco: la obsesión de ser, la obsesión de poder* (Paris, 1976) p. 315.

23 *ABC*, 3 September 1974.

24 *Mundo Obrero*, 24 December 1971; Santiago Carrillo, *Hacia el post-franquismo* (Paris, 1974) pp. 57–62;

25 *Le Monde*, 4–5 August 1974; *Mundo Obrero*, 31 July 1974; Rafael Calvo Serer, *Mis enfrentamientos con el Poder* (Barcelona, 1978) pp. 119–21; Carrillo, FOG/Toledo; Enrique Tierno Galván, *Cabos sueltos* (Barcelona, 1981) pp. 446–9.

26 Calvo Serer, *Mis enfrentamientos*, pp. 248–65; personal observation by the author in Spain at the time.

27 *Le Monde*, 19 October; *Guardian*, 18 October 1974; remarks of Felipe González at FOG/Toledo.

28 *Le Monde*, 7, 12, 13–14 September; *Guardian*, 6 September; *La Vanguardia*, 8 September 1974. See also the interview with Joaquín Ruiz Giménez in *Tele-Express*, 10 September 1974.

29 *Times*, 14 September, *Le Monde*, 15–16, 29–30 September; *Arriba*, 24 September 1974; Ortzi, *Euskadi*, p. 412. See also Lidia Falcón, *Viernes y trece en la Calle del Correo* (Barcelona, 1981) *passim*. Cf. Eva Forest, *From a Spanish Jail* (Harmondsworth, 1975) pp. 9–11.

30 *Le Monde*, 21 September, 4, 8, 18, 30, 31 October; *Guardian*, 27 September, 30 October 1974; José Oneto, *Arias entre dos crisis, 1973–1975* (Madrid, 1975); Ramón Garriga, *Nicolás Franco, el hermano brujo* (Barcelona, 1980), pp. 311–20.

31 *Ya*, 30, 31 October; *ABC*, 30 October; *Cambio 16*, 11–17, 18–24 November; *Le Monde*, 7 November 1974.

32 *Le Monde*, 20, 29, 30 November; *Guardian*, 28 November; *Times*, 28 November; *Financial Times*, 28 November 1974; Alvarez de Miranda, *Del 'contubernio'*, p. 83.

33 *Le Monde*, 3, 4, 5, 6, 18 December; *Ya*, 6 December; *Guardian*, 3 December 1974.

34 *Cambio 16*, 10 June 1974; Ramón Tamames, *Un proyecto de democracia para el futuro de España* (Madrid, 1974) pp. 7–10; Joaquín Garrigues Walker, *Qué es el liberalismo* (Barcelona, 1976) *passim*; Ramon Pi, *Joaquín Garrigues Walker* (Madrid, 1977) p. 40.

35 *Le Monde*, 14 December 1974; *Guardian*, 17 January; *Ya*, 6 February; *Triunfo*, 8 February, 15 March; *Cambio 16*, 17–23 February 1975; Ortzi, *Euskadi*, pp. 412–17.

36 *Guardian*, 6 January, 10 March; *Daily Telegraph*, 7 January; *Financial Times*,

20 February 1975; *Cambio 16*, 15-21 March 1976; Union Militar Democrática, *Los militares y la lucha por la democracia* (n.p., n.d., but Madrid, 1976); Jesus Ynfante, *El Ejército de Franco y de Juan Carlos* (Paris, 1976) pp. 111-12.

37 *Guardian*, 15 February, 4 March 1974; remarks of Adolfo Suárez at FOG/Toledo. See also the interview with Licinio de la Fuente in Bayod, *Ministros*, pp. 240-2.

38 *Le Monde*, 5 March; *Ya*, 5 March; *Guardian*, 5, 6 March 1974.

39 *Cambio 16*, 23-29 June 1975; Figuero, *UCD*, p. 19; Gregorio Morán, *Adolfo Suárez: historia de una ambición* (Barcelona, 1979) pp. 285-96.

40 Suárez, FOG/Toledo; Osorio, *Trayectoria*, p. 183; Figuero, *UCD*, pp. 19-22; Morán, *Suárez*, pp. 74-5, 103-8, 121-7, 169-85.

41 *ABC*, 20 May 1975; Morán, *Suárez*, pp. 297-300.

42 Osorio, *Trayectoria*, pp. 40-5; Carr and Fusi, *Spain*, pp. 204-5; Santiago Pérez Díaz, *Francisco Fernández Ordóñez* (Madrid, 1976) p. 25.

43 Cooper, 'The Church', p. 80.

44 *Times*, 15 May 1975; Noticias del Pais Vasco, *Euskadi: el ultimo estado de excepción* (Paris, 1975) pp. 25-30, 45-77.

45 Javier Sánchez Eraúskin, *Txiki-Otaegi: el viento y las raíces* (San Sebastián, 1978) pp. 260-1, 283-93; NPV, *Euskadi*, pp. 143-51.

46 *Guardian*, 25 August; *Boletín Oficial del Estado*, 27 August 1975. See also the interview with the Under-Secretary of Justice, *Informaciones*, 27 August 1975.

47 *Guardian*, 27 August 1975.

48 *Mundo Obrero*, 4ª semana de junio, 3ª semana de julio 1975. Stock market quotations derive from *Cambio 16* throughout the autumn of 1975.

49 *Ya*, 30 September; *Sábado Gráfico*, 24-30 September; *Guardian*, 26, 30 September, 3, 7 October; *Observer*, 5 October; *Sunday Times*, 5 October 1975.

50 *Cambio 16*, 23-29 June 1975; *Mundo Obrero*, 4ª semana de septiembre 1975; Alvarez de Miranda, *Del 'contubernio'* p. 88.

51 *Cambio 16*, 6-12 October 1975.

52 *Guardian*, 2, 31 October, 7, 12 November; *Sunday Times*, 26 October, 9 November; *ABC*, 7 November; *Times*, 21 November 1975.

53 Joaquín Bardavío, *El dilema: un pequeño caudillo o un gran Rey* (Madrid, 1978) p. 25.

54 *Guardian*, 21, 26, 28 November; *Daily Telegraph*, 21 November; *Times*, 28 November 1975.

55 *Cambio 16*, 17 November 1975.

56 Rafael Calvo Serer, 'Juan Carlos après son père' in *Le Monde*, 29 January 1974; José Luis Aranguren, *La cruz de la monarquia española actual* (Madrid, 1974) *passim*. See also *Le Monde*, 2 February 1974.

57 *Mundo Obrero*, 25 November; *Servir al Pueblo*, no. 45, November; *Correo del Pueblo*, 18 November, 6 December; *Frente Libertario*, no. 57, December 1975.

58 Alfonso Armada, *Al servicio de la Corona* (Barcelona, 1983); Carlos Fernández, *Los militares en la transición política* (Barcelona, 1982) pp. 51-4.

59 *Times*, 27 November; *Guardian*, 1 December; *Daily Telegraph*, 8 December 1975.

60 Rafael Díaz Salazar, *Iglesia, dictadura y democracia: Catolicismo y sociedad en España (1953-1979)* (Madrid, 1981) p. 315; *Financial Times*, 28 November 1975.

61 Bardavío, *El dilema*, pp. 20-4, 42-6; Morán, *Suárez*, p. 16.

62 Areilza, diary entry for 30 December 1975, *Diario*, p. 38.

63 Morán, *Suárez*, pp. 15-20; Samuel Eaton, *The Forces of Freedom in Spain 1974-1979: A Personal Account* (Stanford, 1981) pp. 32-3; *Guardian*, 12 December 1975; Bardavío, *El dilema*, pp. 75-84.

64 Areilza, diary entry for 11 February 1976, *Diario*, p. 84; *Observer*, 1 February 1976; Osorio, *Trayectoria*, pp. 55, 65; Bardavío, *El dilema*, p. 105.

65 Rodolfo Martín Villa, *Al servicio del Estado* (Barcelona, 1984) p. 16.

66 Victor Díaz Cardiel *et al., Madrid en huelga; enero 1976* (Madrid, 1976) pp. 91–150; *Cambio 16*, 19–25 January; *Guardian*, 5, 7, 8, 9, 14, 15, 20 January; *Sunday Times*, 11, 18 January; *Mundo Obrero*, 20, 27 January 1976; Martín Villa, *Al servicio*, p. 17. For a leftist critique of the strike, see *Cuadernos de Ruedo Ibérico*, nos 51–3, May–October 1976, pp. 127–78.
67 Areilza, diary entry for 17 January 1976, *Diario*, p. 54.
68 *Mundo Obrero*, 4, 11 February; *Cambio 16*, 9–15 February; 1–7 March 1976.
69 Mario Onaindía, *La lucha de clases en Euskadi (1939–1980)* (San Sebastián, 1980) pp. 121–6; José María Portell, *Euskadi: amnistía arrancada* (Barcelona, 1977) pp. 37–42, 61–98.
70 'Gasteiz', *Vitoria, de la huelga a la matanza* (Paris, 1976) pp. 117–32, 185–202; Martín Villa, *Al servicio*, pp. 26–8.
71 *Cambio 16*, 29 March to 4 April, 19–25 April, 9–15 August, 23–29 August 1976, 12 February 1978; Amigo, *Pertur*, pp. 94–109, 124–8, 253–74; Garmendía, *ETA*, II, pp. 178–86.
72 Natxo Arregi, *Memorias del KAS: 1975/78* (San Sebastián, 1981) pp. 49–53.
73 *Mundo Obrero*, 27 January, 4, 11 February 1976; Fernando Claudín, *Santiago Carrillo: crónica de un secretario general* (Barcelona, 1983) pp. 231–4; Areilza, diary entry for 12 January 1976, *Diario*, p. 51.
74 Alvarez de Miranda, *Del 'contubernio'*, pp. 92–100; Jáuregui and Soriano, *UCD*, pp. 46, 50.
75 *Mundo Obrero*, 9 April 1976; Osorio, *Trayectoria*, pp. 91–4; Areilza, diary entry for 29 March 1976, *Diario*, p. 122.
76 Areilza, diary entries for 27, 29 March, 9, 10, 15, 23 April 1976, *Diario*, pp. 119–20, 122, 136–8, 146, 153; Emilio Attard, *Vida y muerte de UCD* (Barcelona, 1983) p. 49; Felipe González, FOG/Toledo.
77 *Cambio 16*, 15–21 March 1976; Morán, *Suárez*, pp. 31–2; Osorio, *Trayectoria*, pp. 86–91; 'Gasteiz', *Vitoria*, pp. 117–32; Martín Villa, *Al servicio*, pp. 28–9.
78 Figuero, *UCD*, pp. 23–6; Areilza, diary entry for 30 April 1976, *Diario*, p. 165; Antonio Izquierdo, *Yo, testigo de cargo*, p. 41.
79 Adolfo Suárez, FOG/Toledo.
80 Adolfo Suárez, FOG/Toledo.
81 Minutes of Coordinación Democrática meeting held on 9 April 1976, Oposición Española, *Documentos secretos* (Madrid, 1976) pp. 108–12.
82 Adolfo Suárez, FOG/Toledo.
83 *Newsweek*, 26 April 1976; Areilza, diary entries for 8, 24 March, 2, 8, 15, 28, 29, 30 April, 3, 12 May, *Diario*, pp. 105, 118, 124, 133–4, 146–8, 161–8, 178; diary entries for 14 and 15 July 1976, *Cuadernos de la transición* (Barcelona, 1983) pp. 23–6; Eaton, *Forces of Freedom*, pp. 38–40; *Guardian*, 3 July 1976.

Chapter 4 Reconciling the irreconcilable: the political reform of Adolfo Suárez 1976–7

1 Federico Ysart, *Quién hizo el cambio* (Barcelona, 1984) p. 57.
2 *El País*, 4 July 1976; Osorio, *Trayectoria*, pp. 126–9; Morán, *Suárez*, pp. 55–61; Bardavío, *El dilema*, pp. 150–5; Izquierdo, *Yo, testigo*, p. 41.
3 *El País*, 2 July 1976.
4 *Cambio 16*, 12–18, 19–25 July; *Mundo Obrero*, 14 July 1976; Iniesta Cano, *Memorias*, pp. 240–1; remarks made by Adolfo Suárez at a private seminar held by the Fundación Ortega y Gasset in Toledo in May 1984 (henceforth FOG/Toledo).
5 Alvarez de Miranda, *Del 'contubernio'*, pp. 107–9.
6 *El País*, 6, 21 July; *Cambio 16*, 12–18 July 1976; Areilza, diary entries for 4 and 5 July 1976, *Cuadernos*, pp. 15–16; Osorio, *Trayectoria*, pp. 129–38; Bardavío, *El dilema*, pp. 173–4.
7 Areilza, diary entries for 24 August, 22 September, 22 October, 28 November 1976,

Cuadernos, pp. 39–40, 47–8, 56–8, 71–4.

8 Suárez, FOG/Toledo.

9 *Cambio 16*, 9–15, 23–29 August; *Mundo Obrero*, 26 July to 2 August, 1 September 1976; Joaquín Bardavío, *Sábado santo rojo* (Madrid, 1980) pp. 42–4, 52; Morán, *Suárez*. p. 337.

10 José María Maravall, *The Transition to Democracy in Spain* (London, 1982) p. 13; J.A. Sagardoy and David León Blanco, *El poder sindical en España* (Barcelona, 1982) p. 161.

11 Morán, *Suárez*, pp. 235–44; Osorio, *Trayectoria*, pp. 141–2, 155, 171–4; Figuero, *UCD*, pp. 48–51.

12 *Cambio 16*, 26 July to 1 August, 16–22 August 1976; remarks of Felipe González at FOG/Toledo and to the author; Ysart, *Quién*, pp. 83–4.

13 Bardavío, *Sábado*, pp. 51–8; Morán, *Suárez*, pp. 331–2; Osorio, *Trayectoria*, pp. 162–4; Suárez, FOG/Toledo.

14 Remarks of Santiago Carrillo at FOG/Toledo and to the author.

15 *Cambio 16*, 13–20 September; *Mundo Obrero*, 8 September 1976.

16 Manuel Gutiérrez Mellado, *Un Soldado para España* (Barcelona, 1983) pp. 40–1, 47; Areilza, diary entries for 28 January, 11 February, 23 April 1976, *Diario*, pp. 76–7, 81, 152.

17 *El Alcázar*, 27 October 1976; Fernández, *Los Militares*, p. 63.

18 Figuero, *UCD*, p. 40; Suárez, FOG/Toledo.

19 *El Alcázar*, 23, 27 September; *Cambio 16*, 4–10, 11–17 October 1976; Osorio, *Trayectoria*, pp. 183–9; Fernández, *Los Militares*, pp. 109–13; Colectivo Democracia, *Los Ejércitos... más allá del golpe* (Barcelona, 1981) p. 63; Iniesta Cano, *Memorias*, pp. 242–50; Bardavío, *El dilema*, pp. 184–92.

20 *El País*, 24 December; *El Alcázar*, 28 December 1976; *Cambio 16*, 3–9 January 1977; Martín Villa, *Al servicio*, p. 60.

21 *Mundo Obrero*, 15 September 1976.

22 Osorio, *Trayectoria*, p. 206.

23 Areilza, diary entries for 22 September, 28 November, 6 December 1976, *Cuadernos*, pp. 47–8, 71, 78.

24 Morán, *Suárez*, p. 334; Claudín, *Carrillo*, pp. 238–40; Eduardo Chamorro, *Felipe González: un hombre a la espera* (Barcelona, 1980) pp. 133–6.

25 Suárez, FOG/Toledo.

26 *El País*, 18, 19 November; *Cambio 16*, 22–28 November 1976; Emilio Attard, *La Constitución por dentro* (Barcelona, 1983) p. 76; Suárez, FOG/Toledo.

27 Osorio, *Trayectoria*, pp. 230–46; Areilza, diary entry for 25 November 1976, *Cuadernos*, p. 67; Carr and Fusi, *Spain*, p. 222; Morán, *Suárez*, pp. 312–16.

28 *Mundo Obrero*, 1–7 November 1976.

29 *Mundo Obrero*, 1–7, 15–21, 22 November; *Cambio 16*, 22–28 November, 5 December 1976; Osorio, *Trayectoria*, pp. 208–9; Manuel P. Izquierdo, *De la huelga general a las elecciones generales* (Madrid, 1977) pp. 29–30; Martín Villa, *Al servicio*, pp. 54–7.

30 *El País*, 28 November; *Mundo Obrero*, 6–12 December 1976.

31 *Cambio 16*, 19 December 1976; Chamorro, *Felipe González*, pp. 136–43; PSOE, *XXVII Congreso* (Madrid, 1977) *passim*; Fernando Barciela, *La otra historia del PSOE* (Madrid, 1981) p. 19.

32 *El País*, 14, 15, 16, 17 December 1976; *Cambio 16*, 26 December, 27 December 1976 to 2 January 1977; Osorio, *Trayectoria*, pp. 252–3; Felipe González, FOG/Toledo.

33 Osorio, *Trayectoria*, pp. 212–13.

34 Manuel Durán, *Martín Villa* (San Sebastián, 1979) *passim*.

35 *Cambio 16*, 19–25 July, 2–8, 23–29 August, 11–17, 18–24 October 1976; Portell, *Amnistía*, pp. 170–4.

36 Martín Villa, *Al servicio*, pp. 57–60.

37 *Mundo Obrero*, 20–26 December 1976; Bardavío, *Sábado*, pp. 88–111; Osorio, *Trayectoria*, pp. 254–8; Claudín, *Carrillo*, pp. 2–9, 239–41.

38 *El País*, 12 December 1976; *Cambio 16*, 31 January to 6 February 1977; Pío Moa Rodríguez, *De un tiempo y de un país* (Madrid, 1982) pp. 217–33; Alejandro Muñoz Alonso, *El terrorismo en España* (Barcelona, 1982) pp. 76–85; Durán, *Martín Villa*, p. 79.

39 *Mundo Obrero*, 31 January to 6 February 1977; Bardavío, *Sábado*, pp. 142–7.

40 Morán, *Suárez*, pp. 43–4, 324–8; Osorio, *Trayectoria*, pp. 97–108, 190–7, 291–9.

41 *Cambio 16*, 27 September to 3 October, 18–24 October 1976; Areilza, diary entries for 13, 23 September, 22 October 1976, *Cuadernos*, pp. 43–4, 50, 56; Osorio, *Trayectoria*, pp. 200–5; Pedro J. Ramírez, *Así se ganaron las elecciones* (Barcelona, 1977) pp. 92–108.

42 *Cambio 16*, 6–12 September 1976; *El País*, 24, 29 June, 13, 15 July 1977; Díaz Salazar, *Iglesia*, pp. 353–61; Areilza, diary entries for 27 September 1976 and 21 March 1977, *Cuadernos*, pp. 51, 111; remarks of Gil Robles in an interview with the author; Osorio, *Trayectoria*, pp. 103–8, 191–3; Alvarez de Miranda, *Del 'contubernio'*, p. 126; Figuero, *UCD*, pp. 79–82.

43 Attard, *Vida y muerte*, pp. 34–50; Osorio, *Trayectoria*, pp. 190–7; Alvarez de Miranda, *Del 'contubernio'*, pp. 112–20.

44 Jáuregui and Soriano, *UCD*, pp. 43–8.

45 *El País*, 25 March; *Cambio 16*, 4–10 April 1977; Areilza, diary entries for 6 February, 19, 20, 21, 22, 24 March 1977, *Cuadernos*, pp. 92–4, 108–23; Osorio, *Trayectoria*, pp. 300–2; Attard, *Vida y muerte*, pp. 39–40; Ramírez, *Elecciones*, pp. 29–31.

46 Attard, *Vida y muerte*, pp. 50–3; Figuero, *UCD*, pp. 57–61; Jáuregui and Soriano, *UCD*, pp. 61–4.

47 *Cambio 16*, 16–22 May; *El País*, 6, 7, 8 May 1977; *Diario 16*, 28 January 1978; Figuero, *UCD*, pp. 232–4; Attard, *Vida y muerte*, p. 57; Ramírez, *Elecciones*, pp. 116–21, 139–49, 158–9; Alvarez de Miranda, *Del 'contubernio'*, pp. 127–9.

48 Attard, *Vida y muerte*, p. 52–7.

49 Areilza, diary entry for 21 March 1977, *Cuadernos*, pp. 113–14.

50 Figuero, *UCD*, pp. 173–86, 215–32.

51 *El País*, 1 February; *Cambio 16*, 7–13 February 1977; Colectivo Democracia, *Los Ejércitos*, pp. 75–6.

52 Suárez, FOG/Toledo; Morán, *Suárez*, pp. 320–1; José Oneto, *Los últimos días de un presidente: de la dimisión al golpe de Estado* (Barcelona, 1981) p. 86.

53 *Mundo Obrero*, 7–13, 21–27 March, 4–10, 11–17 April; *Cambio 16*, 18–24 April 1977; Claudín, *Carrillo*, pp. 245–8; Morán, *Suárez*, 338; Bardavío, *Sábado*, pp. 158–68.

54 Izquierdo, *Yo, testigo*, pp. 29, 63–4.

55 *El País*, 15, 16 April; *ABC*, 14 April; *Cambio 16*, 2–8 May 1977; Osorio, *Trayectoria*, pp. 288–91; Martín Villa, *Al servicio*, p. 69.

56 *Cambio 16*, 25 April to 1 May 1977; Suárez, FOG/Toledo; Bardavío, *Sábado*, pp. 196–200.

57 Colectivo Democracia, *Los Ejércitos*; Pilar Urbano, *Con la venia: yo indagué el 23-F* (Barcelona, 1982) p. 16.

58 *Cambio 16*, 14–20, 21–27 March, 23–29 May; 30 May to 5 June 1977; Portell, *Amnistía*, pp. 9–18, 168–239; Onaindía, *Lucha*, pp. 131–4.

59 Arregi, *Memorias*, pp. 285-98; *ETA ante las elecciones: Informe de la Reunión de las fuerzas abertzales* (30 April 1977); *Comunicado de ETA* (28 May 1977); *Carta a la Militancia (Interno)* (no date) – all reprinted in *Documentos Y*, 18 volumes (San Sebastián, 1979–81) vol. 18, pp. 476–7, 509–11, 524–9; Luciano Rincón, *ETA (1974–1984)* (Barcelona, 1985) pp. 50, 61–2.

60 *Cambio 16*, 6–12 June 1977. The author was able to attend numerous political meetings in the course of the campaign.

61 Ramírez, *Elecciones*, p. 52, 127–32, 228–44, 304–6.

62 *Cambio 16*, 13–19 June 1977; author's personal observation.

63 *Cambio 16*, 20–26 June, 27 June to 3 July; *El País*, 15, 22, 29 May 1977; Ramírez, *Elecciones*, pp. 208–11, 248–9, 284–90; Monica Threlfall, 'Women and political

participation' in Christopher Abel and Nissa Torrents, editors, *Spain: Conditional Democracy* (London, 1984).

64. Two interesting works which put this view are Juan Luis Cebrián, *La España que bosteza* (Madrid, 1981) pp. 22–5; Salvador Giner and Eduardo Sevilla Guzmán, 'From despotism to parliamentarism: class domination and political order in the Spanish State' in R. Scase, editor, *The State in Western Europe* (London, 1980) pp. 224–5.

Chapter 5 Building a new world with the bricks of the old: the democratic pact 1977–9

1 Maravall, *Transition to Democracy*, pp. 20–1; Juan J. Linz et al., *IV Informe FOESSA Volumen I: Informe sociológico sobre el cambio político en España: 1975–1981* (Madrid, 1981) pp. 161–3. A gossip-ridden, but informative, account of the 1977 elections can be found in Ramírez, *Elecciones*.

2 Alvarez de Miranda, *Del 'contubernio'*, pp. 138–44; Jáuregui and Soriano, *UCD*, pp. 48–9, 75–92; Figuero, *UCD*, pp. 82–4.

3 Jáuregui and Soriano, *UCD*, pp. 86–7; Osorio, *Trayectoria*, pp. 331–6.

4 Arregi, *Memorias*, pp. 285–98.

5 *Cambio 16*, 4–10 July 1977; Rincón, *ETA*, pp. 14, 46, 57, 66.

6 *Cambio 16*, 29–30 October 1977; Rincón, *ETA*, p. 17.

7 *Cambio 16*, 18–24 July, 8–14, 15–21 August, 5–11 September 1977; Miguel Castells Arteche, *El mejor defensor el pueblo* (San Sebastián, 1978) pp. 78–88, 141–53.

8 *El País*, 11 September 1977; *Cambio 16*, 22–28 August 1977.

9 *Cambio 16*, 24–30 October 1977

10 *El País*, 29 November 1977.

11 Durán, *Martín Villa*, pp. 113–25; *Cambio 16*, 19–25 September, 20 September to 2 October, 3–9 October 1977; Alvarez de Miranda, *Del 'contubernio'*, pp. 157–9, 165.

12 Martín Villa, *Al servicio*, pp. 150–8.

13 Suárez, FOG/Toledo.

14 Unión Militar Democrática, *Los militares*, p. 47; José Luis Morales and Juan Celada, *La alternativa militar: el golpismo después de Franco* (Madrid, 1981) pp. 67–85; Urbano, *Con la venia*, pp. 23–5; Fernández, *Los Militares*, pp. 190–1.

15 *El País*, 20 September; *Cambio 16*, 3–9 October 1977; Fernández, *Los Militares*, pp. 181–3.

16 Juan Pla, *La trama civil del golpe* (Barcelona, 1982) p. 85; Urbano, *Con la venia*, p. 16; Muñoz Alonso, *El terrorismo*, pp. 245–6; Colectivo Democracia, *Los Ejércitos*, p. 96.

17 *Cambio 16*, 24–30 October, 14–20 November 1977; interview held by the author in Madrid with General Prieto in February 1983; Armada, *Al servicio*, pp. 209–13; Fernández, *Los Militares*, pp. 209–13.

18 Osorio, *Trayectoria*, pp. 319–27; Martín Villa, *Al servicio*, p. 176.

19 *Cambio 16*, 11–17 July, 10–16 October 1977; Suárez, FOG/Toledo.

20 *Cambio 16*, 17–23 October; *El País*, 4, 11 October 1977.

21 Castells, *El mejor defensor*, pp. 197–9; Txiki Benegas, *Euskadi: sin la paz nada es posible* (Barcelona, 1984) pp. 80–2.

22 *Cambio 16*, 12–18 December 1977, 26 December 1977 to 1 January 1978, 9–15 January 1978; Manuel Clavero Arévalo, *España, desde el centralismo a las autonomías* (Barcelona, 1983) pp. 46–50.

23 For sane and clear outlines of the complex autonomy problem, see Clavero, *España*, passim and Mike Newton, 'The peoples and regions of Spain' in David S. Bell, editor, *Democratic Politics in Spain* (London, 1983). Cf. Cebrián, *España*, p. 56.

24 *Mundo Obrero*, 16 June, 16 August, 8–14 September, 2–19 December 1977; *Cambio 16*, 17–23, 24–30 October, 31 October to 6 November, 7–13 November 1977; Claudín, *Carrillo*, pp. 275–9.

25 Banco de Bilbao, *Informe Económico 1981* (Bilbao, 1982) pp. 154–61.

26 Izquierdo, *Yo, testigo*, pp. 118–21.

27 *Mundo Obrero*, 20–26 October 1977.

28 The *Ponencia* consisted of Gabriel Cisneros, Miguel Herrero Rodríguez de Miñón, José Pedro Pérez Llorca of the UCD; Gregorio Peces Barba of the PSOE; Miquel Roca of Convergència i Unió; Jordi Solé-Tura of the PSUC and Manuel Fraga of Alianza Popular.

29 *Cambio 16*, 21–27 November 1977; Attard, *La Constitución*, pp. 77–90, 119–23, 223; Antonio Hernández Gil, *El cambio político español y la Constitución* (Barcelona, 1982) pp. 283 ff.

30 Attard, *La Constitución*, pp. 92–107; Martín Villa, *Al servicio*, p. 86; Alvarez de Miranda, *Del 'contubernio'*, pp. 179–95; For ultra-rightist reaction to the military clauses, see *El Alcázar*, 6 July 1978.

31 *El País*, 13 January 1978; *Cambio 16*, 23 July 1978; Durán, *Martín Villa*, pp. 127–9.

32 *Cambio 16*, 5 February, 26 November 1978.

33 *Cambio 16*, 5, 12, 19 March 1978; Attard, *Vida y muerte*, p. 67; Jáuregui and Soriano, *UCD*, pp. 88, 115.

34 Jáuregui and Soriano, *UCD*, p. 125.

35 *Cambio 16*, 29 April, 28 May, 4 June 1978.

36 *Cambio 16*, 28 May, 30 July 1978; Gutiérrez Mellado, *Un soldado*, pp. 77–82, 98–9; Morales and Celada, *La alternativa*, pp. 39–41; Fernández, *Los militares*, pp. 218–20, 227–8; author's interview with General Prieto.

37 *Cambio 16*, 3, 10, 17 September 1978.

38 Durán, *Martín Villa*, pp. 139–48, 167–94.

39 *Cambio 16*, 23 July 1978; Martín Villa, *Al servicio*, pp. 147–8; Durán, *Martín Villa*, pp. 167–94; Benegas, *Euskadi*, pp. 102–3.

40 *Cambio 16*, 28 May, 9 July; *El País*, 29 June 1978; Rincón, *ETA*, pp. 163–6; Benegas, *Euskadi*, pp. 105–8.

41 Conversation of the author with Rodolfo Martín Villa in Madrid in October 1984.

42 *Cambio 16*, 28 May, 4 June, 9 July 1978.

43 *El País*, 30 June, 29 July; *Cambio 16*, 30 July 1978.

44 Izquierdo, *Yo, testigo*, pp. 99–102.

45 *Cambio 16*, 29 October 1978.

46 *El País*, 1 November 1978; *Cambio 16*, 12 November 1978; Rincón, *ETA*, pp. 21–2; Benegas, *Euskadi*, pp. 88–9.

47 *Cambio 16*, 19 November 1978; Muñoz Alonso, *El terrorismo*, pp. 133–40.

48 *El País*, 17, 19 November; *Cambio 16*, 3 December 1978; Colectivo Democracia, *Los Ejércitos*, pp. 78–85; Morales and Celada, *La alternativa*, pp. 43–7; Martín Villa, *Al servicio*, pp. 148–50; Urbano, *Con la venia*, p. 19.

49 Izquierdo, *Yo, testigo*, p. 49; Martín Villa, *Al servicio*, pp. 134–5, 150.

50 José Oneto, *La noche de Tejero* (Barcelona, 1981) pp. 27–34; Antonio Izquierdo, *Claves para un día de febrero* (Barcelona, 1982) pp. 28–9

51 *El Alcázar*, 23 November; *Cambio 16*, 10 December 1978; Morales and Celada, *La alternativa*, pp. 47–8; Izquierdo, *Yo, testigo,*, pp. 68–9.

52 *El País*, 8, 9 December; *Cambio 16*, 17 December 1978; Ministerio del Interior, Dirección General de Política Interior, *Referendum Constitucional: Información sobre resultados provisionales de la votación* (Madrid, 1978).

53 Benegas, *Euskadi*, pp. 89–91.

54 *El Alcázar*, 4, 11 January; *El País*, 3, 4, 5 January; *Cambio 16*, 14 January 1979.

55 *Cambio 16*, 31 December 1978.

56 Rincón, *ETA*, pp. 58, 70–1; Castells, *El mejor defensor*, pp. 154–6.

57 *El País*, 4 March 1979; Pedro J. Ramírez, *Así se ganaron las elecciones 1979* (Madrid, 1979) pp. 185–6.

58 *Cambio 16*, 14 January, 11 February, 4 March 1979.
59 Jorge de Esteban and Luis López Guerra, editors, *Las elecciones legislativas del 1 de marzo de 1979* (Madrid, 1979) *passim; Cambio 16*, 11 March 1979.
60 *Cambio 16*, 18 March 1979; Josep Melià, *Así cayó Adolfo Suárez* (Barcelona, 1981) p. 29. For an amusing and gossip-ridden account of the election campaign, see Ramírez, *Las elecciones 1979*, pp. 179–263.
61 Carlos Elordi, 'El PCE por dentro', *La Calle*, no. 95, 15–21 January 1980.
62 José Félix Tezanos, *Sociología del socialismo español* (Madrid, 1983) pp. 72–8, 89–134.
63 *Cambio 16*, 19 March, 23 April 1978; Barciela, *La otra historia del PSOE*, pp. 51–5.
64 *Cambio 16*, 21, 28 May 1978; Modesta Seara Vázquez, *El socialismo en España* (Mexico D.F., 1980) pp. 14–18.
65 Seara Vázquez, *El socialismo*, pp. 10–14, 20–30; Ramírez, *Las elecciones 1979*, pp. 83–7; *Cambio 16*, 20 May 1979.
66 For an excellent discussion of the issues posed at the XVIII Congress, see Elías Díaz, 'El lado oscuro de la dialéctica: consideraciones sobre el XVIII Congreso del PSOE' in *Sistema*, no. 32, September 1979.
67 *El País*, 19, 20, 22 May; *Cambio 16*, 3 June 1979; Diego Armario, *El triángulo: el PSOE durante la transición* (Valencia, 1981) p. 44.
68 *El País*, 30 June, 10 July; *Cambio 16*, 24 June, 30 September 1979.
69 *El País*, 28, 29, 30 September, 2, 7, October; *Diario 16*, 1 October; *Mundo Obrero*, 2 October; *Cambio 16*, 7 October 1979.
70 *Cambio 16*, 15 April 1979.
71 *El País*, 30, 31 March 1979.
72 *El País*, 4, 5, 6 April; *Cambio 16*, 15 April 1979; Suárez, FOG/Toledo.
73 *Cambio 16*, 22 April, 27 May, 10 June 1979.
74 Martín Villa, *Al servicio*, p. 50.

Chapter 6 Chronicle of a death foretold: the fall of Suárez 1979–81

1 *Cambio 16*, 14, 28 May, 5, 12 October 1978; Ramírez, *Las elecciones 1979*, pp. 81, 103–16; Jáuregui and Soriano, *UCD*, pp. 101–4.
2 *Cambio 16*, 18 March 1979.
3 *El País*, 27, 29 May; *El Alcázar*, 20, 27 May; *Cambio 16*, 10 June 1979.
4 Urbano, *Con la venia*, p. 26.
5 *El País*, 12 May 1979; Armada, *Al servicio*, p. 215; Morales and Celada, *La alternativa*, pp. 51–3.
6 *El País*, 6, 10 June; *Cambio 16*, 10 June 1979; Morales and Celada, *La alternativa*, pp. 43–9.
7 *Cambio 16*, 24 June, 1, 15, 22, 29 July, 5 August 1979; Attard, *Vida y muerte*, pp. 70–2; Jáuregui and Soriano, *UCD*, pp. 129–30.
8 *Cambio 16*, 5 August, 30 September, 4 November 1979.
9 *Cambio 16*, 13, 20 May 1979; Miguel Castells Arteche, *Radiografía de un modelo represivo* (San Sebastián, 1982) pp. 33–8, 129–30.
10 *Cambio 16*, 21 October 1979.
11 *El Alcázar*, 21 September; *Cambio 16*, 7 October 1979.
12 Morales and Celada, *La alternativa*, pp. 74–7; Armada, *Al servicio*, pp. 216–17; Urbano, *Con la venia*, p. 21.
13 *El Alcázar*, 20 October 1979; *El País*, 27 January; *Diario 16*, 25 January; *Cambio 16*, 10 February 1980; Colectivo Democracia, *Los Ejércitos*, pp. 85–91; Morales and Celada, *La alternativa*, pp. 57–61; Urbano, *Con la venia*, pp. 21–3.
14 *Cambio 16*, 25 November 1979; *El Alcázar*, 7 May, 29 June, 3, 9 July; *El País*, 13 September 1980; Colectivo Democracia, *Los Ejércitos*, pp. 91–3.
15 *El Alcázar*, 11, 15, 18, 23, 26 April 1980; author's interview with General Prieto; Urbano,

Con la venia, p. 29; Pla, *La trama civil*, p. 164.

16 Martín Villa, *Al servicio*, p. 90.

17 *Cambio 16*, 16 December 1979.

18 *Cambio 16*, 13 January 1980.

19 *Cambio 16*, 27 January 1980

20 *Cambio 16*, 3 February, 16 March; *El País*, 2, 3 March 1980; Martín Villa, *Al servicio*, p. 90.

21 *El País*, 13, 18 November; *Cambio 16*, 25 November, 2, 9, December 1979, 20 January 1980; conversation of the author with Javier Rupérez in Madrid, October 1984; Javier Rupérez, 'Un secuestro' in *Ideas y debate*, no. 2, 1985.

22 Castells, *Radiografía*, pp. 130–5.

23 *El País*, 18 February; *Cambio 16*, 17, 24 February, 23 March 1980.

24 *El País*, 22 March; *Cambio 16*, 30 March 1980.

25 *Cambio 16*, 2 March, 6, 13 April, 18, 25 May, 21 September 1980: Melià, *Así cayó*, p. 39; Jáuregui and Soriano, *UCD*, pp. 31–3.

26 Melià, *Así cayó*, p. 22; Oneto, *Los ultimos días*, pp. 35, 82.

27 Jáuregui and Soriano, *UCD*, pp. 35–6

28 Martín Villa, *Al servicio*, p. 91.

29 *El País*, 3, 4 May; *Cambio 16*, 18 May, 3 August 1980.

30 *El País*, 21, 22, 23, 29, 30 May; *Cambio 16*, 16 March, 1, 8 June 1980; Martín Villa, *Al servicio*, p. 94.

31 *Cambio 16*, 29 June 1980; Melià, *Así cayó*, pp. 36–7; Oneto, *Los ultimos días*, p. 50.

32 *El País*, 8, 9 July; *Diario 16*, 8 July; *Cambio 16*, 20, 27 July 1980; Melià, *Así cayó*, pp. 45–58; Oneto, *Los ultimos días*, pp. 50–3; Jáuregui and Soriano, *UCD*, pp. 150–3.

33 Jáuregui and Soriano, *UCD*, p. 35.

34 *Cambio 16*, 3 August 1980.

35 *El País*, 30, 31 July; *Cambio 16*, 27 July, 3, 10 August 1980; Jáuregui and Soriano, *UCD*, pp. 37, 156.

36 *Cambio 16*, 13 July, 17 August 1980; Melià, *Así cayó*, p. 42; Jáuregui and Soriano, *UCD*, pp. 15–20, 34–5.

37 *Cambio 16*, 10, 17 August 1980.

38 *Cambio 16*, 17, 31 August 1980; Urbano, *Con la venia*, pp. 31–2.

39 *El País*, 22 June; *Cambio 16*, 13, 20 July, 24 August, 7 September 1980; Rincón, *ETA*, p. 63.

40 *Cambio 16*, 17 August 1980.

41 *El País*, 10 September; *Cambio 16*, 21 September 1980; Melià, *Así cayó*, pp. 51–9.

42 *Cambio 16*, 5, 12 October 1980; Oneto, *Los ultimos días*, pp. 67–8.

43 *El País*, 18, 19 September; *Cambio 16*, 28 September, 12 October 1980.

44 *Cambio 16*, 12, 19 October; *El País*, 2, 13 October 1980; Muñoz Alonso, *El terrorismo*, p. 227.

45 *El Alcázar*, 16, 21 September, 2 December 1980; conversation of the author with Felipe González in Oxford in March 1981; *Cambio 16*, 9 March 1981; Armada, *Al servicio*, pp. 216, 223–7; Santiago Segura and Julio Merino, *Jaque al Rey: las 'enigmas' y las 'incongruencias' del 23-F* (Barcelona, 1983) pp. 53–4, 77–8; Morales and Celada, *La alternativa*, pp. 122–5; Santiago Segura and Julio Merino, *Vísperas del 23-F* (Barcelona, 1984) pp. 297–301; Urbano, *Con la venia*, pp. 33–5.

46 *Cambio 16*, 5, 12, 19, 26 October 1980.

47 *El País*, 24, 25, 26 October; *Cambio 16*, 3 November 1980.

48 *Cambio 16*, 26 October, 3 November 1980.

49 *Cambio 16*, 10 November; *El País*, 11 November 1980.

50 *Cambio 16*, 17, 24 November 1980; Benegas, *Euskadi*, pp. 110–11; Muñoz Alonso, *El terrorismo*, pp. 229–31.

51 Morales and Celada, *La alternativa*, pp. 89–91, 122–5; *Cambio 16*, 17 November 1980; Urbano, *Con la venia*, pp. 24–5.

52. Urbano, *Con la venia*, pp. 29–31, 49; Alvarez de Miranda, *Del 'contubernio'*, p. 145; Attard, *Vida y muerte*, pp. 182–4.

53. Jáuregui and Soriano, *UCD*, pp. 195–9; Attard, *Vida y muerte*, pp. 180–1.

54. Melià, *Así cayó*, pp. 59–63; Oneto, *Los últimos días*, pp. 69–70; *Diario 16*, 12 January; *Cambio 16*, 26 January 1981.

55. Attard, *Vida y muerte*, p. 189.

56. *Cambio 16*, 2 February 1981; Melià, *Así cayó*, pp. 13–19, 68–74.

57. *El País*, 30 January; *El Alcázar*, 30 January; *Diario 16*, 30 January; Oneto, *Los últimos días*, p. 113, 119, 152; Melià, *Así cayó*, pp. 74–5; Morales and Celada, *La alternativa*, pp. 125–6; Urbano, *Con la venia*, pp. 52–7.

Chapter 7 Out of the ashes: the consolidation of democracy 1981–2

1 *El Alcázar*, 24 January; *ABC*, 31 January 1981; Oneto, *Los últimos días*, pp. 74–5; Figuero, *UCD*, p. 4.

2 *Cambio 16*, 9 February 1981; Melià, *Así cayó*, pp. 96–9, 118–19; Oneto, *Los últimos días*, pp. 124–6, 152–3, 159–63.

3 *Cambio 16*, 16 February 1981; Benegas, *Euskadi*, pp. 132–4; Urbano, *Con la venia*, pp. 73–5.

4 *El País*, 17 April; *Cambio 16*, 27 April 1981.

5 *Cambio 16*, 16 February 1981; Rincón, *ETA*, pp. 172–6.

6 *Cambio 16*, 23 February 1981; Rincón, *ETA*, pp. 123–4.

7 *El Alcázar*, 8 February 1981.

8 *El Alcázar*, 17 December 1980, 22 January, 1 February 1981; Morales and Celada, *La alternativa*, pp. 127–30; *Cambio 16*, 22 June 1981; Pla, *La trama civil*, pp. 59–69.

9 *El País*, 7, 8 February; *Diario 16*, 9 February; *Cambio 16*, 16 February 1981; Attard, *Vida y muerte*, pp. 193–207; Martín Villa, *Al servicio*, pp. 94–6.

10 *El País*, 3, 10, 13, 14 February; *Cambio 16*, 23 February 1981; Izquierdo, *Claves*, pp. 99–103, 121–8, 135, 143; Morales and Celada, *La alternativa*, p. 132; Castells, *Radiografía*, pp. 31, 95, 159.

11 *Cambio 16*, 23 February 1981; Pla, *La trama civil*, pp. 46–50; Urbano, *Con la venia*, pp. 76–7

12 *El País*, 22 February 1981.

13 *El País*, 15, 17 February; *Cambio 16*, 23 February 1981; conversation of the author with Félix Pastor in Madrid in February 1981.

14 This account of the *Tejerazo* is derived from *El País*, 24, 25, 26, 27, 28 February; *Cambio 16*, 2, 9 March 1981; Colectivo Democracia, *Los Ejércitos*, pp. 140 ff.; Oneto, *La noche de Tejero*, *passim*; Urbano, *Con la venia*, *passim*; Armada, *Al servicio*, pp. 240–95; Santiago Segura and Julio Merino, *Jaque al Rey: las 'enigmas' y las 'incongruencias' del 23-F* (Barcelona, 1983) pp. 75–188, 220–32; Morales and Celada, *La alternativa*, pp. 135–46; Ricardo Cid Cañaveral *et al.*, *Todos al suelo: la conspiración y el golpe* (Madrid, 1981) *passim*. The Asturian PSOE's declaration was drawn up by the *Alcalde* of Oviedo, Antonio Masip, and a Socialist deputy, Alvaro Cuesta (conversation of author with both in Oviedo, November 1985). See also *La Voz de Asturias*, 24 February 1981.

15 On Armada's extremely confusing behaviour and his contacts with plotters and politicians, see Armada, *Al servicio*, pp. 231, 236; Segura and Merino, *Jaque*, pp. 56–8, 145–6; Martín Prieto, *Técnica de un golpe de Estado: el juicio del 23-F* (Barcelona, 1982) pp. 88–94; José Oneto, *La verdad sobre el caso Tejero* (Barcelona, 1982) pp. 90, 116, 205–35.

16 Colectivo Democracia, *Los Ejércitos*, pp. 360–76.

17 Cid Cañaveral *et al.*, *Todos al suelo*, pp. 205–7; Morales and Celada, *La alternativa*, pp. 146–8.

252 *Notes to pp. 204–223*

18 *Cambio 16*, 23 February, 9, 16 March, 8 June 1981.
19 *Cambio 16*, 9, 16 March; *El Alcázar*, 1 March 1981.
20 *ABC*, 12 April; *Cambio 16*, 20 April 1981; Morales and Celada, *La alternativa*, pp. 166–8.
21 For details of military attitudes to NATO, see Paul Preston and Denis Smyth, *Spain, the EEC and NATO* (London, 1984) pp. 15–21, 53–4.
22 *El Alcázar*, 26, 27, 28 February 1981.
23 *Cambio 16*, 23 March; *El País*, 6, 7, 20, 21, 22 March 1981.
24 *Cambio 16*, 30 March 1981; Colectivo Democracia, *Los Ejércitos*, p. 306.
25 *Cambio 16*, 11 May 1981.
26 *El País*, 5, 6, 8, 9 May; *Cambio 16*, 11, 18 May 1981.
27 *El País*, 22, 24, 26 May; *Cambio 16*, 1, 8 June; *El Alcázar*, 27 May 1981.
28 *El País*, 31 May, 2 June; *Cambio 16*, 8 June 1981.
29 *Cambio 16*, 29 June, 6 July 1981.
30 *Cambio 16*, 25 May, 29 June, 6 July 1981.
31 *Cambio 16*, 22 June, 6 July; *El País*, 22, 23 June; Attard, *Vida y muerte*, pp. 214–32.
32 *Cambio 16*, 29 June, 6, 20 July, 17 August; *El Alcázar*, 27 May 1981.
33 *Cambio 16*, 3, 10, 17 August, 7, 14 September, 23 November; *El País*, 2 September, 4 November 1981; Martín Villa, *Al servicio*, p. 96; Attard, *Vida y muerte*, pp. 232–52.
34 *El País*, 21, 22 October; *Cambio 16*, 26 October, 2 November 1981; Attard, *Vida y muerte*, pp. 263–5.
35 PSOE, *El PSOE ante la situación política* (Madrid, 1981); *Cambio 16*, 21, 28 September 1981.
36 *Cambio 16*, 19, 26 October, 2 November; *El País*, 21, 22, 23, 24, 25 October 1981.
37 *El País*, 20, 21, 22, 23 April 1978; *Mundo Obrero*, 20, 23, 27 April 1978.
38 Claudín, *Carrillo*, pp. 319 ff.; Manuel Azcárate, *Crisis del Eurocomunismo* (Barcelona, 1982) *passim*; Pedro Vega and Peru Erroteta, *Los herejes del PCE* (Barcelona, 1982) *passim*; *Cambio 16*, 28 September, 26 October, 23 November 1981.
39 *Cambio 16*, 9, 16 November; *El País*, 3 November 1981; Attard, *Vida y muerte*, pp. 269–74.
40 *Cambio 16*, 23, 30 November; *El País*, 14, 15, 23 November 1981; Attard, *Vida y muerte*, pp. 274–5.
41 *Cambio 16*, 7 December; *El País*, 7, 8 December 1981; Martín Villa, *Al servicio*, pp. 100, 117.
42 *Cambio 16*, 3, 31 August, 7 December 1981.
43 *Cambio 16*, 14, 21 December 1981, 11 October 1982.
44 *El País*, 14, 15 January; *Times*, 15 January 1982.
45 *Cambio 16*, 21 December 1981, 8 February 1982.
46 *Cambio 16*, 18, 25 January, 1 February 1982.
47 The trial was covered in depth in virtually every issue of *Cambio 16* and *El País* throughout February, March, April and May of 1982. The best accounts can be found in Prieto, *Técnica* and Oneto, *La verdad*. See also Francisco Mora, *Ni heroes ni bribones: los personajes del 23-F* (Barcelona, 1982). An unashamedly pro-*golpista* version is given by Segura and Merino, *Jaque*.
48 *Cambio 16*, 29 March 1982; Pla, *La trama civil*, p. 28.
49 *Cambio 16*, 17, 24, 31 May 1982; Martín Villa, *Al servicio*, p. 100.
50 *El País*, 4, 5, June; *Cambio 16*, 31 May, 7, 14 June 1982; Segura and Merino, *Jaque*, pp. 214–40.
51 *El País*, 31 July; *Cambio 16*, 26 July, 2 August 1982.
52 *El País*, 1 August; *Cambio 16*, 2, 9 August 1982.
53 *El País*, 26, 27, 28 August; *Cambio 16*, 23, 30 August 1982.
54 *El País*, 14, 15 September; *Cambio 16*, 6, 13, 20 September 1982.
55 PSOE, *Por el cambio: programa electoral* (Madrid, 1982); *Cambio 16*, 27 September 1982.

56 *El País*, 3, 4, 5, 6, 7, 8 October; *Cambio 16*, 11, 18 October 1982.
57 *El País*, 14 October; *El Alcázar*, 6, 7 October 1982.
58 *Cambio 16*, 22 October 1982.
59 *El País*, 29, 30 October; *Cambio 16*, 1 November 1982. The best account of the campaign and the results can be found in Muñoz Alonso *et al.*, *Las elecciones del cambio*.

Bibliographical note

The transformation of Spain into a constitutional monarchy was an immensely complex process. As the full bibliography which follows will indicate, there already exists a mountain of books to daunt the uninitiated. This short note aims merely to provide a guide for the non-specialist. Unfortunately, the bulk of the literature exists only in Spanish. Broadly speaking, books on the transition period fall into three categories. Memoirs, of varying degrees of self-interest, have been produced by many of the principal protagonists albeit not by all of the most interesting ones. There has been an abundance of detailed, and often extremely readable accounts by investigative journalists of specific aspects of the process – the Church, the army, ETA, elections, the collapse of UCD and so on. Finally, there have been a number of attempts to provide an explanatory over-view of the entire process.

Among the many general books on the period, I would single out four as worthwhile starting points. On the period up to 1978, the outstanding work is the elegantly written and historically aware study by Raymond Carr and Juan Pablo Fusi, *Spain: Dictatorship to Democracy*. A good introductory survey of the period is provided by David Gilmour's lucid essay *The Transformation of Spain*. Centring much more on the social background to the political turmoil are José María Maravall's rather serious essay *The Transition to Democracy in Spain* and Robert Graham's entertaining *Spain: Change of a Nation*.

Detailed thematic accounts of specific aspects of the transition abound and they are mostly unavailable in English. On the army, the indispensable works are Colectivo Democracia, *Los Ejércitos . . . más allá del golpe* and Pilar Urbano, *Con la venia: yo indagué el 23-F*. On the trial of the military plotters, the most complete accounts are Martín Prieto, *Técnica de un golpe de Estado* and José Oneto, *La verdad sobre el caso*

Tejero. On ETA, all sources are violently partisan. Robert P. Clark, *The Basque Insurgents* and José M. Garmendía, *Historia de ETA* are clear accounts sympathetic to ETA. Two important critical accounts, from a left-wing, non-centralist point of view are Luciano Rincón's acerbic *ETA (1974–1984)* and Txiki Benegas's conversations with Pedro Altares, *Euskadi: sin la paz nada es posible.*

Exciting accounts of dramatic incidents and short periods have become very popular in Spain. The newspaper *El País's* attempt to set up something similar to the *Sunday Times* Insight Team has produced the marvellous volume by Ismael Fuente *et al., Golpe mortal.* Also worth consulting on the assassination of Carrero Blanco is Joaquín Bardavío's highly readable *La crisis: historia de quince días* and the 'ghosted' account of the assassins themselves, 'Julen Agirre' (in reality Eva Forest), *Operación Ogro.* Bardavío has also produced interesting accounts of the legalization of the Communist Party (*Sábado santo rojo*) and of Juan Carlos's first months on the throne (*El dilema*). By far the most convincing works of political commentary in Spain are those produced by José Oneto on the attrition of Arias Navarro, on the fall of Suárez and on the Tejero coup.

The bibliography on the political parties is unbalanced in the extreme. A reasonable starting point would be Jorge de Esteban and Luis López Guerra, *Los partidos políticos en la España actual.* Apart from Elías Díaz's collection of essays, *Socialismo en España,* and José Félix Tezanos's analytical study there is nothing of worth on the PSOE. The situation is even worse for Alianza Popular which has still not inspired a study of any kind. In contrast, the two parties which collapsed in this period, the PCE and UCD, have stimulated a flood of books. On the Communists, apart from Santiago Carrillo's own accounts, the fundamental sources must be Fernando Claudín's brilliant biography of Carrillo, Manuel Azcárate's memoirs and the investigative study by Pedro Vega and Peru Erroteta, *Los herejes del PCE.* On UCD, Fernando Jáuregui and Manuel Soriano, *La otra historia de UCD* is full of intriguing gossip and rather reflects the views of Fernando Alvarez de Miranda. Javier Figuero's *UCD: la 'empresa' que creó Adolfo Suárez* is equally fascinating. Gregorio Morán's biography of Adolfo Suárez provides acute insight into the cut-throat world of the Francoist administration.

The bulk of the political memoirs to have been published so far in Spain has reflected the triumph of publicity over common sense. They sell on a massive scale and then lie unread on people's shelves. They are readable only by specialist academics and journalists and other politicians. They seem often to have been dictated and then sent directly to the printer without passing through the interim stage of copy-editing. Accordingly, they are repetitive and contradictory. The corollary of this, however, is that they can be very revealing. The reader prepared to go through them with a magnifying glass and then to collate them will be richly rewarded. The area best served by memoirs is the creation and collapse of UCD. Absolutely crucial are the urbane and perhaps retouched volumes of diaries by the Conde de Motrico, José María de Areilza. Equally indispensable are the dense memoirs of one of Adolfo Suárez's *eminences grises*, Alfonso Osorio. The works of the amiable Emilio Attard are illuminating. Rodolfo Martín Villa is considered in Spain to be the repository of the dark secrets of the transition. His memoirs are guarded and often dull, but their elliptical insights repay effort.

On the left, there have been few works of note. Carrillo's memoirs are frankly disappointing. No memoir of value has come from the leaders of the PSOE with the exception of Tierno Galván. Recalcitrant soldiers, on the other hand, have written abundantly. Milans del Bosch's views may be found in the works of his lawyer, Santiago Segura, and Julio Merino. Much more interesting are the sibylline memoirs of Alfonso Armada. Even more sibylline, in a different way, are those of General Iniesta who manages to recreate the witch-hunting fervour of early Francoism without giving away anything about his ultra-rightist activities in the democratic period. The memoirs of Colonel San Martín, thought by many to be the brains behind the various plots of the colonels throughout 1981 and 1982, are concerned much more about the early period of his career under Carrero Blanco. Insights about other enemies of the democratic state can be found in memoirs which have emerged from GRAPO and ETA. Pío Moa's *De un tiempo y de un país* tells more about GRAPO than one might have expected but less than one hoped. Miguel Castells's *El mejor defensor el pueblo* is a fascinating account of his work as a lawyer for ETA. It recreates vividly the atmosphere of extreme *abertzalism* and helps explain the long-term survival of support for ETA. Lidia Falcón's *Viernes y trece en la Calle del Correo* presents a bitter vision of ETA violence and the political irresponsibility behind it.

The purpose of this short essay was to introduce the reader to the sources on the period with a view to providing some short-cuts. I fear that anyone who gets as far as reading the more important titles discussed above will not be able to stop. For that reason, a full bibliography is provided for new addicts. The newspaper sources consulted by the author were considerable. Until 1974, foreign and exile sources predominate over the highly censored Spanish press, although *Madrid, Informaciones, Ya* and *ABC* were used. After 1975, *Cambio 16*, and then from 1976, *El País* were the main Spanish newspapers used on a regular basis. Newspaper sources are listed in full in the notes.

Bibliography

Principal diaries, memoirs and printed documents

Agirre, Julen (pseudonym of Eva Forest), *Operación Ogro: cómo y porqué ejecutamos a Carrero Blanco* (Paris/Hendaye, 1974).

Alvarez de Miranda, Fernando, *Del 'contubernio' al consenso* (Barcelona, 1985).

Areilza, José María de, *Cuadernos de la transición* (Barcelona, 1983).

—, *Diario de un ministro de la monarquía* (Barcelona, 1977).

Armada, Alfonso, *Al servicio de la Corona* (Barcelona, 1983).

Attard, Emilio, *La Constitución por dentro* (Barcelona, 1983).

—, *Vida y muerte de UCD* (Barcelona, 1983).

Azcárate, Manuel, *Crisis del Eurocomunismo* (Barcelona, 1982).

Benegas, Txiki, *Euskadi: sin la paz nada es posible* (Barcelona, 1984).

Calvo Serer, Rafael *La dictadura de los franquistas: El 'affaire' del MADRID y el futuro político* (Paris, 1973).

—, *Franco frente al rey* (Paris, 1972).

—, *Mis enfrentamientos con el Poder* (Barcelona, 1978).

—, *La solución presidencialista* (Barcelona, 1979).

Carrillo, Santiago, *El año de la Constitución* (Barcelona, 1978).

—, *Demain l'Espagne* (Paris, 1974).

—, *Hacia el post-franquismo* (Paris, 1974).

—, *Memoria de la transición* (Barcelona, 1983).

Castells Arteche, Miguel, *El mejor defensor el pueblo* (San Sebastián, 1978).

Ciano, Galeazzo, (Malcolm Muggeridge, editor), *Ciano's Diplomatic Papers* (London, 1948).

Claudín, Fernando, *Santiago Carrillo: crónica de un secretario general* (Barcelona, 1983).

—, *Las divergencias en el Partido* (n.p., 1964).

Clavero Arévalo, Manuel, *España, desde el centralismo a las autonomías* (Barcelona, 1983).

ETA, *Documentos Y*, 18 volumes (San Sebastián, 1979–81).

Falcón, Lidia, *Viernes y trece en la Calle del Correo* (Barcelona, 1981).

Fortes, José and Otero, Luis, *Proceso a nueve militares demócratas: las Fuerzas Armadas y la UMD* (Barcelona, 1983).

Fraga, Iribarne, Manuel, *Memoria breve de una vida política* (Barcelona, 1980).

Franco Salgado-Araujo, Francisco, *Mis conversaciones privadas con Franco* (Barcelona, 1976).

Gil, Vicente, *Cuarenta años junto a Franco* (Barcelona, 1981).

Gutiérrez Mellado, Manuel, *Un Soldado para España* (Barcelona, 1983).

Iniesta Cano, Carlos, *Memorias y recuerdos* (Barcelona, 1984).

López Rodó, Laureano, *La larga marcha hacia la Monarquíía* (Barcelona, 1977).

Martín Villa, Rodolfo, *Al servicio del Estado* (Barcelona, 1984).

Moa Rodríguez, Pío, *De un tiempo y de un país* (Madrid, 1982).

Oposición Española, *Documentos secretos* (Madrid, 1976).

Osorio, Alfonso, *Trayectoria política de un ministro de la corona* (Barcelona, 1980).

PSOE, *Congresos del PSOE en el exilio*, 2 vols (Madrid, 1981).

—, *El PSOE ante la situación política* (Madrid, 1981).

—, *Por el cambio: programa electoral* (Madrid, 1982).

—, *XXVII Congreso* (Madrid, 1977).

Ridruejo, Dionisio, *Casi unas memorias* (Barcelona, 1976).

San Martín, José Ignacio, *Servicio especial* (Barcelona, 1983).

Seara Vázquez, Modesto, *El socialismo en España* (Mexico D.F., 1980).

Semprún, Jorge, *Autobiografía de Federico Sánchez* (Barcelona, 1977).

Serrano Suñer, Ramon, *Entre el silencio y la propaganda, la Historia como fue: Memorias* (Barcelona, 1977).

Tierno Galván, Enrique, *Cabos sueltos* (Barcelona, 1981).

Unión Militar Democrática, *Los militares y la lucha por la democracia* (n.p., n.d., but Madrid, 1976).

Books and articles

Abel, Christopher and Torrents, Nissa, editors, *Spain: Conditional Democracy* (London, 1984).

Acqua, Gian Piero dell', *Spagna cronache della transizione* (Florence, 1978).

Aguilar, Miguel Angel, *El vértigo de la prensa* (Madrid, 1982).

Alberola, Octavio and Gransac, Ariane, *El anarquismo español y la acción revolucionaria 1961-1974* (Paris, 1975).

Amigo, Angel, *Pertur: ETA 71-76* (San Sebastián, 1978).

Amover, Francesc, *Il carcere vaticano: Chiesa e fascismo in Spagna* (Milan, 1975).

Apalátegi, Jokin, *Los vascos de la nación al Estado* (San Sebastián, 1979).

Aranguren, José Luis, *La cruz de la monarquía española actual* (Madrid, 1974).

Armario, Diego, *El triángulo: el PSOE durante la transición* (Valencia, 1981).

Arregi, Natxo, *Memorias del KAS: 1975/78* (San Sebastián, 1981).

Arteaga, Federico de, *ETA y el proceso de Burgos* (Madrid, 1971).

Banco de Bilbao, *Informe Económico 1981* (Bilbao, 1982).

Barciela, Fernando, *La otra historia del PSOE* (Madrid, 1981).

Bardavío, Joaquín, *La crisis: historia de quince días* (Madrid, 1974).

—, *El dilema: un pequeño caudillo o un gran Rey* (Madrid, 1978).

—, *Sábado santo rojo* (Madrid, 1980).

—, *Los silencios del Rey* (Madrid, 1979).

Bayod, Angel, editor, *Franco visto por sus ministros* (Barcelona, 1981).

Bell, David S., editor, *Democratic Politics in Spain* (London, 1983).

Ben-Ami, Shlomo, *La revolución desde arriba: España 1936–1979* (Barcelona, 1980).

Bernáldez, José María, *¿Ruptura o reforma?* (Barcelona, 1984).

Blaye, Edouard de, *Franco and the Politics of Spain* (Harmondsworth, 1976).

Borrás Bertriu, Rafael, *et al., El día en que mataron a Carrero Blanco* (Barcelona, 1974).

Busquets, Julio, *Pronunciamientos y golpes de Estado en España* (Barcelona, 1982).

—, Aguilar, Miguel Angel and Puche, Ignacio, *El golpe: anatomía y claves del asalto al Congreso* (Barcelona, 1981).

Cantarero del Castillo, Manuel, *Falange y socialismo* (Barcelona, 1973).

Caparrós, Francisco, *La UMD: militares rebeldes* (Barcelona, 1983).

Carr, Raymond, *The Spanish Tragedy: The Civil War in Perspective* (London, 1977).

— and Fusi, Juan Pablo, *Spain: Dictatorship to Democracy* (London, 1979).

Castells Arteche, Miguel, *Radiografía de un modelo represivo* (San Sebastián, 1982).

Cebrián, Juan Luis, *La España que bosteza* (Madrid, 1981).

Chamorro, Eduardo, *Felipe González: un hombre a la espera* (Barcelona, 1980).

—, *Viaje al centro de UCD* (Barcelona, 1981).

Chao, José, *La Iglesia en el franquismo* (Madrid, 1976).

Chao, Ramon, *Après Franco, l'Espagne* (Paris, 1975).

Christie, Stuart, *The Christie File* (Seattle, 1980).

Cid Cañaveral, Ricardo, *et al., Todos al suelo: la conspiración y el golpe* (Madrid, 1981).

Cierva, Ricardo de la, *Historia del franquismo*, 2 vols (Barcelona, 1975–8).

Clark, Robert P., *The Basque Insurgents: ETA, 1952–1980* (Wisconsin, 1984).

Colectivo Democracia, *Los Ejércitos . . . más allá del golpe* (Barcelona, 1981).

Coverdale, John F., *The Political Transformation of Spain after Franco* (New York, 1979).

Cuadernos de Ruedo Ibérico, Horizonte español 1966, 2 vols (Paris, 1966).

—, *Horizonte español 1972*, 3 vols (Paris, 1972).

Díaz, Elías, 'El lado oscuro de la dialéctica: consideraciones sobre el XVIII Congreso del PSOE' in *Sistema*, no. 32, September 1979.

—, *Pensamiento español 1939–1973* (Madrid, 1974).

—, *Socialismo en España: el Partido y el Estado* (Madrid, 1982).

Díaz Cardiel, Victor, *et al., Madrid en huelga: enero 1976* (Madrid, 1976).

Díaz Salazar, Rafael, *Iglesia, dictadura y democracia: Catolicismo y sociedad en España (1953–1979)* (Madrid, 1981).

Durán, Manuel, *Martín Villa* (San Sebastián, 1979).

Eaton, Samuel, *The Forces of Freedom in Spain 1974–1979: A Personal Account* (Stanford, 1981).

Ellwood, Sheelagh, *Prietas las filas: historia de Falange Española 1933–1983* (Barcelona, 1984).

Elósegi, Joseba, *Quiero morir por algo* (n.p., n.d., but St Jean de Luz, 1971).

Esteban, Jorge de, *et al., Desarrollo político y constitución española* (Barcelona, 1973).

— and López Guerra, Luis, editors, *Las elecciones legislativas del 1 de marzo de 1979* (Madrid, 1979).

— and López Guerra, Luis, *Los partidos políticos en la España actual* (Barcelona, 1982).

Fernández, Carlos, *Los militares en la transición política* (Barcelona, 1982).

Fernández de Castro, Ignacio, and Martínez, José, editors, *España hoy* (Paris, 1963).

Figuero, Javier, *UCD: la 'empresa' que creó Adolfo Suárez* (Barcelona, 1981).

Foltz, Charles, Jr., *The Masquerade in Spain* (Boston, 1948).

Forest, Eva, *From a Spanish Jail* (Harmondsworth, 1975).

Fuente, Ismael, Garcíía, Javier and Prieto, Joaquín, *Golpe mortal: asesinato de Carrero y agonía del franquismo* (Madrid, 1983).

Gallagher, Charles F., *Spain, Development and the Energy Crisis* (New York, 1973).

Garmendía, José María, *Historia de ETA*, 2 vols (San Sebastián, 1980).

Garriga, Ramón, *Nicolás Franco, el hermano brujo* (Barcelona, 1980).

Garrigues y Díaz-Cañabate, Antonio, *Diálogos conmigo mismo* (Barcelona, 1978).

Garrigues Walker, Joaquín, *Qué es el liberalismo* (Barcelona, 1976).

'Gasteiz', *Vitoria, de la huelga a la matanza* (Paris, 1976).

Gilmour, David, *The Transformation of Spain: From Franco to the Constitutional Monarchy* (London, 1985).

Giner, Salvador and Sevilla Guzmán, Eduardo, 'From despotism to parliamentarism: class domination and political order in the Spanish State', in R. Scase, editor, *The State in Western Europe* (London, 1980).

Gómez Santos, Marino, *Conversaciones con Leopoldo Calvo Sotelo* (Barcelona, 1982).

González, Manuel Jesús, *La economía política del franquismo 1940–1970: dirigismo, mercado y planificación* (Madrid, 1979).

Graham, Robert, *Spain: Change of a Nation* (London, 1984).

(Grimau), *¿Crimen o castigo? Documentos inéditos sobre Julián Grimau* (Madrid, 1963).

Gutiérrez, Fernando, *Curas represaliados en el franquismo* (Madrid, 1977).

Heine, Hartmut, *La oposición política al franquismo* (Barcelona, 1983).

Hernández Gil, Antonio, *El cambio político español y la Constitución* (Barcelona, 1982).

Herrero, Miguel, *El principio monárquico* (Madrid, 1972).

Izquierdo, Antonio, *Claves para un día de febrero* (Barcelona, 1982).

—, *Yo, testigo de cargo* (Barcelona, 1981).

Izquierdo, Manuel P., *De la huelga general a las elecciones generales* (Madrid, 1977).

Jáuregui Bereciartu, Gurutz, *Ideología y estrategia política de ETA* (Madrid, 1981).

Jáuregui, Fernando and Soriano, Manuel, *La otra historia de UCD* (Madrid, 1980).

Jerez Mir, Miguel, *Elites políticas y centros de extracción en España 1938–1957* (Madrid, 1982).

Krasikov, Anatoly, *From Dictatorship To Democracy: Spanish Reportage* (Oxford, 1984).

Lieberman, Sima, *The Contemporary Spanish Economy: A Historical Perspective* (London, 1982).

Linz, Juan J., 'An authoritarian regime: Spain' in E. Allardt and Y. Littunen, editors,

Cleavages, Ideologies and Party Systems (Helsinki, 1964).

—, et al., *IV Informe FOESSA Volumen I: Informe sociológico sobre el cambio político en España: 1975–1981* (Madrid, 1981).

Lizcano, Pablo, *La generación del 56: la universidad contra Franco* (Barcelona, 1981).

López Pintor, Rafael, *La opinión publica española: del franquismo a la democracia* (Madrid, 1982).

Lurra, *Burgos, Juicio a un pueblo* (San Sebastián, 1978).

Maravall, José María, *Dictatorship and Political Dissent: Workers and Students in Franco's Spain* (London 1978).

—, *The Transition to Democracy in Spain* (London, 1982).

Martín Aguado, José Antonio, *Asalto a la democracia* (La Coruña, 1981).

Martín Prieto, *Técnica de un golpe de Estado: el juicio del 23-F* (Barcelona, 1982).

Melià, Josep, *Así cayó Adolfo Suárez* (Barcelona, 1981).

Miguel, Amando de, *Sociología del franquismo* (Barcelona, 1975).

Ministerio del Interior, Dirección General de Política Interior, *Referendum Constitucional: Información sobre resultados provisionales de la votación* (Madrid, 1978).

Mohedano, José María and Peña, Marcos, *Constitución: cuenta atras ETA-Operación Galaxia y otros terrorismos* (Madrid, 1978).

Mora, Francisco, *Ni héroes ni bribones: los personajes del 23-F* (Barcelona, 1982).

Morales, José Luis and Celada, Juan, *La alternativa militar: el golpismo después de Franco* (Madrid, 1981).

Morán, Gregorio, *Adolfo Suárez: historia de una ambición* (Barcelona, 1979).

—, *Los españoles que dejaron de serlo: Euskadi, 1937–1981* (Barcelona, 1982).

Morodo, Raul, *Por una sociedad democrática y progresista* (Madrid, 1982).

—, *La transición política* (Madrid, 1984).

Moya, Carlos, *El Poder económico en España* (Madrid, 1975).

Mujal-León, Eusebio, *Communism and Political Change in Spain* (Bloomington, 1983).

Muñoz Alonso, Alejandro, et al., *Las elecciones del cambio* (Barcelona, 1984).

—, *El terrorismo en España* (Barcelona, 1982)

Naredo, José Manuel, *La evolución de la agricultura en España*, 2nd edition (Barcelona, 1974).

Noticias del País Vasco, *Euskadi: el último estado de excepción* (Paris, 1975).

Onaindía, Mario, *La lucha de clases en Euskadi (1939–1980)* (San Sebastián, 1980).

Oneto, José, *Arias entre dos crisis, 1973–1975* (Madrid, 1975).

—, *La noche de Tejero* (Barcelona, 1981).

—, *Los últimos días de un presidente: de la dimisión al golpe de Estado* (Barcelona, 1981).

—, *La verdad sobre el caso Tejero* (Barcelona, 1982).

Ortzi (pseudonym of Francisco Letamendía), *Historia de Euskadi: el nacionalismo vasco y ETA* (Paris, 1975).

Paniagua, F. Javier, *La ordenación del capitalismo avanzado en España: 1957–1963* (Barcelona, 1977).

Paricio, Jesús M., *Para conocer a nuestros militares* (Madrid, 1983).

Parti Communiste Français, *2 meses de huelgas* (Paris, 1962).

Pérez Díaz, Santiago, *Francisco Fernández Ordóñez* (Madrid, 1976).

Pi, Ramón, *Joaquín Garrigues Walker* (Madrid, 1977).

Pla, Juan, *La trama civil del golpe* (Barcelona, 1982).

Portell, José María, *Euskadi: amnistía arrancada* (Barcelona, 1977).

—, *Los hombres de ETA*, 3rd edition (Barcelona, 1976).

Preston, Paul, *The Coming of the Spanish Civil War* (London, 1978).

—, 'The dilemma of credibility: the Spanish Communist Party, the Franco regime and after' in *Government and Opposition*, vol. 11, no. 1, Winter 1976.

—, 'The PCE in the struggle for democracy in Spain' in Howard Machin, editor, *National Communism in Western Europe* (London, 1983).

—, 'The PCE's long road to democracy 1954–1977' in Richard Kindersley, editor, *In Search of Eurocommunism* (London, 1981).

—, editor, *Revolution and War in Spain 1931–1939* (London, 1984).

—, editor, *Spain in Crisis: Evolution and Decline of the Franco Regime* (Hassocks, 1976).

— and Smyth, Denis, *Spain, the EEC and NATO* (London, 1984).

Ramírez, Luis (pseudonym of Luciano Rincón), *Franco: la obsesión de ser, la obsesión de poder* (Paris, 1976).

Ramírez, Pedro J., *Así se ganaron las elecciones* (Barcelona, 1977).

—, *Así se ganaron las elecciones 1979* (Madrid, 1979).

Ramos Espejo, Antonio, *El caso Almería* (Barcelona, 1982).

Reinares, Fernando, editor, *Violencia y política en Euskadi* (Bilbao, 1984).

Rincón, Luciano, *ETA (1974–1984)* (Barcelona, 1985).

Roa Ventura, Agustín, *Agonía y muerte del franquismo (una memoria)* (Barcelona, 1978).

Rodríguez Armada, Amandino and Novais, José Antonio, *¿Quién mató a Julián Grimau?* (Madrid, 1976).

Romero Maura, Joaquín, 'After Franco, Franquismo? The armed forces, the Crown and democracy' in *Government and Opposition*, vol. 11, no. 1., Winter 1976.

Ruiz de Ayúcar, Angel, *Crónica agitada de ocho años tranquilos: 1963–1970* (Madrid, 1974).

Rupérez, Javier, 'Un secuestro' in *Ideas y debate*, no. 2, 1985.

Sáez Alba, A., *La otra cosa nostra: la Asociación Católica Nacional de Propagandistas y el caso de EL CORREO de Andalucía* (Paris 1974).

Sagardoy, J.A. and León Blanco, David, *El poder sindical en España* (Barcelona, 1982).

Salaberri, Kepa, *El proceso de Euskadi en Burgos. El sumarísimo 31.69* (Paris, 1971).

Sánchez Eraúskin, Javier, *Txiki-Otaegi: el viento y las raíces* (San Sebastián, 1978).

Sanz, Jesús, *La cara secreta de la política valenciana: de la predemocracia al Estatuto de Benicasim* (Valencia, 1982).

Segura, Santiago and Merino, Julio, *Jaque al Rey: las 'enigmas' y las 'incrongruencias' del 23-F* (Barcelona, 1983).

— and —, *Vísperas del 23-F* (Barcelona, 1984).

Sevilla Guzmán, Eduardo and Giner, Salvador, 'Absolutismo despótico y dominación de clase: el caso de España' in *Cuadernos de Ruedo Ibérico*, nos 43–5, January–June 1975.

Silva Muñoz, Federico, *La transición inacabada* (Barcelona, 1980).

Soriano, Ramón, *La mano izquierda de Franco* (Barcelona, 1981).

Southworth, Herbert R., *Guernica! Guernica! A Study of Journalism, Diplomacy, Propaganda and History* (Berkeley, 1977).

Tamames, Ramón, *Un proyecto de democracia para el futuro de España* (Madrid, 1974).

Tezanos, José Félix, *Sociología del socialismo español* (Madrid, 1983).

Torres, Lorenzo, 'The Spanish left: illusion and reality' in *The Socialist Register* 1966.

Tusell, Javier, *La oposición democrática al franquismo* (Barcelona, 1977).

Urbano, Pilar, *Con la venia: yo indagué el 23-F* (Barcelona, 1982).

Vega, Pedro and Erroteta, Peru, *Los herejes del PCE* (Barcelona, 1982).

Vilar, Sergio, *La oposición a la dictadura: protagonistas de la España democrática*, 2nd edition (Barcelona, 1976).

Villacastin, Rosa and Beneyto, Maria, *La noche de los transistores* (Madrid, 1981).

Viñas, Angel, *Los pactos secretos de Franco con Estados Unidos* (Barcelona, 1981).

Viver Pi-Sunyer, C., *El personal político de Franco 1936–1945* (Barcelona, 1978).

Ynfante, Jesús, *El Ejército de Franco y de Juan Carlos* (Paris, 1976).

—, *La prodigiosa aventura del Opus Dei: génesis y desarrollo de la Santa Mafia* (Paris, 1970).

Ysart, Federico, *Quién hizo el cambio* (Barcelona, 1984).

Index